No. 2644
$25.95

111 YARD AND GARDEN PROJECTS

from boxes and bins
to tables and tools

PERCY W. BLANDFORD

TAB BOOKS Inc.

Blue Ridge Summit, PA 17214

FIRST EDITION
FIRST PRINTING

Copyright © 1986 by TAB BOOKS Inc.
Printed in the United States of America

Library of Congress Cataloging in Publication Data

Blandford, Percy W.
111 yard and garden projects.

Includes index.
1. Gardening—Equipment and supplies. 2. Garden
tools. 3. Garden ornaments and furniture. 4. Garden
structures—Design and construction. I. Title.
II. Title: One hundred eleven yard and garden projects.

SB454.8.B55   1986   635   85-27680
ISBN 0-8306-0344-1
ISBN 0-8306-0444-8 (pbk.)

Contents

Introduction

A garden is primarily a place where you hope things will grow. You might be mainly interested in producing vegetables and fruit. Your inclinations might be more toward flowers and shrubs. You might have enough land to divide into vegetable plots, formal gardens, and informal areas. There could be a large expanse of lawn with borders of flowers, bushes, and trees. At the other extreme, you might have little more than a few potted plants and a window box.

Whatever your form of gardening, you will need tools and equipment. There might be a need for just a few tools. Even if your property is so extensive that you must have powered tools to work it, there are many gardening jobs that can only be done with hand tools. The equipment you need will range from such things as labels and boxes, through carts and bins, to a shed and a greenhouse.

Almost certainly you will have to fence your garden or yard and provide gates. There might have to be terraces. Climbing plants will need supports of varying complexity. Coupled with all this could be a deck to give balance to the garden layout.

Even if you are only an average handyman, you can make many of the items of equipment and tools you need. Although you might not think you have much ability in working wood or metal, a large number of useful projects can be completed with the minimum of skill and very few hand tools.

If you are more of a workshop enthusiast with extensive equipment, you can make almost all the items you need to be a successful gardener. Besides saving money with everything you make, you can fashion tools to suit your particular needs—build fences, sheds, and other equipment that exactly fit—as well as get the double satisfaction of combining gardening and craftsmanship. Obviously, there are a few things that cannot be made with the usual home-shop facilities, but you can satisfy nearly all your gardening needs with things you make yourself.

And that is what this book is all about. May you enjoy the combination of successful gardening and satisfaction in your craftsmanship.

Note: Unless otherwise indicated, sizes are in inches and they are quoted in descending order of dimensions: length, width, and thickness. It is common to allow a little extra on lengths when obtaining wood.

Chapter 1

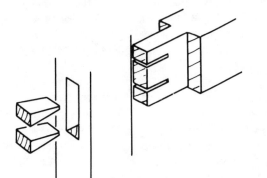

Craftmanship

The combination of crafts enthusiast and gardener in one person opens up so many interesting possibilities that you might be carried away with the idea of making your own tools instead of buying them. Taken to extremes, you could spend all your time in the shop making things and have no time left to go outside and use them. That could happen if you tried to make all the projects in this book; you have to be selective.

Few of the products require a high degree of skill or very elaborate facilities. What you choose to make depends on your needs, inclinations, shop equipment, and your ability to make the best use of what you have. Most beginner craftsmen can tackle basic woodworking. As many outdoor wood projects are made without cut joints, construction is very easy and can be done with few hand tools. Power tools will help by lessening labor and sometimes increasing accuracy.

It is the working of metal that will worry some readers. A few enthusiastic woodworkers have a prejudice against working in metal. If you have some skill at woodwork, basic metalwork should come naturally. For most projects involving metal, you only have to saw, file, drill, and bend. A substantial metal vise is valuable, but the other tools needed are simple and you might have them already.

Whether or not to tackle some of the more advanced projects involving metal depends on your facilities for joining parts. If you have welding equipment almost anything is possible. Without it you can still make strong joints by brazing—using the flame of a propane torch. Easier, although less strong, is soldering. A combination of rivets with brazing can provide good tool strength.

You must also consider if you can work steel in larger sizes. If you are an expert blacksmith, with the facilities that go with the job, you might do such work, but most of us will use only strips and rods. This means that using steel for any tools bigger than a hoe are beyond the scope of most of us. Spades, shovels, digging forks and similar things are better bought. Mechanical things, whether hand or power operated, are also mostly better bought.

1

You can make things that pivot on bolts or rivets and have only a simple action, but if the device has rotating parts as well you will almost certainly need a metalworking lathe. This, and the fact that most machines need special parts not always easy to obtain, makes the production of garden machines unsuitable for the majority of metalworking gardeners.

Although most readers will not have a metalworking lathe, more will be able to turn wood. Wood turning is not essential—you can produce acceptable parts without a lathe—but turned parts, where appropriate, give the tool or equipment a better appearance. This is particularly so with handles. An attraction for the user of a wood-turning lathe is that handles and other parts can be made to exactly fit their needs. This is not always so with some manufacturers that use stock handles for a variety of the tools they sell.

An attraction of making your own tools and outdoor equipment is that you are dealing with one-off projects, made to exactly fit a need. A deck will be exactly the size you want it. A tool shed can fit a space exactly. It can accommodate equipment measured to fit. If you are tall or short, tool lengths can be made to suit.

Overall you have the satisfaction of knowing that the complete concept is under your control. When laying out the whole or part of your property you can make things to suit and you suddenly will not find that a purchased seat, shed, gate, or other item cannot be made to fit. You make it and it will fit.

There is also the satisfaction of being able to make things that cannot be bought. For many of the tools described here there is no store-bought equivalent. You can make tools to suit a purpose and need. Those tools offered in a store suit average needs. In many cases purchased tools are satisfactory, but when you make a tool it should be right for you every time.

Very low on the list of priorities for a craftsman gardener is economy. Advantages of making things to exactly suit their purpose and the sheer satisfaction of saying, "I made that," outweigh considerations of cost. Usually, of course, the homemade

tool is less expensive than the purchased equivalent (if there is one).

That is assuming you are not allowing yourself a wage. Making individual tools for sale would involve a high selling price if the scheme is to be viable. With larger projects, there might be no mass-produced item to compare. You might find a prefabricated tool shed or seat to compare, but a fence, gate, arch or other item fitted to its surroundings will not be like anything you could buy. Economically you will have a very good deal compared with paying someone else to do the job.

Planning is important. Do not rush into making things, particularly large projects, and then find they will not fit or do not match their surroundings. It is helpful to draw a plan of the garden and yard—with the house and other fixtures shown on it—even if your property has a simple square outline. If the drawing is to scale and you draw additions to scale or cut their outlines to shape on loose paper to move around, you will avoid most mistakes. Even things like widths of paths or gates in relation to wheel tracks of carts to be used need advanced planning. If you are making a shed or tool locker, measure the contents first or you will feel silly having to shorten a handle to get it in.

You might already have some garden tools and equipment. Do these things function as they should? Before rushing into making new tools, you might be able to think of ways of altering or improving existing tools. Even if you decide to make replacements, there might be old parts you can recycle. Handles of discarded tools can be used again. Any old mild steel strip or rod will often find a new use. Pieces of tool steel are worth having even if they have not been tools. Springs are tool steel. Sheet mild steel can be cut from many discarded domestic appliances.

An advantage of wood that has already been used is that it can be assumed to be well seasoned. Obviously, if there are signs of rot or worm holes, you will not want to use the wood again, but much useful wood can be obtained from old furniture, crates, and similar things.

In a garden you will probably want to make bins and containers to hold soil or store crops. Although new wood can be used, an assembly of recycled wood can be just as effective. Even plywood with non-waterproof glue might last several months in dry weather. Another advantage of old wood is that its appearance will probably blend into its surroundings.

If you are an enthusiastic gardener but you live in an area where, for many months of the winter, you cannot work outside, making tools and equipment—prefabricating parts of sheds, seats, fences and other large projects—can keep your gardening interest alive. When you can work outside again, it will not take long to install your new work and then get on with the serious business of sowing, planting, and all the activities your garden will demand of you.

Chapter 2

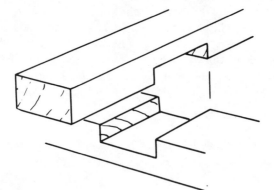

Wood

Most amateur craftsmen make things from wood. It is assumed that the reader of this book has some familiarity with wood and the basic techniques of working it with hand and power tools. Wood is a good choice for making a great many things, and it has many applications in tools and equipment for the garden and yard.

Almost any wood has possibilities. You can buy lumber, you can recycle wood that has been used in some other construction, or you can cut and convert wood growing on your own land.

Broadly, woods are divided into hardwoods and softwoods. The names are not strictly true definitions as the differences are botanical rather than descriptions of relative hardness. The majority of hardwoods are harder than most softwoods. The softwoods available are mostly firs, spruces, and pines. Some softwoods are not durable, but if they are resinous they have a longer life. Most hardwoods, such as oak, can be assumed to be much longer-lasting. Hardwoods tend to be heavy. For tools where lightness is important, it would be advisable to choose softwood and accept the fact that

it will not last as long. Softwood can be protected with paint and preservative and by storing it in a place when not in use.

Wood straight from the tree contains a considerable amount of moisture in the form of sap. There is less sap if the tree is felled in the winter, but there is still more than can be accepted for anything except rough construction. If you are planning rustic work where stability of the wood is not important, you can go ahead with it straight away. For anything else, the wood should be dried to a small moisture content by the process called seasoning. If wood is not seasoned, it will shrink and warp after being built into something, and it might develop lengthwise shakes (cracks).

Natural seasoning is done by stacking boards in a sheltered place, but where air can circulate, and then leaving them for some time (1 year for each 1 inch of thickness is appropriate). Commercially there are faster methods of seasoning. Lumber bought from a regular supplier should be correctly seasoned. Even then it is a good idea to buy well ahead of your needs and keep the wood for perhaps two months before using it. Then you can see if the wood will retain its shape and size.

Softwoods are sold in a standard sections so it is advisable to plan projects to suit them. Everyone knows about 2 × 4s, but there are many other sizes. With hardwoods it is advisable to check what sections your supplier has rather than present him with a cutting list of different sections. Otherwise he will charge you extra. Of course, if you have your own power saw of sufficient capacity you could buy economical larger sections and cut them down yourself.

Wood is typically sold in the size it is quoted as sawn. Although 2 inches by 4 inches might be the true sawn size, a planed 2 by 4 will actually be 1 7/8 inch by 3 7/8 inch (or less), and you should allow for that in your projects. There are several outdoor projects that can be made with wood that has not been planed, but an advantage of buying planed wood is that you are better able to see any flaws quickly rather than discover them later.

Natural wood, either round as it comes from the tree or just split down the middle, has many uses in the garden for making fences, arches, and similar things. Even smaller plant pot containers or other more compact constructions can be made with small pieces of poles or branches. You must first decide whether to use the wood with its bark on or to strip it off first. Most fir, spruce, and similar softwoods tend to shed their bark as they dry and shrink. What might look attractive when first constructed could eventually take on an untidy appearance where some bark is retained and other has fallen off. That wood is better stripped of its bark before making the wood into a project.

Some woods have bark that is very securely held. You could decide to leave it, but in general it is better to remove bark. Insects and other pests tend to gather between bark and wood. It is better for the life of the wood, and possibly for things growing nearby, to strip the poles or branches down to the wood.

Plywood has many uses in outdoor constructions; make sure you get the type bonded with a waterproof glue, which is described as *exterior* or *marine* grade. The latter is more expensive and not usually necessary. Veneers mainly affect appearance. For something like a compost container, the lowest veneer category might be just as useful as the more costly higher-quality plywood. If your project is a piece of patio furniture, the better-looking, high-grade plywood would be preferable.

Hardboard is not suitable for outdoor use. Even the oil-tempered type will not stand up to weather for long. Particleboard and some of the other manufactured boards might have exterior uses, but check what the manufacturer says about specific grades. In general, you are more likely to be satisfied with solid wood and the appropriate plywood for exterior work.

Not so long ago joints in exterior woodwork required mechanical fasteners because there were no glues that would stand up to moist conditions indefinitely. Otherwise there had to be wedges or interlocking joints. All of these techniques are still used, but there are modern, fully waterproof glues that will make secure joints unaided or to complement mechanical fasteners. Some of these glues are in two parts to be mixed before use or applied separately to the surfaces before bringing them together. Others are one-part glues. Unfortunately, trade names do not always give you a clue to the chemical content. If the glue is a two-part product or described as suitable for boats, it should be fully waterproof and strong enough.

NAILS

Many wood things for use in the garden or yard are nailed together, which is quite satisfactory for most assemblies. Usually there is not much to worry about, providing you use sufficient nails of sufficient length and you take care to hit the nail and not your own.

Common nails are made from round wire. These and the similar "box" nails are suitable for most garden carpentry. They are made of mild steel (which will rust) so it is advisable to buy them protected with zinc or other coating. Lengths usually available are from 1 inch to 6 inches, with increases in diameter to suit. They are sold by penny sizes, from 2d for a 1-inch nail through 6d for a

2-inch nail, and 20d for a 4-inch nail to 60d for a 6-inch nail.

If you are joining two pieces of wood, it is the amount of nail in the lower piece that provides strength. Therefore, you must choose a nail that will have enough penetration. How much penetration needed is more a matter of experience than a matter of rule, but you need a greater length in softwood than in hardwood and more in end grain than in side grain.

For many assemblies you can drive nails without drilling, but it might help you to drill the top piece to the same size as the nail diameter. This makes for easier driving and reduces any tendency to split the top piece, and it is advisable near an edge—even if you drive without drilling further along.

You can increase the strength of a nailed joint by dovetail nailing (Fig. 2-1A), with alternate nails sloping opposite ways. It also increases strength in the joint to put end nails closer together (Fig. 2-1B).

With thin wood you might only be able to get sufficient strength by taking a nail through and clenching its point. This will also provide a pivot if two parts have to move on each other. An example is a trellis that will fold when not required to be opened out. The best way to clench is to drive the nail through, with enough point projecting (Fig. 2-1C), and then curve the point over a spike while the other side is supported on an iron block (Fig. 2-1D). While still supporting the other side, bury the point diagonal to the grain (Fig. 2-1E), rather than along the grain (which might start a split).

SCREWS

Screws can be described as *wood screws* to distinguish them from *metal-thread* screws, that are used with nuts. Screws provide a more positive fastening than nails, with joints that are pulled

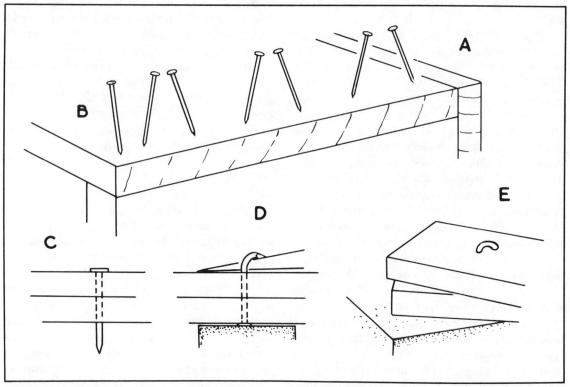

Fig. 2-1. The strength of a nailed joint is increased if nails are driven dovetail fashion.   With thin wood, a nail will go through and can be clenched.

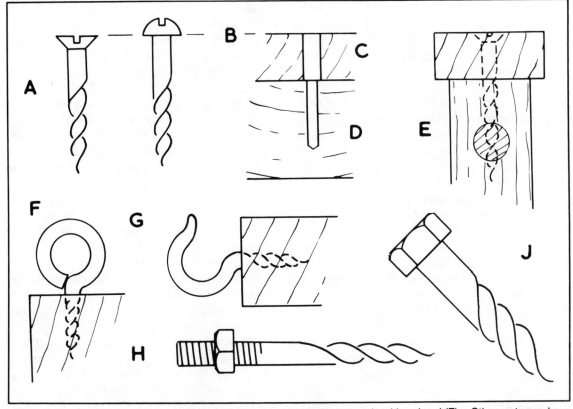

Fig. 2-2. Wood screws need holes (A-D) and can be strengthened in end grain with a dowel (E). Other parts can have screw ends (F-J).

closer and stronger. It is also easier to withdraw a screw with less risk of damage to the wood. Screwed construction is considered superior to nailing and is preferred for better work.

There are several types of screws, but for most purposes flat-headed ones are appropriate (Fig. 2-2A). Round-head screws are the only other type you are likely to need (Fig. 2-2B). The types with slotted heads for a common screwdriver are all you need, but other types with socket heads are really intended for quantity production and require special screwdrivers.

Screws are described by their length from the surface of the wood and are obtainable in several gauge thicknesses for each length. In small sizes, there are single-gauge number differences, but in lengths from about 1 1/2 inches up, your supplier will probably only have even-number gauge sizes.

Table 2-1 shows the most-used screw sizes.

Common screws made from mild steel can be bought protected from rust by various platings. They might be made of brass, which has a good resistance to moisture, or one of several other metals that usually are more costly but also have a good resistance to corrosion.

Table 2-1. Common Screw Sizes.

Length (inches)	Gauge sizes available
1	6, 8, 10
1 1/4	8, 10, 12
1 1/2	8, 10, 12
2	8, 10, 12, 14
2 1/2	10, 12, 14
3	14, 16, 18
4	16, 18, 20

The threaded part of a screw is about two-thirds of its length, and it is the pull of this in the lower piece of wood that draws the top piece tightly down. There is nothing to be gained by having the screw a tight fit in the top piece.

There should be a clearance hole for the shank of the screw in the top piece (Fig. 2-2C). If that wood is thin and part of the parallel shank enters the lower piece, you could also take the clearance-size drill a little way into that. Otherwise the plain shank forcing its way there may lift fibers on the surface and interfere with the joint pulling tight. With a small-diameter screw in softwood, you can start the screw in the lower piece with a tap from a hammer and let it cut its own way in as you turn it. In most cases, it is better to drill an undersize hole in the lower piece (Fig. 2-2D). In softwood, it need not be as large nor go as far as a hole in hardwood.

With many woods, a flat head will pull itself in flush with the surface. With harder wood, you can use a countersink bit to prepare the hole. Even then it is advisable to only partly countersink to allow for some pulling in. Round heads are more often used to hold metal to wood, but otherwise it is worthwhile putting a washer under the head to spread the load and increase pressure.

Screws are generally stronger than nails so they can be more widely spaced, but there should still be a good penetration of the lower wood and a greater length allowed in end grain. Screws can be installed closer to an edge. For an assembly like a box corner, you could use a screw for strength near the open top, while nails are used in the joint further down.

The grip in end grain is much less than in cross grain, particularly in some softwoods. This can be improved by putting a dowel across so that the screw goes through its cross grain (Fig. 2-2E).

Wood screw ends are provided in some other applications. Screw eyes (Fig. 2-2F) have uses in many outdoor projects such as hanging containers. There are several sizes and forms of screw hooks (Fig. 2-2G) that have obvious applications. Less obvious is the hanger screw or bolt (Fig. 2-2H). This is used where you want to drive a wood screw—

usually because you cannot take a bolt right through—and then attach a metal part. To drive a hanger bolt, tighten two nuts on it against each other, and then use a wrench on the top nut to turn the screw into a hole in the wood. Release the nuts by using two wrenches.

Very large and thick screws would be very difficult to turn tight with an ordinary screwdriver. Therefore, lag screws or coach screws (Fig. 2-2J) have heads to take wrenches. They must be started by hammering into the top of an undersize hole.

JOINTS

For much exterior woodwork it will be sufficient to put one piece of wood over another and either nail or screw it there. In some constructions, such as seats and tables, the joints will have to be more like those for interior furniture. Even then there are some variations advisable to suit the exterior situation.

If you want to positively locate one part over another, even if the fastening is to be a nail or screw, it is a help to notch one of the pieces (Fig. 2-3A). Notch both pieces if accuracy of location is needed both ways. This is helpful to retain symmetry even with rustic poles. The notches can be quite shallow.

If parts have to cross at the same level, whether square to each other or not, you must cut a halving joint (Fig. 2-3B). This weakens the wood. If you can cross without bringing surfaces to the same level, the notches can be shallower and the wood stronger.

Dowel construction is possible for some things, but you are then dependent upon only glue. It is better to build in some mechanical strength. That is more easily done with mortise and tenon joints. If the ordinary mortise and tenon joint has the tenon right through (Fig. 2-3C), there can be one or two saw cuts across the tenon end and wedges can be driven in (Fig. 2-3D). Do this with the wedges in the direction that expands the wood of the tenon toward the end grain of the mortised part.

A good way of coupling mechanical and glued

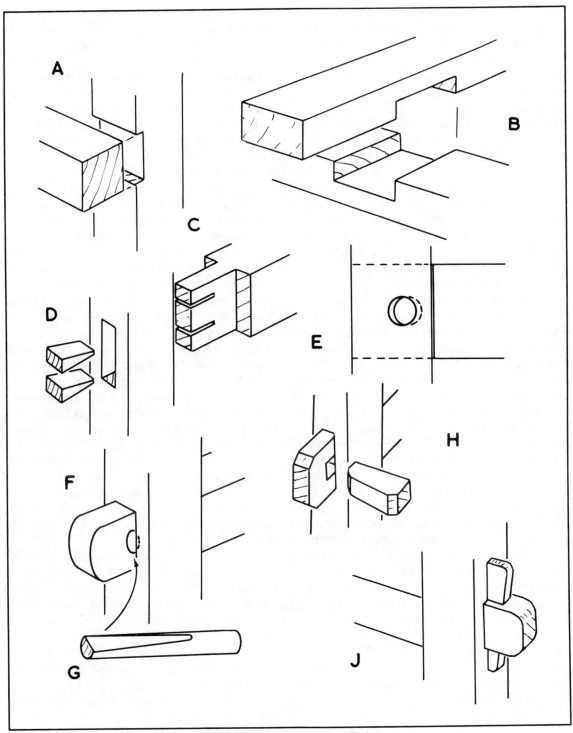

Fig. 2-3. Parts can be notched together (A, B) or tenoned with wedges (D-J).

strength is to draw-pin a mortise and tenon joint. For large seats and similar things, where it would be difficult to use clamps, draw-pinning pulls joints together. Cut a mortise and tenon joint, and then drill across the mortised part, either central or toward the side where the tenon shoulder will come. In the tenon, mark and drill a similar hole, but slightly toward the shoulder (Fig. 2-3E). How far you move this depends on the wood, but 1/8 inch is probably right for a 1/2-inch hole. Taper the end of a dowel rod longer than the thickness of the wood. Glue the parts and fit them together. Drive in the tapered dowel to pull the joint tight, and then cut off the extending tapered and top parts.

Another way to tighten a mortise and tenon joint is with external wedges through what are called *tusk tenons*. This can also serve as decoration. In its simplest form, let the end of the tenon extend and drill a hole across that will have its edge below the surface of the other part (Fig. 2-3F). Plane a taper on the side of a dowel that fits the hole in order to make a wedge (Fig. 2-3G), and drive that through the hole with the flat surfaces together. This pulls the tenon tighter into its mortise. The end of the tenon can be shaped and the dowel cut so it projects evenly after driving.

A wedge with a rectangular section might look better than a tapered dowel. The important thing is to cut the slot for the wedge so its inner edge is below the surface of the mortised part. This way the wedge forces outwards against the wood of the tenon. The slot should taper to match the wedge (Fig. 2-3H), which can have decorated ends.

It may be better in some constructions to have the wedge the other way through the tenon (Fig. 2-3J). In all of these wedged tenons there is a considerable thrust on the end grain. It is advisable to only use the method on compact hardwoods and then to allow adequate wood outside the slot.

Variations on these and other joints are described in this book with particular projects to which they apply. For most exterior woodwork, simpler joints are preferable to some of the more complicated ones appropriate to indoor constructions.

EDGE JOINTS

For some outdoor projects it is necessary to join pieces of wood to make up sufficient width. Where a wide board is available it is usually preferable, but there may be a risk of warping and that is often counteracted by different grain patterns in several boards joined to make up a comparable width. If you are buying wood, the wide pieces might be disproportionately more costly due to their rarity.

Gluing is the obvious way to join boards edge to edge, and modern waterproof glues should be just as successful outdoors as indoors, providing the wood has been seasoned to only a small moisture content. No glue can be very effective on wood containing an excess of water. If the wood is unsuitable for gluing, it is still possible to make a mechanical joint that will be satisfactory in many outdoor situations. Even with simple glued joints, there might be a problem in an assembly that has to stand up to all the rigors of year-round exposure. The glue line might hold, but wood fibers nearby might fail. Therefore, it would be advisable to do more than merely glue surface to surface.

For many assemblies, strips can be joined with cleats or battens across at the back or underneath (Fig. 2-4A). These pieces can be just nailed or screwed. If you are putting something together fairly wide that might have to withstand rain and sunlight, there ought to be an allowance for expansion and contraction. This will apply to a door or tabletop, possibly 30 inches wide, when a 1/4-inch alteration in total width could be expected at different seasons.

The variations can be taken care of by slot screwing. If equal expansion has to be allowed for, use round holes for central screws, but put those further out in slots (Fig. 2-4B) up to 1/4 inch long or more toward the outside. If it is an assembly where one side should remain unaltered, put screws at that side in round holes and have the others in slots getting progressively longer towards the other side.

If dry wood is to be glued edge-to-edge, plane both edges straight and try them together to see

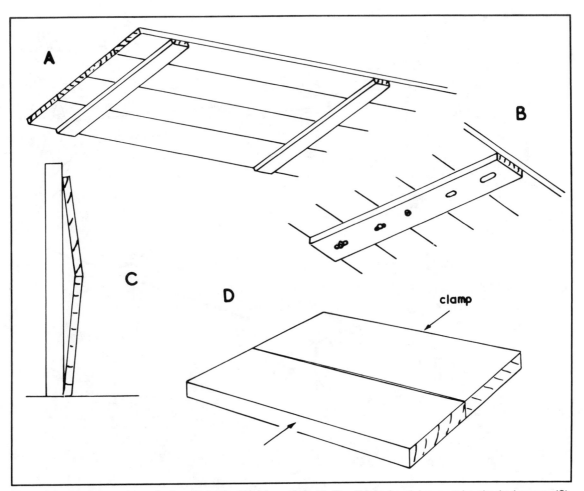

Fig. 2-4. A wide top can have the boards held with strips across (A, B). Edges for gluing must be checked square (C), and a slight hollow helps in clamping tightly (D).

that they will not finish out of true on the surfaces (Fig. 2-4C). Trouble comes with ends of joints opening. This can be avoided by making the meeting surfaces very slightly hollow in the length, and then a central bar clamp can be used to close the joint and the ends will be forced tighter than the center (Fig. 2-4D). If there have to be several edge joints to make up a width, it is wiser to make them one at a time. This will reduce the risk of the boards buckling out of true while clamping.

If increased strength is wanted in an end joint, dowels can be included. How many and their spacing depends on circumstances. For example,

a joint in a tabletop of 1-inch boards might have 3/8-inch dowels at 6-inch intervals. Care is needed in marking out. Put the planed edges together and mark across, and then gauge from what will be the top surfaces (Fig. 2-5A). Drill slightly too deep. Dowels going 1 inch into each piece should be sufficient (Fig. 2-5B). Taper the ends of the dowels so they will enter easily. A saw cut along each dowel is worthwhile because it lets air and surplus glue escape as the joint is clamped.

Secret slot screwing is a good way of strengthening a joint and pulling it together. This is just as suitable for outdoor as indoor woodwork.

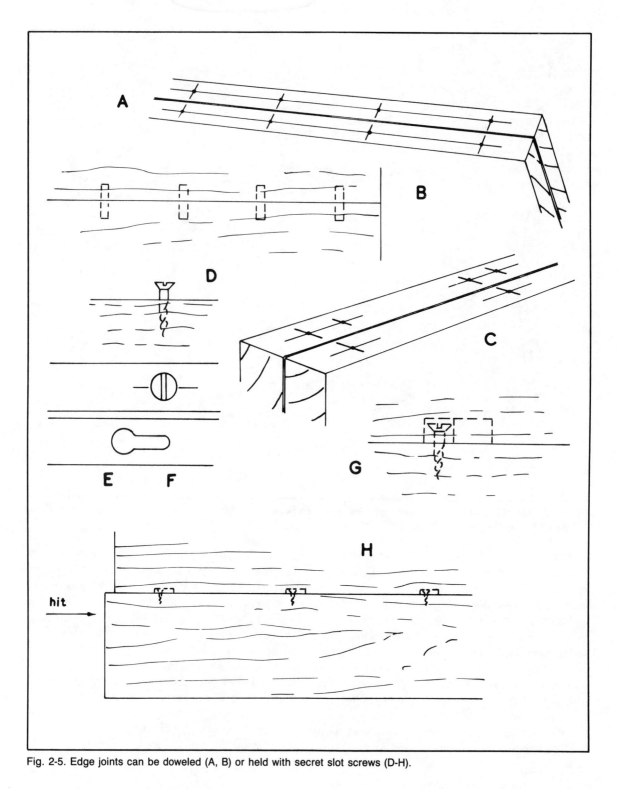

Fig. 2-5. Edge joints can be doweled (A, B) or held with secret slot screws (D-H).

It is intended for use with glue, but even without glue it will lock edges together in addition to battens or in place of them. The method uses screws in one edge, with their heads projecting into slots in the other piece. Careful marking out is essential.

For boards about 1 inch thick, suitable fasteners are steel screws 1 inch by 8 (or 10 gauge). If you are using hardwood, choose thicker screws because they have to resist bending. Space the screws according to the strength needed, but 6-inch intervals will probably be satisfactory.

Put the boards together and mark hole positions as if for using dowels, and then mark more hole centers 1/2 inch away (Fig. 2-5C). Drive screws into the board with single-hole positions, going far enough in to bury the threads and leave about 1/4 inch projecting (Fig. 2-5D). In the other board, drill holes, at the second position, large enough to clear the screw heads (Fig. 2-5E). At the points opposite the screws in the other board, drill holes of a size to clear the neck of the screws. All of the holes should be slightly deeper than the projection of the screws. Make slots from the small holes into the larger ones. Some of the waste can be drilled away and the slots trued with a chisel (Fig. 2-5F).

Bring the boards together with the screw heads in the large holes (Fig. 2-5G). Hit one board along so the screw head cuts its way along the slot (Fig. 2-5H). Knock it back again and coat the surfaces with glue. Tighten each screw one-quarter of a turn and assemble the joint again. As you drive one board along the other, the joint should pull very tight.

Brass screws might seem more suited to outdoor use, but they might bend during tightening, except in very soft wood. The screws are buried and protected with glue so there is little risk of steel rusting.

Chapter 3

Metal

Basic metalwork is as interesting and no more difficult than woodworking. A considerable amount of metalwork can be done with hand tools, and for most of the projects described in this book you will not need power tools, other than an electric drill.

Many tools and equipment for the garden and yard combine wood and metal. This combination offers some interesting work, and probably a greater satisfaction to the maker than something in wood or metal alone. A knowledge of metals and alloys helps in selecting suitable material and knowing about the effects of heat treatments gives you scope for interesting constructions. Some general metalworking techniques are described in this chapter, but others are described where they apply to particular projects.

IRON AND STEEL

Most tools for garden and farm have their principal parts made of what is loosely termed "iron." That is a convenient general term, but it is not strictly correct any more than talking of a "tin" roof. Tin is a fairly valuable metal and a roof made of it would be very expensive. The roofing material is really iron coated with zinc. This combination has a good resistance to corrosion. Tin is used as a very thin protective coating on iron for cans and other things because it is safe in contact with foodstuffs. Tin is not used on roofs.

Pure—or almost pure—iron is rare today. It is sought after by blacksmiths for the ease with which it can be worked, but now they have to be satisfied, usually, with mild steel. Cast iron is a form of iron, often with many impurities, that can be melted and poured into a mold. It is of use when a part has to be cast, but it is unsuitable for working in bar and strip and cannot be made into sheets. As the heat needed to melt iron to be cast is greater than anyone except a specialist worker would have, cast iron (except as ready-made parts) is of no interest to the maker of tools to be used on the land.

Steel is iron containing a proportion of carbon (which alters iron's characteristics). It is sometimes spoken of as an alloy, a mixture of metals, but as carbon is not a metal the term is not strictly correct. A small amount of carbon in iron does not have much effect on it. Such *mild steel* is usually inferred today when "iron" is used. Mild steel is not as ductile as pure iron, but it can still be bent and shaped or forged to a sufficient degree. Steel is more prone to rust than pure iron.

Rust is oxidation of the surface due to the effect of moisture in the atmosphere. The corrosion is a layer of ferrous (meaning iron) oxide. On pure iron, the first corrosion is slight and this forms a skin that restricts further corrosion. On steel, corrosion will go on progressively if unchecked by protective coatings. This could be a coating of other metal with a good resistance to corrosion, painting, or occasional wiping with oil or grease (which is the most usual treatment for outdoor tools).

Anything that does not have to cut can be satisfactorily made with mild steel, sometimes termed *low-carbon steel*. With an increased amount of carbon, the steel will accept heat treatment so that it can be hardened and tempered (the dual treatment for giving it the required hardness) or annealed (which brings it to its softest state). This is *high-carbon* or *tool steel*. Straightforward tool steel made into many tools can be heat treated satisfactorily with the facilities available to most craftsmen or the operators of small shops. There might not be the precision that is available for heat treating at a large manufacturing plant, but simple methods and approximate temperatures should give a satisfactory result.

Today there are a large number of steels with other metals alloyed to give special characteristics, including stainless and nonmagnetic. Unfortunately, these steels require careful temperature control when heat treating and, therefore, are unsuitable for most makers of individual tools. When something harder than mild steel is required, the choice should be straight tool steel.

For practical purposes nothing you do to it will affect the characteristics of mild steel enough to notice. It can be hammered, bent, drilled, machined and forged to different shapes, then its characteristics will still be the same.

HARDENING

If you heat tool steel to redness and cool it rapidly in water, it will be hardened. It is then as hard as it can be, but unfortunately it is also brittle. If it is given a cutting edge, it will crack or splinter if you try to use it. If you dropped the tool it might break. Metal-cutting files are left fully hard, or almost so, but this state would be unsuitable for other tools.

ANNEALING

If you heat tool steel to redness and let it cool extremely slowly, it will be annealed to the softest state it can be. New tool steel might be already fully annealed and described so by the makers. If you want to anneal tool steel yourself, the best way is to heat it in a fire and leave it to cool overnight with the fire. If you heat it with a blow-lamp flame, surround it with coke or other fuel, so that is heated as well, and then leave it all to cool. Annealing is important if you want to machine or drill the steel. In any state but not fully annealed, you would blunt the drill and probably not make a hole. The drill is also tool steel; it cannot be expected to cut through something as hard as itself. Today, drills are usually alloyed with other metals to give increased toughness, but they still cannot cut through unannealed tool steel.

TEMPERING

For most of the things we want, the final hardness of the steel has to come between the fully hardened and fully annealed states. By reducing some of the hardness, the tendency to brittleness is also reduced. The required hardness for a particular tool is found by tempering, which is done after hardening. The steel is heated to redness and quenched to harden it. It is again heated to a certain temperature, which varies according to the intended use, when it is quenched again.

If we had to measure the temperature, most of us with limited equipment would be in difficulty. Fortunately, there are colored oxides that form on a smooth bright surface of tool steel at definite temperatures. By watching the formation of these oxides and quenching at the right moment, you can get the correct temper without special equipment. The oxides will still be there after quenching; you can check results. Remember that the oxides are only a clue to temperature. You can get the same colors on mild steel, but that does not mean you have done anything to the hardness of the metal. When you are dealing with tool steel, it is only the part that was previously brought to redness in hardening that will be tempered. Nevertheless, you will see the oxide colors on other parts.

The oxide colors come in rainbow formation in a definite sequence. They can be seen on a clean, polished surface. Heating to harden takes away the polished effect. If you start with a bright surface, it can be rubbed bright again, after heating and quenching, by using emery cloth or a piece of sandstone.

To familiarize yourself with the colors, have a length of flat steel, perhaps 12 inches long, with one surface rubbed bright. Hold it by one end and heat near the middle with a flame. Once colors have started appearing there, withdraw the flame and only return it briefly, if necessary, until the whole set of colors are spreading from the heated part. If you keep the heat to the minimum necessary, each band of color will widen as it spreads so you get a better idea of the color sequence and the way the colors blend into each other. Overheating, or quick heating, will produce much narrower bands of color. The sequence of colors and their shades, with examples of tools that are tempered to those colors, is shown in Table 3-1.

Annealing should be done before working on the steel, but then you usually completely make the tool before hardening and tempering it.

As a practical example of hardening and tempering, make a screwdriver from a piece of 1/4-inch round tool steel. If it is newly annealed steel, file the taper at the end (Fig. 3-1A). If you prefer an awl, you could make a point. At the other end, file a square point for driving into a handle. Brighten the working end with abrasive. If you do not know if the steel has been annealed, your first attempts at filing will show you. If you cannot file,

Table 3-1. Tempering Colors.

Color of oxide	Tools
Light yellow	Files
Yellow	—
Dark yellow	Chisels
Brown	Shears, scissors
Dark brown	Knives, punches
Brown/purple	Axes
Light purple	Hoes, spades
Dark purple	Saws
Blue	Screwdrivers, springs

do not continue because that would ruin the tool. Anneal the steel before going further.

Heat the screwdriver end to redness for a distance of up to 1 inch and quench in water. Lower vertically into the water (Fig. 3-1B). If the tool goes in sideways, the slight unevenness of quenching might cause cracking. The end is now hardened and brittle; treat it gently. Brighten all of that end with emery cloth or other abrasive.

Use a blow-lamp flame to heat the rod a few inches back from the end (Fig. 3-1C). Watch the oxide colors form. They will spread outward. Those that go away from the working end are of no consequence. Keep the heating to a minimum once the colors form so that they spread in wide bands. When the blue color reaches the end, again quench the steel vertically in water. If you are satisfied that you have the right color at the end, clean off the colors and the whole tool with emery cloth, and fit a handle.

If you make a mistake and quench too late or too early, you must go back to hardening again before making another attempt at tempering. This method works with any pointed tool or even one with a broad end, like a chisel. You can harden and temper a chisel for cutting rock or metal or deal with the end of a pick ax or other end-cutting tool.

If you work quickly, it is possible to harden and temper such a tool end with one heating. Heat the end to harden it, as just described, but when you quench the red hot end do not plunge the whole tool into water. Immerse enough to cool the red end and a little further, leaving plenty of

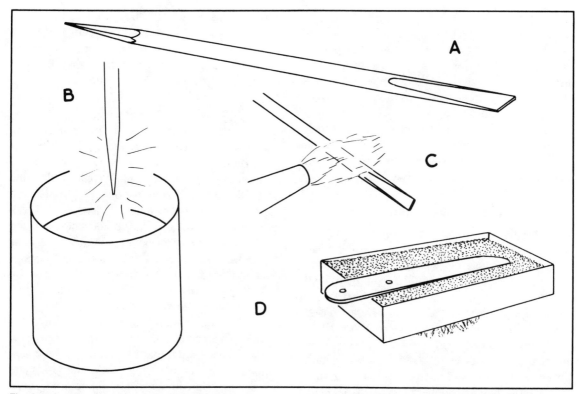

Fig. 3-1. A screwdriver end is hardened and tempered with a flame (A-C). A blade may be heated on sand (D).

heat still in the bar a few inches from the end. Quickly rub the end, and a few inches back, bright with abrasive and watch for the oxide colors coming along from the hot part. When you get the correct color on the end, immerse the whole tool endwise and it will be correctly tempered.

If you want to harden and temper a larger area—as would be necessary for the cutting edge of a knife, hoe, or other tool with a long or broad edge—you have to adopt a different method because local heating would give a patchy result. It might be possible to fan a blow-lamp flame over an area to get the degree of temper, but that is a chancy method.

For a piece of plate steel or other tool, such as a knife blade that is broad and not very thick, have it cleaned bright, and then heat it just to redness as evenly as possible all over the part that includes the cutting edge to harden it. Quench it quickly and clean it bright again.

Have a tray of sand ready. It should be a metal container rather larger than the metal to be heated for tempering and the sand should be about 1/2 inch thick. Put this over a flame to drive out moisture in the sand. Put the steel on the sand (Fig. 3-1D) and heat from below. The sand will spread the heat fairly evenly. At first you could immerse the steel in the sand to quicken its heating, but once the sand and steel get warm have the steel on top and watch as oxides form. Once they begin to appear, they will change quickly. Be prepared to act as soon as the color you want comes. Use pliers or tongs to lift the steel and drop it in the water. If you get it wrong, you must go back to hardening again before trying tempering a second time.

There is obviously a limit to the size of the tool that can be hardened and tempered by these methods, but many garden and farm cutting tools are within the practical range. If a tool part needs to be stronger than could be expected with mild steel, it is possible to use tool steel without hardening and tempering it and still find the results satisfactory. It is only when a cutting edge that will last has to be provided that hardening and tempering is essential. Tools that have to cut wood and metal are obvious examples, and tools to cut hay and other crops are other examples. For a tool such as a garden hoe that only has to cut soil, a reasonable life can be expected from an untreated blade. And its edge can be revived by filing.

NONFERROUS METALS

Most metals used in garden and yard tools are varieties of steel, but some others (described as nonferrous, because they lack iron) have their uses. The term *metal* is loosely applied to alloys as well as pure metals. None of the other common metals are as strong as steel, but most of them are easier to work and have better resistance to corrosion.

Copper is a soft, reddish metal that is now little used without being alloyed to other metals. Copper has been used for pipes because it suits their manufacture and copper pipes are easily bent. The only way that copper can become hard is by work hardening. If it is hammered, rolled, or otherwise worked, it could reach a stage where it gets hard; so much so that if nothing is done about it, it will crumble and crack. It can be annealed by heating to redness, and then by either cooling quickly or slowly. To a certain extent it will age harden if left as is, but in the annealed state it is very ductile.

Sheet copper can be hammered into quite deep bowl shapes, but it will have to be annealed many times in the process. If something made of sheet copper is to be brought to maximum hardness after the desired shape has been reached, it has to be *planished* (hammered all over), while supported on a stake or anvil, so the metal is squeezed at each blow between the hammer and the supporting steel surface.

Zinc is a metal that is seldom used alone today. It is a drab grey color and difficult to polish. At one time it was used for kitchen utensils because of its considerable resistance to corrosion and the ease with which it could be soldered. Perforated zinc sheets can still be obtained. They had much use in pioneer days for food storage cabinets, before the days of refrigeration, as they let cooling draughts through but kept flies out.

BRASS

Zinc is alloyed with copper to make brass. The quality and characteristics of the resulting alloy depend on the proportions of the two base metals. In any case the result is yellow: paler if the zinc proportion is high and more golden if there is more copper. Sheet brass is made with a fairly high copper content and it can be worked and annealed in the same way as copper (although it is never as soft or ductile). Brass takes a good polish to produce an attractive appearance. Brass parts on something mainly wood or another metal always gives a high-quality appearance.

Brass for machining contains more zinc. Rods can be machined cleanly, but this quality brass will break if an attempt is made to bend it. Where bending rather than machining is intended, rods and strips are made with copper and zinc proportions more like sheet material. Brass tubes will take slight bends, but they will also machine; pieces of brass tube make attractive ferrules on handles.

SPELTER

The melting point of an alloy is always lower than the melting points of its individual metals. This is taken advantage of in the making of *hard solder* or *spelter* for use in brazing joints using a flame. Copper and zinc in the correct proportions for a low melting point will form the spelter used in these joints. It is possible to vary the proportions so a spelter with a low melting point can be used near a joint made with a spelter having a higher melting point, and without the first joint separating. The melting point can be made even lower by adding silver. The resulting *silver solder* is obviously expensive and unlikely to be used on garden tools. However, there are low-melting-point hard solders obtainable with less expensive alloyed metals.

Brass and copper will corrode, but not to the same extent as iron and steel. Polishing gives a resistance to corrosion. When corrosion occurs, it is a greenish powder that rarely goes very deep. The initial corrosion provides a barrier to further corrosion. This can be seen in the green roofs of some old buildings where the copper sheathing has turned green, but will then last a very long time.

TIN AND LEAD

Tin can be alloyed with copper to make bronze; the sheet alloy is sometimes called *gilding metal*. Bronze has a better resistance to salt water corrosion than brass so it is used on boats. In an extreme case, saltwater will take the zinc out of brass so that screws and other parts crumble. Bronze has characteristics and appearance otherwise very similar to brass. The alloy could be used in similar situations on garden tools, if available, although it is not an alloy to choose specially.

Lead is a dull grey, heavy metal. Its concentrated weight governs most of its uses. If you want the most compact weight, it must be lead. Its melting point is low enough for it to be melted with an ordinary flame. Therefore it is possible to make a mold and pour in molten lead while using quite simple equipment.

Lead is obtainable as sheets that are very easily bent and formed. It has uses in gutters and as a valley between parts of a roof where it can be bent and cut to shape in position. Water pipes were once made of lead, but it is now known to be unsafe for carrying drinking water. In making tools, lead is more likely to be used to provide weight. There is no way of hardening or softening lead, but it has almost complete resistance to corrosion.

SOLDER

Lead and tin are alloyed together to make common or "tinman's" solder. The melting point is such that the solder can be made to flow with a soldering iron (actually a copper bit) or a flame. The proportions of the two metals affect the melting point and characteristics of the solder. At one time, a solder with a high lead content was used to make joints in lead pipes by *wiping*. This solder remained ductile enough before fully cooling for it to be wiped

to shape with a suitable cloth or moleskin.

When most pots and pans were made of tinplate, soldering played a big part in construction and repairs. A tinsmith or tinman was a busy craftsman, while the travelling tinker made his living from repairs.

In making garden and yard tools and equipment, soldered tinplate can be the best way to make special containers, measures, planters, and similar things. For a one-off item, soldered tinplate can provide better and easier results than fabricating from other materials.

ALUMINUM

Aluminum is well known as a lightweight, silvery metal with a good resistance to corrosion but not much strength. Pure aluminum is very soft. Most material loosely described as aluminum has other metals alloyed, in very small quantities, for hardening and strengthening. Most aluminum tubes are of this type.

Sheet aluminum might be used for making special containers and similar things, but it cannot be soldered by normal methods. Therefore, joints have to be screwed, riveted, or joined in some mechanical way or by specialized welding.

Corrosion of aluminum is usually slight and it takes the form of a fine powder that can be brushed off. Many structures of aluminum used outdoors are left untreated. Iron and most other metals require paint or other protection from the weather. There is no way to anneal or harden aluminum to any appreciable extent.

RIVETS

Rivets are used to make more permanent joints in metal than screws or bolts and nuts. They can provide all the strength needed in themselves, but in many garden tools one or more rivets are used to keep the parts in the correct relation to each other while they are brazed or welded. In that case, the rivet is not expected to provide much strength in the finished tool. Therefore, it can be thinner. Because most parts being joined are steel, the rivets should normally be iron or steel. For purely locating purposes copper rivets are easy to work. Aluminum is not compatible with brazing. If the rivets have to provide strength without the assistance of brazing or welding, they should be iron or steel.

In most small tools, the rivets can be 1/8 inch, 3/16 inch, or 1/4 inch diameter. They can be made from rod or you can buy rivets with prepared heads on one end. The common head is round (Fig. 3-2A) and sometimes called a *snap rivet*. It can be countersunk (Fig. 3-2B) and there are several others. Heads can be shaped in position with a ball-pane hammer (Fig. 3-2C), although a cross-pane (Fig. 3-2D) has uses in getting a head edge close to the surface.

A tool called a *snap* or *set* has a hollow to match a particular rivet head and might have a hole to match the diameter of the rivet (Fig. 3-2E). The hole is used over the end of the rivet to set down tightly the metal parts the rivet end projects through (Fig. 3-2F). The hollow can be used to support a prepared head, with the tool held in a vise, while the other head is formed. If you hammer a round head to a reasonable shape, the snap can be used over it to finish its surface. Without the support of a snap, a prepared head resting on an iron block will flatten, but that might not matter. Without a snap, you can support a prepared head on a lead block to avoid damage to it.

A hole for a rivet should be a close fit to avoid bending the shank when the end is hammered. If you want the head to finish level, countersink the hole properly to make a head that will have sufficient strength. Estimate the amount of rivet end left standing to be enough to fill the countersink (Fig. 3-2H).

If you have to make a rivet from rod, cut it to sufficient length to make two heads. Support one end on an iron block or with a snap and start forming one side. After a short time, work on the other side (Fig. 3-2J), and do this progressively until you have two good heads (Fig. 3-2K).

Rivet centers should be at least two diameters from an edge (Fig. 3-2L) and usually three or four diameters apart (Fig. 3-2M).

OTHER METAL FASTENERS

If you want to take a joint apart, as when making a tool with alternative heads, the parts can be held with nuts and bolts. If you need a "bolt" with a screw thread almost to its head, ask for a machine screw (Fig. 3-3A). If you ask for a "bolt," it will only be threaded a short distance from its end (Fig. 3-3B). If there is no good reason for using any other screwed connection, choose hexagonal nuts and bolt heads that are made with precision and suit standard wrenches. Normally, put washers under bolt heads and nuts (Fig. 3-3C).

If one or more parts have to rotate on a bolt, something has to be done to prevent the nut from loosening. The traditional way is to add a plain locknut (Fig. 3-3D), and then with two wrenches the lower nut is tightened against the upper one. There are many nuts available with friction of some sort built in (Fig. 3-3E). They hold without further assistance. A castellated nut (Fig. 3-3F), with the bolt end drilled for a cotter pin, is more often used in machinery and is less likely to be needed in garden equipment. However, a cotter pin and washer (Fig. 3-3G) is a good way of retaining a loose part on a rod.

If one part is thick enough and you have the necessary screwing equipment, you can dispense with a nut by driving a bolt end into a threaded hole (Fig. 3-3H).

A nut tightened with a wrench is most secure, if you want to be able to change a part or make an adjustment, but you have to find the wrench. To avoid that, you can use a hand-operated nut. For a small part it can be knurled (Fig. 3-3J). For more leverage it is better to use a wing or butterfly nut (Fig. 3-3K). In some situations, it might be better to cut a thread through a hole at the end of a flat strip (Fig. 3-3L). This will give you more of a wrench action.

CONICAL DEVELOPMENTS

Some long-handled tools are attached to the wood handles with tapered tubular parts, usually secured with one or two screws through holes. The conical part can be cut square across (Fig. 3-4A) or it

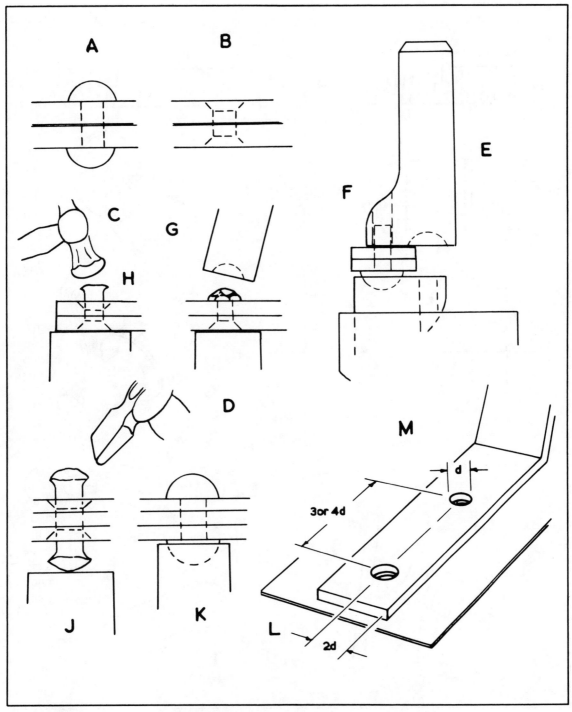

Fig. 3-2. Rivets can have round or countersunk heads and are closed with a hammer and set.

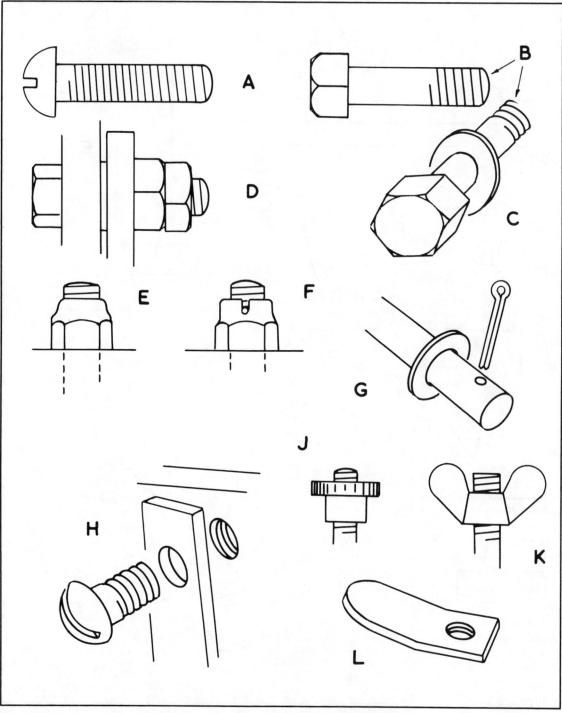

Fig. 3-3. Screws and bolts are used with several types of nuts (A-F). A cotter pin (G) holds parts on a rod. A thread in a part can take the place of a nut (H). Some nuts can be turned without a wrench (J-L).

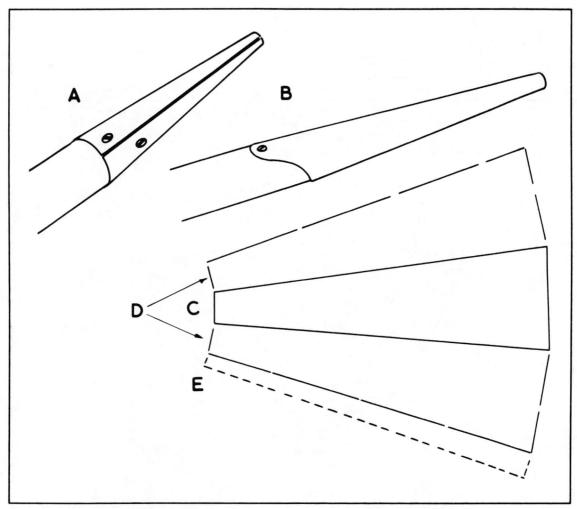

Fig. 3-4. Sheet metal for a tapered socket can have its developed shape set out approximately.

looks neat if shaped to a central screw hole (Fig. 3-4B). The lower side can be open. Therefore, it is possible to get a reasonable shape for the sheet steel before bending by doing little special marking out.

For a simple truncated cone, you can draw the size you want the finished part to be (Fig.3-4C) and mark each side of it the same (Fig. 3-4D) using a card template. That gives you a width of three times the diameter. For a full-width closed cone, it should be three and one-seventh (the relation between diameter and circumference of a circle) times the diameter. The odd fraction can be left as the gap

at the bottom or you can add a little when you cut out (Fig. 3-4E).

Round the ends and you have a shape that can be rolled to the final cone (as nearly accurate as it needs to be on most tools). If the top is to be shaped, you can draw in the outline freehand on half of the development, and then reverse it on the other side.

For a more exact truncated cone, particularly if the large end is to be curved, the shape should be set out geometrically. Draw a side view (Fig. 3-5A). If you want a shaped top, continue to where the point would be if cut square (Fig. 3-5B). At the

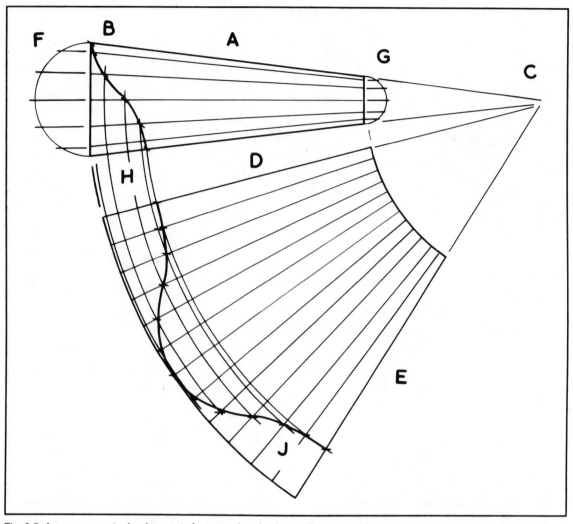

Fig. 3-5. A more accurate development of a tapered socket has ordinates transferred from a side view to the open shape.

small end, extend the lines until they meet (Fig. 3-5C). With that point as center, draw curves that will be the ends of the developed shaped. Draw a line for one edge to the center (Fig. 3-5D) and measure three and one-seventh times the diameter around the outer curve for a line to mark the other side of the development (Fig. 3-5E). That gives you the shape to cut the metal to roll into a square-ended conical object, if that is what you need.

If there is to be a curved end or there is any other shaping to be done, you have to draw lines (ordinates) on the side view and repeat them in ap-propriate places on the development. You can then mark points on the curve and join them up. Draw semicircles on the ends (Figs. 3-5F and G) and divide them into equal divisions; six should do (making 12 in a full circle). Project the points to the ends and join them. Divide the outer curve of the development into 12 and draw lines toward the center. Working around the center, project crossings on the side view lines to the matching lines on the development (Fig. 3-5H). Draw through these points to get the developed shape of the end curve (Fig. 3-5J).

Chapter 4

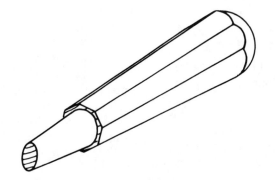

Tool Handles

Most tool handles are made of wood. There is a resilience and spring, as well as comfort, not found in other materials. It has a pleasing feel that is difficult to define, but a tool with a wood handle will usually be considered superior to one with a handle made of metal or plastic. For anyone making tools away from quantity production facilities or an elaborately equipped shop, wood has the advantage of being easier to work with simpler equipment than the possible alternatives.

If a long handle has to be made for a tool that is to have a chopping action (such as a hoe) or it is to be levered (as in a spade), the wood used should be springy or it will soon crack or break. The best woods for this purpose are ash and hickory. If the handle is not to receive the shock of blows, it is better made of a light wood. Straight-grained fir or pine provide lightness in a tool to be used for a long period and this allows you to continue working for a greater time without fatigue. Old-time hay rakes are examples of ultimate lightness in tools. Willow was used for rakes even

though it does not possess much strength or durability.

For short handles, such as those for trowels, hardwood is preferable. There might not be much load on the wood handle and weight is not of much importance, but a nicely shaped hardwood handle, finished with varnish, is attractive and pleasant to use. Certainly a wood handle is much better than plastic or the metal extension sometimes seen on such a small tool.

The handles of some tools can be made from metal tubes and aluminum alloy is usually chosen because of its lightness. For a tool such as a fruit picker, where lightness with length is important, this would be preferable to wood. There is little resilience or spring in aluminum tubing, so it would be a bad choice for a hoe or other chopping tool, but for a more gentle action, such as that of a rake, aluminum tube might be a good alternative to wood. Metal tubing does not provide a comfortable or firm grip, and something must be done to improve the grip where it is held. For some tool handles, aluminum tubing can be used with wood. The tube provides the length and wood makes the gripping handle at one end and, possibly, the tool attachment at the other end.

CUTTING WOOD HANDLES

One way of cutting wood for handles, particularly where the strength of continuous grain is more important than perfect straightness, is to split or *rive* the wood. The traditional tool for doing this is a froe (Fig. 4-1A), which is a long thick knife with a wedge section and a handle projecting square to the cutting edge at one end. This is driven into the end grain, usually with a crude mallet made from a log (Fig. 4-1B). Once it has started a split (Fig. 4-1C), the handle is moved from side to side to open and continue the cut (Fig. 4-1D). The split will follow the grain; therefore, its lines are parallel to the cut.

You finish with a piece of wood of an even thickness. If the grain lines wander, so does the shape of the piece of wood. If you have chosen

a piece of wood with reasonably straight grain lines, the handle you produce will be acceptable as it is and you know it has maximum strength because of the full-length grain. For some tools there is an advantage in having a curved handle.

Another way to cut wood for a handle is to choose a young tree or a branch from a larger one, of the right thickness, and peel the bark off it. It might not be exactly straight, but the grain lines follow the outside (as in a riven piece). Round wood prepared like this should be seasoned in the same way as flat boards. In some cases, the wood will split as it dries. Season more than you need to allow for some waste. When flat boards are seasoned, the ends may open.

SQUARE TO ROUND

Many handles will have to be made from wood bought as square pieces at a lumberyard. If you have a lathe, you should be able to turn short handles and you will certainly want to make those for trowels and other short tools in that way. Never-

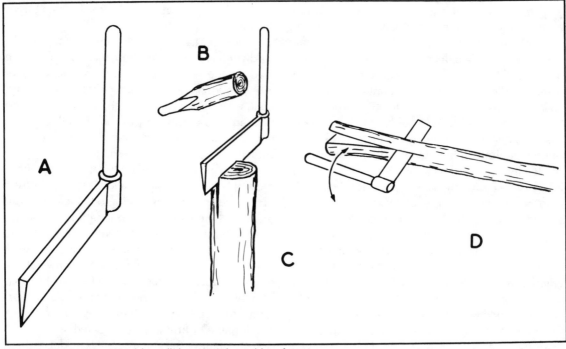

Fig. 4-1. The traditional tool for splitting natural wood is a froe.

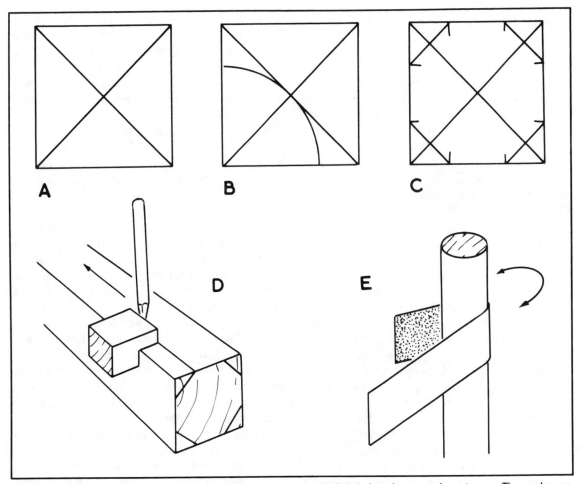

Fig. 4-2. To convert a square piece of wood to round, it is first marked and planed to a regular octagon. The angles are removed before sanding round.

theless, many garden and farm-tool handles have to be quite long in relation to their diameter. Most lathes will not accommodate 6-foot-or-so-long stock, and if they would there are problems in turning long, thin strips. Long handles are better converted from square to round in a different way. Fortunately, perfection in cross section is not important. Actually there are some tools where it is better to have a part with an elliptical section, in order to get greater strength in the direction of the load, that cannot be shaped with a lathe.

A rounded section can be obtained by planing either by hand or by machine. To secure reasonable uniformity as the cross section is

changed to round, it is first made into a regular octagon. Forming an octagon on a square is a simple piece of geometry. Draw a square of the size of the wood on paper or trace the end of the actual wood. Draw two diagonals (Fig. 4-2A). Set a compass to half a diagonal, and then put its point on a corner and swing it to mark two sides (Fig. 4-2B). You can do this at each corner and join the places where the arcs cut the sides (Fig. 4-2C), but doing it from one corner gives us all the information we need.

Mark the corners of the octagon along the wood, making eight lines in all. You can do this with a marking gauge. If you want to avoid scratches, cut a notched piece of wood and use a pencil (Fig. 4-2D).

Plane off the corners and you should finish with eight surfaces of equal width. Further shaping can be done by eye. Plane off the eight angles until you can see that you have sixteen surfaces of about the same width. It helps to have your light source, whether natural or artificial, on the other side of the bench so that you look across the wood and the plane marks are more easily seen. Almost certainly, there will be some unevenness to correct. A block plane in one hand, while you move the wood with the other hand, is useful at this stage.

From this point, final rounding is best done with abrasive (preferably cloth-backed) paper. Use a strip that you can pull backward and forward around the wood (Fig. 4-2E). The wood can be placed in a vise and moved round as necessary. It is also possible to hold the wood on a trestle, by sitting on it, and then it is easy and quick to release pressure for the many times you have to turn and move the wood. Of course, for some tools you may not need the fully sanded finish, and the handle can be left from planing.

If the handle is to be oiled or varnished, you should give the wood a good surface by doing a final sanding along the grain to remove the scratches made by the abrasive around the wood.

Some round handles have to be tapered. If it is a straight taper, you can mark out the octagons at opposite ends and join them with lines drawn with a straightedge. You cannot use a simple gauge because of the diminishing width. Some handles are further complicated by having to be thicker at some point, then taper toward the ends, and probably by different amounts. There is no basic way to mark this. You can estimate the shape, but there is a fairly simple method borrowed from boat spar makers who use a special gauge. Cut the wood to the intended lengthwise shape, tapered straight or curved, or with one or more thicker parts.

If it is a one-off job, work to a square the same size as the largest section. If you expect to have to deal with other squares, work to a square of the largest section you expect to have when making the special gauge (which can then be used on any square-sectioned wood smaller than that). Draw the square and mark the points on one edge for the corners of an octagon (Fig. 4-3A). Make a block of hardwood to fit over the square. Exact size is not important, but for a 2-inch-square maximum handle it could be 1 inch square and 5 inches long, with a notch 1/2 inch deep (Fig. 4-3B). There have to be two points to scratch lines along the wood. Mark on the gauge where the corners of the octagon come and drive in two nails. Cut them off 1/4 inch or less from the wood and file points on them (Fig. 4-3C).

This would serve for marking a piece of wood of the original size, but for narrower and tapered pieces the gauge has to be angled for the sides of the notch to bear on the wood. So that only the centers bear, cut back the notch ends but leave their centers unaltered (Fig. 4-3D). How much you taper the notch ends depends on the variations in width of wood with which you expect to deal.

In use, turn the gauge so both sides of the notch bear against the wood, and keep them there while you pull it along (Fig. 4-3E). If there are variations in the width of the wood, the angle of the gauge will alter, but the proportions of the widths marked will remain the same so long as you keep the side surfaces in contact.

With the octagonal sections marked even when the wood tapers or is irregular in the length, finishing is similar to that of a parallel piece of wood: plane off the corners to get regular octagonal sections, plane off the sharpness of the eight angles, and then remove any high spots. Sand with strip abrasive around the wood to finalize the shape and sand lengthwise to get a good finish.

FITTING TO A TOOL

Usually the top end of a long handle has to be rounded. If you are to wrap your hand over the end, it is important that this is an even shape and smooth (if you are to avoid blisters). The common shape to aim at is half a sphere, but perfection is unlikely. Nevertheless, that is what you should be aiming to produce. Have the end cut square across, and then go round cutting at about 45 degrees to

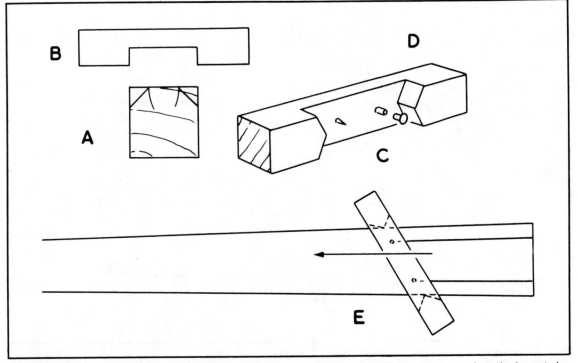

Fig. 4-3. When an octagonal section has to be marked on wood that is not parallel, a gauge made to the largest size can be used by altering its angle as it is drawn along.

the wood. You can use a plane or chisel, but a Surform tool is particularly suitable. You can hold the wood over the edge of a bench and rotate it with one hand, while cutting with the other (Fig. 4-4A). If you make a bevel all round, comparable with the width left on the end, you will be working similarly to the way an octagonal section is achieved in the length. Then it is easy to take off the angles (Fig. 4-4B) and finish rounding with more Surform work and some abrasive paper.

At the other end, you might have to taper the wood to fit a socket in a tool head. With practice you can do this by eye. If you taper too much, you can cut off the end so more of the wood goes into the socket, or even cut right back and try again (assuming there is some wood to spare in the total length).

If you want to work with precision, it is better for the taper to be marked out. Draw a circle the small end is to be on the wood (Fig. 4-5A). At the limit of the taper, you need a line around the cylin-

drical wood. A freehand line is sufficient, but mark it accurately with the straight edge of a piece of paper wrapped around as a guide for the pencil (Fig. 4-5B).

You can put the wood in a vise and plane the taper a little at a time. You could use a belt or disc sander and rotate the handle against it to remove surplus wood. Another way is to use a plane light enough to hold in one hand, and then rest the wood over the edge of the bench and plane the taper while rotating the wood with the other hand (Fig. 4-5C).

Some tool heads have a spike to drive into the end of a handle. It is unwise to attempt this without strengthening the end. The usual way to resist splitting is to fit a ferrule, (a tight-fitting piece of metal tube). Special ferrules, cupped to close over the wood end, can be bought but for most tools a piece of metal tube can be used. For small hand tools, the ferrule can be brass, copper, or aluminum. For such things as hoes and rakes,

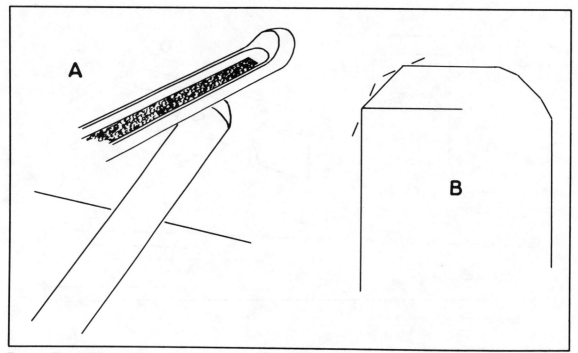

Fig. 4-4. The end of a handle can be rounded by first beveling.

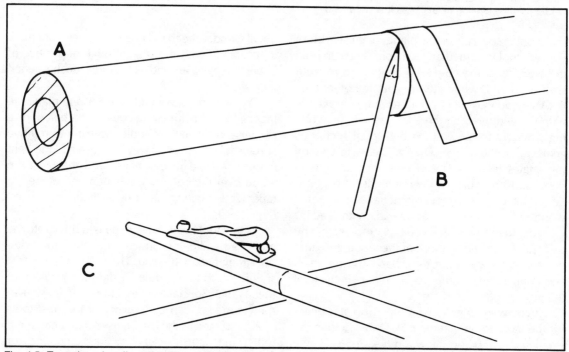

Fig. 4-5. To make a handle end to fit a socket, mark the size of the end and the length of the taper.

needing larger ferrules, steel tubing is better. If you expect to make many tools, it is worthwhile to accumulate a stock of odds and ends of tubes of many sizes for use as ferrules.

As a general guide, a ferrule made from tubing can be about the same length as its diameter, but you might want to vary this to suit a particular tool or just for the sake of appearance. On thicker wood, the tube length can be rather less than the diameter.

You will have to taper the wood slightly so the ferrule is a drive fit (Fig. 4-6A). For many tools, a tube ferrule on the surface is all that is needed. For neatness you can reduce the end of the wood so the outside of the ferrule is flush with the main part of the handle (Fig. 4-6B). Cut in at the ferrule limit, and then reduce the wood carefully up to the cut. Try not to cut the shoulder too deep and do not reduce the end too much because either of these things would defeat the object and the wood might split. It is usual to let the wood project a little through the ferrule (say 1/8 inch on a 1 1/2-inch diameter).

Drill for the spike or tang of the tool. In nearly every case, it is unwise to attempt to drive the metal point in without making a hole first. Despite the ferrule, there is far too great a risk of splitting. How much to drill depends on the wood. Holes can be smaller in softwood than hardwood. You can let the tang point penetrate the last of the depth without a hole going all the way in softwood, but in hardwood there should be a hole as far as the metal is expected to go. Holes should be drilled in steps (Fig. 4-6C). For a short distance, the hole might be nearly the full size of the metal, and then reduced two or three times. In wood that tends to clog the drill, start large. If the wood drills cleanly, go all the way with a small drill first because that guides the other drills and it is easier to keep the final stepped hole straight. A depth gauge on the drill, or careful measuring, will prevent drilling too much or too large.

You have to estimate how much undersize to make the hole. If the tang is square, work to the sizes across the flats; the corners will provide grip as they penetrate the wood. Measure the length of the tang, before you drive it in, so you know when it has gone in the required amount. Usually, the tightness of the fit is all that is needed to keep handle and tool head together. You could smear

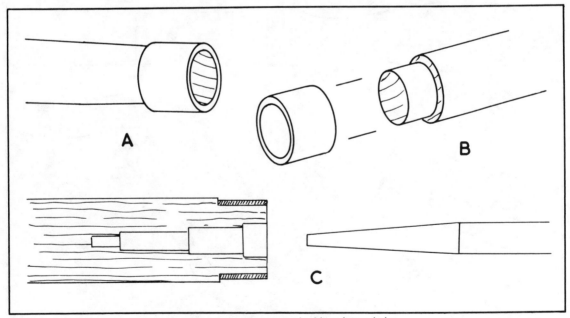

Fig. 4-6. A metal ferrule prevents wood splitting when a tang is driven into a hole.

epoxy glue inside the hole to bond the wood and metal. If you are unfortunate enough to drill too much, so a tang would not grip, all is not lost. Mix sawdust with epoxy glue and put it in the hole around the metal. The mixture will set and fill any gaps.

METAL HANDLES

Solid metal rod would be too heavy on most tools, but for some long handles, metal tubing makes an alternative to wood. In particular, aluminum alloys make lightweight, stiff handles. They are unsuitable for tools that have to deliver blows because spring in the tubing is minimal and a jarring action would be transmitted to a hand or a tube might break or buckle. As an example, a long handle for a rake

made of aluminum tube should be at least as good, and probably lighter, than a wooden rod.

A common fault with aluminum handles is that they are often of too small a diameter to be comfortable in long use. An outside diameter of 1 to 1 1/4 inches is needed for a comfortable grip.

The end of a tube can be left open, with any sharpness filed off, but it is better plugged. There are plastic plugs available that are intended for use with parts of tubular furniture. There also are rubber and plastic feet for tubular metal chairs that can be adapted. Obviously, these have to be matched; get tubes and plugs at the same time. Quite often diameters are less than you want. For larger tubes, it is better to turn wooden plugs. The plugs could be just short pieces (Fig. 4-7A), extended for decoration, to permit a hole for a hanging cord (Fig.

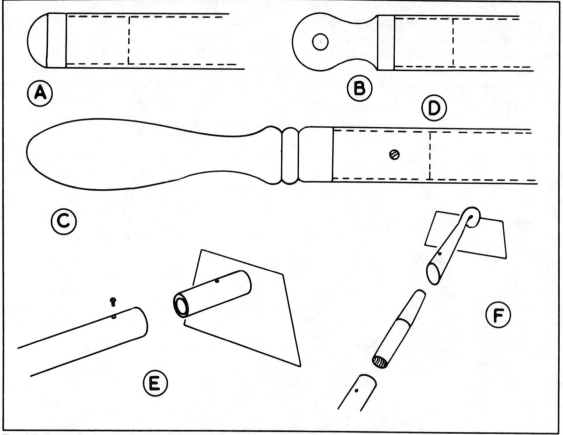

Fig. 4-7. A metal tube can have wooden ends to make handles or a means of attaching to a tool.

4-7B) or even longer to make a better grip than is offered by the metal tube (Fig. 4-7C). A plug can just be driven in, but then shrinkage might cause it to loosen. It could be held in with epoxy adhesive or you could drill the tube for a small nail or screw (Fig. 4-7D).

At the other end there can be a rod or tube extending from the tool head to telescope in the handle (Fig. 4-7E), to be held with a screw or rivet. If you are making a tube handle to replace a wooden one, there could be a tapered wood plug in the tube (Fig. 4-7F).

Except for brief use, a metal tube does not provide a satisfactory grip. Although it might be clean, your hands will turn black and it is slippery. Even if it does not look very attractive, binding with electrician's tape will produce a good grip. There are some flexible plastic sleeves that can be softened in hot water and stretched over to provide a grip. If the size is right, bicycle handlebar grips can be used.

Metal tubing is useful if you want to make a long handle to take apart. That might be needed for a fruit picker (which is easier to store if reduced to half-length). It might be that you want to put a long tool in the car trunk and it has to be in two parts.

Some aluminum tubing is available in telescopic sizes; each diameter fits easily into the next size above. If you can get those tubes, it is easy to make a take-down joint. One tube can push into the other as far as a bolt or rivet stop (Fig. 4-8A). If you want both parts to be the same size, there can be a tube held with screws in one piece so the other pushes on (Fig. 4-8B). An overlap of each part of about 4 inches would be about right. If the parts ought to be locked together, you could use a self-tapping screw (Fig. 4-8C). For that you need a screwdriver, but for a safe joint without tools for assembly the end of the outside tube can have L-shaped slots to engage with a screw on one or both sides (Fig. 4-8D) or there could be a rod through (Fig. 4-8E).

The two parts need not both be metal tube. There could be a wooden handle on the tool, and then a tube used when it has to be extended. In that case, the wood end goes inside the tube (Fig. 4-8F) in the same way as an inner metal tube. The only problem with using a wood plug piece is the probable expansion and contraction of the wood, which would cause variations in the fit. An improvement is a metal sleeve on the end of the wood part (Fig. 4-8G). Both parts could be wood with short pieces of tube to make the joint (Fig. 4-8H).

SHORT HANDLES

Trowels and many other small tools that a gardener uses are best fitted with hardwood handles. A varnished handle, possibly with a brass ferrule where appropriate, is a pleasant thing to use and much better than a plastic or metal extension of the working end of the implement. Wood handles can be made in a great variety. Anyone with a lathe can produce many attractive handles that are often of better design than some on manufactured tools. Certainly they are more individual. Short handles, as described in this section, are those up to about 20 inches long.

Without a lathe, handle shapes are confined to straight types or those that can be carved. A simple square, with the corners taken off, can be practical but rather unattractive (Fig. 4-9A). If it is tapered and given a regular octagonal section, it immediately looks more attractive (Fig. 4-9B). It might need a tapered end to fit a socket (Fig. 4-9C), or for a tang on the tool it should have a ferrule (Fig. 4-9D).

A carved handle can be made to fit your hand, with an enlarged part for the fingers and an extension at the end to prevent your hand sliding off (Fig. 4-9E). On a square piece of wood, cut and mark the view from the side (Fig. 4-9F), and then draw the outline of the top view (Fig. 4-9G). If there is to be a tubular ferrule, fit that at this stage (Fig. 4-9H), and then carve or whittle the handle shape. When it is finished, there should be none of the flat cross-sectional surfaces remaining.

For turned handles there are some basic shapes to use as guides. Most common is what can be called a file-handle shape (Fig. 4-10A). A variation on this has a parallel part for the grip (Fig. 4-10B).

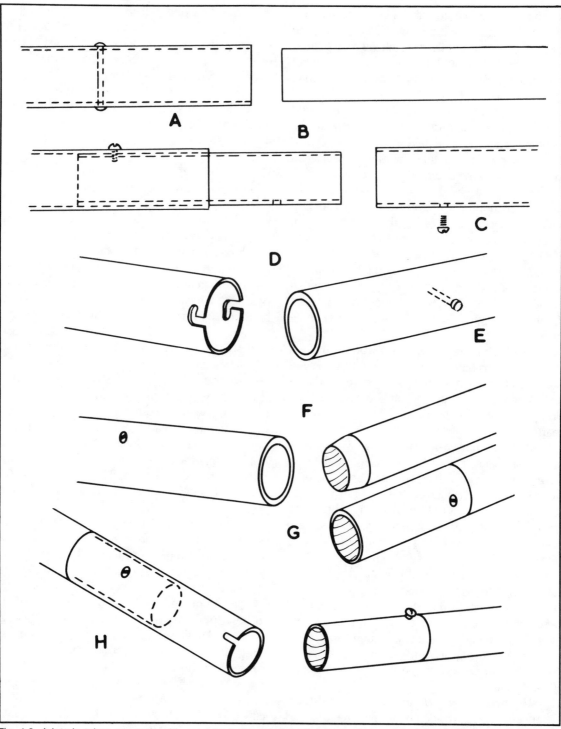

Fig. 4-8. Joints in tubes are made with one tube inside another. Tubes can be used for joints between wooden rods.

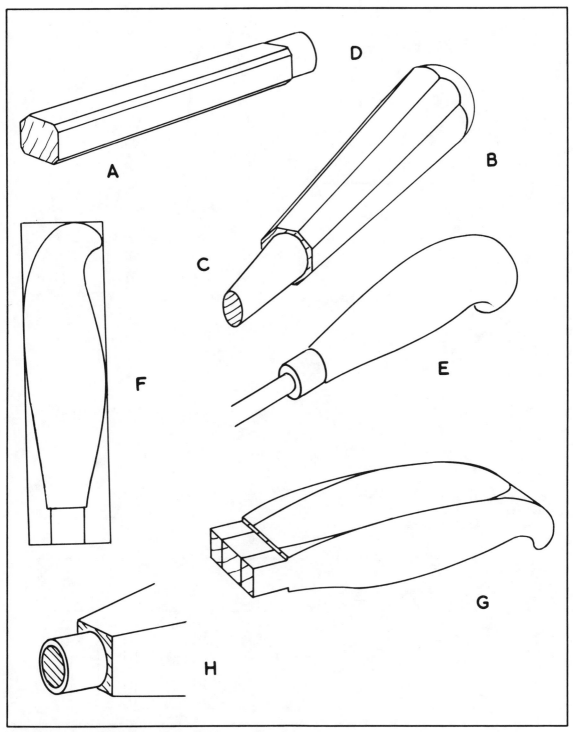

Fig. 4-9. Wood handles can be square, tapered, or carved.

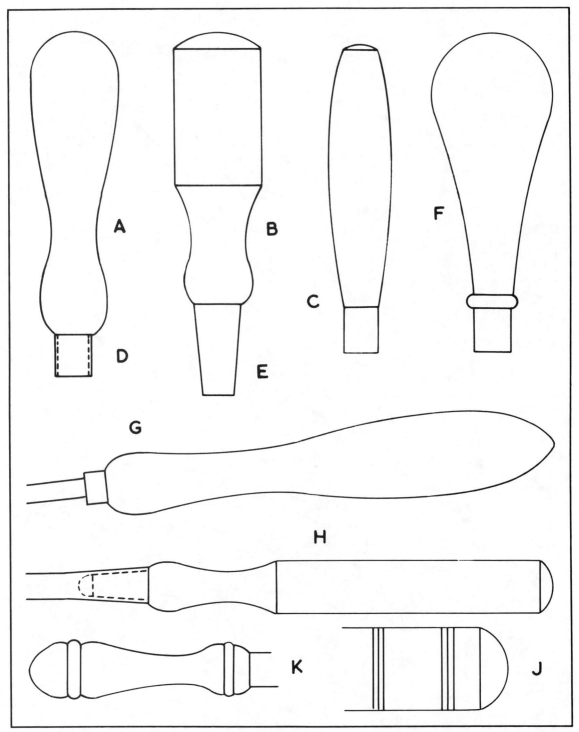

Fig. 4-10. Turned handles can take many forms to suit the tool.

The barrel-shaped chisel handle pattern (Fig. 4-10C) has some uses on garden tools, but it is not so good for end thrusts. Any of these, about 5 inches long and with a 1-inch or 1 1/8-inch maximum diameter, will provide a good one-hand grip. There could be a tubular ferrule to take a tang (Fig. 4-10D) or a tapered end to go in a socket (Fig. 4-10E). Make the taper so that it binds against the socket to get a tight fit before its end reaches the limit inside. Testing before completion of turning will show where the wood is rubbing and what has to be taken off.

If the tool is one where most of the work is pushing, turn more of a knob on the end (Fig. 4-10F) for the palm of the hand to push against.

If you want a longer reach, the file handle shape can be stretched (Fig. 4-10G) or the design with the parallel part can be given whatever length is needed (Fig. 4-10H). In both cases, there is enough space for two hands. Rings (Fig. 4-10J) or beads (Fig. 4-10K) will decorate a handle and strengthen your grip. Beads for the whole length of a parallel handle would be useful and attractive.

On any handle that will require a thrusting action, make sure the end is well rounded in order to reduce the risk of sore hands. A hole drilled through near the end of a handle can take a cord for hanging the tool on the wall or on your belt. Countersink the hole each side to remove roughness.

Chapter 5

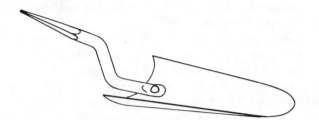

Small Hand Tools

Much gardening around the home has to be done with small tools, many of which can be controlled with one hand. Sometimes the tool has a long handle, for use when standing, but when the work is done kneeling or the soil is in a raised bed, a tub or a window box, the tools are better with short handles.

An advantage of making your own tools is that they can be the size and shape you prefer or which suit the particular circumstances. Someone in an urban situation, with a "garden" consisting of window boxes, can have light, narrow tools that are smaller than those obtainable in a tool store. Someone with extensive flower beds might want tools bigger than usual to get through the tasks quicker.

Small tools have the attraction of not needing much material, and in most cases the work can be done with simple equipment. Although some more ambitious tools really require the use of a well-equipped shop, hand gardening tools can usually be made with hand woodworking and metalworking tools only—which seems appropriate.

The tools described in this chapter involve several methods of construction and the sizes given are average. Even if you only want to make one of the tools described, at least look through the instructions for the others. You can then select an alternative detail to incorporate. An example could be a tang instead of a socket to connect to the wood handle or rivets to join parts without the help of brazing or welding.

If you are doubtful about your ability to work in wood and metal, you will find it worthwhile tackling some of the small hand tools first. When you are more certain of your skills, move on to larger and more complicated things. In many cases, you will find that a larger project only requires a greater quantity of simple work and not necessarily anything more difficult.

TROWEL

One advantage of making your own trowels is that you can choose your own sizes instead of accepting what the makers provide. You can also make several trowels of different sizes for less than the cost of one manufactured tool. If the tool is only to be used for small plants or seedlings in a box or greenhouse, it would be better made smaller and more slender. For dealing with heavier work in the garden, the tool could be made larger.

The method of construction suggested includes a tang on the tool to fit into a handle. The handle could be a plain piece of wood, but it is better to have a turned handle with a ferrule to resist any tendency to split (Fig. 5-1). The handle can be any length.

For one-handed use when working with the hand close to the ground, the handle need be no more than 6 inches long. If you prefer not to bend as much, the handle could be 18 inches or longer. For use in a standing position, you could have a handle 48 inches or longer. In any case, a ferrule at the end is advisable. With longer handles, there is a greater inclination to apply more leverage, and that puts a strain on the joint. For longer handles, it is better to make a trowel with a socket handle.

1. The trowel is shown with a blade of moderate curve (Fig. 5-2A). Besides giving a useful shape, the curve provides stiffness.

2. Cut the blade with a slightly tapered outline (Fig. 5-2B). At the narrow end, the metal can be semi-circular or taken to a slight point (as drawn). Do not make a slender point that would be weak and soon bend or wear away.

3. Curve the blade over an iron rod, extending from the side of a vise, or over the beak of an anvil. The rod should be a smaller diameter than the curve of the blade (Fig. 5-2C). It should be possible to bend the blade by a combination of pressure and hammering; one side can be hammered while the other side is held with pliers or tongs. Carry the curve along the blade, as close as possible to the point, to ensure stiffness there. It should be possible to shape the blade without heating.

4. If making the shaft without the use of heat, flatten the end that will be attached to the blade by hammering and filing. Use a vise to make the double bend. The rod can be hammered over or

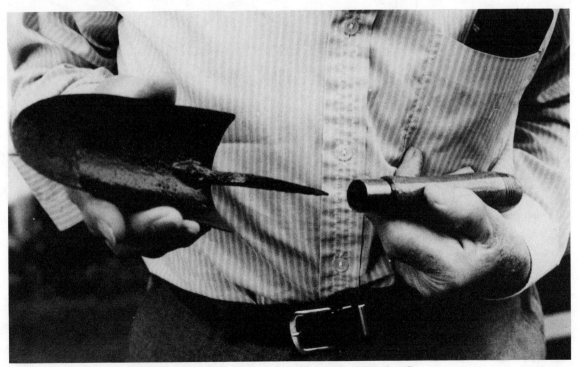

Fig. 5-1. This trowel has a shaped sheet steel blade and a tang to drive into a handle.

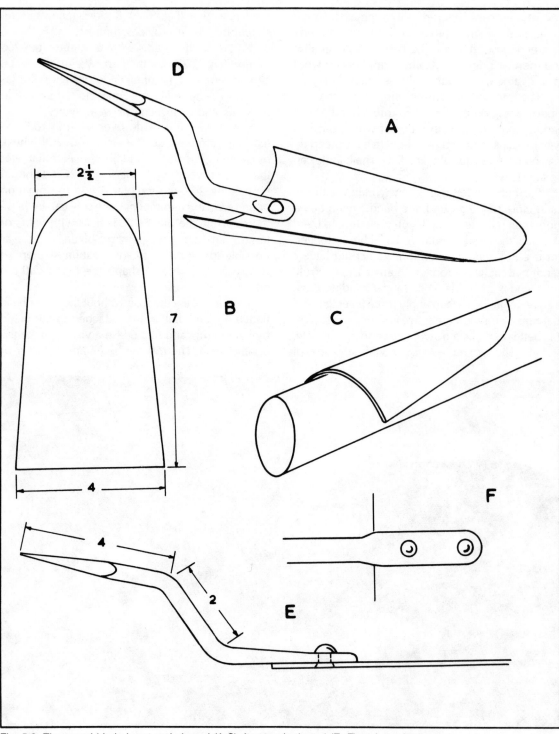

Fig. 5-2. The trowel blade is cut and shaped (A-C). Its tang is riveted (E, F) and can be brazed.

levered to shape with a tube slipped over it. Cut off to length and file the square tang to go into the handle (Fig. 5-2D).

5. If you are using heat, flatten the end that wil take the rivet, by hammering to about half thickness, and then hammer the double bend over an anvil or iron block. Cut off the rod and hammer the square-pointed tang end.

6. Drill the shaft and blade for the rivet; a 1/8-inch or 3/16-inch diameter will be suitable. Countersink the hole in the blade underneath (Fig. 5-2E).

7. File or scrape the meeting surfaces bright, and then rivet the parts together. Braze or hard solder the joint. If you do not have facilities for doing this, or for welding, you could flatten the rod far enough to allow two rivets in line (Fig. 5-2F). It would then be advisable to allow for raised heads on the rivets underneath. This gives more strength than might be provided by countersunk heads in thin metal.

8. There is no need to paint the working part of the blade, but the tool looks best if you paint the shaft and the blade to just ahead of the joint.

Fig. 5-3. The sheet steel blade of the trowel extends to form a socket for the handle.

Materials List for Trowel

All mild steel
1 blade	7 × 4 × 16 gauge
1 shaft	10 × 3/8 diameter
1 or 2	3/16 rivets

SOCKETED TROWEL

The alternative to giving the metal part of a trowel a tang to go into a hole in a wood handle is to provide it with a socket into which the tapered wood handle can be thrust (Fig. 5-3). This can be done with a handle of any length, but it is particularly suitable for longer handles because the socket joint is stronger. Even when there is a ferrule, levering the tool will make a tang try to split the wood. With a socket the wood is compressed and less likely to break.

The trowel and its socket can be made of one piece of sheet mild steel. Heat is necessary to get a good shape and you need some sort of tapered steel former no bigger than the taper is to be. That might be the beak of an anvil or a sheet-metalwork bick iron. A piece of round rod could be filed or turned on a lathe and held in a vise.

1. Cut a piece of sheet mild steel to shape (Fig. 5-4A). This gives a blade of average size, but it could be increased or decreased without affecting the method of construction. The socket tapers down from about 7/8 inch diameter, to go on a handle of any length (Fig. 5-4B).

2. The socket tubular taper has to be continued into a hollow in the blade to provide stiffness between the socket and blade (Fig. 5-4C). To form this hollow, have the vise jaws open slightly more than the thickness of the metal and the tapered rod end. Heat the steel to redness and hold it over the vise jaws and hammer the tapered rod into the socket end of the blade between the jaws for a distance that overlaps the blade by about 2 inches (Fig. 5-4D). In preparation for uniformly curving the metal, flatten the blade on each side of the hollow.

3. Heat the metal again and curve the blade to a suitable shape (Fig. 5-4E), with the curve taken the full length to provide stiffness toward the point.

4. On the end of a bick iron or the tapered rod held in the vise, hammer the hot metal to shape for the socket (Fig. 5-4F).

5. Check that the shapes are symmetrical. Drill for a screw to secure the handle in its socket.

6. Leave the working end of the blade untreated. Paint the socket and perhaps a short portion of the blade.

7. To get a good bearing inside the metal for as far as possible, use the socket as a guide when tapering the end of the wood handle.

FLAT HAND FORK

A hand fork can be made as part of a set with a trowel. It can have its tines flat if it is intended to lift soil as well as loosen it. Such a fork is useful for lifting small plants for potting or setting them out in the garden (Fig. 5-5). The fork shown in Fig. 5-6A has three tines, but it could have four and they could be tapered or splayed out. The parallel form is simple to make and quite effective.

Because the fork does not get any stiffness from curves, the part forming the blade should be stiff

in itself. It could be mild steel, 1/8 inch thick. If tool steel is used it need only be about 3/32 inch thick (preferably then hardened and tempered). Because thicker material is not easy to form into a socket with ordinary hand tools, a separate tang handle is recommended. The wood handle could be any length. It might even be long enough for use at a standing position. The handle shown in Fig. 5-5 is a file type about 5 inches long.

1. Cut the steel for the blade to the overall size and mark it out (Fig. 5-6B).

2. The spaces have to be sawn and filed, but their bottoms can be shaped by drilling 3/8-inch holes (Fig. 5-6C) that then can be sawn into to remove the waste.

3. Round the end of the wide part and taper the tines to rounded ends (Fig. 5-6D). If they are shaped to very fine ends they will quickly wear away. If stout metal has been used, you can taper and round the ends in thickness.

4. The tang handle should be filed or forged to a square point to go into a hole in the wood handle (Fig. 5-6E), and then bent in the vise (Fig. 5-6F) so that the handle slopes at a convenient angle to the blade.

5. Cut off the rod at the blade end. Heat it to redness and flatten it so that it can be drilled and rounded to take a rivet.

6. Drill the rod and the blade for a rivet. The rivet need not be very thick because its only purpose is to hold the parts together while brazing them (Fig. 5-6G).

7. Scrape or file the meeting surfaces bright, and then rivet the parts together. A round head on top and a countersunk one underneath will be suitable, but it would not matter if both heads were round.

8. Braze, hard solder, or weld the parts together.

9. Work in soil will soon rub any paint off the working ends of the tines, but the appearance of the tool is improved if the steel is painted (except for about 2 inches of the pointed ends).

10. Drill a hole to the full diameter of the tang for a short distance into the handle, and then taper to smaller holes so the tang will drive in tightly.

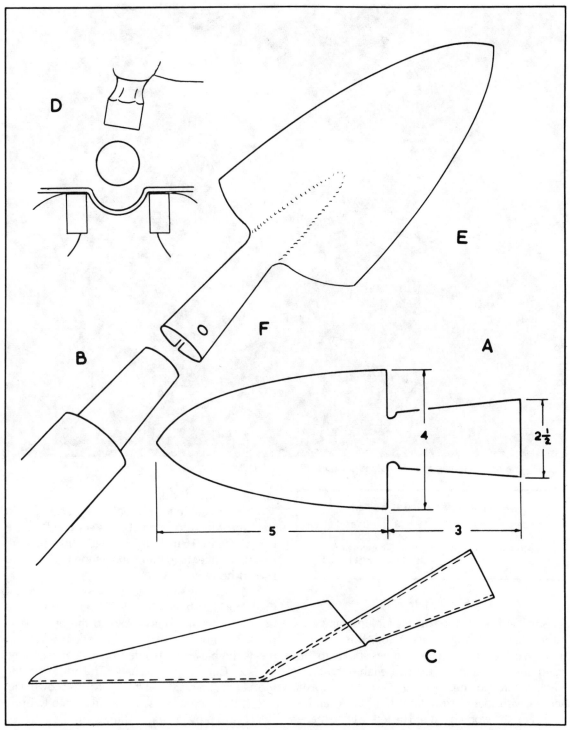

Fig. 5-4. The developed shape of the trowel (A) has its end curved to fit the handle (B-F) and the blade is shaped.

Fig. 5-5. The hand fork has a flat blade and a tang to fit into a handle.

Materials List for Flat Hand Fork	
1 blade	5 × 3 × 1/8 (mild steel) or 3/32 (tool steel)
1 piece mild steel rod	10 × 3/8 diameter
1	3/16 inch rivet to suit

TWISTED TINE FORK

If a small fork is intended mainly for loosening soil, rather than for lifting plants or soil, it is better if the thin direction of the tines comes square to the main area of the tool. This will enable the tines to slice through the soil (Fig. 5-7). This tool is shown with four narrow tines (Fig. 5-8A) and a socket for the wood handle. The fork can be made with a tang handle that is similar to that described for the flat hand fork.

It is advisable to use tool steel because mild steel tines tend to bend. Tool steel need not be thicker than 1/16 inch or 16 gauge. This will work easily, but after hardening and tempering the tines should be quite stiff.

1. Cut the steel sheet to the overall size and mark out the shapes (Fig. 5-8B). Notice that the points of the tines curve toward the outsides in pairs. The hollowed edges where the socket part meets the blade are needed to facilitate shaping.

2. Cut the steel to shape. The hollows at the roots of the tines are better elliptical, as shown (Fig. 5-8C), than semicircles. Ellipticals make twisting easier and provide some stiffness in the finished tines.

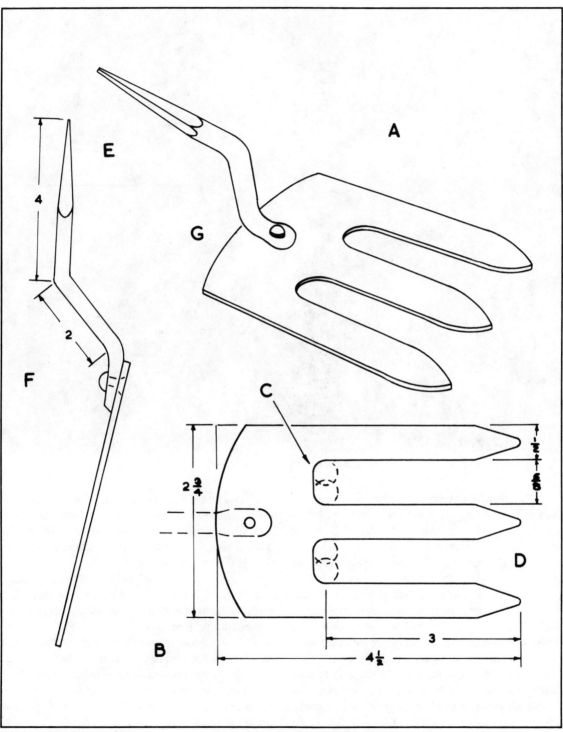

Fig. 5-6. The blade of the fork is sawn and filed (A-D). Its tang is riveted and brazed.

Fig. 5-7. The tines of this fork are twisted and the handle fits into a socket.

3. Shape the socket before twisting the tines. This is best done over the beak of an anvil or a sheet-metalwork bick iron, but it could be done over a round rod held in a vise.

4. Continue the hollowing into the wide part of the blade in order to provide stiffness (Fig. 5-8D). It will help in shaping this part if you hammer a rod into the metal over a partly open vise (Fig. 5-8E). Hammer the parts flat on each side of the hollow. This shaping can probably be done with the steel cold. If you have to heat the steel do not cool it by dipping it in water because that will harden tool steel. Try to get a good conical shape to the socket. If the edges do not meet closely underneath, it does not matter (Fig. 5-8F).

5. When twisting the tines, two are dealt with each way (Fig. 5-8G). With the wide part of the blade held in a vise, you can grip each tine with pliers (preferably the type that lock on) or with a hand vise. Grip at the same height each time so that you can get matching twists.

6. Try to make all twists the same amount and in the same plane so that, in side view, the tines are parallel and the socket slopes up at a convenient angle (Fig. 5-8H).

7. Drill a hole for a screw through the socket into the tapered end of the wood handle (Fig. 5-8J).

8. If a tang handle is to be used, cut the sheet metal straight across where the metal for the socket would come, and then make a tang and braze it on in the same way as described for the flat hand fork.

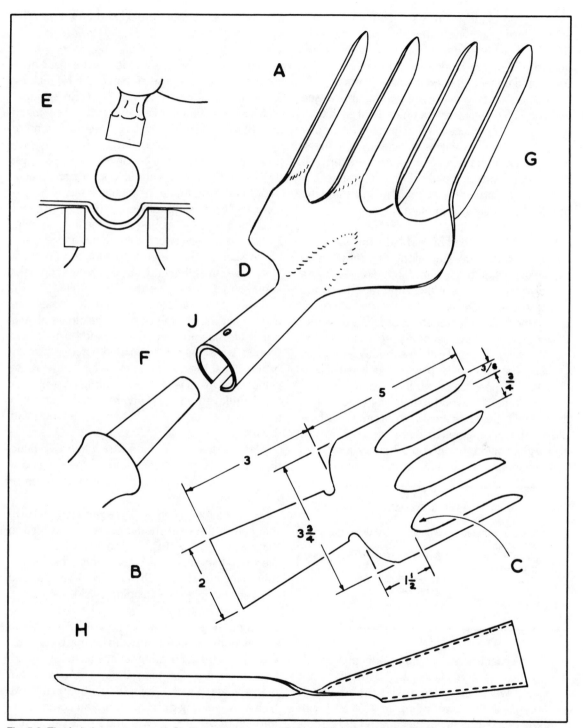

Fig. 5-8. The fork tines are sawn (A-C), the socket is made (D-F), and the tines are twisted (G, H). Drill a hole for a screw into the handle (J).

9. The blade might have enough stiffness without heat treatment, but the tines will hold their shape and be better able to spring back (if roughly treated) if they are hardened and tempered. The socket and upper part of the blade can remain soft. Clean the steel bright—so you will be able to see the oxide colors—at least on one side of each tine.

10. Use a propane torch to heat the broad part of the blade and the lengths of the tines to redness, and then quench the tool in water. Carefully rub bright those parts you had previously brightened. Be careful because the steel will be brittle and the narrow tines could be broken.

11. Reheat, with most of the flame directed at the broad upper part of the blade, but watch for the oxide colors traveling along the tines. Try to spread the action of the flame so the oxides along the tines travel at about the same rate. Keep the heat gentle, once the colors have started traveling, so that the bands of color are as broad as possible. When the points have become purple, quench the steel in water. The tool is then correctly tempered.

12. The steel can be painted, but leave at least 2 inches of the ends of the tines bare.

13. Taper the wood handle to fit the socket, then drive it in and secure it with a screw. The handle in the photograph extends about 5 inches above the socket, but it could be any length, to suit a standing or kneeling working position.

Materials List for Twisted-Tine Fork

1 piece tool steel	8 × 4 × 1/16 or 16 gauge
If with tang:	
1 piece tool steel	5 × 4 × 1/16 or 16 gauge
1 piece mild steel	
rod	10 × 3/8 diameter
1	3/16 rivet to suit

WEEDER

A small weeder is useful for lifting individual weeds among flowers and plants, and particularly for removing weeds on a lawn with the minimum disturbance to the surrounding grass. A tool with a forked end (Fig. 5-9) will get around deep roots and pull them without breaking off the tops. The tools described here are basically strips of flat mild steel, but some variations are suggested.

For most purposes a weeder can be made from strip mild steel with a section about 1 1/4 inch by 3/16 inch. For more delicate work in window boxes and hanging baskets, the tool can be made of light material while for larger weeds in a more extensive garden it can be larger. For many purposes, the tool need not be longer than 12 inches. If you want to use it without stooping too much, a tool could be made 24 inches long.

1. For the simplest weeder (Fig. 5-10A), drill a 1/4-inch hole for the bottom of the fork slot (Fig. 5-10B). Next, draw two lines from this and saw and file to shape. File the ends to rounded points.

2. At the other end, cut two hardwood slabs about 5 inches long for the handle (Fig. 5-10C). Drill one of them and the steel with clearance holes for two screws. Mark through on the other slab and drill undersize holes for the threaded parts of the screws. The slabs can be shaped before assembly or most shaping can be done after screwing together. The wood is shown with simple bevels, but the handle could be fully rounded. For extra security, use epoxy glue between the wood and the metal.

3. By levering or hammering in a vise, bend the blade a short distance behind the cut end.

4. Paint the steel, and either paint or varnish the handle.

5. If a round handle is preferred (Fig. 5-10D), that end of the steel should be sawn and filed to make a tang (Fig. 5-10E). Drill so this will drive into the wood handle, but also cut a slot across the ferrule so the broad part will fit in (Fig. 5-10F). Round any parts of the metal extending outside the ferrule.

6. Increased leverage can be obtained by putting a tube across the main part (Fig. 5-10G). If it extends outside the width of the blade, this gives an increased bearing surface on the surrounding soil or grass. A tube about 1 1/4 inches in diameter and 3 inches long should be suitable. Attach it by welding or brazing, or you could screw through or use rivets—with the inside heads sup-

Fig. 5-9. A weeder with a forked end will get round roots. A plain version makes a scraper for cleaning muddy tools.

ported on an iron rod—while you form the outside heads.

7. Another way of increasing leverage, although it does not spread the bearing surface like a tube, is to put a double bend in the blade (Fig. 5-10H). This can be done, in a vise, by hammering one way and moving to the second position to hammer the other way. The bends do not have to be sharp and are better left rounded.

8. The forked end can be made wider than the shaft part if the iron is split instead of sawn to shape. Have an anvil or an iron block ready to work on. Use a chisel and a heavy hammer. It helps if you make the fork on the end of a long piece. This way you can hold it without getting your hand hot, and then cut the piece to length afterward. Heat the end to redness in a fire or with a propane torch and split it centrally with the chisel (Fig. 5-10J). You can start with a central saw cut if you prefer. Because no metal has been removed, the jaws will spread out to give a greater spread (Fig. 5-10K).

9. Figure 5-9 shows a mud scraper. This is just a strip of metal, like a weeder without its forked end, thinned a little to make a scraping edge.

HOE

Garden hoes come in a surprising variety to suit particular purposes and regional preferences. Nevertheless, those available in your local tool

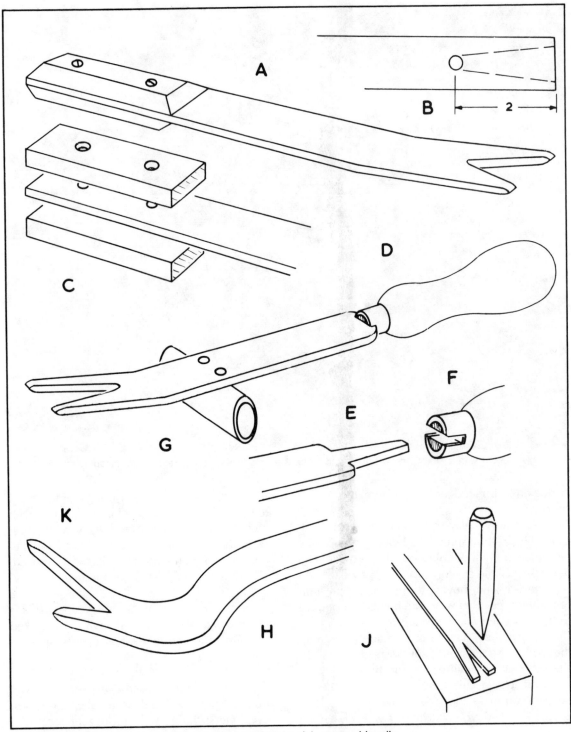

Fig. 5-10. The weeder made from flat strip steel can have a slab or round handle.

store might not be the size and shape to suit your own needs. It is not difficult to make hoes, and you can make yours exactly to your own pattern. There are several ways to make hoes. The example described here is simple if you have facilities for brazing. Welding would be even better.

This hoe has a small blade (Fig. 5-11), and it is arranged at a moderate angle not far from the end of the handle (Fig. 5-12A). For this size tool, it should be satisfactory to make all the parts out of mild steel. The tool will stand up to reasonable use for a long time. The blade could be tool steel, which would be stronger and need sharpening less frequently, even if left untempered. If hardened and tempered it would be the ultimate in durability.

1. Mark out and cut the steel for the blade (Fig. 5-12B). Mild steel should be 14 gauge or thicker, and tool steel could be about 18 gauge. Exact thickness is not crucial.

2. Prepare a piece of 3/8-inch-diameter rod. Heat one end to redness and flatten a part to bear against the blade and provide sufficient area for a rivet hole (Fig. 5-12C).

3. Bend to a suitable curve, with a straightened part to go along the handle, so the blade will be at an angle of 70 to 80 degrees to the handle (Fig. 5-12D).

4. Cut off the rod and flatten the end sufficiently for two rivets to the ferrule.

5. The ferrule is a piece of steel tube to suit the wood handle. An outside diameter between 1 and 1 1/4 inches should be suitable (Fig. 5-12E).

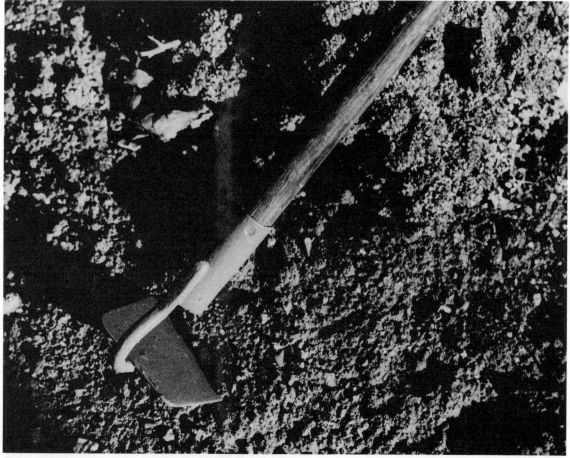

Fig. 5-11. The hoe is joined to its handle with a long ferrule.

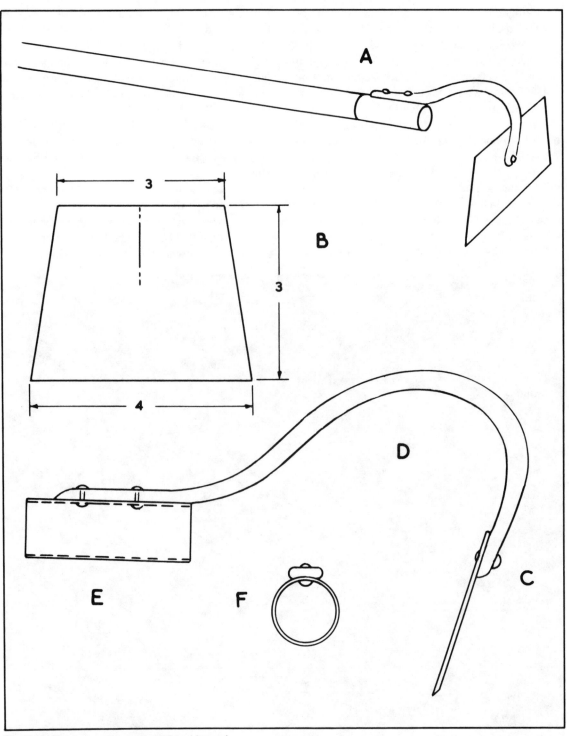

Fig. 5-12. The hoe parts are riveted and brazed.

6. Rivets at both ends of the rod are mainly to hold the parts in the correct relation while brazing. They need not be very thick; any diameter between 1/8 inch and 1/4 inch will do.

7. Scrape or file the meeting surfaces bright, and then rivet the parts together. Those rivets positioned through the tube should have prepared heads, which come inside (Fig. 5-12F), so they can be supported by an iron rod in the tube while heads are formed with a hammer outside.

8. Braze or weld the joints at both ends of the rod.

9. Drill one or more holes, for screws in the tube, for securing the tube to the wood handle.

10. The end of the handle can be reduced to fit into the ferrule or it can go into it full size. Make the length to suit yourself, but 48 inches should be suitable for use when standing. A shorter handle could be fitted for work on raised beds or other nearer-the-soil surfaces.

11. Sharpen the blade by filing the outer surface to a chisel section. Although a knife edge would cut into the soil easily, it would quickly blunt and it is wiser to leave a little thickness on the edge.

12. Paint the metal, if you prefer, but leave about 1 inch from the edge bare.

```
              Materials List for Hoe

All steel except handle
1 blade               4 × 3 × 14 × or 18 gauge

1 rod                 15 × 3/8 diameter
1 tube                3 × 1 1/8 × 18 gauge

rivets to suit
1 handle              58 × 1 1/8
```

ONION HOE

A broad hoe with a long swan-neck shaft is sometimes called an onion hoe (Fig. 5-13A), but it can obviously have many gardening uses besides dealing with an onion patch. Because the blade is fairly wide, it should be made of tool steel for stiffness, but the shaft can be made of mild steel.

In Fig. 5-14 a tang is shown into the handle but it could be attached to a ferrule (as described for the ordinary hoe). The blade and shaft are joined by brazing or welding.

The amount of curve given to the shaft depends on personal preference, but the blade should be 10 inches or more from the end of the handle, so you get a clear view of where the blade is cutting, then you do not cut off the young shoots that you are supposed to be working around.

1. Mark out the steel for the blade (Fig. 5-13B). If the tool steel is received in a hard state, it will have to be annealed first (by heating to redness and allowing to cool slowly). If the tool is to be hardened and tempered, that can be down after joining on the shaft.

2. Round the end of the shaft and saw down its center carefully to a depth of about 1 inch (Fig. 5-13C).

3. Lever open the saw cut (Fig. 5-13D) with a screwdriver or similar tool. If the surfaces are very uneven, you can file them but the surface left from the saw is satisfactory for brazing.

4. Scrape the blade bright where the joint will come and close the opened end of the shaft over it (Fig. 5-13E). Squeezing in a vise is a good way of closing the ends. Seperate the parts until after the rest of the shaft has been shaped.

5. Bend the shaft to a suitable shape that will bring the blade below the level of the handle and at an angle of about 70 degrees to it (Fig. 5-13F).

6. Cut the shaft to length and forge or file a point on the end.

7. Put the cut shaft end over the blade and drill through for a rivet (Fig. 5-13G).

8. Braze or weld the shaft to the blade. The rivet will hold the parts together, but make sure they are supported so they will be joined without twisting.

9. The blade can be left untempered, but it would be more durable if hardened and tempered. To do this, heat the whole length of the blade to redness for about 1 inch back from the cutting edge and plunge the blade into water. Enter vertically with the edge level in order to reduce the risk of the steel warping. Rub most of the blade bright

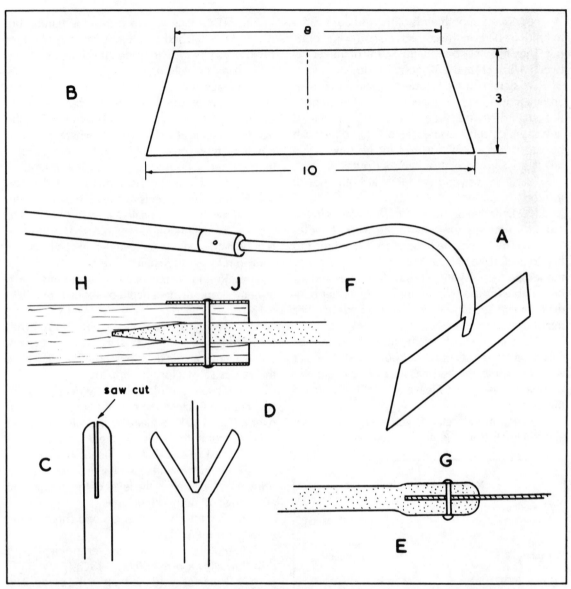

Fig. 5-13. The onion-hoe blade fits into a slot in the shaft. The tang is held with a rivet through the ferrule.

with sandstone or emery cloth. Heat by fanning the flame along the top of the blade until you see the colored oxides appear. When the edge has turned purple, quench the blade in water again.

10. Sharpen the blade with a bevel on the outside surface.

11. Fit the wood handle with a tubular ferrule about as long as the diameter of the wood. Drill centrally to almost the full diameter of the shaft for about the length of the ferrule. Make undersize holes of reducing sizes for the point to drive in (Fig. 5-13H).

12. Drive the shaft into the handle, then drill through for a pin to keep the shaft in place (Fig. 5-13J). The pin could be a long thin rivet, but a stout nail would do.

Fig. 5-14. An onion hoe with a long rod shaft.

Fig. 5-15. A rake can be made from flat strip with round rod tines. This one has a tapered socket for the wood handle.

RAKE

Rakes of many sizes are useful in the garden. This example can be made in various widths (Fig. 5-15), but it is drawn as a narrow type (Fig. 5-16A) with five round prongs and two more are formed with the ends of the frame. If it is to be made very wide, the single, centrally attached shaft to the handle can not be stiff enough. The alternative then is to have double shafts, as described for the Dutch hoe, with the ends of the parts engaging with the tops of two prongs instead of just the central one.

If a lathe is available, the shoulder parts and the points of the prongs can be turned, but it is easy to make the prongs with hand tools. Great precision is unnecessary. A tang into a hole in the handle is the simplest attachment, but a socket is also shown. In either case, a handle long enough for the tool to be used when standing is the usual choice.

1. Mark out a 10-inch strip, for the frame, with the hole positions center-punched.

2. Taper the ends to rounded points (Fig. 5-16B). Fine points would soon wear away in use.

3. Drill for the prongs. If the prongs are made from 1/4-inch rod, the holes should be 3/16 inch. For 5/16-inch rod they should be 1/4 inch.

4. Cut the pieces of rod slightly too long for the prongs. Shoulder the tops to fit into the holes with enough projecting to make rivet heads (Fig. 5-16C). Allow about 1/8 inch extra on the center prong to go through the shaft as well. With a lathe, the shoulders can be turned. Otherwise use a file, on a prong held in a vise, with a piece of scrap sheet metal to prevent the file coming into contact with the vise jaws (Fig. 5-16D). Test each shouldered end in a hole; it should make a push fit.

5. Bend the ends of the frame by hammer-

ing over in a vise. Check squareness.

6. Use the bent ends of the frame as a guide for marking the lengths of prongs. The prongs should project so that their ends come in line with the points at the ends.

7. Shape the prongs to rounded points. The ends can be central (Fig. 5-16E) or the points can be toward the side the rake will be pulled (Fig. 5-16F). Carried a stage further, the points could be curved over (Fig. 5-16G) by hammering on the beak of an anvil or on a round rod.

8. Make a tang shaft. Its length will depend on how far you want the rake to project ahead of the handle; 4 or 5 inches should be suitable. Flatten one end to a wide enough palm to allow for a hole to be drilled for the top of the central prong (Fig. 5-16H). Forge or file the other end to drive into a hole in a handle (Fig. 5-16J).

9. If a socket for a handle is preferred, make a similar palm on the end of a rod, but a short distance behind that cut the rod off and make a shouldered end (Fig. 5-16K).

10. Roll a sheet-metal cone so that its large end is the same as the handle diameter and the small end fits over the shouldered piece of rod (Fig. 5-16L). For the method of setting out the cone see Chapter 3.

11. Arrange for the cut edges of the socket to be downward when you braze the cone to the shouldered rod. Drill holes on opposite sides of the socket for screws into the wood handle (Fig. 5-16M), but stagger their positions so they come into different parts of the wood.

12. After cleaning the meeting surfaces ready for brazing or welding, fit the handle extension over the central prong top and rivet it there. Support the parts squarely while joining.

13. Drive the tang into stepped holes in the

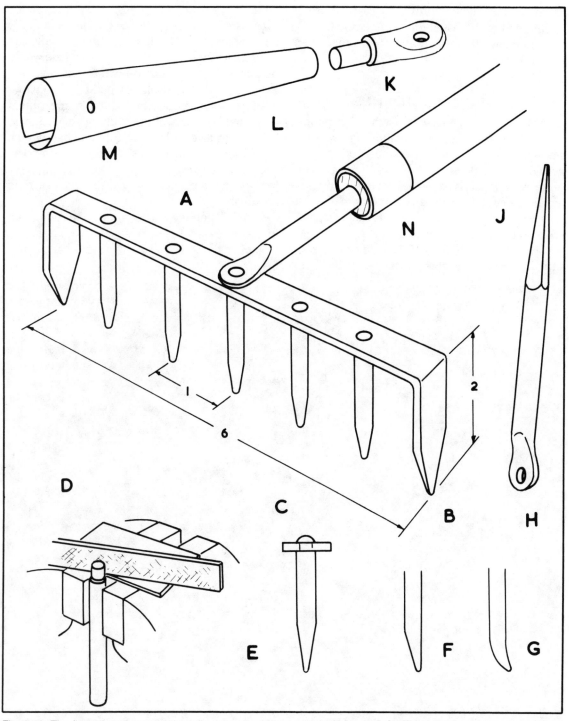

Fig. 5-16. The flat strip is bent and the rake tines shouldered and riveted to it (A-G). There can be a tang or socket to attach to the handle (H-N).

end of a handle with a ferrule (Fig. 5-16N) or taper the end of the handle to fit the socket.

14. Paint the metal parts and varnish the wood, if you wish.

ONE-HAND DUTCH HOE

A small Dutch hoe, for use in one hand, can form part of a set with a trowel and a fork for work on small soil containers, in a greenhouse, or in a congested part of a flower bed where work has to be done on your hands and knees. Its particular uses are in freeing soil of surface weeds before they get an opportunity to develop and for breaking a hardened soil surfacein order to aerate it.

The hoe shown in Fig. 5-17 is of simple construction and can be joined with rivets only, if you do not have brazing facilities, because not much strain is ever likely to be put on the joint. A file type of handle is suitable, but a longer handle can be used. It is not likely that this size of blade would be put on a handle for use when standing.

1. Mark out the blade (Fig. 5-18A) by working each side of a centerline. Cut to shape. Round the upper corners. Thin the cutting edge slightly, but do not take it down to a knife edge (which would soon blunt). Bend the blade on the marked line (Fig. 5-18B). The amount of bend is not very important, but between 10 and 15 degrees would be suitable.

2. Flatten the end of a rod to make a palm long enough to take two rivets (Fig. 5-18C) and put a point on the other end to drive into a handle (Fig. 5-18D).

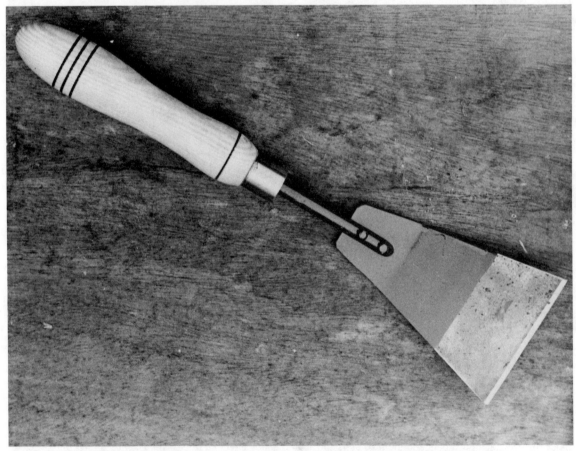

Fig. 5-17. A small Dutch hoe can be used in one hand for work in flower borders and window boxes.

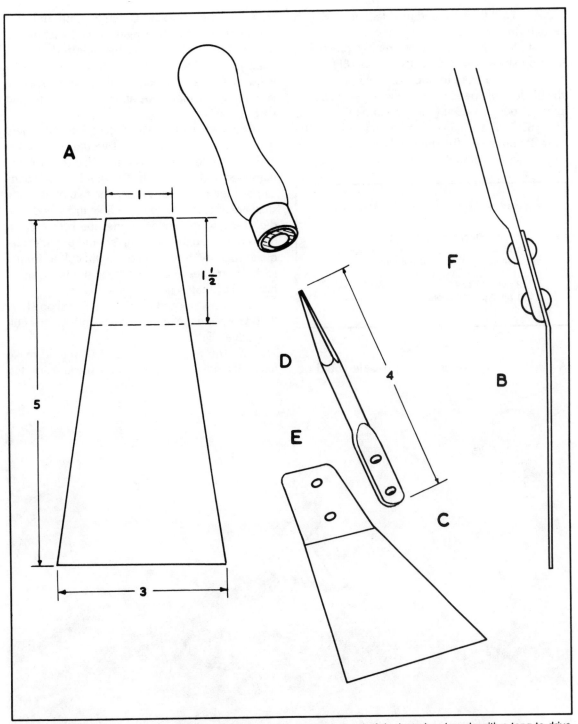

Fig. 5-18. The Dutch hoe blade is shaped and bent (A, B), and then the shaft is riveted and made with a tang to drive into a handle (C-F).

3. Drill the shaft and the blade for 1/8-inch or 3/16-inch rivets.

4. Join the parts with rivets, preferably forming shallow round heads (Fig. 5-18F).

5. If you want to braze or weld the shaft to the blade, there need only be one rivet to keep the parts in position during heat treatment.

6. Drill a suitable handle and drive in the tang. If you prefer, the shaft and upper part of the blade can be painted.

Materials List for One-Hand Dutch Hoe

All mild steel except the handle
1 blade   5 × 3 × 16 gauge
1 shaft   4 × 3/8 diameter

2 rivets to suit
1 file type of handle

DUTCH HOE

A push hoe for use on a long handle could be made like the one-hand Dutch hoe, but unless it was rather narrow the single, central shaft might not be stiff enough to resist bending and twisting loads in use. The Dutch hoe shown in Fig. 5-19 is given a broader support with a double shaft. It could have a wider blade and still retain sufficient rigidity.

The blade could be mild steel, but if tool steel is used it will be thinner and would be stronger and less liable to wear on the edge (even if not hardened and tempered). The divided shaft parts can be mild steel in any case. The two parts of the shaft are intended to go into a hole in a wood handle. Because the action of the hoe is thrust and tends to tighten the joint, this should provide adequate security. It would not be difficult to form a socket from sheet metal and braze shortened shafts into it, but that is not described here.

1. Mark out and cut the blade to shape (Fig. 5-20A). Round the upper corners and thin the cutting edge slightly.

2. The two sides of the shaft should make a pair. It is advisable to set out the blade shape and

Fig. 5-19. This Dutch hoe has a double shaft tapered to fit into a handle.

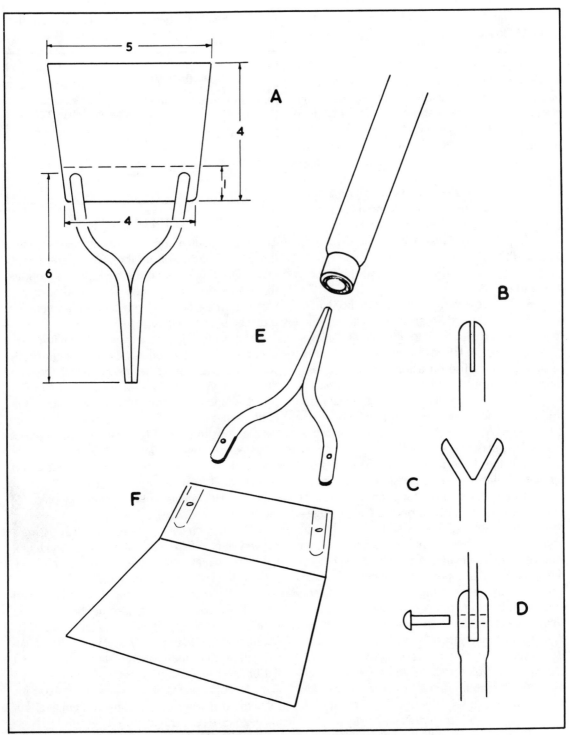

Fig. 5-20. The double shaft fits over the blade and is tapered to fit into the handle.

a centerline on scrap wood. One side can be shaped to that drawing and then the other side can be made the same.

3. Cut the two pieces for the shaft a little overlong and prepare the ends that will fit on the blade before doing any other shaping. Round the ends and saw centrally about 3/4 of an inch deep (Fig. 5-20B). Open these ends by levering with a screwdriver (Fig. 5-20C), and then close them over the blade (Fig. 5-20D) by hammering and squeezing in a vise.

4. Bend the shafts to shape with matching curves that bring them together centrally. Cut them to length and file the meeting surfaces so as to reduce the total width that will go into the handle (Fig. 5-20E).

5. Bend the blade to about 15 degrees across the marked line.

6. The tapered meeting parts of the shaft do not have to be joined because they will be pulled together when driven into the handle. Nevertheless, it helps in keeping the parts in the correct relative positions if they are brazed (not necessarily throughout the full length of the meeting surfaces).

7. Position the shaft ends on the blade and drill through for rivets (Fig. 5-20F). File or scrape the meeting surfaces before riveting, and then braze the joints.

8. If the blade is not to be hardened and tempered, that completes construction. If it is to be heat treated, use a propane torch to heat the blade—about 1 inch back from the cutting edge—to redness, after rubbing its surface bright with abrasive paper. Then quench it in water. Rub the surface bright again and heat the blade by fanning the flame along its upper part until the oxide colors appear. Continue heating gently so the colors spread toward the cutting edge. Move the flame so the spread of colors is as even as possible. When the edge becomes purple quench the blade again. If you prefer, clean the steel bright.

9. Drill holes in graduated steps in the handle end. The mouth of the hole can be widened slightly with a chisel or gouge to admit the double thickness of rod, but further in the tapered parts should drive without difficulty.

10. Paint the shafts and a short way on to the blade.

Materials List for Dutch Hoe

All steel except the handle

1 blade	5 × 4 × 1/8 mild steel or 3/32 tool steel
2 shafts	10 × 3/8 diameter
2 rivets to suit	
1 handle	48 × 1 1/8

PUSH-PULL HOE

The normal Dutch hoe only cuts off weeds or stirs the surface of the soil on the push stroke. If it is given a cutting edge on the back, it will work in the reverse direction as well. This could be an advantage when dealing with awkward weeds or those close to a wall.

The blade has to be arranged so that its edges are presented to the soil at the correct angle (both ways) without altering the angle at which the handle is held. While the push-pull hoe shown in Fig. 5-21 is shaped to suit most users, the angles of the cutting edges and the handle can be altered for very tall or short users. The blade is best made of tool steel because it retains its sharp edges longer than mild steel (even when not hardened and tempered). The shafts are mild steel.

1. Mark out and cut the rectangular piece for the blade (Fig. 5-22A).

2. Sharpen the cutting edges, but avoid making very thin knifelike edges that would soon blunt. It is better to make the angles fairly steep and leave a slight thickness along the edges.

3. Bend the blade along the marked bend lines. The amount of bend need not be much, but if the center is about 1/4 inch above the edges (Fig. 5-22B) that should be sufficient. If you will be dealing with a very sandy soil, the blade could be left flat or given only slight bevels.

4. Forge palms on the ends of the two rods that will form the shafts, and bend them at about 30 degrees (Fig. 5-22C).

5. Bend the pair of rods inward so they meet.

Fig. 5-21. A push-pull Dutch hoe will cut in both directions.

Cut them off so the parallel parts are about 2 inches long.

6. Grind or file the meeting surfaces (Fig. 5-22D) so they make a tapered tang to go into the handle (Fig. 5-22E). Put rivets loosely in the holes so you can check that the two parts of the shaft make a pair and the tang will be central.

7. Scrape or file the meeting surfaces, and then rivet the shafts to the blade (Fig. 5-22F). Clamp the tang ends together while brazing the shafts to the blade.

8. If the blade is to be hardened and tempered, do this now.

9. Prepare the wood handle with a tube ferrule at least 1 1/2 inches long (Fig. 5-22G).

10. Drill for the tang and drive the parts together. There will probably be enough friction in the joint to resist pulling apart in use, but if you want to make sure a nail can go through a hole in the ferrule and tang as a rivet. Alternatively, you could raise a few teeth in the tang parts with a cold chisel (Fig. 5-22H) before assembly.

11. Paint the metal, except for the bent parts of the blade, and varnish the wood handle.

Materials List for a Push-Pull Hoe	
1 blade	4 × 3 × 16 gauge tool steel
2 shafts	10 × 3/8 diameter mild steel
2 rivets to suit	
1 wood handle	48 × 1 1/8 with tube ferrule

WEEDING HOE

Clearing badly weeded land sometimes calls for a standard straightedged hoe. At other times a

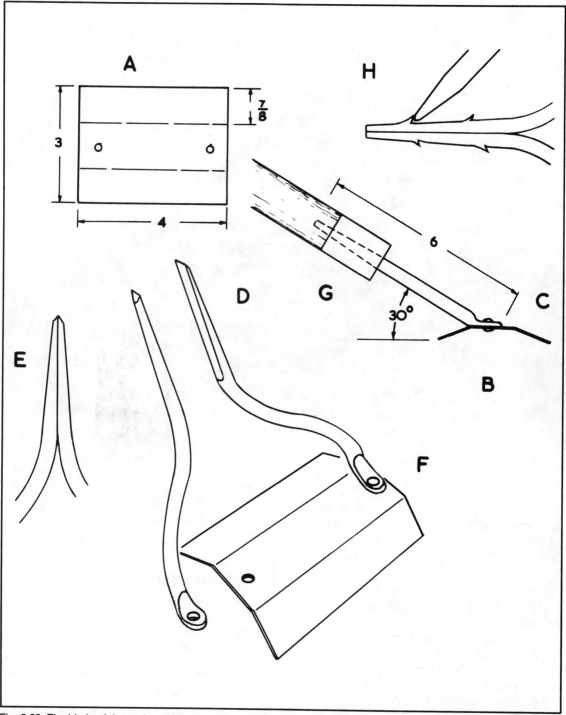

Fig. 5-22. The blade of the push-pull hoe has a double shaft riveted and brazed to it (A-G). Its tang end can have teeth cut in it to resist pulling out of the handle.

pointed hoe will be of more use. The weeding hoe shown in Fig. 5-23 is reversible; one tool does both jobs. You could have a forked end (Fig. 5-24A) instead of a point. This is sometimes helpful for getting around large roots or breaking up lumps of earth.

The blade should be made of tool steel and be fairly stout; 1/8 inch is suggested. The tube that forms the socket for the handle has to be brazed or welded on. Because this joint takes all the chopping strains, it needs to be as strong as you can make it. If you are brazing, use the hardest spelter that the available flame will melt.

1. Mark out the rectangle for the blade, and then curve to a central point at one end (Fig. 5-24B) or saw the forked end. You can get a symmetrical curved shape by drawing a freehand curve at one side of the centerline on a piece of paper, and then cut this out and reverse it on the metal to mark the other side.

2. Cut the blade to shape. The straight-end edge can be given a bevel, but the other edges should be rounded or left square.

3. The tube should be mild steel, it should have walls about 1/16 inch thick, and it should have a diameter to suit the chosen handle. The handle should be 1 1/8 inches or 1 1/4 inches. Either file or turn the ends of the tube true (Fig. 5-24C).

4. File or scrape the surfaces bright where the brazed joint will come—including the inside of the end of the tube—so spelter can build up inside.

Fig. 5-23. The weeding hoe has a central handle and straight and pointed cutting edges. This one has been fitted with a natural wood handle.

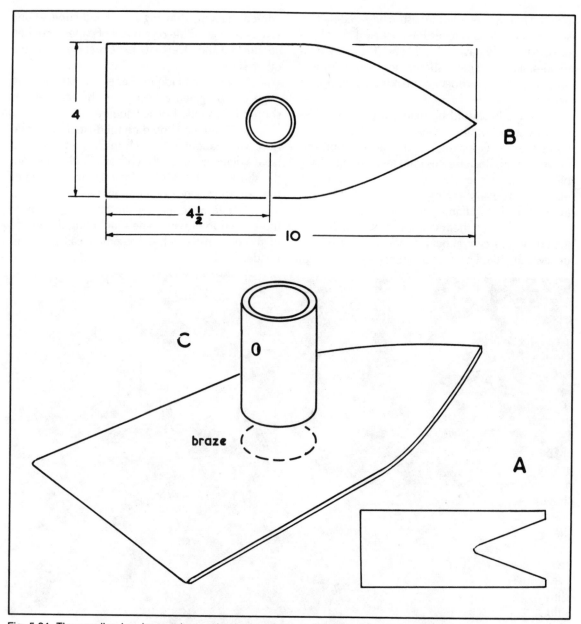

Fig. 5-24. The weeding hoe has a tube to take the handle brazed to the center of the blade.

5. Have the blade level and the tube standing on it. Wire it or hold it in place with a weight. Besides flux it will help to put some pieces of spelter inside the tube. This will augment the spelter fed on to the outside of the joint when you heat. Then you should get the maximum amount of spelter fillets built up each side of the joint.

6. Drill the tube for one or two screws into the wood handle. This could be a round rod, but the handle shown in Fig. 5-23 reveals how a natural piece of wood with the bark peeled off can be used.

7. If you prefer to harden and temper, treat the two ends separately. Clean the steel bright to within 1 inch of each end. Heat an end to brightness and quench it. Brighten the surface again and fan the flame above it. Watch the oxide colors spread until the purple reaches the edge, and then quench. Do the same at the other end.

8. Drive in and secure the handle.

9. Paint the metal except for 1 inch bands at the cutting edges.

Materials List for Weeding Hoe	
1 blade	10 × 4 × 1/8 or thicker tool steel
1 tube	3 × 1 1/8 diameter mild steel
1 handle	40 × 1 1/8 or 1 1/4 diameter hardwood

OTHER HOE BLADE SHAPES

It might be thought that any hoe would suit any gardening purpose, and except for differences in size there would be no need for many hoes. There are, however, regional preferences and those engaged in different branches of horticulture have their own preferences. This means that there are actually a tremendous range of hoes in use and anyone making their own can settle for the locally accepted shape. This is true even if your neighbors have difficulty in explaining why they prefer the shape they use.

When making a hoe blade of special size and shape, you must consider the choice of steel and its thickness. Large hoes that get heavy use should be tool steel (preferably hardened and tempered). This would also be the better choice for small hoes, but it is possible to use the more easily worked mild steel if the blade is kept a little thicker. For normal use in the garden and yard, mild steel blades should have a reasonable life. They can be resharpened with a file, but a tempered tool steel blade would have to be ground.

A few special blade shapes are shown in Fig. 5-25. The warren hoe (Fig. 5-25A) would be about 6 inches deep and made of steel at least 1/8 inch thick in order to stand up to a chopping action in heavy soil. A narrow triangular hoe with a long point downward might be 4 inches deep (Fig. 5-25B). It goes on a long handle and would be used for weeding and cultivating in places where there might be danger of a wider blade cutting off shoots or roots.

When a hoe is being used for long periods, anything that will lighten it and reduce strain on the arms is valuable, but there has to be weight at the cutting edge. A light handle is helpful, but it must be strong enough and of sufficient diameter to provide a comfortable grip. Weight where it is not needed can be reduced by cutting off the top corners of a wide blade (Fig. 5-25C). This should not go so far down the sides as to reduce the effective blade area when hoeing deeply, but if the blade is deeper and narrower the bevels can be steeper (Fig. 5-25D).

It might be the association with pretty and attractive-looking produce that makes a worker in a flower garden favor curves instead of straight lines in his or her tools. The more severe straight lines would work just as well. Some hoes have curved arched tops (Fig. 5-25E) or the whole upper edge might sweep in curves to the bottom (Fig. 5-25F).

SEED DRILL TOOL

The instructions on the packets of many seeds instruct you to plant them perhaps 1/4 inch or 1/2 inch deep. Scraping a drill or trench as shallow as this with the corner of a hoe or other large tool is rather clumsy. The one-hand tool shown in Fig. 5-26 will scrape a seed drill at any depth you want. You could put in seeds as you progress and use the flat side of the tool to draw the soil back over them.

Exact sizes are unimportant and you could use oddments of available material, but those shown (Fig. 5-27) will produce a tool that should suit most gardeners. There is not much load on the tool so all parts can be made of mild steel. Tool steel for the blade would give maximum durability.

1. Cut the blade as an equilateral triangle with a 1/4-inch hole at the center (Fig. 5-27A).

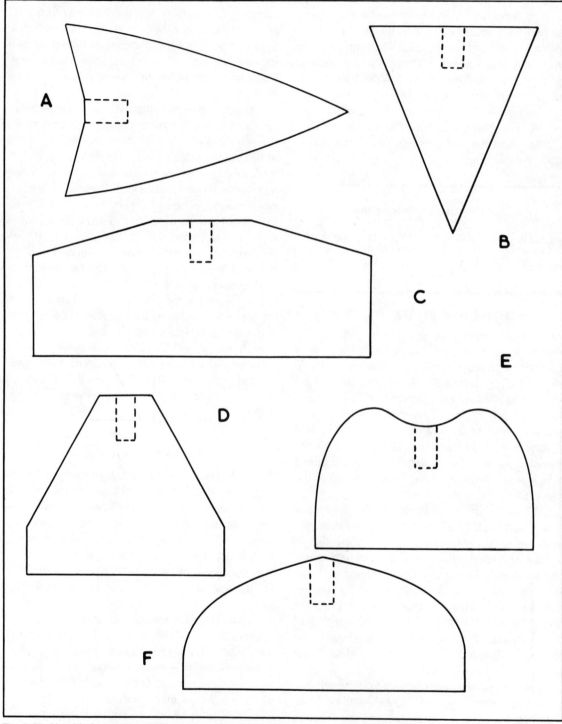

Fig. 5-25. Hoe blades can be made in many shapes to suit requirements and preferences.

Fig. 5-26. A tool for scraping seed drills in the ground has a triangular blade and is intended for use in one hand.

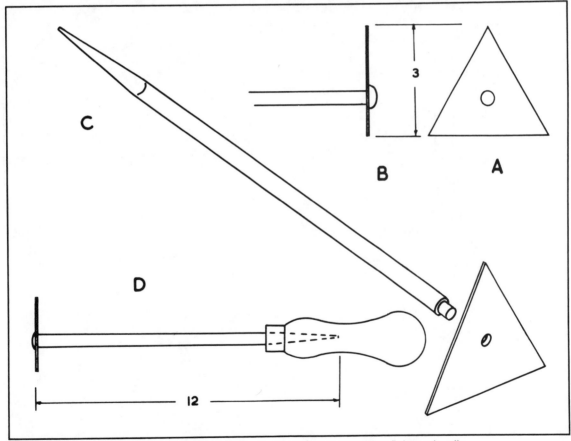

Fig. 5-27. The seed drill tool has its shaft riveted to the blade and is tapered to fit into a handle.

2. Shoulder the end of the shaft by filing or turning to go through the hole and project enough for a good head to be riveted (Fig. 5-27B).

3. At the other end of the shaft, file or forge a point to go into the handle (Fig. 5-27C). Make the shaft long enough to keep the handle well back from the blade (Fig. 5-27D) so that you can work comfortably and see how the blade is making a groove in the soil.

4. Attach the shaft to a file type of handle. Paint the shaft and varnish or paint the handle, but the blade should be left untreated. There is no need to thin the edges of the blade unless you expect to use it like a small hoe to break up soil.

Materials List for Seed Drill Tool	
1 blade	3 × 3 × 14 or 16 gauge mild steel or tool steel
1 shaft	12 × 3/8 diameter mild steel
1 file-type handle with ferrule	

Chapter 6

Simple Equipment

All of the things you use to prepare soil, plant seeds, and attend to growing crops can be called tools, but it is convenient to regard only those items you have to handle regularly as tools (described in Chapter 5). Things that have a more static use can be described as equipment. If you have to dig, cultivate, remove weeds, harvest crops, or generally handle an implement, you are using a tool. If what you are using defines an area, provides storage, or has an otherwise more passive purpose, it is equipment. Equipment described in this chapter can be made mostly with simple woodworking and metalworking tools.

LINE WINDER

To keep rows straight when planting seeds, a stretched cord is the usual guide. It is much better to have a prepared line, with its winder and peg, than to use any odd piece of string with sticks that you pick up. The winder shown in Fig. 6-1 is made of wood. Suggested sizes can be varied to suit available material (Fig. 6-2A). Hardwood should be more durable than softwood. For the spool around which the line is wound, you could use solid wood, with the grain across, or 1/4 inch exterior or marine plywood would be suitable. The other parts can be made from wood about 1 inch square.

For a line that will last and not kink in use, it is worthwhile getting braided synthetic cord not more than 3/16 of an inch thick. Cut ends can be sealed by heating with a flame from a match or cigarette lighter, and then rolling the semimolten ends between moistened finger and thumb.

1. Prepare the wood by planing to size, if necessary.

2. Mark out and cut the spool (Fig. 6-2B). Do not make the hollows too deep or the turns of cord will be small and you will take a long time winding it on.

3. Make both sticks the same length and whittle points at their lower ends.

4. For the simplest tops, thoroughly round the wood (Fig. 6-2C).

5. For a better top, that makes it easier to

Fig. 6-1. A garden line winder can be made from wood, with one part carrying a spool for winding surplus line.

thrust hard into stubborn ground, make T handles (Fig. 6-2D). Such handles should be with mortise and tenon joints (Fig. 6-2E). Well round all the parts you will grip. You could round the lower parts that will penetrate the ground, but a square section is just as good.

6. The stick with the spool might try to turn in the ground when the line is strained. To prevent this, make a little spike at one side of the spool (Fig. 6-2F). It could be just a flat piece nailed on one side, but it is better made to notch into place in order to be glued and screwed (Fig. 6-2G).

7. For the most durable results, assemble the parts with waterproof glue as well as screws or nails. The wood can then be treated with a preservative or be painted.

METAL LINE WINDER

The metal line winder shown in Fig. 6-3 serves the same purpose as the wooden one, but it will appeal to the craftsman who prefers to work metal. It should be more durable. There is also the advantage of the thinner spikes being easier to thrust into hard ground. The parts are iron or mild steel in sections that can probably be bent cold. If heat is needed, you can use a propane torch or similar flame. The materials list suggests suitable sizes, but these are not crucial; other available sizes may be just as satisfactory.

Synthetic line, of the type suggested for the wooden line winder, can be used and tied to the two parts.

1. Make the strips for the top and bottom of

the spool (Fig. 6-4A). Drill central holes that will turn easily on the rods and holes toward the ends to suit the rivets (any size between 1/8 inch and 1/4 inch diameter can be used).

2. Cut the strips for the two bowed parts of the spool (Fig. 6-4B). Bend the two ends to about 45 degrees (Fig. 6-4C), and then spring or hammer the central parts to curves so the ends are parallel and about 3 inches apart (Fig. 6-4D). Check to be certain the two pieces match each other.

3. Bend and shape a spike (Fig. 6-4E) to press into the ground from one end of the spool.

4. Rivet these parts together. Make sure the top and bottom are parallel and that there is no twist in the assembly.

5. The rod that takes the spool and the one at the other end of the line can be made the same, but they are shown with different tops to suggest alternative handles. For the T-shaped top (Fig. 6-4F), bend back about 4 inches by hammering in

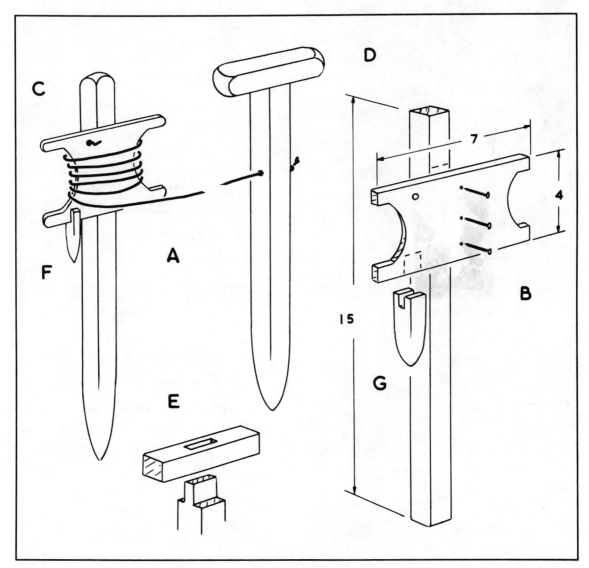

Fig. 6-2. There are alternative tops to the line winder. The spool has a peg to press into the ground and prevent unwinding.

the vise. Then fold over to make the top and cut off to length for a balanced shape. File the end rounded for comfort.

6. For a round top (Fig. 6-4G), bend back about 5 inches in the vise, and then hammer the eye to shape over a round rod held in the vise or over the beak of an anvil.

7. The bottoms of the rods can be filed to rounded points (Fig. 6-4H) or filed or forged square ends (Fig. 6-4) might cut into the earth better.

8. To keep the spool in place on its rod, use two washers that fit easily over the rod (Fig. 6-4K) and two cotter pins through holes in the rod (Fig. 6-4L) with the points turned over (Fig. 6-4M). Position the washers and pins so the spool will turn easily.

9. The line winder should have quite a long life if left untreated, but it will look better and be made durable if treated with anti-rust solution and painted. A bright color, such as red, will help you find the tool if you mislay it among the mainly green foliage and vegetables in your garden.

Materials List for Metal Line Winder

All iron or mild steel

2 pieces	18	× 5/16 round rod
2 pieces	7	× 3/4 × 1/8 flat strip
2 pieces	6	× 3/4 × 1/8 flat strip
1 piece	4	× 3/4 × 1/8 flat strip

2 washers, 2 cotter pins, and 4 rivets to suit

SECTIONAL COMPOST BOX

You might not always want to make compost or to keep rubbish or leaves together in your garden. Nevertheless, it is convenient to be able to assemble a container for such things as you have the need. Figure 6-5 shows a box without a bottom that can be taken apart and stored as a stack of boards when not required. It assembles into a bin of reasonable capacity.

As drawn, the capacity is about 24 inches square and deep, but sizes can be varied to suit

Fig. 6-3. An all-metal line winder works in the same way as the wooden one, but the spool is made from strip metal and it rotates on a round rod.

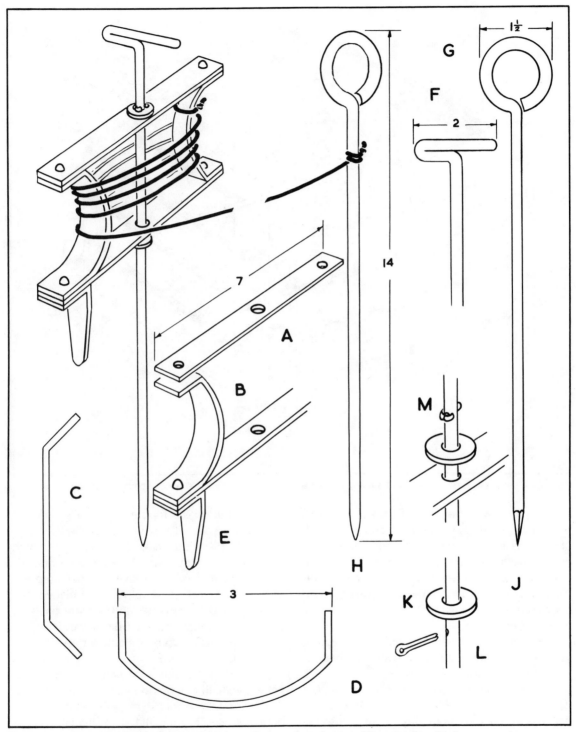

Fig. 6-4. The spool of the garden line winder is made from riveted strips. Alternative handle shapes are shown.

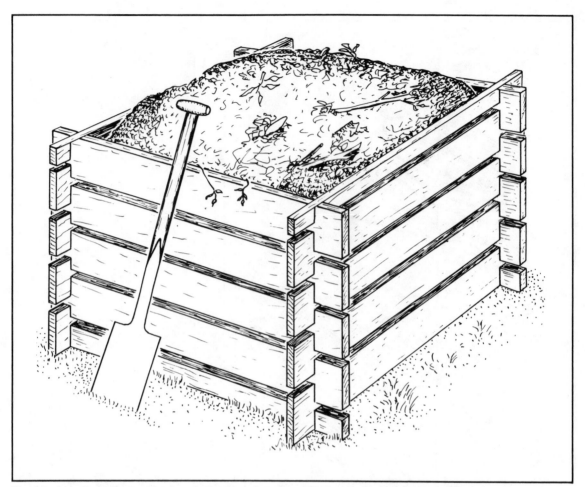

Fig. 6-5. A sectional compost box can be made up into any size. The parts will store compactly when out of use.

your needs or available wood. Except for four narrower pieces used to level the top and bottom, all of the parts are the same. Any number of parts can be put together to make an assembly of any depth. You can extend upward with more pieces or you can reduce the box after some of the contents have been used. The removed parts can be used to make a second container.

The wood should be a durable hardwood or you can use softwood treated with preservative. As shown, the pieces are 5 inches wide and 7/8 inch thick. Other sizes will be just as suitable, but it would be inadvisable to use thinner wood because the pressure from inside could cause the wood to bow outward. Gaps of 1 inch are allowed

between the boards for ventilation (Fig. 6-6A).

1. Prepare all the wood. For the assembly shown, you have to make 16 pieces that match each other and four narrow pieces with notches to match them. It is best to have the wood prepared in long runs. It does not have to be planed, but planed wood looks better and is more likely to have a consistent thickness. Consistency is important if the parts are to be suitable for assembly in any sequence.

2. Mark out the wide parts (Fig. 6-6B) together, with all notches the same at the ends (Fig. 6-6C). From these boards, mark the notches in the narrow pieces (Fig. 6-6D). Use the actual wood to get the widths of the notches; they should be cut

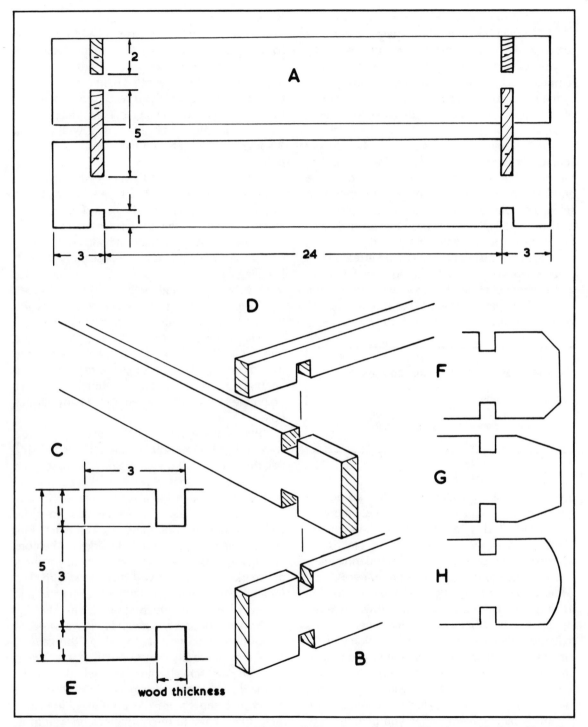

Fig. 6-6. The main parts of the compost box are all the same (A-C), with narrow strips (D) at top and bottom. Alternative end shapes are possible (E-H).

to make an easy fit on the wood (Fig. 6-6E).

3. It will be helpful to prepare the end of a scrap piece of wood carefully with notches exactly as you want them to be, and then use this as a template to check marking out and cutting as well as the fit across the wood. Make a trial assembly of the parts and adjust any notches where necessary.

4. The ends of the strips can be left cut square across. Sharpness and roughness should be removed, but if you prefer you can decorate the ends. There are a large number of ends to trim so select a simple pattern. You could cut the corners at 45 degrees (Fig. 6-6F), choose a flatter angle (Fig. 6-6G), or round the ends (Fig. 6-6H).

5. If you make sure the ground is reasonably level where you assemble the box, the parts will go together better and have a longer life because they will not get distorted. Make sure it is put together squarely when viewed from above.

Materials List for Sectional Compost Box

All wood

| 16 pieces | $30 \times 5 \times 7/8$ |
| 4 pieces | $30 \times 2 \times 7/8$ |

SQUARE LINE

If you want to lay out a formal garden, set out the ground corners "square" or 90 degrees; otherwise the plot will lack symmetry. Even when you are planting many rows of seeds across a plot, it is a help to start off squarely to avoid wandering lines. It is very easy to have rows getting progressively wider or narrower apart at one end or becoming increasingly out of true. If the first row is marked square and the other rows are measured parallel to it, the pattern will be kept neat and you will not be annoyed with yourself every time you look at an unevenly arranged growing crop.

This technique also allows you to square your layouts for paths, patios, decks and other comparatively large patterns when you plan the way

you want to use the land around your home.

Fortunately it is very easy to lay out one line square to another whatever the size involved. Suppose you have a straight path or border, you can mark a line at 90 degrees to it right across the plot and measure other lines you need parallel to it. The method is based on the fact that any triangle with its sides in the proportion 3:4:5 will have a 90-degree angle between the 3 and 4 sides (Fig. 6-7A).

To adapt this fact to your needs requires a length of cord—preferably a type with no stretch in it—and four metal rings about 1 inch in diameter. Decide on the greatest length you expect to have to set out on the ground and relate this to the "4" side of the triangle. Suppose this is 20 feet. Dividing it by 4 gives us a unit of 5 feet. Therefore, the sides of the triangle will be 15 feet, 20 feet, and 25 feet. The length of cord needed will be the total of this (with a little over, for example 65 feet).

Tie a ring to one end of the cord, measure three units (15 feet in the example), and then tie in another ring. Go four units (20 feet) and tie in another, and then a further five units (25 feet) to tie on the last ring (Fig. 6-7B). Cut off any surplus cord.

Put the three-unit ring at the point where you want the end of the square line to be and push a peg through it. Pull the cord along the base, path edge, or border that you are working from and push a peg through the first ring (Fig. 6-7C). Lay out the cord loosely in a triangle and hook the other end ring over the same peg as the first. Pull at the remaining ring until both sides of the cord are equally tensioned. The corner where you want the marked line to be will then be square (Fig. 6-7D). Push a peg into that further corner ring and you will have your square line (Fig. 6-7E).

You will probably not want to leave this cord in position when you start work on the garden. Mark the square line location with another cord between pegs, scratch a line in the soil, draw a line on the deck, or otherwise mark in a way that will ensure that the square-line position is indicated later if you have to measure other lines from it.

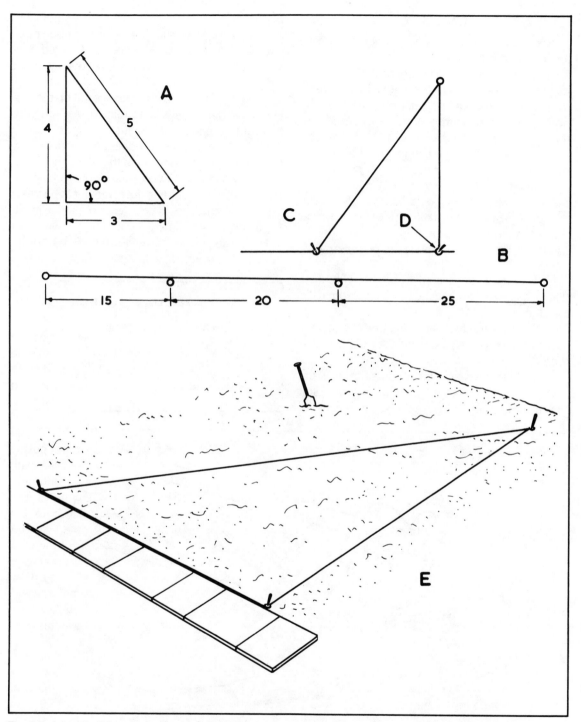

Fig. 6-7. A length of line marked in the proportions 3:4:5 can be used to set out lines squarely on the ground.

TOOL BOX

A box to carry small tools, seed packets, gloves, and other odds and ends that a gardener needs is a worthwhile piece of equipment that is easy to make. Figure 6-8 shows a box with a handle made from a dibber that can be withdrawn for use. The box could also hang from any long-handled tool that you will need for the work in hand. If you do not need this facility, the handle could be a piece of 1-inch dowel rod permanently in place.

Although sizes are suggested (Fig. 6-9), this is the sort of project that could be arranged to suit available materials or adapted to carry particular things. Almost any wood is suitable. This is especially true if it is finished with preservative or paint.

1. The key parts are the uprights with holes (Fig. 6-9A). Leave drilling the holes until you make the dibber.

2. Make the two ends (Fig. 6-9B) to lengths to match the first two pieces and the sides to match them (Fig. 6-9C).

3. Before assembly, drill holes to fit easily on the tool handle that will carry the box or to suit the dowel, if either is the chosen means of transport.

4. If a dibber is to double as a handle, make it (Fig. 6-9D). It could be a piece of 1 inch dowel rod nearly as long as the box, with a rounded point and a handle tenoned on.

5. Drill the uprights for an easy fit on the dibber. You should be able to remove it easily, but it would be better not too loose.

6. Assemble the box parts and add a bottom (Fig. 6-9E). Nails or screws in the joints should be adequate, although if you are a woodworking enthusiast corners could be dovetailed. If the bottom is plywood, that should be exterior or marine grade for damp resistance.

7. Cleats under the ends (Fig. 6-9F) can be added, if you wish.

Materials List for Tool Box	
2 uprights	7 × 6 × 5/8
2 ends	6 × 3 × 5/8
2 sides	20 × 3 × 5/8
1 bottom	20 × 7 1/4 × 3/8
2 cleats	8 × 1 × 5/8
1 dibber from	26 × 1 diameter

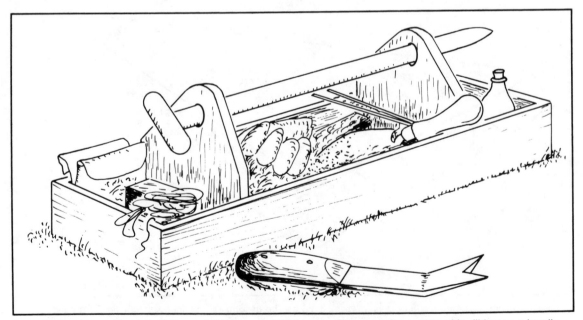

Fig. 6-8. A tool box will carry all the small things a gardener needs. This one uses a removable dibber as a handle.

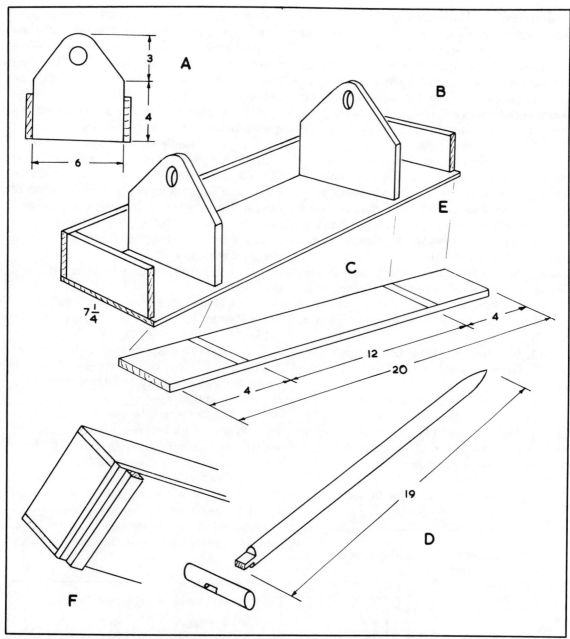

Fig. 6-9. Parts of the tool box are nailed together and holes are made large enough for the dibber to slide through easily.

STACKING SEED BOXES

Seed boxes are often preferred in larger numbers than can be spread on the available shelf or bench space. It is then helpful if the boxes can be arranged with enough space between them for the contents to get air, to be watered and to sprout. If the bottom box rests firmly, a stack of six or more would be quite feasible and make good use of available space.

By the nature of their use, seed boxes tend to

be neglected and do not last long. If they are well made—even from the least-expensive woods—you should get many years of use out of your boxes. It would be unwise to use paint or preservative on the wood because they might affect soil or seeds.

The boxes shown in Fig. 6-10 should suit average needs, but the sizes given (Fig. 6-11A) can, if you prefer, be altered considerably.

1. For the sake of standardization, it is advisable to decide how many boxes you need and make all the parts at the same time. The bottoms can be made of any number of narrow strips or single pieces of exterior plywood. If the wood parts are sawn accurately, you need not plane them.

2. Have all the sides and ends ready and nail them together (Fig. 6-11B).

3. Nail on the bottoms. Check squareness as you do this. If you are assembling a large quantity, it will help to have a jig made from two strips square to each other attached to the bench (Fig. 6-11C).

4. Nail in the square corner posts (Fig. 6-11D). Be careful that these all finish at the same height.

5. Put strips across (Fig. 6-11E) to act as handles.

6. Make locating blocks (Fig. 6-11F) to go under the corners. When a box stands alone they act as feet; when stacked they keep the boxes in place. They need not fit very closely to the posts. If the fit is loose, that will allow for slight variations in the construction of the boxes.

Materials List for One Stacking Seed Box

2 sides	18 × 3 × 1/2
2 ends	11 × 3 × 1/2
1 bottom	18 × 12 × 1/2
4 posts	6 × 1 × 1
2 handles	12 × 1 × 1/2
4 locating blocks	2 × 2 × 1/2

KNEELER

It is usually unwise to kneel on damp ground and it is always better to spread your weight if you are dealing with a prepared surface. It might be sufficient to use any available odd board, but many gardeners, even if fairly agile in other ways, have difficulty in getting up and down from a kneeling position. A board with handles would be welcomed.

Handles permanently in place could make a kneeler bulky for storage. The example shown in Fig. 6-12 has a handle stout enough to lean on at each end, but when out of use the two handles fold flat. Although the kneeler might be acceptable in almost any wood, it would be strong if made of close-grained hardwood. If lightness is an important consideration, softwood can be used. For rigidity at the joints, keep any wood to at least the specified thickness.

1. Prepare all wood to the same width and thickness.

2. Cut the piece for the base with notches that will let the handles set in about 1/4 inch (Fig. 6-13A).

3. Cut the bottoms of the handles to fit into the notches (Fig. 6-13B). They must not project below the bottom surface and should be an easy, but a loose, fit.

4. Cut the finger holes (Fig. 6-13C) by drilling the ends and sawing between. Round the tops (Fig. 6-13D), and then well round the edges of the holes and outsides where the hands will grip.

5. Use two 3-inch stout hinges at each end (Fig. 6-13E). There is no need to let them into the wood. Fit them while the handles are held in position square to the base. Test the folding action. The wood can be left untreated or treated with preservative.

Materials List for Kneeler

1 base	18 × 9 × 1
2 handles	9 × 9 × 1

KNEELER/TOOL CARRIER

There is no need for anyone to be uncomfortable while gardening, but for anyone with difficulty in kneeling, close work on such things as flower

Fig. 6-10. Stacking seed boxes conserve space. They can be separated when needed.

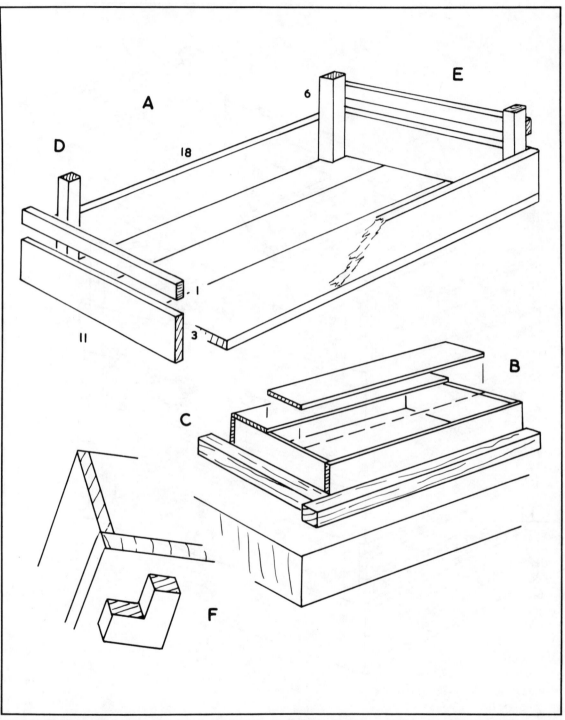

Fig. 6-11. The boxes (A) are nailed together, but a simple jig (B, C) keeps them square during assembly. Posts with handles (D-F) fit the boxes together.

Fig. 6-12. A simple kneeler will fold flat when out of use.

borders becomes impossible without some aid. The combined tool carrier and kneeler shown in Fig. 6-14 is intended to give padded comfort under the knees, handles high enough to lean on when getting up and down, and boxes at the ends to carry hand tools, seed packets, string, and other small items.

The base and boxes could be light softwood, but the handles are better made of hardwood. The base and the upholstered board could be plywood. Exact sizes are not crucial, but for comfort do not reduce the gap for the knees between the handles.

The boxes can be altered and could be given compartments for specific tools. The whole assembly can be nailed or screwed together, but dovetails or other appropriate joints could be used at the corners. Even with other parts nailed, it would be stronger to tenon the handles into the base (as suggested below).

1. Set out the base (Fig. 6-15A) first because that controls many other sizes.

2. Cut the wood for the handles (Fig. 6-15B). If this is to be nailed or screwed through the base, cut the bottom square across. For mortise and

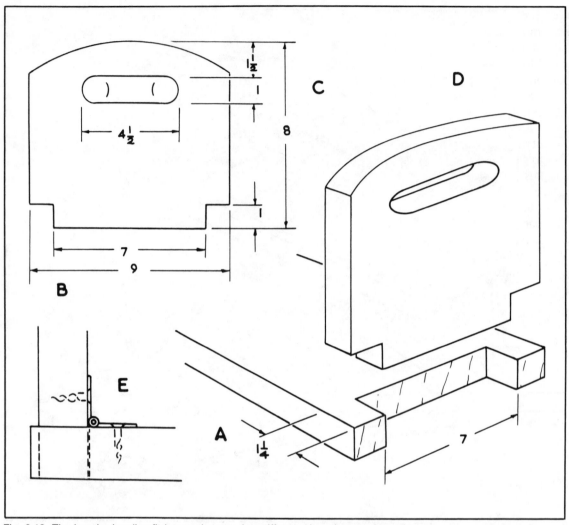

Fig. 6-13. The kneeler handles fit into sockets to give stiffness when they are leaned on.

tenon joints, mark out the parts and cut them (Fig. 6-15C). When you assemble, drive wedges into saw cuts in the tenons (Fig. 6-15D) to supplement glue.

3. Cut the hand holes (Fig. 6-15E) by drilling the ends and sawing between. Round the tops and take off all sharp edges where the hands will grip.

4. Make the box parts (Fig. 6-15F).

5. Join the handles to the base; check that they are square across and stand upright. Assemble the box parts to them and to the base.

6. The upholstered pad is based on a piece of solid wood or plywood, screwed through the base, so that it can be removed if it ever needs attention. The padding is a piece of plastic or rubber foam about 2 inches thick. The covering should be plastic-coated fabric that will be unaffected by dampness. Cut the pad wood for an easy fit between the handles. Allow for the thickness of the covering material. Drill two 1/2-inch holes in the base and pad. These are to let air in and out as the foam compresses and expands. Also drill for two holes for screws (Fig. 6-15G).

7. Cut the foam slightly oversize to allow for

compressing. A thin-bladed knife, kept wet, will cut most foam. Bevel around the underside to about half thickness (Fig. 6-15H). This allows the edge to be pulled to a neat curve by the covering material (Fig. 6-15J).

8. Use tacks (Fig. 6-15K). Position one near the center of each edge, then work out to the corners. a spacing of 1 1/2 inches will probably be about right. Experiment with tensions of the material to get a good appearance on top, then cut off surplus material underneath and screw the pad in place.

9. If the equipment is to be painted, remove the pad until after that has been done.

Materials List for Kneeler/Tool Carrier

1 base	24 × 8 × 1/2
2 handles	11 × 8 × 1
2 box ends	8 × 4 × 1/2
4 box sides	4 × 4 × 1/2
1 pad	15 × 8 × 1/2
1 piece foam	15 × 8 × 2
1 piece covering material 21 × 13	

ROW MARKERS

When you plant a row of seeds, you need to mark the ends to show where the row is and to indicate what seeds are in that row. Too often any odd stick is thrust in and any marking soon becomes indecipherable. Better row markers are easily made in quantity if you have a table saw that will cut to at least 1 inch thickness.

Cut the profile you want on an offcut of wood. A thickness between 3/4 inch and 1 inch and a length of 7 inches or so will do (Fig. 6-16A). Set the fence on the saw to about 1/4 inch and cut off as many markers as you require (Fig. 6-16B). If the saw is fine and you feed the wood slowly, the surface left should be good enough to take lettering from a waterproof felt pen. Otherwise you can plane or sand it. A refinement is to give one side of the marker a coat of nonglossy white paint so that the lettering will show better.

Longer pieces made in the same way can be cut for supports for flowers or plants, possibly with holes drilled to take string. Although wood of any sort will do for markers, choose straight-grained pieces free from knots for the longer supports.

Fig. 6-14. This kneeler has an upholstered center and boxes at the ends to carry small tools and other equipment.

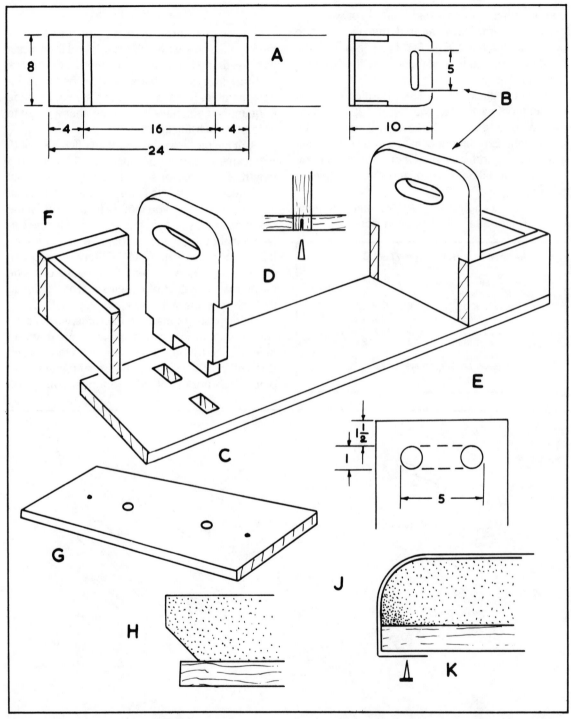

Fig. 6-15. Strength is given to the kneeler by tenons between the handles and the base (A-G). Foam is used for the upholstery (H-K).

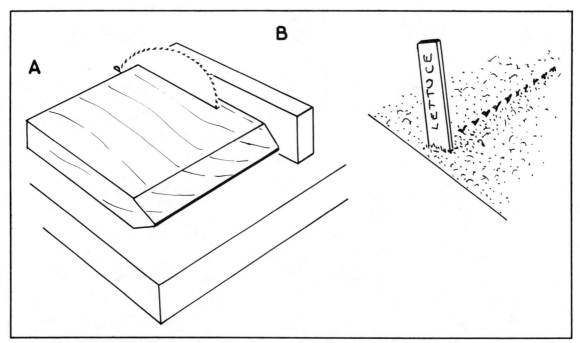

Fig. 6-16. Row markers can be cut from a shaped block of wood with a table saw.

EDGES

To keep soil within bounds, particularly if you are making a raised flower bed, there has to be some sort of edging to define limits. A simple assembly is made from thin boards with pieces to thrust into the ground (Fig. 6-17). This looks neatest if the uprights are inside, but that puts a load the wrong way on the nails if they are straight. It is advisable to take them through and clench the ends (Fig. 6-18A). It is better to use sections rather than try to make a long border piece. Allow for the lower edge to come slightly below the surface and give

Fig. 6-17. Edges can be made with boards or logs.

89

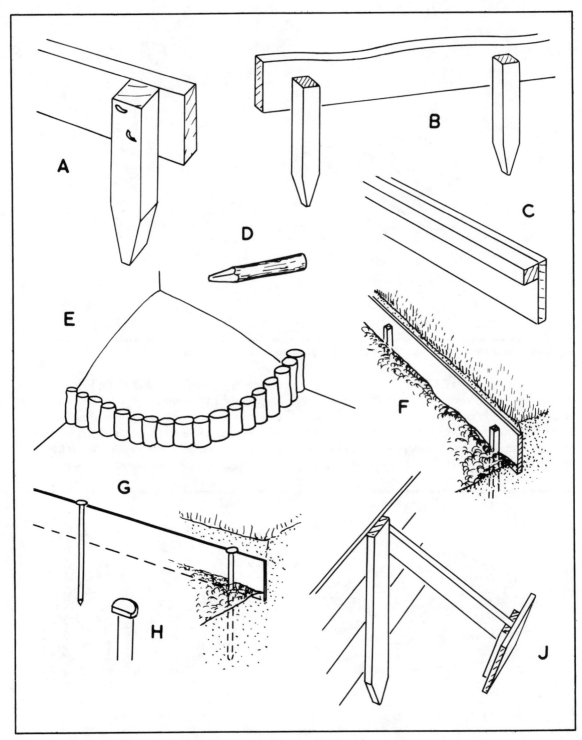

Fig. 6-18. Garden edges can be kept in place with stakes into the ground.

the uprights enough length to withstand the soil pressure, which could be considerable when you are digging or cultivating.

The top edge can be shaped (Fig. 6-18B), but do not make the curves excessive or soil will escape over the top. Thickening a straightedge (Fig. 6-18C) will help to resist warping and can improve appearance. A painted finish should look attractive.

If you have plenty of natural wood, a series of short stakes (Fig. 6-18D), about 2 inches or 3 inches in diameter, can be driven with level tops or arranged in a pattern. For a corner, the tops can sweep down to the center (Fig. 6-18E). If your natural wood is thicker, you can split it and use it in the same way with the flat sides inward.

The edge of a lawn is often matched by a flower garden that might be a few inches lower.

Trimming this edge can be a chore that you would rather not have. Grass grows out of the side and spreads into the garden. Periodically you have to straighten the edge and generally tidy up. If you fit a wood or metal edge below the grass surface level, the lawn should keep a neat appearance for a long time.

If wood is used, pieces about 3 inches by 3/8 of an inch would be suitable, but they should be resinous or other durable types. Small supporting stakes can be located about 9 inches apart (Fig. 6-18F). Not all stakes need be attached to the lengthwise wood, but the end ones and some at about 24-inch intervals could be nailed.

A more durable lawn edge can be made with a metal such as aluminum. Steel would rust but that is unlikely to matter. In both cases a thickness

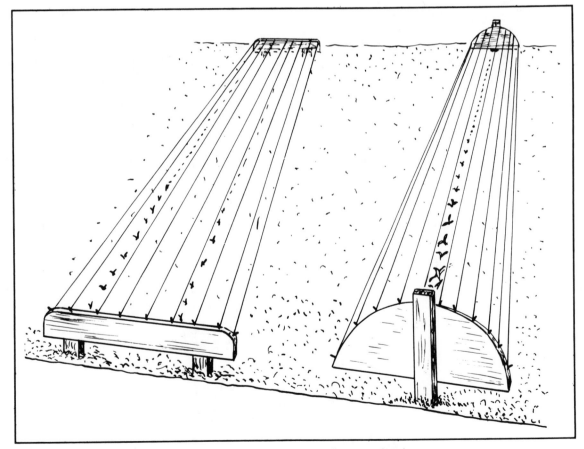

Fig. 6-19. Seedlings can be protected from birds with cotton strands on wood ends.

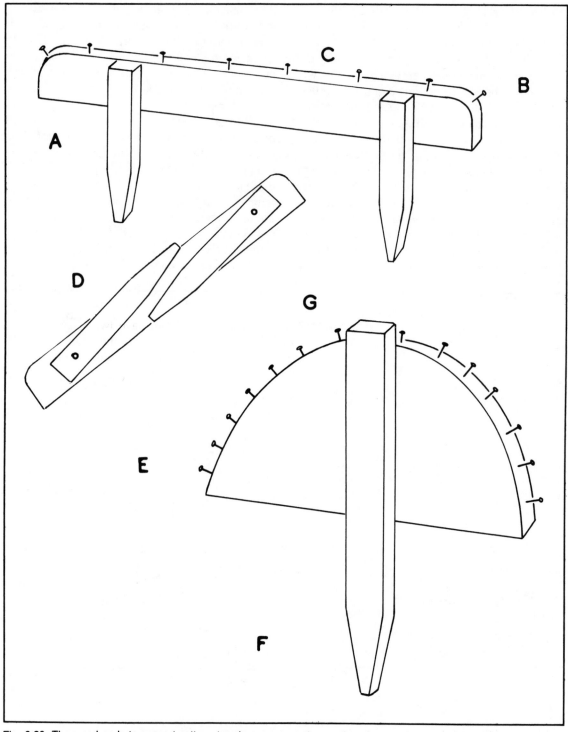

Fig. 6-20. The wood ends to support cotton strands are mounted on stakes that can be arranged to fold.

of about 1/8 inch is advisable. Thinner metal would tend to buckle unless the supports were very close. Stakes can be 6-inch nails; the heads are hooked over the sheet metal to keep it in place (Fig. 6-18G). An occasional nail could be on the lawn side of the strip to help in retaining it. For neatness the extending side of a nail head could be filed off (Fig. 6-18H).

If you want to make a high support for soil, possibly behind a sloping bank of flowers, any wood structure is liable to bow outward after some time. Struts on the outside would prevent this. If you want to avoid struts, there will have to be some internal bracing. One way of arranging this is to fit diagonal internal struts below what will be the soil level and have quite wide pieces across their bottoms (Fig. 6-18J) so that soil packed around them will resist the pull when the back tries to bow.

BIRD PROTECTORS

Birds will devour many small seedlings, and the usual way to scare them away is to arrange cotton thread stands almost invisible above the rows of sprouting plants. This is often done with a few sticks pushed into the ground at the ends of the rows.

Something more substantial is worth making and the same parts can be used year after year. The supports shown in Fig. 6-19 can be arranged at the ends of rows. On very long rows more can be used intermediately. The supports can be positioned soon after sowing and strands can be strung between them before the first shoots appear. The sup-

ports should be high enough for birds to tangle their legs before they are very close to the ground. Strands raised up to 6 inches should be satisfactory.

1. If there are two rows of seeds fairly close together, the simplest supports are straight pieces with legs to thrust into the ground (Fig. 6-20A). The ends can be rounded, and then you drive nails partly into the edges for attaching the strands (Fig. 6-20B).

2. Arrange the legs to come to the top edge (Fig. 6-20C). If you have to hit the supports to get them into the ground, your blows can come directly on these pieces.

3. The legs can be pivoted on bolts so that they will swing up to reduce bulk during storage (Fig. 6-20D).

4. For a single row, particularly if it is a crop that needs protection until the leaves are several inches high, it is better to make a semicircular end (Fig. 6-20E).

5. The end can have two legs, similar to those on the straight end, or there might be a central piece (Fig. 6-20F) extending a short distance above the shaped part (Fig. 6-20G), for thrusting or hitting into the ground.

6. The center leg could be carried higher if you want to mount a scarecrow, flag, or other additional bird scarer.

Materials List for Bird Protectors
First end: 1 piece 24 × 4 × 1 and 2 pieces 12 × 2 × 1
Second end: 1 piece 12 × 7 × 1 and 1 piece 18 × 2 × 1

Chapter 7

Special Hand Tools

Most garden work, particularly on the land around your home, can be done with a few standard hand tools. Such tools have stood the test of time and have evolved into patterns that are generally acceptable. They form the mainstay of gardeners' tool kits. One advantage of making your own tools is that besides these standard tools you can make others that will do jobs better or are more suitable for your needs. You can have tools for which there is no manufactured alternative. Some of the tools might be similar to those found in a tool store, while others might be special designs.

The tools described in this chapter are not all new designs. They are mostly the types of hand tools that can be regarded as extra to the basic gardening tools that every gardener should have. You might not find a need for all of them, but others will be preferable to some basic tools. A special tool does not have to be difficult to make while allowing you to perform a task better than the tool it replaces.

TURF EDGER

You can trim the edges of the grass alongside a flower border with a spade, but because of its curved cross section it will not produce a uniform line when you look along the edge of the turf. A spade is not a sharp cutting tool; its edge does not go easily through matted turf. It is better for straightness of cut and ease of working to have a turf edger (a cutting tool made straight in section). The tool shown in Fig. 7-1 has a blade made from a piece of steel taken from discarded farm machinery. The edger could have been made from new tool steel, but mild steel would not be stiff enough and would not keep its edge for long.

The edger is used with a double action. It is thrust down to make the first cut, and then it is rocked both ways to lengthen the cut. Its top should have a handle suitable for your hand to push down and it will also help to have a foot position to give a greater thrust. Some variations are shown (Fig. 7-2).

Fig. 7-1. A turf edger with a blade made from a discarded piece of farm equipment.

1. The blade can be cut to a regular curve, which is part of a circle (Fig. 7-2A), or the end can be taken to a slight point (Fig. 7-2B). Exact sizes are unimportant, but too wide a blade will be weak and difficult to use. A narrow blade will have to be thrust more often and straightness of the cut edge will be more difficult to maintain.

2. The simplest construction has a tang into the end of a handle with a tube ferrule (Fig. 7-2C). Even with brazing, the load on the tang is such that it should be wider than on many other tools and it is better secured with two rivets.

3. For the tang, have a strip of mild steel—about a 5/8-inch-by-3/8-inch section—and forge one end to go into the handle (Fig. 7-2D). Cut off with enough left to make the palm and hammer this down to a piece wide enough for two 1/4-inch rivets (Fig. 7-2E).

4. Clean the meeting surfaces, and then rivet the parts together and braze or weld them. See that the tang is square to the blade in both directions.

5. Another method of attaching the blade puts both handle and blade between steel cheek strips (Fig. 7-2F). With a 1 1/4-inch-diameter handle the strips can be about 7/8-inch-by-3/16-inch-section mild steel.

6. Taper both sides of the end of the handle for about 6 inches to the thickness of the blade (Fig. 7-2G). Cut the strips to fit against the wood and the blade. One may have its top straight and the other turned out for a step (Fig. 7-2H). Round the ends of both pieces and bend them slightly to fit closely in position.

7. Drill for 1/4-inch rivets through the handle and blade in the steel strips and the blade. Rivet and braze the strips to the blade.

8. Grind the curved edge on both sides to make a knifelike cutting edge. This could be followed by use of an oilstone or a water stone. Final sharpness is better left until after hardening and tempering. Rub the steel bright for about 1 inch from the cutting edge and heat the whole length to redness. Make sure the steel blade is glowing fairly evenly, and then plunge edgewise into water. Rub the steel bright again.

9. It is difficult to fan a flame on a blade of this length so the oxide colors can spread to the edge evenly, but it can be done. If you try and are not satisfied with the result, you must reharden and try again. Another way of tempering the broader area is to have a tray of sand heating over a flame. The blade rests on top. Watch carefully for the oxide colors that will build up over the whole piece. With both methods, plunge the blade into water when the edge becomes purple. If you see oxide colors on the mild steel strips, it does not matter because heating does not have any effect on the hardness of mild steel.

10. Fit the end of the handle and drill and rivet through the strips. For protection against rust, paint the meeting surfaces before attaching the handle. The long rivets can be made from cut 1/4-inch rod. Heads are formed on each side (Fig. 7-2J).

11. To stand up to the levering ation of cutting, the handle is best made of a wood, such as ash or hickory, that withstands flexing loads. At the top tenon on a cross grip (Fig. 7-2K), thoroughly round all the wood there for comfort.

12. If the blade is attached to the handle with a tang, it can be left without a step for foot pressure. One way of adding this is to put a steel rod through the handle (Fig. 7-2L). It should be satisfactory to put a 3/8-inch rod through a parallel 1 1/4-inch diameter handle. To compensate for any weakening, due to drilling, the shaft of the handle could be made about 1/4 inch thicker where the hole comes and taper off toward top and bottom.

13. Paint the steel to within about 1 inch of the sharpened edge and varnish the wood handle to complete the turf edger.

ADAPTABLE HOE

If a hoe is provided with blades that can be changed, its scope is increased. Blades can then be of different sizes and their shapes can be varied. Constructionally, there is the advantage that only the blade need be made of tool steel. This simplifies hardening and tempering. The other part can be mild steel.

The hoe shown in Fig. 7-3 can be made in two possible forms, and with some alternative constructions. The blade can be square to the line of the handle, so it may be used with a chopping action, or it can be set at a more acute angle to the line of the handle so it will function as a push-pull or Dutch hoe. The general method of construction is the same, but the first instructions are for a push-pull hoe with the metal parts bolted or riveted to the handle. Variations are described later.

1. Mark out the strip that forms the body of the hoe (Fig. 7-4A). The lines across for the bends diagonal to the edges can be at 60 degrees, but these affect the angle at which the blade will be to the handle. You might want to try bending a strip of paper or card to find what angle would suit your needs best.

2. Mark the positions of holes and drill those for the bolts through the blade. It is better to leave the holes for rivets through the handle until after shaping, or only drill one side, so that you can drill through the handle and the other side at the same time during fitting.

3. Bend the strip on the diagonal lines (Fig. 7-4B) by hammering over in a vise.

4. Curve the ends that will fit against the handle (Fig. 7-4C). This can be done by hammering a rod over the hot metal resting on a partly open vise.

Materials List for Turf Edger	
1 blade	9 × 4 1/2 × 5/32 or thicker tool steel
If tang is used:	
1 tang	from 6 × 5/8 × 3/8 mild steel
1 ferrule	2 × 1 1/4 × 1/16 mild steel tube
If cheeks are used:	
1 strip	7 × 7/8 × 3/16 mild steel
1 strip	9 × 7/8 × 3/16 mild steel
1 rod	for rivets 10 × 1/4 diameter mild steel
In both cases:	
1 wood handle	30 × 1 1/4 diameter
1 step, if required,	8 × 3/8 diameter mild steel

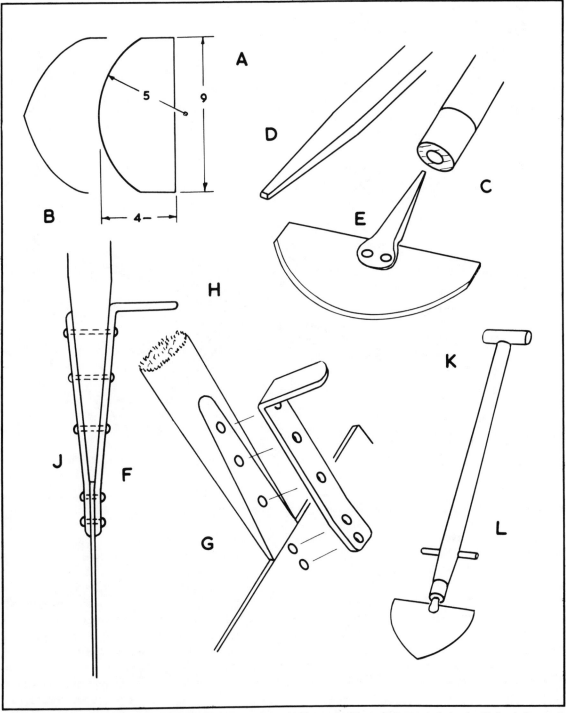

Fig. 7-2. The blade of the turf edger can be riveted to its tang (A-E) or a double arrangement of cheeks (F-J) can be used. The handle (K) can be given a step (L) for foot pressure.

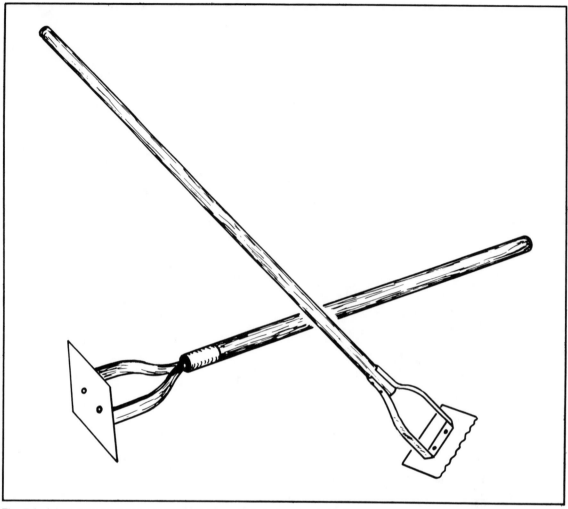

Fig. 7-3. A hoe may be made adaptable if different blades can be bolted on.

5. Bend the two sides in toward the handle equally (Fig. 7-4D). They will also have to be given a slight twist to bring the ends into line at the handle.

6. Fit the end of the handle between the frame sides and drill through for rivets or bolts (Fig. 7-4E). Paint or varnish where the metal and wood meet, and then join these parts together.

7. The basic blade is a piece of tool steel cut to a rectangular shape (Fig. 7-4F). If you make it slightly thicker than if you intend to heat treat it, it could be used without hardening and tempering. Drill for the bolts and make a trial assembly.

Sharpen the cutting edges. If you harden and temper, bring the edges to purple oxide colors.

8. It helps in cutting some small surface weeds if the cutting edge is serrated like a saw or cut with small curves (Fig. 7-4G). The edges do not have to be straight across. You may prefer to have an edge cut diagonally so that there is one long corner for digging into stubborn weeds. The edge could be curved (Fig. 7-4H) or pointed (Fig. 7-4J).

9. If you want to make a chopping type of hoe, instead of making bends at an angle across the body strip bend them squarely. The part across the end will finish square to the handle and you

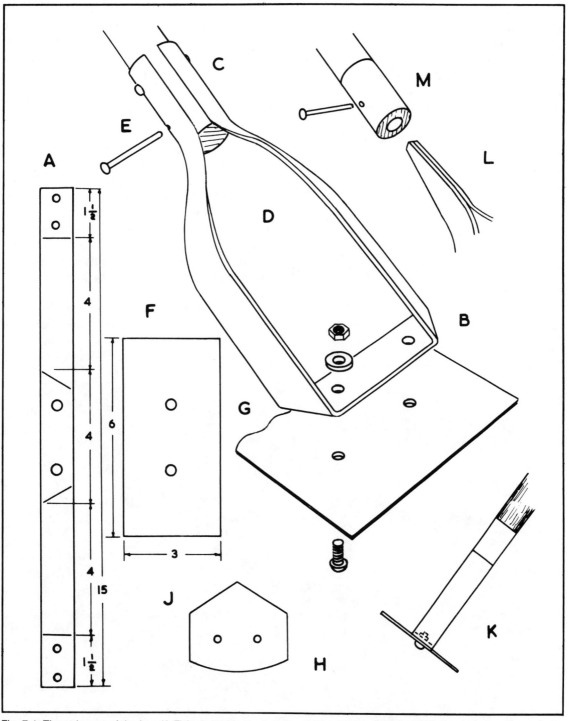

Fig. 7-4. The strip part of the hoe (A-E) is riveted to the handle and the blades (F-K) are drilled to bolt on. Alternatively, the strip can fit into the handle (L, M).

can bolt on a blade that can chop from either side (Fig. 7-4K).

10. Having the sides riveted or bolted through the handle will be strong enough for the push-pull action of hoeing, and this will be satisfactory for a chopping action if the handle is hardwood and is taken far enough through the metal sides to resist splitting.

11. There could be a tubular ferrule on the end of the handle and the sides of the tool frame brazed to it. The ferrule compresses the wood and resists any tendency to split.

Materials List for Adaptable Hoe	
1 frame	15 × 1 × 3/16 mild steel
1 or more blades	6 × 3 × 16 or 18 gauge tool steel
2 bolts with nuts and washers	3/4 × 1/4 diameter
2 3/16 rivets to suit handle 1 wood handle	48 × 1 1/8 diameter

12. The two ends of the frame could be brought together and pointed (Fig. 7-4L), then the handle end strengthened with a long ferrule. After driving the metal into the hole, a rivet through the ferrule and all parts will secure it (Fig. 7-4M).

SIMPLE TOOLS

There are several very simple tools that a manufacturer might not bother with, yet the craftsman/gardener can make to aid his hobby. Some of these tools are appropriate to use with window boxes, hanging plant holders, and other small gardening situations where tools of standard size would be too bulky. Sometimes rather toylike tools are offered for the purpose, but it would be better to have substantial tools within their limitations. The tools shown in Fig. 7-5 may easily be altered and developed to suit individual needs.

Reversible Hand Hoe. A reversible hand hoe can be made from a strip of mild steel that is 3/4 inch by 1/8 inch and about 10 inches long. Bend one end to make the hoe and file its edge thin (Fig.

Fig. 7-5. Small tools are convenient for working in small spaces and dealing with pots and boxes.

7-6A). The other end could be left square as a little Dutch hoe or filed to a rounded point (Fig. 7-6B). A handle could be made by binding with electrician's tape, but it would be better to fit two wood slabs (Fig. 7-6C) about 4 inches long. Drill the top slab and the steel to clear two screws, and then drill undersize holes for the screw threads in the lower slab. Partly shape the slabs before assembly.

Hook Tool. In its smallest size, a hook tool acts as a hoe or cultivator. It has about a 2-inch cut when flat or a 1-inch cut when on edge for use in confined spaces. It could be made larger for more general use. For the small version use steel 1-inch-by-1/16-inch section. Bend to shape (Fig. 7-6D) and file the cutting edges thin. The example is shown with a tang to fit into a file handle (Fig. 7-6E), but it could be made with a wood slab handle (Fig. 7-6F).

Paving Stone Hook. When a path is formed with stone slabs, whether squared blocks or natural shapes as crazy paving, weeds will grow in the gaps. The paving stone hook is intended for removing those weeds. It should reach into even the narrowest crevices. The hooks are on a strip of 1/4-inch-diameter steel about 15 inches long. Tool steel is advisable if the double hook is to have a long life. The handle is a piece of 3/4-inch wood dowel rod, 5 inches long, and drilled to fit the rod (Fig. 7-6G).

Bend one end and forge and file it to a thin blade (Fig. 7-6H) in line with the rod. Slide on the handle up to that end while you bend and forge the other end to a chisel section (Fig. 7-6J). If tool steel has been used, harden and temper the cutters to blue or purple. Slide the handle out of the way as you heat treat each end. Smear the center of the rod with epoxy glue to secure the handle there.

Paving Stone Knife. A hook might not be substantial enough for weeds in large cracks. The knife shown in Fig. 7-6K is better able to stand up to hacking and chopping to greater depths. The blade is cut from sheet tool steel (1/8 inch thick should be satisfactory) and it is shown with a slab handle (Fig. 7-6L). There is no need to thin the edge

because it is not intended to cut in line, but its tip works more like a chisel or tiny hoe. It is the temper at the point that is crucial. Harden the end, and then temper by heating near the angle so that the oxide colors spread slowly to the point, which should be quenched when purple.

Materials List for Simple Tools	
Reversible hand hoe	
1 blade	10 × 3/4 × 1/8 mild or tool steel
2 slabs	5 × 3/4 × 3/8 wood
Hook tool	
1 blade	10 × 1 × 1/16 mild or tool steel
1 handle:	either 2 wood slabs 5 × 1 × 3/8 or a file handle
Paving stone hook	
1 rod	15 × 1/4 diameter tool steel
1 handle	5 × 3/4 diameter wood
Paving stone knife	
1 blade	10 × 3 × 1/8 tool steel
2 slabs	5 × 1 × 3/8 wood

BULB PLANTER

When something as large as a flower bulb has to be planted, a rather large hole is needed. If this hole is made by pushing a stick or a dibber into the ground and then levering it round to make the hole bigger, the effect is to compress the soil around the hole. Compressed soil makes it hard for the delicate roots to enter and there is a risk that the roots will be broken as the bulb is inserted. It is better to remove enough soil so that what is left is at its normal consistency. If a trowel is used to dig a hole, more soil has to be removed than is needed. A piece of parallel tube could be thrust in, but there would be difficulty in removing soil from inside it each time. It would be better to make a tapered tubular planter. The hole it makes is better for planting and any soil inside is easily pushed through.

The planter shown in Fig. 7-7 should suit most

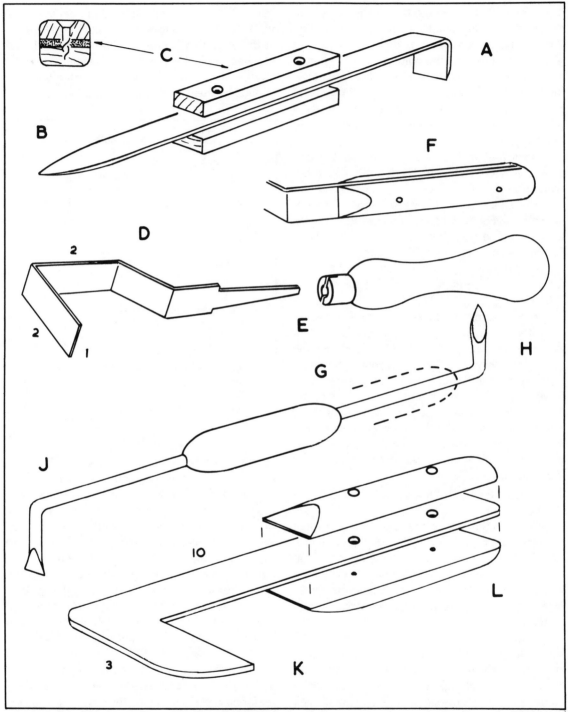

Fig. 7-6. The reversible hand hoe has flat slab handles (A-C). A hook tool can fit into a round handle or have slabs (D-F). The paving stone hook has a wood handle (G-J). A paving stone knife can have a slab handle (K, L).

Fig. 7-7. A bulb planter removes sufficient soil without disturbing the surrounding area.

flower bulbs and other large seeds or plants. It will make a tapered hole up to 6 inches deep. The conical tube part has a dowel rod handle attached with strip steel pieces (Fig. 7-8A). Riveted construction is shown, but the sheet-metal cone could be brazed or welded.

1. Draw a side view of the cone (Fig. 7-8B). Based on this, draw the developed shape as described in Chapter 3 (Fig. 3-5). Allow enough metal for the edges to overlap about 1/2 inch.

2. Mark a centerline on the development for the position of the handle strip opposite the joint. Rivet holes can be drilled along one edge before rolling the metal to a cone. Allow for two 3/16-inch rivets for each handle strip, but the others can be 1/8 inch.

3. Bend the conical tube. Drill through for the 1/8-inch rivets and fit them to hold the tube in shape (Fig. 7-8C).

4. Bend the strips for the handle (Fig. 7-8D). They follow the slope of the cone, but should have parallel ends to take the wood handle. Drill those ends for central wood screws (Fig. 7-8E). Drill and rivet the other ends to the tube.

5. Cut and fit a piece of dowel rod between the strips and screw it in place. If you have a wood lathe you might prefer to turn a shaped handle.

6. Not everything you plant will need to go the full depth of the tool, and it is helpful to know how much of the tube is in the ground, by making deep scratches at 3 inches, 4 inches, and 5 inches from the bottom (Fig. 7-8F).

7. The handle parts can be left plain or painted, but the tube is best left untreated.

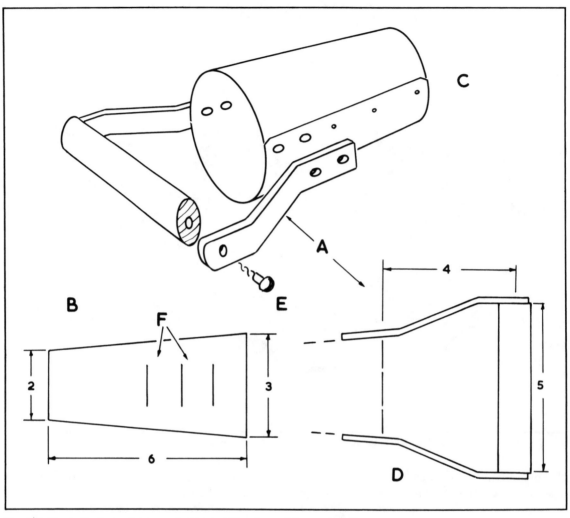

Fig. 7-8. The bulb planter has a conical body with strips to join to a handle.

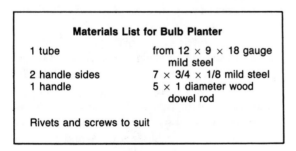

Materials List for Bulb Planter

1 tube	from 12 × 9 × 18 gauge mild steel
2 handle sides	7 × 3/4 × 1/8 mild steel
1 handle	5 × 1 diameter wood dowel rod

Rivets and screws to suit

RIDGER

For planting seeds you have to make a groove or furrow in the ground. When plants are growing in rows, you will have to scoop soil from between the rows to build up around the plants. A ridger or furrower is a tool primarily used for the second purpose, but it will also make planting furrows or drills.

The tool can be small and short-handled for some work, but for most jobs it should be long enough to use when standing and wide enough to form grooves and ridges where rows of plants are 12 inches or more apart. The tool shown in Fig. 7-9 has a blade like some snow plows and large farm double ploughs. It is used with a pulling action so that you do not walk on the part you have worked.

1. The blade shown in Fig. 7-10A is cut from a square piece of sheet metal. This gives a corner folded at 45 degrees. Other angles are possible. You can experiment with paper and use the shape you prefer as a template. The ends do not have to be shaped, but they improve appearance (Fig. 7-10B) and facilitate curving the bottom edges outward.

2. Fold the blade on the bend line. There is no need for a sharp fold, particularly at the top. Aim at about 60 degrees at the top (Fig. 7-10C), but the angle can be wider near the bottom. Curve out the bottom edge (Fig. 7-10D).

3. The stem is a piece of 3/8-inch-diameter rod that can be attached to the handle in any of several ways. At the blade it should go inside about 1 1/2 inches (Fig. 7-10E). File it and the blade bright where they meet so that the rod makes a fairly close fit inside the curved bend, and then braze or weld together.

4. Form the rod into a swan neck. The end may be given a point to drive into a hole in a handle with a ferrule (Fig. 7-10F), where it is secured with a rivet.

5. The stem could be riveted and brazed to a tube (Fig. 7-10G), to fit on a long handle, with a securing screw. The stem might have a shouldered end to braze into a conical piece to fit over the tapered end of the wood handle (Fig. 7-10H). Both methods have been described for earlier tools.

6. If the tool is painted, leave the lower half of the blade untreated, as any paint there would soon wear away.

Materials List for Ridger	
1 blade	from 10 × 10 × 18 gauge mild or tool steel
1 stem	from 15 × 3/8 diameter mild steel
1 ferrule, as needed	
1 handle	48 × 1 1/8 wood

THISTLE HOOK

If you have to deal with a small amount of thistles, nettles, or brambles that are beginning to overrun

Fig. 7-9. The ridger lifts soil between rows to build up around plants.

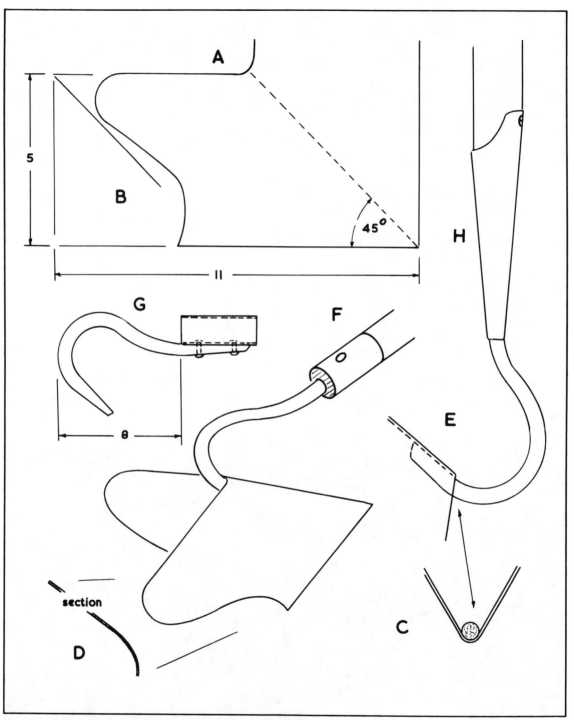

Fig. 7-10. The ridger blade is cut square and bent to shape (A-E). The stem curves to fit and can go into the handle, be riveted to a ferrule or be continued into a conical socket (F-H).

the crop you are trying to grow, the tool to remove them has to have a working end small enough to go where you want it without cutting the standing crop. This hook shown in Fig. 7-11 is intended for that purpose.

The hooked cutting edge has sharp teeth to grip and cut the stems of tough weeds. The handle can be any length from about 6 inches, but will probably be most useful if it is 15 inches (giving an overall length of about 20 inches).

1. The blade should be tool steel thick enough not to buckle in use. Sheet about 1/16 inch should be satisfactory. Although it could be thicker, it would be more laborious to cut and shape. Cut the metal to the outline (Fig. 7-12A).

2. File large triangular teeth in the hollow edge (Fig. 7-12B), and then use a large, half-round file to bevel both sides to make a cutting edge. Finish the edge with a small oilstone (used like a file). You will have to complete sharpening after hardening and tempering, but the edge should be near its final state at this stage.

3. Make the handle of hardwood. Whatever its length, taper it slightly in thickness so that your hand grip is strengthened by pulling against a thicker section.

4. Start with the square-sectioned handle. Cut the slot for the blade (Fig. 7-12C). Drill for two rivets (Fig. 7-12D), which could be pieces of nail about 1/8 inch diameter.

5. When you are satisfied with the shape of the blade, harden and temper it. Tempering would

Fig. 7-11. A thistle hook will pull and cut off tougher weeds.

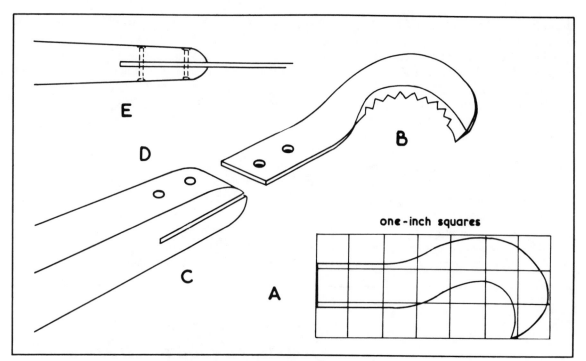

Fig. 7-12. The thistle hook blade (A, B) is riveted into its handle (C-E).

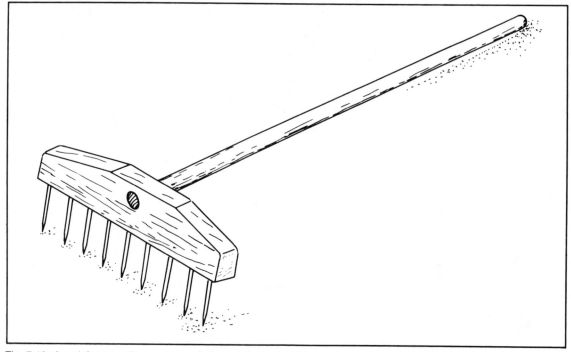

Fig. 7-13. A satisfactory rake can be made from nails and wood.

be best done on a tray of sand, as described in Chapter 3 (Fig. 3-1), but it could be done by fanning a flame carefully around the outside of the curve. Stop when dark brown or purple oxides reach the cutting edge.

6. Complete the shaping of the handle before assembly or leave final shaping until after riveting. The section could be fully rounded or you could leave it with a square section with rounded corners.

7. The loads on the rivets are mainly across them and the heads have to do little more than pre-vent them falling out, so countersink the holes only lightly and cut the rivet ends with just enough projecting to hammer into them (Fig. 7-12E).

8. Paint or varnish the handle. Leave the steel untreated.

Materials List for Thistle Hook	
1 blade	from 7 × 3 × 1/16 or thicker tool steel
1 handle	from 16 × 1 1/2 × 1 1/2 hardwood

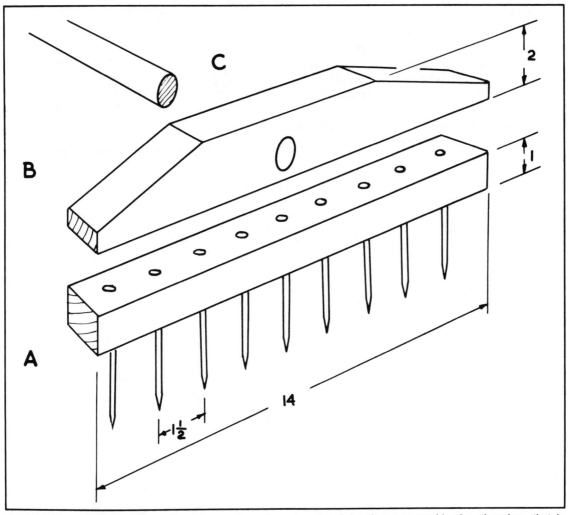

Fig. 7-14. The nails in the rake go through one piece of wood, and their heads are covered by the other piece that is also drilled for the handle.

WOOD AND NAILS RAKE

To be successful a tool does not have to be complicated or difficult to make. A satisfactory rake can be made from wood and nails for ordinary garden use or for gathering large grass cuttings and weeds.

The rake shown in Fig. 7-13 has eight tines made from nails spaced about 1 1/2 inches apart (it could be made to other sizes). The head is in two parts so that the nails are prevented from being forced back if they strike stones or are dropped on hard surfaces. You might want some weight in the head, but a light hardwood is recommended. The nails suggested are 4 inches long.

1. Start with the strip to take the nails (Fig. 7-14A). Mark the positions of the nails and drill for them before cutting the ends to length. This will reduce the risk of end-grain splitting. The ends need not be cut off until after assembly. Drill the nail holes slightly undersize (how much smaller depends on the wood). It will be worthwhile to experiment on a scrap piece of the same wood to see what size gives a tight grip on the nail without splitting. Drill squarely, with the aid of a drill press, if possible. Lightly countersink for the nail heads.

2. Make the cover piece (Fig. 7-14B) and drill it for the handle (Fig. 7-14C).

3. Drive the nails so the heads finish level with the surface.

4. Join the two parts of the head with glue and screws (which can be driven from below between nails). Four screws should be enough.

5. Glue in the handle. For further security, you could drive a screw down through the head or you could saw a cut across the end and drive in a wedge.

6. Paint the rake if you prefer.

Materials List for Wood and Nails Rake

1 head	14 × 1 × 1
1 head	14 × 2 × 1
1 handle	48 × 1 1/8 diameter

nine 4-inch nails

Chapter 8

Boxes and Bins

There are needs for containers of many sorts in the yard and garden. A few of these might be metal or concrete, but the majority, as described in this chapter, can be made of wood. Some containers can be filled with soil and used to grow things, others can hold or carry plants in pots, and still others hang and either hold soil or enclose one or more pots. Compost is best made and kept within bounds by using a container. Many tools and other equipment can be kept in a lidded box if you do not want to use a storage shed.

Containers that are used for growing plants can extend your garden and provide attractive edges for decks or patios. They allow flowers to be grown on the tops of walls that would otherwise be bare. For anyone with limited garden space, window boxes, hanging containers, and other arrangements of flowers in boxes can extend the apparent size of a garden and make an attractive display where there would otherwise be a barren outlook.

Open boxes or trays have their uses for starting seedlings indoors or in a greenhouse. Too often these are crude and simple things that might

not even survive one use. It is preferable to use better wood and a little more skill and care to produce longer-lasting trays. The stacking seed boxes shown in Fig. 6-10 are one way of dealing with seed growing, but boxes and trays of other sorts are also needed in the well-equipped garden.

Some boxes are needed to contain plants in pots for permanent display or to transport plants from greenhouse to garden. The containers do not have to be soiltight and are better with some gaps for cleaning and ventilation. Some containers might even appear to have more gaps than wood.

Tool storage boxes need to be substantial, and it might be necessary to provide a lockable lid if the garden is remote from the house. The box could be a horizontal chest with a lid that serves as a seat or one that slopes to shed rain. The tool storage container might be upright and more like a shed, but not so large that you could get into it.

The wood used might be a resinous type that has a good resistance to moisture, but other woods that can be protected with paint or preservative will probably have to be used. If seeds are to be grown in soil close to the wood, check that there is no risk of the particular preservative affecting the crop. It is possible to use plywood, but that should be exterior or marine grade plywood that has a glue unaffected by moisture. Where solid wood is difficult to obtain is suitable sections, plywood will make satisfactory boxes. It needs care in cutting to avoid ragged edges and it is more difficult to form corner joints.

Much can be done with natural wood or boards that are not prepared to the stage where they would be suitable for better carpentry or cabinetwork. Pieces cut from poles or branches can be built into attractive containers. When a lumberyard cuts planks and boards from round logs, it removes slabs from the outside. The slabs are flat inside and curved outside. Much of that outside wood is discarded and burned. It could make parts of plant pot stands.

When boards are cut through the log, one or both edges will have an outline following the profile of the log. This *waney edge* would be cut off and the edge of the board made straight, but in some boxes or wall troughs a board with the natural edge would look attractive and more in keeping with its surroundings than a straight board.

BASIC BOX VARIATIONS

Boxes are not necessarily all "hammer and nail" projects. You can build boxes that way in some cases, but for others it is better to cut joints. Variations from the simple box are needed for special purposes. Most boxes are rectangular, but sloping sides improve appearance and help if the contents

Fig. 8-1. Garden boxes have several sizes and patterns.

have to be tipped out. The basic method of construction allows for a great many variations (Fig. 8-1).

1. If the box is longer than it is wide, it is usual to nail the longer sides to the ends (Fig. 8-2A) and to nail the bottom underneath (Fig. 8-2B). This is satisfactory for most purposes.

2. At the corners, the nails have to go into end grain, which does not provide the best grip. Penetration into end grain should be at least twice the thickness of the wood. Instead of straight nailing, it is stronger to alter the angles of the nails or use dovetail nailing, with the top two nails closer than the others (Fig. 8-2C).

3. The pieces making up the bottom can also be attached to the sides and ends, with dovetail nailing, using closer spacing across the ends than will be needed at the sides.

4. If plywood is used for the sides and ends, that does not provide a very good grip for nails and it tends to split. It is better to cut the corners with tongues to fit into each other (Fig. 8-2D). Thinner nails can be used, to reduce the risk of splitting, and the joints will be locked by having nails both ways.

5. The greatest load comes on the bottom of a box and that has to be taken in the usual construction by nails end-on, in the direction most likely to slip.

6. It is better to enclose the bottom within the sides (Fig. 8-2E). This should be done for any heavily loaded box, but it involves more careful workmanship and a bottom thick enough to take nails in its edge. The nails take the load across their thickness (Fig. 8-2F), instead of end-on, and the bottom is more secure.

7. Cleats under the ends of a box (Fig. 8-2G) are not essential, but they serve at least two purposes. If the box is to stand on damp earth, they keep the bottom clear and they help to strengthen the attachment of the bottom to the ends.

8. If you want to provide a box with handles for lifting, the easiest way is to put strips across the top edges at the ends (Fig. 8-3A). If the ends of the strip are nailed into the ends of the sides, they help to prevent the sides being forced out.

9. More comfortable handles on a box or tray used for carrying pots or equipment are formed by building up the ends so slots can be cut (Fig. 8-3B). If the ends are fairly thick and the slots are about 5 inches long and at least 1 1/4 inch deep—and well-rounded—quite heavy loads can be carried comfortably.

10. If you want to make a box of thin wood, particularly if it is plywood that cannot be expected to take nails safely in its edges, the box ends can be framed (Fig. 8-3C) so that the nails from the sides have thicker wood to grip.

11. This box is shown with the framing outside. That gives a clean, smooth surface inside and the top part of the framing also acts as a handle. If it is more important for the outside to be smooth, the end framing would be just as strong inside.

12. There might be a problem of nailing a bottom to a thin side. If so, there can be framing strips on the sides—either outside (Fig. 8-3D) or inside—added after the other parts of the box have been assembled.

13. Sloping sides can improve the appearance of a box or trough containing plants. The front of a window box could slope (Fig. 8-3E). The back of a box could also slope without bringing any structural problems, but it is inadvisable to slope all four sides—at least, not very much. If a box is to be made flaring out, so the top is much larger than the bottom, there are compound angles at the corners. If you merely cut ends square across, the joints will be poor. You can accept this or alter the angles by trial-and-error, but getting the angles correct by geometry is not really worthwhile for garden woodwork.

WINDOW BOX

Flowers growing in a box under a window enhances the appearance of the house, and it adds an extra area for the enthusiastic gardener to use. How the box is arranged in relation to the window depends on the house construction. In some town houses, there is a fairly wide sill under the window. Even if this slopes, it is possible to wedge a box level on it. A width of 6 inches is about the minimum if a box is to have enough room in it for

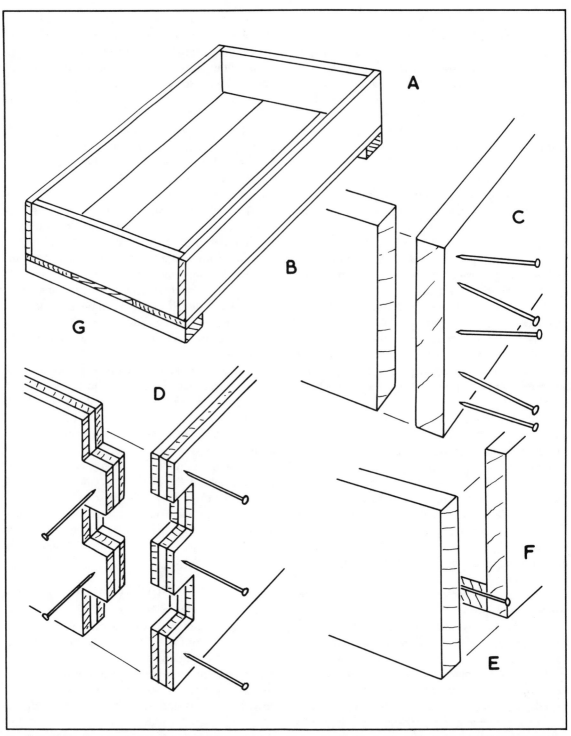

Fig. 8-2. A nailed box (A-C) can be strengthened with interlocking ends (D). The bottom is better held if it is inside (E, F).

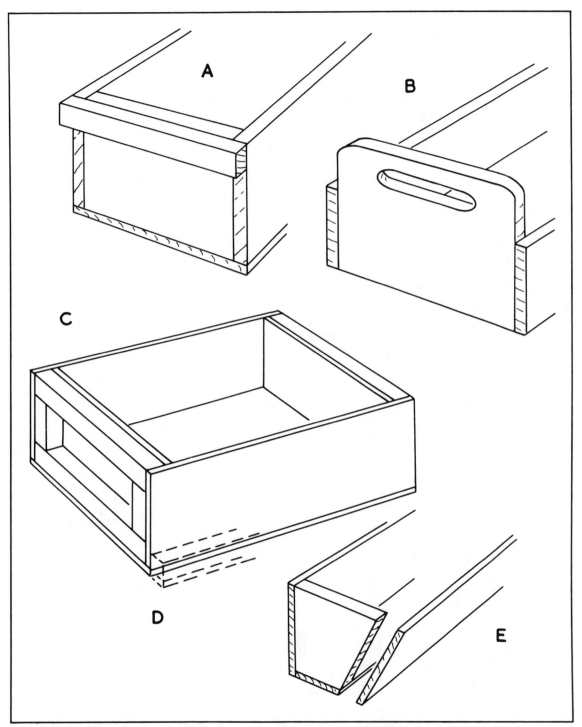

Fig. 8-3. A strip (A) will make a handle or there can be a slot (B). Plywood may be framed outside (C, D). One or more sides can be sloped (E).

spreading roots. If the window is not set back much, the box can be supported on the wall below it. In that case, its length is not so restricted and a longer box full of colorful flowers can make a very effective display.

A long box full of earth is quite heavy. This puts a strain on the box itself and on its supports (which might not be immediately apparent). After some time, boards in the box might warp or sag while brackets or other supports might collapse or buckle. In any case, the box should be deeper than the amount of soil you intend to put in it, in order to provide stiffness and to retain its contents as plants grow. With a width of at least 6 inches, soil could be 3 inches deep for small plants. If you want to make a good, large display, there should be a soil depth of 6 inches.

A box should be mounted securely, but it is advisable not to have it close against the wall. A box attached tightly to a wall would encourage rot and might harm the wall (whatever its construction). An air gap would prevent this. It would be advisable to make the box removable, making it easier to turn out soil, and paint the wood or service the wall behind or below. A typical box and various supports are described as follows, with some suggested sizes as guides to proportions. Sizes will have to be adapted to suit circumstances.

1. The section of a box can be parallel. That will be appropriate for a shallow one standing on a window sill, but in most cases the box looks better if the front slopes. The back can be slightly higher (Fig. 8-4). Do not make a considerable slope (Fig. 8-5A). The available wood will govern sizes. Allow for the bottom coming inside the back and front (Fig. 8-5B). Nailing from below might put more load on the nails than they would stand for over a long period. Cut the two ends.

2. Nail the parts together. It is preferable to use nails with zinc or other coating to resist rust. Drive in a dovetail-nailing pattern at the ends. Screws instead of nails would provide extra strength into the ends near the tops of front and back (Fig. 8-5C).

Fig. 8-4. A window box is decorative and provides additional space to grow plants.

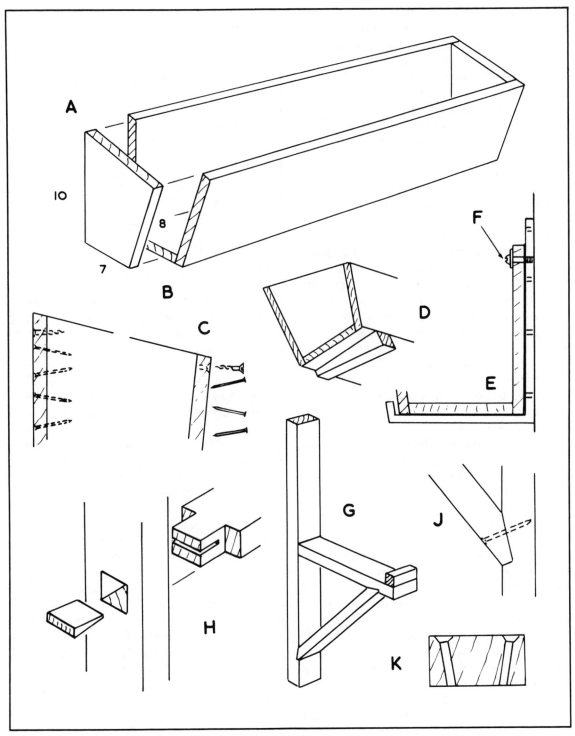

Fig. 8-5. The window box is nailed and supported on brackets.

3. Drill some holes in the bottom for drainage. To prevent soil from falling through, tack fine metal mesh, perforated zinc, or something similar over each hole. An alternative is to merely put suitably shaped pieces of stone or tile in place when you fill the container with soil.

4. Most window sills slope in order to shed rainwater. Bring the box level with wedges (Fig. 8-5D). Secure to the window framing with screwed blocks or metal brackets.

5. Unobtrusive supports for a box below a window can be made of mild steel, almost wholly behind the box (Fig. 8-5E). The supports have to be fairly stout; bending them might require more heat than could be produced by a propane torch. If the supports were too light, they would gradually sag under the load. One way of reducing the tendency to sag would be to screw the backboard to each bracket. So the box can be removed, the bracket must have a threaded hole so the screw can be driven in from the front. Put a large washer under the screw head to spread the load (Fig. 8-5F).

6. A wood bracket should extend below the box (Fig. 8-5G), but if the back of the bracket extending up behind the box keeps the rear board away from the wall it allows one or more high fixing screws (where they are most effective).

7. Use a tenon joint between the horizontal and upright parts, with glue and a wedge (Fig. 8-5H). Strength at this joint is important. If you have doubts about the joint, put a small steel angle bracket inside it.

8. Set out a fullsize side view of the bracket to get the size of the strut. To allow for settling, arrange the piece across under the box to slope upwards a few degrees. The best way to arrange the diagonal piece to take the thrust is to notch it into the other parts (Fig. 8-5J), where it can be held with glue and nails or screws.

9. Screw holes in the top part of the bracket can be straight, but arrange those lower at a slight angle so a screwdriver can be used beside the diagonal strut (Fig. 8-5K).

10. How many brackets to provide, whether wood or metal, depends on the size and weight of the box, but a spacing of 24 inches to 30 inches will take the weight and limit any tendency of the box to sag.

Typical Materials List for Window Box				
2 ends	10	×	8	× 1
1 back	48	×	10	× 1
1 front	48	×	8	× 1
1 bottom	48	×	6	× 1
For each bracket:				
1 bracket back	24	×	2	× 1
1 bracket rail	10	×	2	× 1
1 bracket strut	15	×	2	× 1

PLANT POT CONTAINER

Flowers and plants in pots need something more than the plain pot to complement the foliage. If they have been grown in the pots, however, it might be unwise to disturb them by transplanting into boxes. A wood container for the plant in its pot can stand on a deck or patio, and a number of similar containers will enhance your outlook over the yard. When one plant has passed its prime, it can be exchanged for another in the box without the problem of having to dig up one and replace with another.

The container shown in Fig. 8-6 is intended for the more enthusiastic woodworker who favors traditional construction. A container described later in this chapter provides a similar effect with simpler methods. If the container is to be well made, it is worthwhile starting with a good hardwood that can be finished by varnishing. Softwood could be used and painted to match other work in the garden or yard.

1. The choice of plywood will affect other parts. Groove the legs centrally for the plywood (Fig. 8-7A). A depth of 3/8 of an inch should be sufficient. There is no need for the grooves to extend below the bottom rail position, but with most methods of grooving it is easier to cut right through and the part below is not very obvious in the finished container.

2. Groove the rails in the same way (Fig. 8-7B).

118

Fig. 8-6. A plant pot container can be made with plywood panels in solid wood.

3. Mark out the legs (Fig. 8-7C). Cut tenons on the ends of all rails (Fig. 8-7D). The tenons should be long enough to just meet in the legs (Fig. 8-7E); deepen the slots to make mortises accordingly. Be careful to mark all legs and all rails together, so that sizes are the same. Otherwise the container will not assemble squarely.

4. The bottom is a piece of plywood resting inside the side plywood panels on the bottom rails (Fig. 8-7F). Cut this to size before completing assembly. You will not be able to fit it in after all four sides have been joined.

5. Assemble two opposite sides. Waterproof glue alone should be sufficient, and particularly if the assemblies are clamped until the glue sets. Thin nails can be driven from inside into the tenons if you prefer. Check that they are square, without twisting, and that they match each other.

6. Assemble the parts the other way and include the bottom. That will keep the assembly square (as viewed from the top). Check squareness the other way, and stand the container on a flat surface, with a weight on top if necessary, so that the legs stand without wobbling.

7. The top (Fig. 8-7G) has its inner edges level with the insides of the legs and rails (Fig. 8-7H). Miter the corners and fit the parts with glue and nails or screws.

Materials List for Plant Pot Container

4 legs	16 × 2 × 2
8 rails	12 × 2 × 1
4 tops	14 × 3 × 1
4 panels	12 1/2 × 11 1/2 × 1/2 plywood
1 bottom	11 × 11 × 1/2 plywood

NAILED PLANT POT CONTAINER

If you prefer a simpler construction than mortise and tenon joints with plywood grooved in, it is possible to make satisfactory containers using a mainly nailed construction. This container looks very similar to the one shown in Fig. 8-6, but uses simpler methods. The framing wood is fitted to the surfaces of the plywood and two pairs of assemblies are joined together to make the box.

The suggested construction uses 1/2-inch plywood and strips of 1-inch-by-2-inch wood. You could use softwood finished with paint. The completed container is comparable with the previous example, but sizes easily can be altered. The container does not have to be square, but if it is square the assemblies one way have to be narrower by the thicknesses of the two assemblies the other way. It would help to make the container stronger and more durable if waterproof glue is used, as well as nails, for all joints.

1. Cut the plywood panels for the two larger sides (Fig. 8-8A).

2. Join the legs and rails to them by nailing from inside.

3. Deduct twice the total thickness of one assembly to get the width to cut the plywood for the other panels (Fig. 8-8B). Make up these sides in the same way. Check that all legs are the same length. Put the bottom support strips on the narrow panels only at this stage (Fig. 8-8C). If necessary, plane leg and panel edges true.

4. Join the parts by nailing the wider assemblies to the narrower one (Fig. 8-8D). Below the overlapping panels, fill in the gaps between the legs with pieces of plywood.

5. Put bottom support strips on the wider sides between the strips already on the narrow panels. Fit the bottom plywood to these supports (Fig. 8-8E).

6. The top is made from four mitered strips similar to those in the previous example, but they should come about 1/2 inch inside the top of the box (Fig. 8-8F).

Materials List for Nailed Plant Pot Container

8 legs	16 × 2 × 1
4 rails	9 × 2 × 1
4 rails	6 × 2 × 1
4 tops	14 × 3 × 1
4 bottom supports	9 × 3/4 × 1/2
2 panels	13 × 12 × 1/2 plywood
2 panels	13 × 9 × 1/2 plywood
1 bottom	9 × 9 × 1/2 plywood

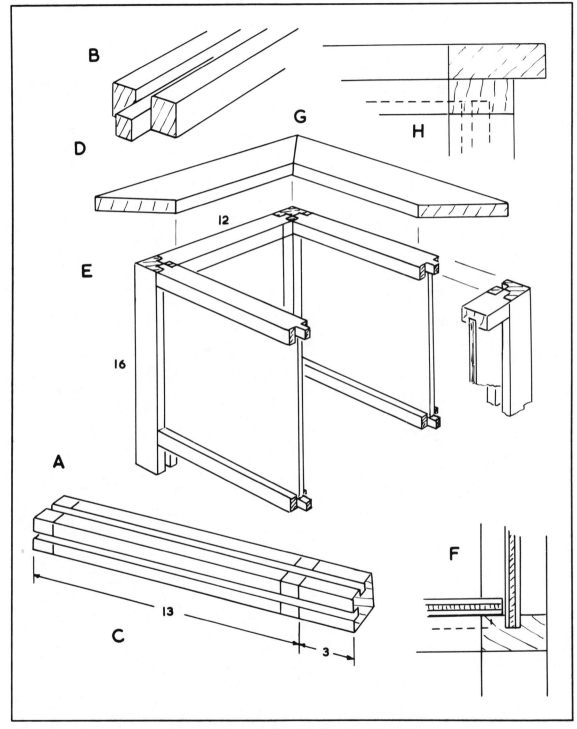

Fig. 8-7. The suggested construction uses grooves for the plywood and mortise and tenon joints.

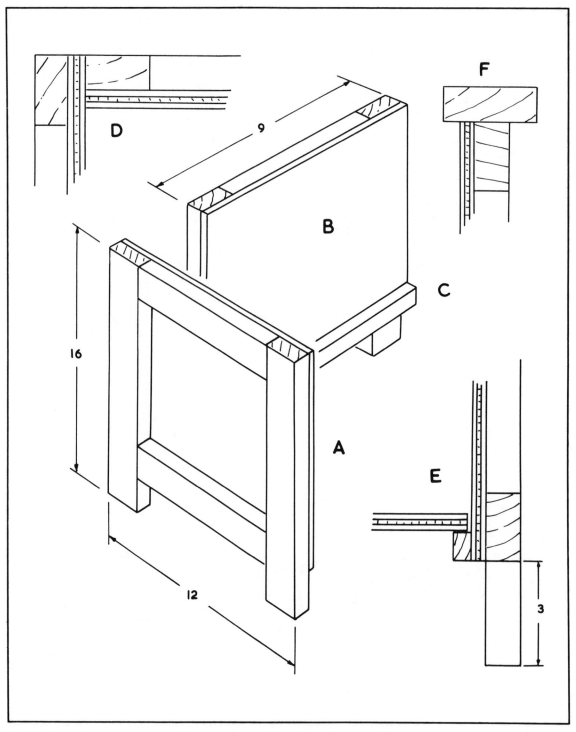

Fig. 8-8. For a simpler plant pot container, the plywood is nailed inside the solid wood.

WALL BOX

A box on top of a wall allows a display of flowers where there would otherwise be a rather blank expanse of brick or stone. The box could be made of planed boards, but this is a place where waney-edged boards would look attractive. Perhaps you could have the front board showing waney edges at the top and where it overhangs the wall (Fig. 8-9).

A box could be any length, but practical difficulties limit it to not more than about 60 inches because of weight and the availability of suitable boards. Unless it is quite a small box, the wood should be at least 1 inch thick. If only the front of the box will normally be visible, the bottom of the back can be straight above the wall (Fig. 8-10A). If both sides will be seen, it will be better to have the back extending below (Fig. 8-10B) in the same way as the front. In any case, there will be suffi-

cient weight to keep the box in place without any special attachments.

1. Make the bottom first. It is a parallel board and governs the sizes of other parts (Fig. 8-10C).

2. Drill some drainage holes in the bottom and add two or more cleats (Fig. 8-10D) to raise the bottom off the top of the wall and allow water to run away.

3. The ends could be straight across the top or have waney edges there (Fig. 8-10E).

4. Front and back could have straight ends that are either level with the box ends or projecting slightly. If two or more boxes are to fit against each other, their ends must be finished level.

5. Alternative ends carry on the waney edge theme by cutting to irregular curves (Fig. 8-10F).

6. Nails should be protected with zinc or other coatings. The box will be stronger if you drive the nails in a dovetail manner, possibly with screws at the tops, as suggested for the window boxes.

Fig. 8-9. A box to mount on a wall can have the natural waney edges of the boards.

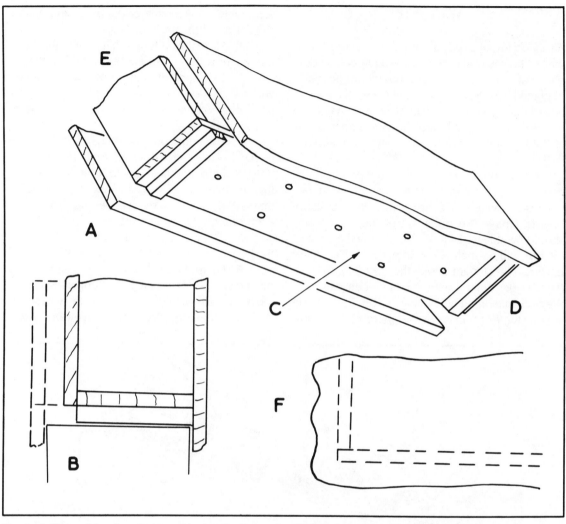

Fig. 8-10. The wall box is nailed together, but the bottom is raised and provided with drainage holes.

ROD HANGING POT HOLDER

Hanging plant or flower holders are broadly divided into those that actually have soil contained in them and those that are containers for potted plants. Both can be in various sizes, but this example is intended to hold a pot of moderate size (Fig. 8-11), such as might hang in a porch, either alone or as a series of similar ones, to give a colorful display of potted flowers. An advantage is that the same holders are used for other flowers, with minimum trouble, when the first ones are finished. Such a hanging holder can also be taken indoors

for further use when the outside weather becomes unsuitable.

The base of the holder is a piece of plywood. The sides are made of wood rod, which is conveniently cut from dowel rod, although old broom handles or similar things could be used. The parts are then threaded on rope.

1. The guiding shape is the truncated cone that passes through the base and the rods (Fig. 8-12A). Measure the diameters of the rods and set out the shape to allow for the chosen number of these thicknesses. This gives you the location of

Fig. 8-11. A hanging pot holder can be made of dowels or roughly rounded rods.

the centers of the holes in each layer of rods. Allow for the rods extending about 1 inch outside the holes.

2. The ends can be cut squarely across and any raggedness can be sanded away. If you have a lathe, they can be bevelled or rounded.

3 Although close-fitting holes would have to be drilled at an angle, there is no need for this if you drill the holes large enough to be a very easy fit on the rope. Drill the holes in the rods and the base, and then lightly countersink above and below to reduce the risk of chafe on the rope.

4. Almost any rope can be used, but synthetic fibers will stand up to the weather better than natural fibers. Quite light cord would be strong enough, but for appearance it is better to use rope 3/16 inch or 1/4 inch diameter. It does not matter if it is plaited or three-strand construction.

5. Cut double lengths to cross underneath the base (Fig. 8-12B), and then thread on the parts (Fig. 8-12C). Tie a knot in each rope close above the top rods to prevent movement of the parts, and then continue up to tie all four parts together. How far you go depends on the situation where the pot holder is to hang. Long ropes look better and are easier to arrange among foliage (if there is space to have them).

Materials List for Rod Hanging Pot Holder

1 base	8 × 8 × 1/2 plywood
Rods from	240 inches of 1 inch dowel rod

NATURAL WOOD HANGING POT HOLDER

A hanging holder for a plant pot that looks very similar to the one made from dowel rods could be made with natural wood. That is more suitable for larger construction, and possibly for a situation where the holder is to hang among trees or from a rustic arch rather than in a porch or similar position. Because pieces of natural wood vary, the holder will have to be designed to suit the available pieces of pole or branch. The pot that is to be held will govern the approximate internal measurements.

Although an interesting pattern can be obtained by using pieces of wood that are not straight, too many varying shapes will make it difficult to get a holder that is reasonably symmetrical and looks right. Fir poles will yield a good supply of fairly straight and almost parallel pieces. There will be tapers, but if alternate layers are reversed the overall effect should be fairly true.

Whether to leave the bark on or not depends on the wood. If it can be removed fairly easily, that is advisable, as if left it would probably come away in sections later and it tends to harbor insects.

The holder shown in Fig. 8-13 is intended to be made with 1 1/2-inch-to-2-inch-diameter wood to hold a pot about 12 inches in diameter and 14 inches high. Because it would be difficult to set out the shape in the way described in the preceding project, because of the varying wood sizes, it is better to work upside down—using the pot as a guide to the progressing shape that is built up.

1. Select the piece of wood and cut the first pieces for the top to length. So far as possible, have opposite pieces in each layer of matching thickness. Start with the top four pieces and arrange them to easily fit around the top of the pot.

2. Drill for nails (Fig. 8-14A). The hole should be clearance size in one piece and slightly undersize in the other piece. How much undersize depends on the wood, but the nail must grip without splitting the wood. Use zinc-coated nails.

3. Check squareness by measuring diagonals, although do not expect perfection. Drive the nails (Fig. 8-14B) so the heads are buried.

4. As you build up the pile, use the inverted pot as a guide to the amount of taper (Fig. 8-14C). The number of pieces of wood will depend on their diameters.

5. The bottom is a piece of exterior plywood (Fig. 8-14D). Give it a good bearing surface on the bottom two strips by planing flats on them. It may be better along these joints to use screws instead of nails.

6. Put large screw eyes in the corners at the top and attach hanging ropes to them, taken up to be knotted together or to a metal ring.

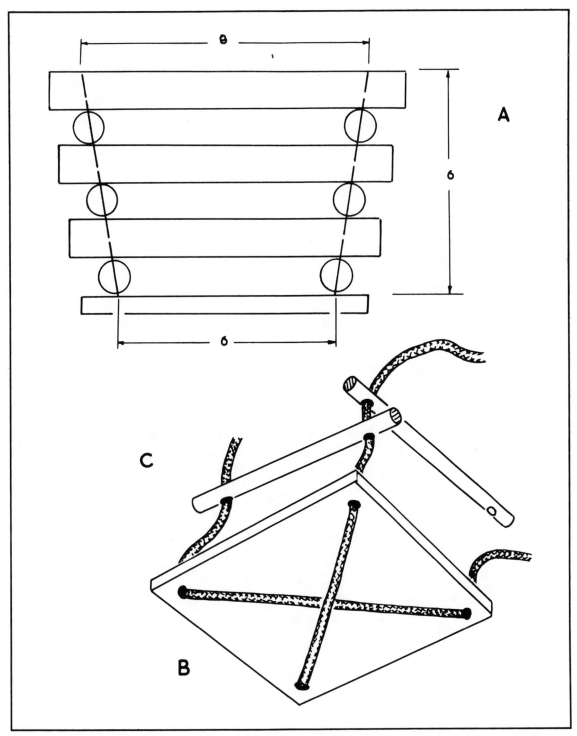

Fig. 8-12. The rods of the hanging pot holder are drilled so that the assembly tapers to suit the pot.

Fig. 8-13. For a large pot holder made from natural wood, the strips are nailed together.

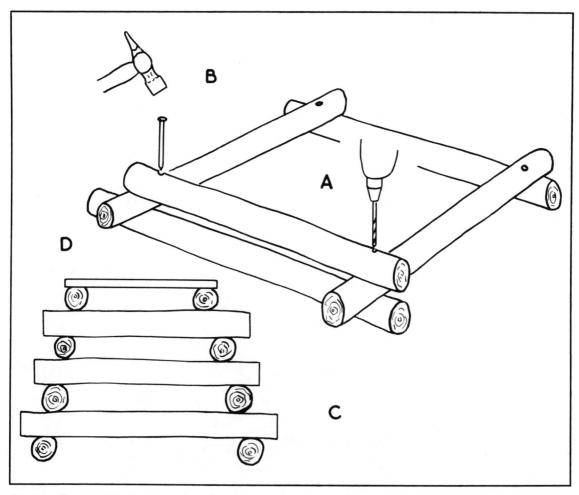

Fig. 8-14. The pot holder is built up by nailing in layers from the top downward.

PLYWOOD HANGING POT HOLDER

Anyone interested in the use of a scroll or jigsaw may welcome an opportunity to decorate a hanging plant holder. Plywood is the most convenient material for this type of decoration. This project is a box with plywood sides to hold the usual plant in a pot (Fig. 8-15). Exterior plywood can be used, and then painted so that the cutouts show a contrast. Fir plywood will not allow for much detail in the shaping so a bold treatment is advised. Mahogany or similar plywood will take all the fine detail you want, but a pot holder is something normally viewed at a distance so fine work would not be appreciated.

Suggested sizes are given in Fig. 8-16. If the parts are joined with waterproof glue, only fine nails or panel pins need be used in assembly.

1. Two plywood panels overlap the edges of the other two (Fig. 8-16A), so the two inner ones (Fig. 8-16B) should be narrower if the box is to finish square.

2. For the outlines of the top edges (Fig. 8-16C), make a card template of half the shape and use it each side of centerlines on the plywood.

3. The cutouts can be leaf shapes or anything else you prefer (Fig. 8-16D). Clean off any raggedness of the edges.

4. Frame the insides of the wider pieces

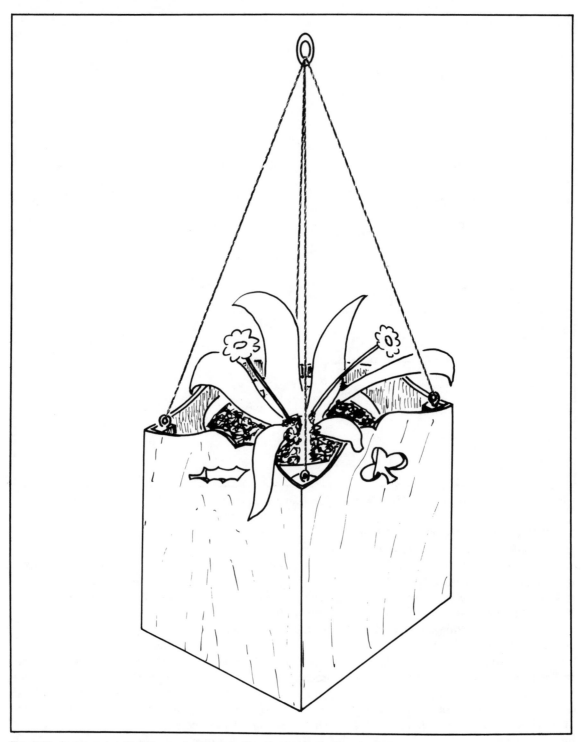

Fig. 8-15. A plywood pot holder can be decorated by piercing and edge shaping.

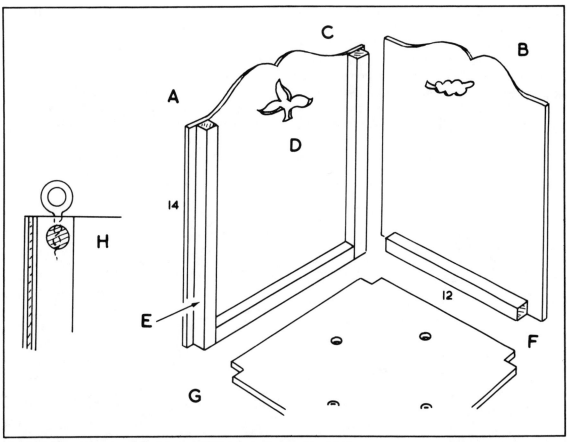

Fig. 8-16. The plywood panels of the pot holder are nailed to strips inside.

(Fig.8-16E); allow for the thickness of the other pieces at the edges.

5. Assemble to the narrower pieces and add the strips at the bottom (Fig. 8-16F) to support the bottom.

6. Make the bottom (Fig. 8-16G) with notches at the corners and a few holes to provide drainage. Fitting it will keep the box in shape and provide rigidity.

7. The screw eyes at the corners will have to be driven into end grain. Unless they are very long, the end grain areas will not provide enough grip on the threads to take the considerable load. This can be improved by putting dowels across so the screws go through their cross grain (Fig. 8-16H).

8. Use ropes from the screw eyes to a ring for hanging.

Materials List for Plywood Hanging Pot Holder	
4 panels	16 × 12 × 1/2 plywood
1 bottom	12 × 12 × 1/2 plywood
4 corners	14 × 1 × 1
4 bottoms	12 × 1 × 1

BOARD TOOL BOX

In many situations, garden tools and equipment can be kept in a garage or in a shed large enough to walk into and use for potting, putting seeds in trays, and similar things. If you only want to store hand tools and some of the other equipment you tend to accumulate for gardening, it might be better to make a box or locker. If the garden or yard is extensive, you will be glad to have such a box at some point distant from the main storage area.

The box can be made with solid wood or plywood. Plywood construction is described in the next project. The boards used could have square edges, but if you are able to get tongued-and-grooved boards they will make a weatherproof box. Check what stock sizes of boards are available and scheme the overall sizes to make the best use of them without having to cut much to waste. If you have tongued-and-grooved boards you must allow for cutting tongue or groove off some boards that come at edges. Measure the longest tools you will want to store. Some long handles might fit in diagonally if you want to keep the length to the minimum.

As shown in Fig. 8-17, the lid slopes slightly to shed rain, but it also comes at a height that makes it suitable for a seat. When open it is held just past upright by ropes.

1. The pair of ends are the key pieces that

Fig. 8-17. A large tool box will store tools near where you use them and can be used as a seat.

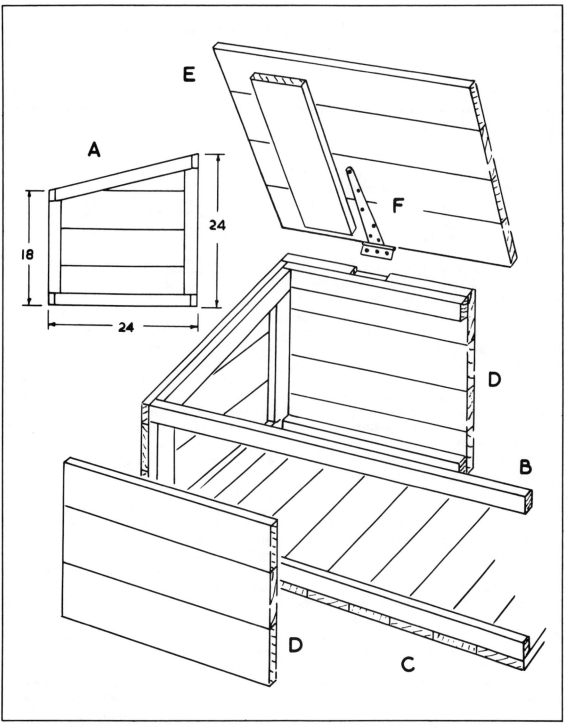

Fig. 8-18. The large tool box is made with boards on framing.

settle several other sizes. Frame the ends with strips, but leave gaps at the corners for the lengthwise pieces (Fig. 8-18A). If you are using square-edged boards, bring the edges tightly together as you assemble. If they are made of normally seasoned wood, they will expand a little outdoors and become even tighter. With tongued-and-grooved wood, it is better to not force the edges very tight.

2. Join the ends with the four lengthwise strips (Fig. 8-18B). Make sure outer surfaces come level. Nails into end grain at the corners will be sufficient at this stage because the boards fitted next will secure the corner joints.

3. Check squareness by measuring diagonals.

4. Nail on the bottom. This is shown with boards across the narrow way. You could use long boards, but by using short pieces there is less risk of the bottom warping and the assembly will be slightly stronger (Fig. 8-18C). With the bottom boards on, the assembly should keep its shape. Further check squareness as you fit the other boards.

5. Nail on the front and back boards (Fig. 8-18D). If the box is very long and there might be a risk of the boards warping later, fit one or more uprights intermediately. These boards should overlap the bottom.

6. The lid comes level at the back, but it should overlap the ends and the front by about 1 inch. Cut the boards to suit and join them with pieces across (Fig. 8-18E). It might be sufficient to put a piece near each end, but for extra strength, particularly with square-edged boards, you could have another piece at the middle.

7. Large T hinges are recommended (Fig. 8-18F.) Preferably, the hinges should reach halfway across the lid. They can go on the surface of the lid, but let the other part in enough for the lid to shut with only a small gap along the back.

8. Put screw eyes in the lid and ends for supporting ropes (Fig. 8-17).

9. There could be strips of leather or plastic screwed with loops under the lid to take small tools.

10. If the box will stand on concrete or be supported on stones, the bottom can be left unaltered. To keep it away from earth, and the risk of rot, fit cleats across at the ends and perhaps intermediately.

11. Finish the wood with paint or preservative. There could be a handle and a hasp and staple for a lock, as described for the next project, if you like.

Materials List for Board Tool Box	
8 end frames	24 × 2 × 1
8 end boards	24 × 6 × 1
4 lengthwise strips	60 × 2 × 1
7 lengthwise boards	60 × 6 × 1
10 bottom boards	24 × 6 × 1
4 or 5 lid boards	63 × 6 × 1
2 lid cleats	24 × 6 × 1
2 bottom cleats	26 × 2 × 2
2 T hinges to suit	

PLYWOOD TOOL BOX

Plywood is convenient to use. Exterior or marine grades will withstand exposure to the weather. The box shown in Fig. 8-19 is generally similar in form to that described in the previous project, but the main parts are 1/2 inch plywood. Framing is shown on the outside of the plywood. This gives a smooth interior and offers protection to many plywood edges, where moisture might otherwise seep into the veneers if inadequately protected by paint or other finish.

Suggested sizes are intended to allow you to cut many parts economically from the usual 48-inch-by-96-inch plywood sheet. If your long tools will not go into a box this size, you will have to cut the plywood to suit and find other uses for some of the offcuts.

1. Start by making the pair of ends (Fig. 8-20A and B). You could use waterproof glue as well as nails, for this and other framing. Plane the framing pieces level on the edges where other parts have to fit.

2. Cut the front and back plywood to size and stiffen top and bottom edges (Fig. 8-20C).

3. Join these parts to the ends and check squareness.

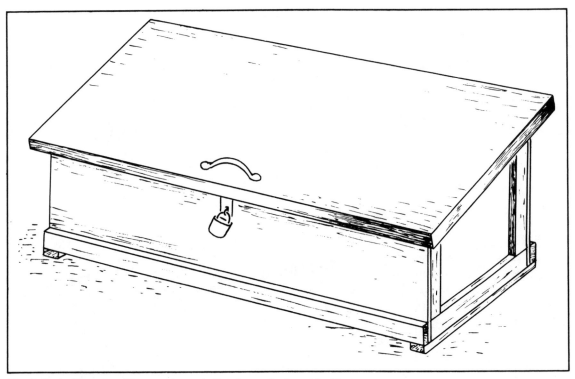

Fig. 8-19. A plywood tool box can be a similar size to the board tool box.

4. The bottom could be a piece of plywood (Fig. 8-20D) overlapping the other parts. This could be vulnerable in a very damp situation, and it might be preferable to fit a solid wood bottom, as suggested for the previous project. In any case, put cleats across underneath (Fig. 8-20E) to raise the bottom slightly.

5. The plywood lid should be framed around to fit loosely over the top of the box (Fig. 8-20F). For neatness, the strips can be mitered at the corners (Fig. 8-20G), and the edges of strips and plywood well rounded.

6. You cannot hinge the lid directly to the edge of the box as the framing strip on the lid would prevent the parts swinging clear of each other. Put blocks where the hinges will come (Fig. 8-20H). They can be longer than the hinges and their tops should match the slope of the box top. Three 4-inch hinges would be suitable.

7. Fit tool loops, if you prefer, similar to those shown for the previous box (Fig. 8-17).

8. There could be a lifting handle and a hasp and staple for a lock (Fig. 8-19).

9. Finish the box inside and out with paint or preservative. Any exposed edges of plywood would be well covered to prevent the entry of water. A good way of sealing them is to coat them with waterproof glue before painting all over.

Materials List for Plywood Tool Box	
2 ends	24 × 24 × 1/2 plywood
8 end frames	24 × 2 × 1
1 back	48 × 24 × 1/2 plywood
1 front	48 × 24 × 1/2 plywood
4 lengthwise strips	48 × 2 × 1
1 bottom	48 × 28× 1/2 plywood
2 cleats	28 × 2× 1
1 top	51 × 1 × 1
2 top frames	29 × 1 × 1
2 top frames	8 × 1 1/4 × 1 1/4
3 hinge blocks	
3 four-inch hinges	
1 handle to suit	
1 hasp and staple	

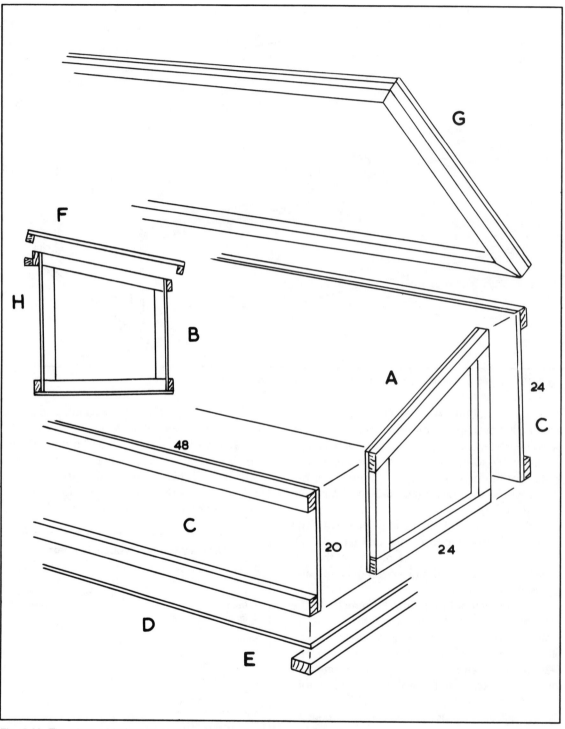

Fig. 8-20. The plywood is framed on the outside and raised on battens from the ground.

VERTICAL TOOL LOCKER

An alternative to a horizontal box for tool storage is an upright locker that looks like a small shed, but is not large enough for a person to enter. It could be freestanding, but it is probably better against a wall or fence. If made freestanding, the corner uprights might have to be lengthened to enter the ground to provide stability, or there could be posts bolted to the outside.

The locker shown in Fig. 8-21 is intended to

Fig. 8-21. A vertical tool locker provides storage, but is not large enough to enter.

be just high enough for the longest handles and roomy enough for a good selection of hand tools and equipment. It could be made larger for power tools. If it is to fit against a fence, that may decide the height. The locker is shown made from solid wood, but it could be covered with plywood. A comparison of the two previous boxes will show the differences in construction. If tongued-and-grooved boards are used, the covering should be more weatherproof than if square-edge boards are used. The roof is shown made up of boards, but that could be plywood and can be covered with a waterproof roofing material. The widths of available boards might settle the final sizes of the sides of the locker.

1. Make a pair of sides. Boards are brought close together and framed with strips on all edges. At the front, cut back for the top (Fig. 8-22A) and bottom (Fig. 8-22B) strips. Allow for the strips at top and bottom of the back (Fig. 8-22C).

2. Make the back assembly (Fig. 8-22D). The central cross member can be cut to fit between the side framing. There is no need to notch it into the uprights.

3. Cut the top and bottom front pieces to fit into the notches and hold the assembly to the same width at the front as at the back.

4. Join all these parts. The locker can stand directly on the ground without a bottom of its own, but if you want a closed bottom nail boards across. Check squareness (particularly in the door opening).

5. Make the roof with boards level at the back and overhanging at the sides and front (Fig. 8-22E).

6. Assemble a door (Fig. 8-22F) to fit easily into the opening. Except for not making it so loose as to admit vermin, there is nothing to be gained by making it a precision fit. The weather will cause expansion and contraction and affect its fit.

7. The door can be hinged either side. Two 4-inch hinges should be satisfactory. At the opposite side arrange a latch or other fastener (with a lock if necessary). The door can be prevented from swinging too far in with strips inside overlapping the framing at top and bottom.

8. Racks and hooks for tools can be fitted inside and to the back of the door. If there are many tools to stow, more can be put in if they are kept loose.

9. Finish the wood with paint or preservative.

Materials List for Vertical Tool Locker	
6 side boards	60 × 6 × 1
4 side frames	60 × 2 × 1
6 side frames	18 × 2 × 1
3 back boards	60 × 6 × 1
3 back frames	18 × 2 × 1
4 roof boards	22 × 6 × 1
3 door boards	50 × 6 × 1
2 door boards	15 × 6 × 1
2 four-inch hinges	
1 latch or lock to suit	

SECTIONAL COMPOST CAGE

Making compost is not always a year-round activity, and it is convenient to have a compost container that can be taken down and packed flat when not required. The compost cage shown in Fig. 8-23 consists of four identical frames that can be hooked together for use or reduced to a pile about 10 inches thick for storage. The suggested sizes are for a cube about 36 inches each way, but sizes can be varied to suit your needs and the amount of composting you expect to do.

In each section, the wood frame has its corner joints made with plywood gussets. If you want to show your carpentry skills, the corner joints can be mortises and tenons. Good access for air is needed, and this is provided by making the main area of a side of a mesh about 1/2 inch size. You could use chicken wire or any of the other metal mesh obtainable from a hardware store. The sections are shown with one leg pointed for driving into the ground and the tops of the legs extended slightly so they can be hit. If your compost cage will be on a hard surface, cut off the points.

1. Cut the wood for the posts and rails (Fig. 8-24A and B). Allow for the posts standing about 1 inch above the top rails. The amount you allow for the pointed end into the ground depends on

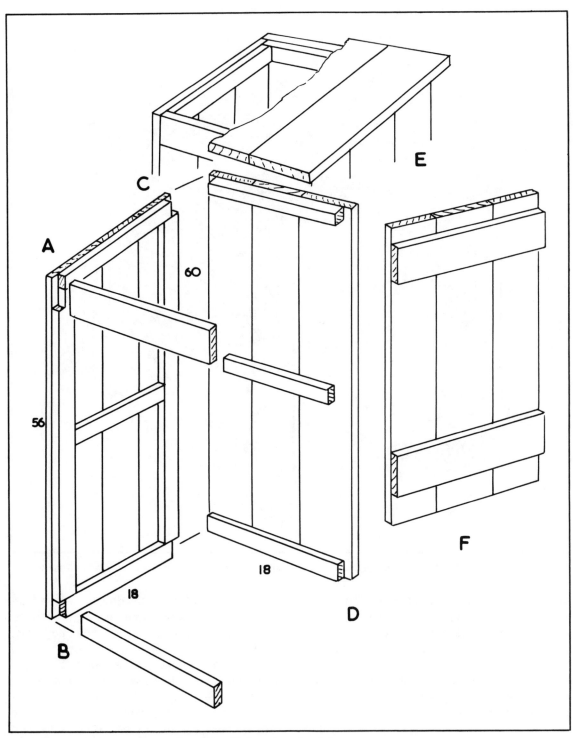

Fig. 8-22. A vertical tool locker can be made with boards on framing.

Fig. 8-23. This cage for making compost has four sides hooked together so that they can be taken apart and stored flat.

the softness of your soil, but a projection of 6 inches should be enough (Fig. 8-24C).

2. Make the gussets by cutting squares of plywood and dividing them diagonally (Fig. 8-24D).

3. Join the posts and rails with the gussets on the outside only, checking squareness and that the four sections match (Fig. 8-24E).

4. Trim the wire mesh so it comes within about 1/2 inch of the outsides of a section. Attach it with staples or by partially driving nails and turning over their heads. Further security is obtained by nailing the inside gussets over the mesh (Fig. 8-24F).

5. The temporary corner joints are made with hooks and eyes screwed to the posts. Bring a corner together and get the positions for the screwed eyes by experiment (Fig. 8-24G), so the parts are held reasonably close. There is no need to have to force the hooks and eyes tight, par-

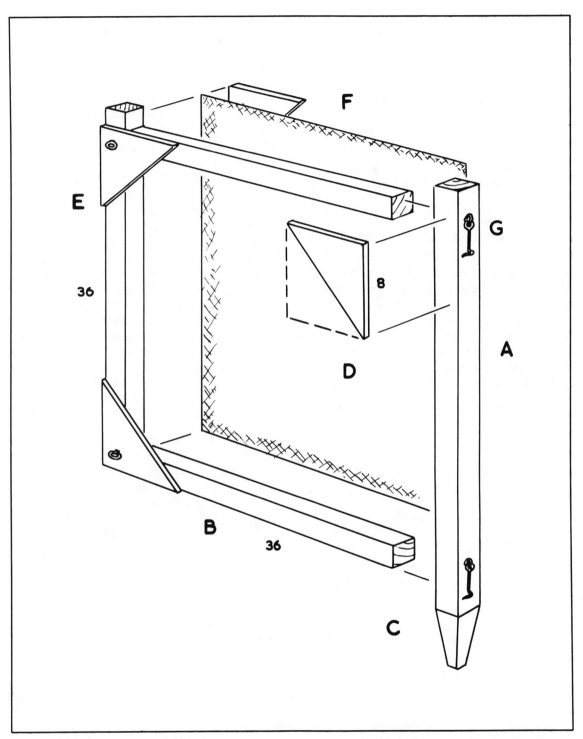

Fig. 8-24. The side of a compost cage has plywood gussets at the corners and one leg extends into the ground.

ticularly if the posts go into the ground to provide rigidity.

6. Finish all parts with several coats of paint.

Materials List for Sectional Compost Cage

4 posts	36 × 2 × 2
4 posts	42 × 2 × 2
8 rails	32 × 2 × 2

gussets from 8 pieces 8 × 8 × 1/2 plywood
8 hooks and eyes, about 2 inch.

STACKING COMPOST BIN

Compost is something that is often plentiful at one time and sparse at another time. A large bin to hold the maximum quantity is a nuisance when you have very little compost with which to deal. Therefore, it is helpful to have some means of enlarging or reducing a bin to suit your needs. The bin shown in Fig. 8-25 is made in sections that can be assembled to make a structure of any height, depending on how many sections you make.

If the sections are to stack in any position, there has to be some uniformity of size. Assembly can be fairly loose, but even then there is not much tolerance to allow for discrepancies of size. One way of reducing the problem is to avoid a square shape. With four sides supposed to be equal, there are four ways each section needs to match any four ways of the one below. If the sides are longer one way than the other, there are only two ways each section can be expected to match. The sections have short posts in the corners, and these fit on to each other so there is a gap of 1 inch between the boards. This should be enough to allow air to the contents. If more air is needed, holes can be drilled in the boards. That would be better than widening the gaps (which might then let too much of the contents slip through).

The bin is intended to rest on the ground, with the post extensions of the bottom section pressed into the ground. If the bin is to rest on a hard surface, the bottom section should have the posts cut off flush. If you want the bin to be self-contained, the lowest section can have a bottom nailed on.

1. Decide on the number of sections you

Fig. 8-25. A compost bin made like open boxes can be assembled to any height required.

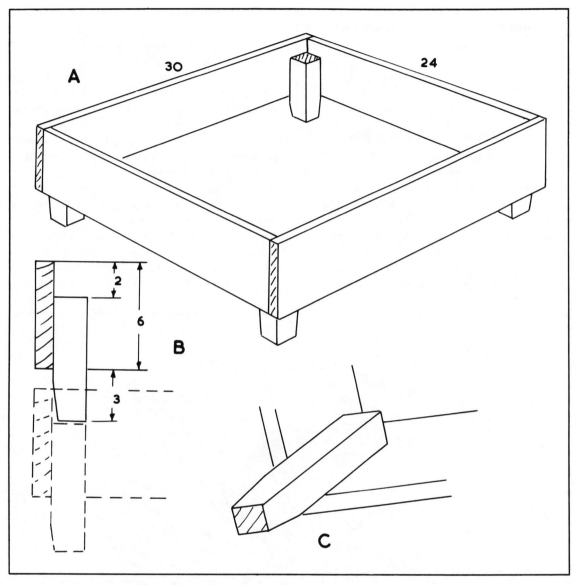

Fig. 8-26. A unit of the stacking compost bin has legs to fit the parts together and control separation.

want and make all parts at the same time so that sizes match. Suitable sizes are suggested (Fig. 8-26A). The wide boards need not be planed, but the posts will make a better fit if they are planed.

2. Make the posts so they will come 2 inches below the top edges and extend 3 inches below the bottom edges (Fig. 8-26B).

3. Taper the outer surfaces of the bottom ex-

tensions of the posts so they will fit easily inside the section below (Fig. 8-26C).

4. Screw or nail the parts securely together and use the first assembly to check subsequent ones. Check that they will fit together either way. If you do not succeed in making all parts interchangeable, mark those which fit together best.

5. Finish the wood with preservative.

143

PERMANENT COMPOST BIN

If there is a corner of the garden where you will always make compost, it might be better to assemble a permanent means of keeping it all together than to rely on take-down or other semi-temporary structures. The obvious way to do this is to drive posts into the ground and fit covering around them, but there has to be some means of access. This is particularly true when the contents are low. The permanent bin shown in Fig. 8-27 is all wood, and it has a front that will swing down or lift away completely.

Sizes will have to suit your available space and probable required capacity, but sizes shown suit a bin 36 inches square. The sections of wood could be the same up to nearly twice that overall size, but this is the sort of project that can be adapted to suit available materials.

1. Prepare the posts (Fig. 8-28A) with points to drive into the ground, and probably too long, so the tops can be trimmed level later if all posts do not penetrate to the same depth.

2. If the ground is not level already, it should be brought to a reasonably level surface for the area the bin is to cover. Otherwise it will be difficult to assemble the parts. Boarding around the sides that are not near horizontal will look unsatisfactory, even if it does the job just as well.

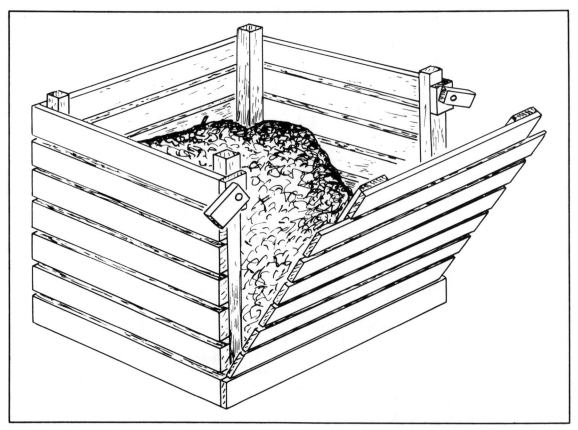

Fig. 8-27. A permanent compost bin can be made with boards nailed to posts. A removable side allows access.

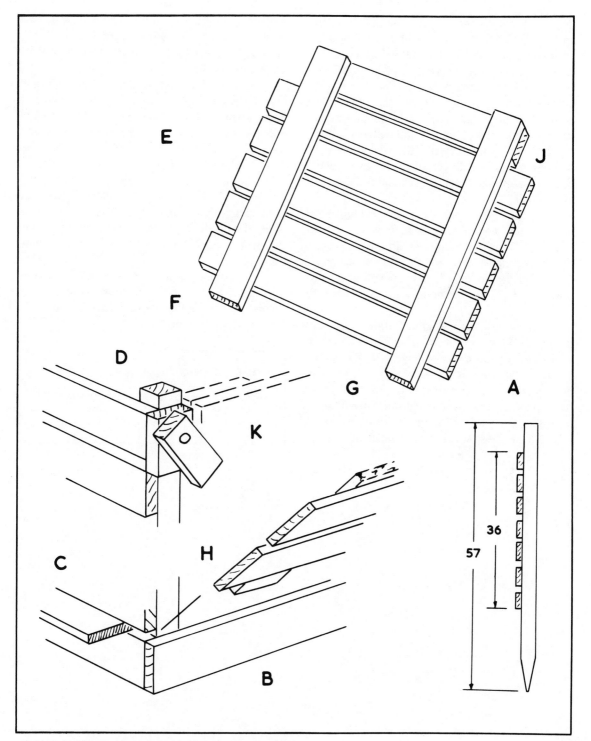

Fig. 8-28. One side of the compost bin is arranged to lift out.

3. Measure the size you want on the ground and start holes for the posts with a spike or other tool so that the posts enter in the correct places. Check that the posts are upright as you drive them.

4. Fit the lowest boards all round (Fig. 8-28B). It does not matter if they do not make a close fit on the soil all round. It is more important to get them level individually and with each other. It will probably be advisable to drive a few nails part of the way in until you have checked that the boards are level and in the best positions; then nail them flush.

5. Continue up the three sides, adding more boards, using a board on edge to measure the gaps (Fig. 8-28C). As hammering could push the posts out of true, nail temporary pieces of scrap wood across their tops to keep them in the correct relative positions until there are enough outside boards to steady them.

6. Nail sufficient boards to three sides, and then cut off the tops of the posts, either level or projecting a short distance (Fig. 8-28D).

7. The front is a separate assembly (Fig. 8-28E). Have sufficient boards long enough to overlap the sides. Join them with strips at a distance from the ends that will fit easily inside the posts (Fig. 8-28F). These strips come level at the top, but project about 2 inches at the bottom (Fig. 8-28G) to hook over the piece across the bottom of the front (Fig. 8-28H). Have the ends of the top boards level with the upright strips (Fig. 8-28J).

8. When the front is put in, its bottom is held in place by the hooked extensions. At the top there have to be large turnbuttons on the posts. Pack out with pieces the same thickness as the boards, and then use strips turning on bolts or screws (Fig. 8-28K). The outward pressure on the front of a large, full bin could be considerable. Therefore, the pivots should be long, stout wood screws or bolts taken right through the posts. Use washers under the heads to spread the load and others between the turnbuttons and the posts to ease turning.

9. It would be advisable for most woods to treat the bottoms of the posts with preservative before driving into the ground. Treat all woodwork before using the bin.

Materials List for Permanent Compost Bin

(sizes are for approximate 36 inch cube capacity)
32 boards	42 × 4 × 2
4 posts	60 × 3 × 3

Chapter 9

Display Equipment

While much of the beauty of a garden or yard comes from what is actually growing in the ground, additional attraction can come from flowers, plants, and ferns growing in boxes, troughs and pots such as those described in Chapter 8. If the amount of ground is limited or nonexistent, the entire display will have to be arranged. Some of the boxes might not need special support or have legs built-in. If they are intended to hang, suitable supporting places might exist or you may have to provide brackets. Other containers will have to be provided with supports if they are to be raised above ground level.

Thought given to arranging displays can increase the growing potential of your existing available area considerably, and the total effect of what you provide in additional display facilities can give you a more effective and satisfying garden.

There can be a certain amount of improvisation. Supporting a box or pot on bricks might be just as satisfactory as building a special support. You might be uncertain about what display arrangements will be best and have to assemble temporary shelves or other supports. In any case, whatever you build as display equipment only has a secondary role to play to the display of flowers or foliage. Permanent display equipment should be built strongly, but in many cases it should not be treated as a decorative feature in its own right. There are exceptions—such as designs like miniature paling fences around pots—but in general what you are making is just functional.

You can expect that what you make will probably be ignored and neglected once it is in position. This means that it should be made strong and able to fulfill its purpose without much maintenance.

Untreated softwood is unlikely to last long if left outside throughout the year. Treating it with preservative will lengthen its life, but it is better to start with a more durable hardwood or a softwood containing resin.

Consider loads. A long trough that extends over supports might not have much effect on a shelf, but if you stand individual pots along a shelf each applies a more localized load. Large pots full of soil are heavy. A new shelf might appear to be supporting them adequately, but in six months time you could see a definite sag and pronounced downward curve. Make sure your shelves are thick enough to be stiff and arrange supports fairly close together. The two requirements are related. If the only support locations have to be wide apart, you

need a stiffer board for the shelf than if supports are more frequent.

WALL SHELVES

The simplest shelf is a board supported on two brackets screwed to the wall (Fig. 9-1A). If screws through the bracket can get a good grip into

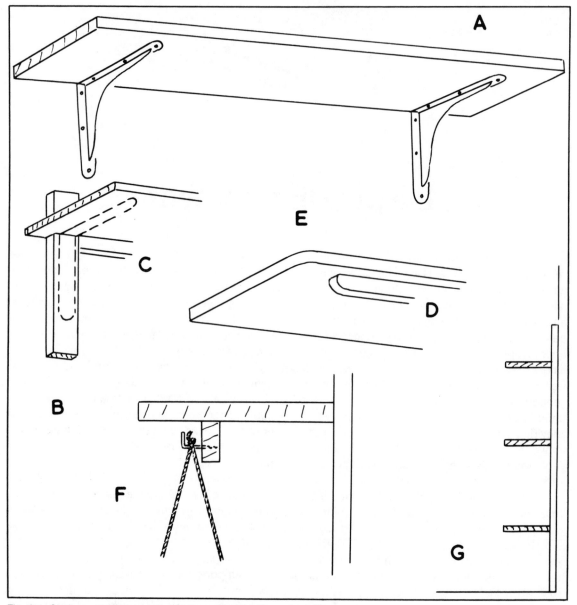

Fig. 9-1. Shelves can be bracketed to the wall and will require stiffening.

something capable of supporting the weight, this is satisfactory but make sure you are not just screwing to cladding (that will pull away) or plugging a brick or stone wall that is so soft that it will crumble around the screws.

Check that the shelf is level. You can measure up from the floor, but it is not always as level as you think. It is better to use a level on the shelf, as you fit it, or on a line drawn on the wall as a guide. Put one screw through a bracket and move the shelf up and down, pivoting on it to a level position before marking the first screw hole at the other end.

1. In many situations, strong points in the wall or fence and the positions you want to drive screws will not coincide. It is better then to attach battens to the wall and screw the brackets to them (Fig. 9-1B). You can arrange the battens long enough to allow for driving screws in the best positions. Leveling the shelf on its bracket becomes easier. Make the battens thick enough to take screws long enough through the brackets to support the intended weight.

2. You could notch the shelf around the battens, and then a strip can be fitted under it between the battens (Fig. 9-1C). This does two things: it helps the shelf resist sagging, and it is a place to put more screws into the wall. Alternatively, the shelf could merely come against the battens so that its rear edge is away from the wall. This would be better for cleaning. You can stiffen the front of a shelf with a strip underneath (Fig. 9-1D) that is either level with the front or set back a short distance. Round or bevel the ends of the shelf and this stiffener (Fig. 9-1E).

There could be a single stiffener near the center of the shelf width. This makes a good place to put hooks for hanging plant holders (Fig. 9-1F).

3. Several shelves can be arranged on the same battens. It is a good idea to let the battens reach the floor (Fig. 9-1G) because this gives additional vertical support.

4. Although steel brackets are convenient shelf supports in many situations, it is possible to make satisfactory wood brackets. If solid wood is used, the grain should run diagonally for maximum strength. The front can be decorated by shaping (Fig. 9-2A). This type of bracket has to be fixed by screwing through the shelf and batten (Fig. 9-2B). That means the bracket must be attached to the battens before they are screwed to the wall. Screwing down through the shelf can be done in position. If you are certain you will not want to take the assembly apart later, it is worthwhile using waterproof glue as well as screws.

5. A rather cruder bracket can be made with plywood. Arrange a batten under the shelf, the same width as the upright batten, and nail plywood to one or both sides (Fig. 9-2C). If you like, the space between could be filled with solid wood. When making this or any other bracket, it is advisable to assume that the front edge of the shelf will sag slightly under load. If the bracket is made to lift the front edge a little in the first assembly, it should settle level eventually. If the wall batten is truly upright, that means making a bracket that is about 92 degrees instead of square. If the wall is not plumb, use a level to check the actual angle needed.

6. A wide, heavily loaded shelf is better supported with brackets having diagonal struts. Attach the shelf to the upright batten with a lengthwise strip (Fig. 9-2D) and arrange another batten under the shelf (Fig. 9-2E). Set out the full size of the shape of the bracket. Allow for the slight rise of the front of the shelf. The angle of the strut can be about 45 degrees, but is better slightly more upright.

7. The ends of the strut should be notched in (Fig. 9-2F). Keep the notches shallow and cut their outer ends square. Secure these joints with nails or screws, but the notches will take the thrust.

SHELF END SUPPORTS

It might be better to support some shelves with uprights at one or both ends. There could also be brackets along the shelves, but an upright support would be better near an external wall corner. The upright can then carry hooks or brackets for hanging displays.

End supports usually take the load to the floor and so relieve the wall fasteners of some of the load. An end can be solid or open and may be

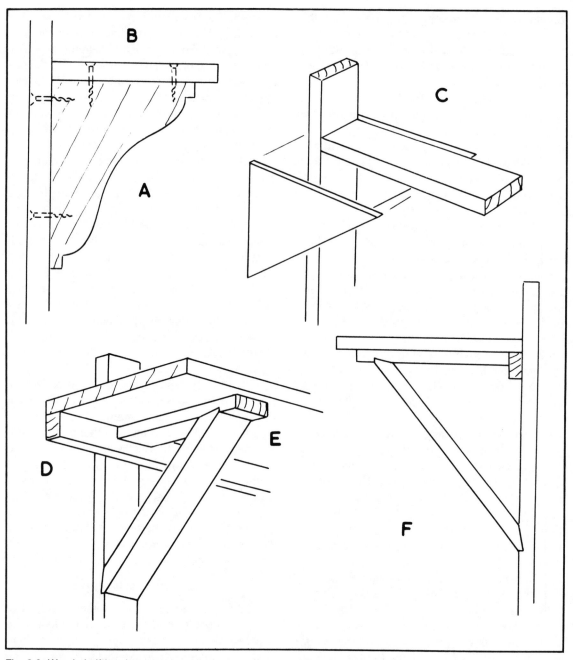

Fig. 9-2. Wood shelf brackets may be solid (A, B), made with plywood gussets (C), or built up (D-F).

plain or shaped. It does not have to be the full width of the shelves, but that would provide the best support.

    1. The simplest end support is a board the same width as the shelves (Fig. 9-3A). You could support the shelves with dado joints (Fig. 9-3B), but for most outdoor assemblies it will be sufficient to nail pieces across (Fig. 9-3C). Probably the best

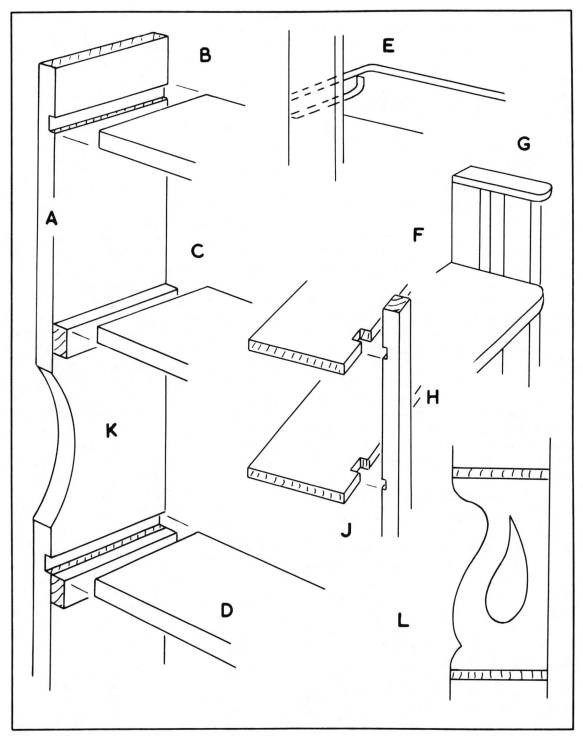

Fig. 9-3. End supports are better than brackets for providing strength and stiffness.

arrangement is a combination of the two with a shallow dado locating the shelf end (Fig. 9-3D).

2. If the end is not as wide as the shelves, supporting pieces should be carried forward to prevent the shelves from sagging (Fig. 9-3E). Pieces inside the ends, either from shelf to shelf or only as required, can take screws into the wall.

3. For an open end, two narrow uprights could be used (Fig. 9-3F) with dadoes or supporting strips across. They could be taken above the shelf and capped in order to prevent anything slipping off the end (Fig. 9-3G).

4. It might be that brackets provide ample support, but an exposed corner of a block of shelves needs supporting and strengthening. If a full end is not required, there could be a fairly light upright (Fig. 9-3H). This is best let in, with each shelf and the upright notched (Fig. 9-3J), so that the parts cannot move under load. The upright could be at the end or a short distance along the shelves. The same method can be used if intermediate support for the front edges is needed elsewhere along the shelves (Fig. 9-4).

5. A plain, full-width end might be considered ugly, and it might restrict the view of plants displayed or limit the amount of sunlight getting to them. The front edge between shelves could be scooped out (Fig. 9-3K) or given a decorative outline and holes to let light through (Fig. 9-3L).

FREESTANDING WALL SHELVES

If shelves are screwed to a wall or fence, there is no reason to fear them falling over and wrecking the pot plants or other display, but you might not always want to have shelves permanently in position or you might not want to make holes in or mark the wall. If you can have a stack of freestanding shelves, the whole assembly can be moved to another position if you want to alter the layout of a deck or garden. You could move the assembly under cover for the winter.

For stability, it is important to give freestanding shelves a broad base. You cannot have a stack of narrow shelves, similar to those attached to a wall, without providing feet that extend some way. Such feet could be a nuisance; it is better to make the

lower shelves wider. This way the need for extending feet can be avoided. The arrangement shown in Fig. 9-5 will go flat against a wall, but the spread front legs prevent tipping forward (except with the most abnormal usage).

1. Decide on the end view that will suit your purpose. Suggested sizes are given as a guide to wood sizes (Fig. 9-6A). Set out one leg assembly.

2. Make up a pair of leg assemblies. It will probably be sufficient to arrange battens across to support shelves (Fig. 9-6B). There could be another at the top, but that part will look better if you halve the two parts together (Fig. 9-6C). Use dadoes at the shelf positions if you prefer.

3. Make the shelves by building up widths as necessary. There could be battens across intermediately to prevent the boards warping in relation to each other. If the shelves are fairly long, stiffen them with lengthwise pieces and put struts between shelves (Fig. 9-6D).

4. If the legs are to rest on a hard surface, there is no need to do anything to them. If they are going on soil or other soft surface, put feet under them to spread the load (Fig. 9-6E).

5. Nail or screw the shelves to the end assemblies. Besides nails into the supporting battens, you can put screws through the legs into the end grain of the shelves. Keep the rear edges of the shelves level with the edges of the uprights.

6. The block of shelves might seem steady after the first assembly, but they would tend to loosen if not given extra stiffness lengthwise Brackets between the ends and the shelves would help, but it would be better to provide diagonal bracing at the back (Fig. 9-6F). This is best done

Materials List for Freestanding Wall Shelves				
4 legs	50	×	3	× 1
2 tops	8	×	3	× 1
8 shelf supports	14	×	3	× 1
1 shelf	48	×	9	× 1
1 shelf	48	×	10	× 1
1 shelf	48	×	12	× 1
1 shelf	48	×	15	× 1
2 braces	56	×	2	× 1

Fig. 9-4. Particleboard shelves can be supported by posts notched into the front edge.

Fig. 9-5. Freestanding wall shelves can be supported on end frames, with diagonal bracing at the back for stiffness.

after the other parts are assembled and checked for squareness.

7. Lay the pieces that will make the braces across the other parts and pencil where they come. Notch for them, screw them in place, and then cut off their ends level.

STEP SUPPORT

If pot plants are to be displayed, many of them need to go higher than the usual gap between shelves, and it is necessary to arrange the shelves so that a lower one is clear of the next one above and the foliage or flowers can stand in front of the upper shelf. It might be satisfactory, as in the previous example, to have the shelves only partially overlapping. If you want the whole shelf width to be clear of the one above, a series of shelves will have to project a long way from the wall. Unless there is a considerable amount of space available, it would be wise to limit this arrangement to two shelves.

A simple way of supporting shelves against a wall is with sloping ends (Fig. 9-7). They can be

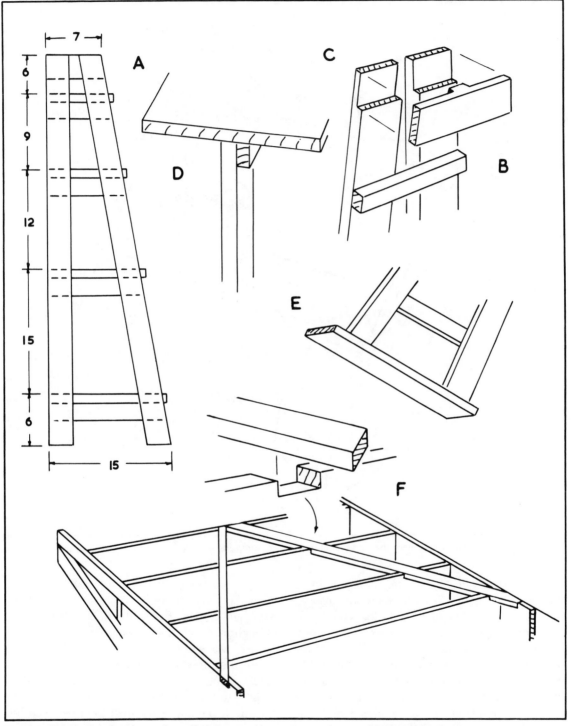

Fig. 9-6. The shelf assembly can be nailed, but notching parts together provides mutual support.

Fig. 9-7. For plants that reach higher than one shelf to the next, supports can slope and be screwed to the wall.

screwed to the wall at each side. There should be no need to secure the lower ends to the ground, but there could be similar blocks for screws into wood or concrete, or small stakes could be used into soft ground. Besides the two shelves, pots or boxes can stand between the legs and the whole assembly of three layers of plants can make a very decorative display. The suggested sizes can be modified, but it is unwise to use this method for a very big or a multishelf stand.

1. Set out an end view full size (Fig. 9-8A). Draw the end views of the shelves first (Fig. 9-8B) with their supports and let the sloping ends follow through to match their positions.

2. Make the pair of ends and mark on them where the other parts come (Fig. 9-8C). Attach blocks at the top that will screw to the wall (Fig. 9-8D). Fit the supporting blocks for the shelves.

3. Make the lower shelf to fit between the sides and the top long enough to overlap the screw

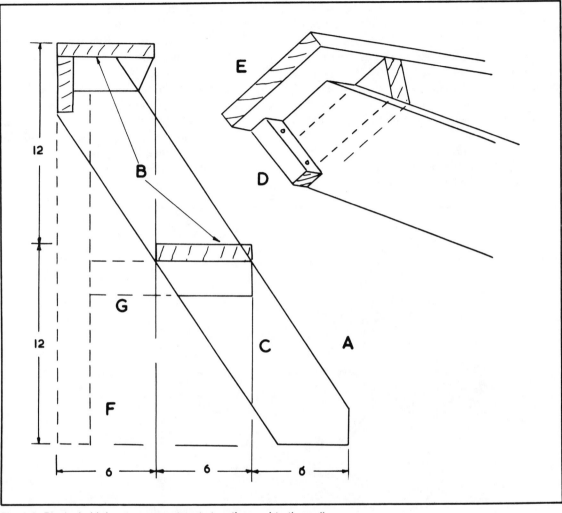

Fig. 9-8. Blocks hold the step support parts together and to the wall.

Materials List for Step Support

2 legs	36	× 6 × 1
1 shelf	30	× 6 × 1
1 shelf	26	× 6 × 1
4 shelf supports	7	× 2 × 1
If free-standing		
2 legs	24	× 2 × 1
2 rails	12	× 2 × 1

blocks (Fig. 9-8E). Attach them to their supports.

4. When attaching to the wall, use your full-size drawing height to check the position of the top shelf on the wall and use a level on the top shelf to see that it does not slope forward.

5. The assembly could be made freestanding. Fit rear legs vertically (Fig. 9-8F) and extend the lower shelf supports to join them (Fig. 9-8G).

SLATTED PLANT STAND

Pot plants require frequent watering, and considerable water will land on the shelves. Therefore

157

it is a good idea to have gaps in the shelves for water to run through. This is best done by arranging a series of strips—that have to be thicker than the board that would otherwise be used—to resist warping unevenly. The use of strips or slats makes the building up of shelves of any width easier. If the stand is to take larger plants in tubs or other big containers, stepped supports can be made to any required size.

The plant stand shown in Fig. 9-9 has three wide-slatted shelves that are clear of each other, when viewed from above, so foliage on any level can extend upwards without hindrance. The construction suggested has the lower front shelf supported by diagonal struts. The weight of the assembly, plus any pots on the other shelves, should prevent any risk of tipping, but if very heavy loads are to be put on the lowest shelf it could be given vertical legs at the front.

1. Get all the wood first. The whole assembly is intended to be made of 2-inch-by-2-inch stock. Check the actual dimensions of the wood you have and then set out and cut the joints to suit.

Fig. 9-9. A slatted plant stand will drain water away and this arrangement allows for high growth.

2. The parts can be made without setting out an end full size (Fig. 9-10A), but you might find it helpful to do so. Heights are to the tops of shelves.

3. So far as possible, mark out all pieces in the same direction together so that the spacing of joints will match and the assembled ends will stand square. Mark the joints on all the uprights (Fig. 9-10B). Put the wood for the rails together and mark their joints (Fig. 9-10C). Gauge the depths of the joints from the same surface of all pieces, and then cut the joints.

4. For the diagonal struts, cut the notches in the way described for shelf brackets (Fig. 9-2).

5. Assemble one end. Waterproof glue and a central screw in each joint should be sufficient. Check squareness and use the first end as a pattern for making the other one to match.

6. Cut all slats to the same length and remove any raggedness from the ends.

7. The slats could be attached with long screws or nails, but a neat way that uses shorter screws is to counterbore the holes (Fig. 9-10D). Drill holes deep enough to suit the screws, then plug them with dowels after driving the screws.

8. Arrange the slats evenly spaced (Fig. 9-10E) and let them overhang the end frames by about 2 inches. To keep the assembly in shape while making up the shelves, fit a slat at the back of the top and another at the front of the bottom shelf. Measure diagonals to check squareness, then add the other slats without disturbing the shape.

9. The assembly may be rigid enough, but if the stand is to be heavily loaded there should be some bracing added. This may come at the back and is most simply arranged with two struts (Fig. 9-10F) between the rear legs and the top rear slat.

Materials List for Slatted Plant Stand	
4 legs	36 × 2 × 2
2 legs	24 × 2 × 2
rails from four pieces	36 × 2 × 2
2 struts	15 × 2 × 2
15 slats	36 × 2 × 2
2 struts	48 × 2 × 2

Although the ends of the struts could be notched in, it should be sufficient to nail or screw them in place.

RAISED RUSTIC TROUGH

If a supply of stout boards cut across a log are available, a substantial rustic-effect holder for plants can be made with end legs that raise it above the ground. The wood can have a sawn surface and any waney edges can be incorporated. The trough looks best if it is fairly large. It could be made with boards about 1 1/2 inches thick and an overall size of about 72 inches by 18 inches with a height about 24 inches. It can then stand on the edge of a deck or similar place, but it looks particularly good in less formal surroundings such as at the edge of a path further out in a wilder part of the garden.

If the wood is cut from your own trees or from local recent felling, it is advisable to keep the boards as long as possible before using them, to fully or partially season, so that any warping or splitting can occur before you cut parts to size. For this type of assembly, natural flaws can be regarded as decorative if changes of shape or size and any opening of shakes are not too pronounced. Usually it is the ends of boards that open in cracks. Keep pieces over length until you have seen what is likely to happen before final cutting to size.

1. The trough is shown with legs splayed outward slightly and the lower edges of the side pieces with waney edges (Fig. 9-11). Proportions and sizes will have to suit the available wood and the locating of the finished trough.

2. The key parts are the two ends (Fig. 9-12A). Make them symmetrical about centerlines. Recess the sides to take the long pieces, and then spread below to widen the legs and give increased stability.

3. The center V cut could be made by just two saw cuts meeting, but it helps to drill first and saw into the hole (Fig. 9-12B). This makes cleaner cuts, looks decorative, and reduces the risk of a split starting from the opening as the wood dries out further.

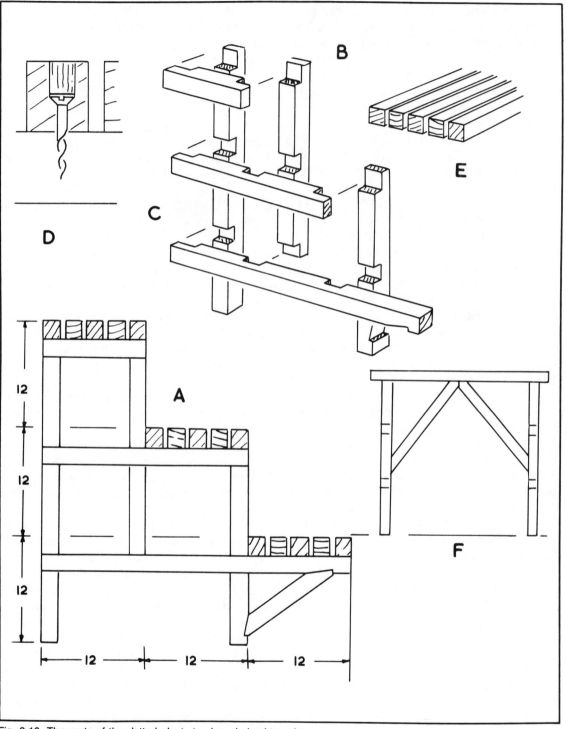

Fig. 9-10. The parts of the slatted plant stand are halved together.

Fig. 9-11. A trough can be made with natural boards and be raised on its own legs.

4. The lengthwise spread of the legs need only be slight (possibly 2 inches further at the bottom than the top). This is not really enough to affect the angle at the bottom of the recesses (which could be cut square across).

5. Make the bottom to fit between the sides (Fig. 9-12C), using the ends as a guide to its width.

6. Cut the two sides (Fig. 9-12D). Keep their tops level with the ends. You may have to notch the waney edges to fit into the ends. Mark on the sides the intended splay of the ends. It will probably be best to leave cutting off any extensions until after nailing the parts together.

7. Put a few drain holes in the bottom.

8. Assemble with nails, but screws at the top corners will provide extra strength where the greatest loads come.

9. The trough could be left at this stage, but warping of the ends can be minimized and the corner joints strengthened if strips are put across (Fig. 9-12E), with screws into the sides as well as the ends.

Materials List for Raised Rustic Trough

2 ends	25 × 25 × 1 1/2
1 bottom	72 × 18 × 1 1/2
2 sides	72 × 12 × 1 1/2 waney edge
2 strips	22 × 4 × 1 1/2

FORMAL RAISED TROUGH

A trough on legs, which has been made of planed seasoned boards and finished with white or other paint, is more appropriate to the patio or deck than the rougher trough just described. It could be used to contain plants in pots or there could be soil put directly into it (Fig. 9-13).

Many sizes are possible; much depends on where you want the trough to be located. If it is going near a wall, it might be made higher than if it is free and could be knocked over. So far as possible, the height and width should not be very different. The trough should have enough dead weight to be quite stable. Length does not affect stability and can be anything reasonable. Remember the weight if the trough has to be moved. Great length will result in bulging sides after long use. Stiffeners inside will reduce this risk. The sizes suggested in the materials list are intended as a guide to proportions.

1. The sides and ends are shown as made up of two boards (Fig. 9-14A). There should be no need to glue the boards together, but it will help to keep them in line along the sides if there are dowels at about 12-inch intervals (Fig. 9-14B). The bottom can be two or three boards with dowels arranged in the same way. Prepare the boards before marking out and cutting to size.

2. Nail the end boards to the legs, checking squareness and seeing that opposite ends match.

3. Prepare the bottom to width to fit between the sides. Drill drain holes.

4. Nail in the bottom between the ends and the sides to ends and bottom (Fig. 9-14C). Assemble on a flat surface and check that the trough stands firmly and without twist.

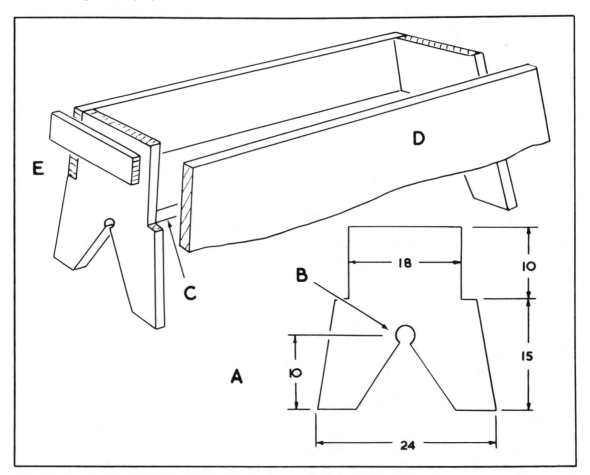

Fig. 9-12. The box sides fit into the leg recesses; these are splayed to provide stability.

Fig. 9-13. A raised trough can be made with boards on square legs.

5. Fit capping pieces at the ends (Fig. 9-14D), level with the inside surfaces, but extending about 1/2 inch outside.

6. The main drawing shows the ends cut square, but some decoration can be provided by curving the ends of the side boards and the edges of the capping pieces (Fig. 9-14E).

7. If the trough is to stand on a soft surface, the load can be spread by putting strips across below each pair of end legs.

8. Finish the trough with paint inside and out.

Materials List for Formal Raised Trough	
4 sides	48 × 6 × 1 1/4
4 ends	14 × 6 × 1 1/4
3 bottoms	48 × 6 × 1 1/4
4 legs	16 × 3 × 3
2 caps	16 × 5 × 1

PALING POT CONTAINER

Although most supports, boxes, and troughs for pot plants are made to be inconspicuous, there are many places where the container will draw more attention to itself and be attractive even when pots have been removed temporarily. The container shown in Fig. 9-15 is intended to be more of a decoration than some others. The front and back are arranged like the upright palings of a fence. This container is intended to hold several fairly large pots. Their contents should grow to at least as high again as the depth of the holder.

It would be advisable to decide on the pots that will usually be put in the container. Make sizes to suit so that the pots almost reach the tops of the surrounding rails and a convenient number can be put in the length. The suggested sizes would comfortably take three pots of about 16-inch diameter and depth. The wood sizes are light, but the parts depend on mutual support when built into the

163

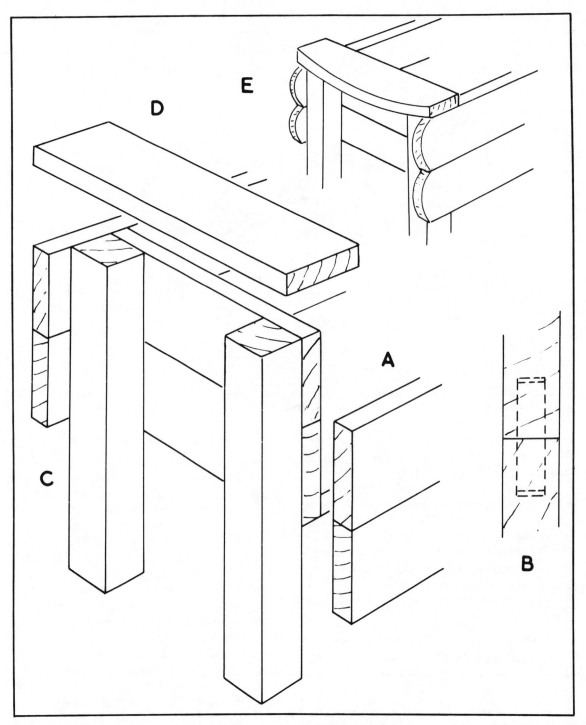

Fig. 9-14. Boards can be glued or doweled (A, B), and then nailed to the legs (C) with top cover pieces (D) and shaped ends (E) if you prefer.

Fig. 9-15. A paling arrangement and splayed legs gives an unusual appearance to a container for several plant pots.

complete assembly. The splayed legs are decorative. You could fit upright legs if the container is to stand near a wall or fit into a limited space and you do not want the rear legs to extend behind. As shown, the container is intended to stand where it may be viewed from any direction.

1. Choose the wood sizes. In particular, get the wood for the palings. This is shown 3 inches wide with 3 inches between pieces (Fig. 9-16A). Both could be wider or narrower. Space out the chosen wood in relation to the length you estimate will be needed and settle on the overall length in that way. The width between the sides should give ample space for the pots to be put in and out.

2. The design is based on two identical frames (Fig. 9-16B) that should be joined securely at the corners. Nails only there would not be strong enough.

3. The corners could be joined with small metal angle brackets (Fig. 9-16C).

4. Alternatively, cut joints. Glued dovetails will resist pulling apart if the tails are on the crosswise pieces (Fig. 9-16D). Another suitable joint is a comb or tongue (Fig. 9-16E) that gives a good area for waterproof glue. There could also be a nail or screw down through most of the tongues.

5. The bottom (Fig. 9-16F) can be solid

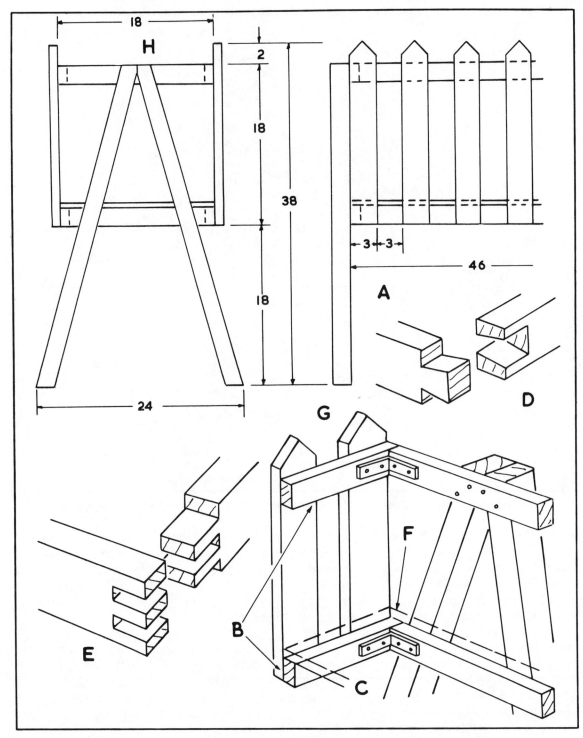

Fig. 9-16. Strength is needed in the corners; they can be dovetailed, bracketed, or tongued together.

boards in either direction, but it is most simply made from exterior plywood. Put a few drain holes in it and attach it to the bottom frame. Do not make up the whole assembly and try to put the bottom in last; that cannot be done.

6. The upright palings should be identical (Fig. 9-16G). They can be cut by the use of square and miter fences on a table saw, or you can mark out and carefully cut by hand. Take the sharpness off exposed edges.

7. Space the palings evenly on the sides of the frames. Fit the end ones on both sides and check squareness before adding the other pieces.

8. Make a full-size setting out of the main lines of the legs and ends to obtain the angles to cut the legs. At their tops bevel the meeting surfaces (Fig. 9-16H).

9. Join the legs to the ends with waterproof glue and long screws from inside.

10. Finish the wood with paint inside and out.

Materials List for Paling Pot Container

2 sides	46 × 2 × 1
2 ends	18 × 2 × 1
1 bottom	46 × 18 × 1/2 plywood
16 palings	20 × 3 × 1
4 legs	40 × 2 × 2

TAKE-DOWN TROUGH STAND

A trough or box on legs makes a good display, but there is an advantage in having the trough separate from the legs that support it. This allows some flexibility in the display. There could be a fairly large box containing deep-rooted plants that depend mainly on their foliage for display. During some seasons, particularly spring and early summer, you might want a display of flowers that will not last for long, but which are very attractive for the period they are in bloom. Many of these flowers are better in a shallow box. You can lift out the deep box of plants and replace it temporarily with a shallow one containing flowers. Carried a stage further, you can replace a box with a piece of plywood and you then have a seat or an outdoor coffee table. The example shown in Fig. 9-17 has a deep box, but the same stand would take a shallow box or a seat board.

The legs have to withstand a moderate strain and it is not advisable to depend only on nailed or screwed construction in the stand. The rails could be doweled or tenoned. If the stand is to be much higher than it is wide, a shelf underneath will stiffen the assembly as well as provide storage space. Although a durable hardwood would be a good choice, a softwood assembly finished with paint should have a long life.

Fig. 9-17. This trough fits into its stand and can be lifted out.

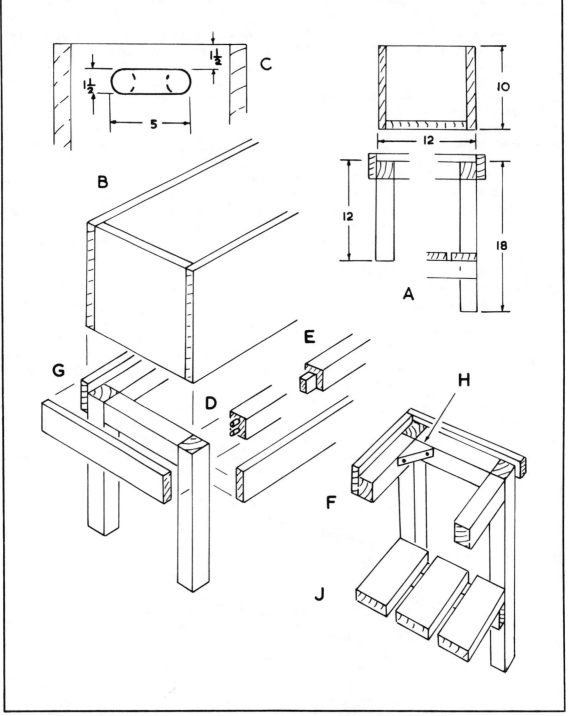

Fig. 9-18. The trough stand can be doweled or tenoned, and could be high enough to have a shelf.

1. Decide on the size, particularly if the stand is to be tall, with a shelf (Fig. 9-18A). The suggested sizes are intended to give an indication of suitable proportions. The box might be made of sawn boards, but the wood for the stand is better planed.

2. The box (Fig. 9-18B) is a simple nailed or screwed construction, with the bottom contained within the sides and ends for strength. Put drainage holes in the bottom.

3. So the weight of a deep loaded box can be lifted easily there can be hand holes in the ends. Drill holes and saw between them (Fig. 9-18C). Well round the hole edges.

4. Mark out and cut the four legs together so as to get them the same.

5. The stand should be an easy fit around the box, so make the box first and allow at least 1/4 inch extra all round for the stand.

6. Make the four rails. For doweled joints (Fig. 9-18D) square the ends to length. For tenoned joints allow for the extra wood needed for the tenons (Fig. 9-18E).

7. Assemble opposite sides and check that they match and are square, then join them with the rails across. Leave for the waterproof glue to harden.

8. Frame around the top with strips that stand about 1 inch above the surface (Fig. 9-18F and G) to keep the box in place.

9. Corner joints can be strengthened, if thought necessary, with metal angle brackets or triangles of wood glued and screwed in (Fig. 9-18H).

10. If there is to be a shelf, put battens across the legs and fit strips to them (Fig. 9-18J).

11. If there is to be an alternative shallow box, make one like the other (but about 4 inches deep). For a seat, cut a piece of 1/2-inch plywood to fit inside the border.

12. Finish all wood with preservative or paint.

Materials List for Take-down Trough Stand			
2 box sides	36 ×	10 × 1	
2 box ends	10 ×	10 × 1	
1 box bottom	34 ×	10 × 1	
2 rails	36 ×	2 × 2	
2 rails	12 ×	2 × 2	
2 borders	38 ×	3 × 1	
2 borders	14 ×	3 × 1	
4 short legs	12 ×	2 × 2 or	
4 long legs	18 ×	2 × 2 and	
2 battens	12 ×	2 × 1	
3 shelves	36 × 3 1/2 × 1		

Chapter 10

Climbing Supports

Many things that grow depend on clinging to supports as they climb upward. This applies to flowers, vegetables, vines, and other growths. For vegetables, the supports can be temporary and as simple as possible, without much thought for appearance. If the support is for climbing flowers, it should be better designed and more permanent so that it looks attractive or at least does not mar the appearance of the garden when nothing is climbing on it. If the support is for a vine or climbing tree, it might have to be fairly massive and built more like the structure of a building.

Supports for the flower garden and vegetable garden can be made entirely of wood, but there is a use for fiber rope and wire in single strands or as nets or meshes. The wood structure can be planed wood or it could be natural poles. Construction with natural poles is described in Chapter 11.

Supports for climbers can also provide backgrounds or dividers between parts of a garden, and perhaps even to the extent of being more like fences with archways and gates. Arranged in this

way, climbers look better than unadorned fences and gates between such things as a formal garden and a natural one, or between the vegetable patch and a flower garden. A divider covered in foliage or blossoms makes a good background to the garden as viewed from the house windows. This is true even when it is almost bare in winter.

The larger arbor or support for vines or trees will have to be planned as an extension of a building, as a shelter for seats, or as a roofed avenue from one part of the garden to another.

Temporary supports for such things as a vegetable crop can be made of almost any wood. The parts can be put into a dry store when not needed, but more permanent supports that have to withstand winter weather should be made of more durable wood. This is particularly important for the uprights that enter the ground; they should be treated with preservative.

It might be better to use short concrete posts in the ground and bolt the wood to them above the surface. A common fault is to not take the posts deep enough. A height of 6 feet or so of fairly dense screening or climber support can offer considerable obstruction to wind. Strong winds will loosen the grip of shallow posts in the ground. If the display arrangement is in an exposed position, there should be plenty of gaps in it to let the wind through, and there will have to be some diagonal struts. For most floral displays, an arrangement that is not too tightly packed looks better in any case.

EXPANDING WOOD TRELLIS

Criss-crossing trelliswork forms a good base for climbing plants to cling to. Its diamond pattern looks good even when there is no foliage on it. It will not stand unaided, but it is easily attached to a few uprights or more extensive framing for a large area. It can also be attached to a fence or wall permanently or just for the growing season. If it has to be taken down, this trellis will fold to a compact bundle for storage. If made as described, it also gives you scope for adjusting overall sizes. You can pull or push it to the width you want. This is accompanied by variations in the height, but it is usually possible to change sizes of a particular piece of trellis within a fairly wide range to get a shape to match a particular area to be covered.

In most circumstances, this type of trellis looks best when it is opened to a diamond shape (Fig. 10-1). You might prefer top angles about 60 degrees (Fig. 10-2A), but it is still attractive with squares (Fig. 10-2B). It is less satisfactory when it is pulled too wide and the diamonds are the other way (Fig. 10-2C). If you know the area you want to cover, it is probably best to scheme the laths to form the trellis so you allow for opening to square shapes. You can add one or two pieces, depending on the overall size, so that you do not have to pull the assembly to the full width and the openings will finish taller than they are wide.

The wood chosen should have fairly straight grain and be free of large knots. Convenient sections are between 3/4 inch by 1/8 inch and 1 1/4 inch by 3/8 inch. You might have to cut your sections down from larger stock. If you cannot get wood in single lengths to suit a large area, the trellis

can be made in several sections. Two sections that open to matching shapes may not be apparently much different in appearance from one large trellis. They will be easier to make and fit. For convenience in making, strips no more than 60 inches are advised.

1. Decide on the size mesh you want and draw the centerlines of the strips on a layout. Meshes at 5-inch centers are suggested and the lines are at 45-degrees to the borders (Fig. 10-2D).

2. At the outside, allow for the ends extending about half a mesh size (Fig. 10-2E).

3. With the layout as a guide, mark sufficient strips of full length (which are the same both ways) and others to make up the shorter pieces at the ends (Fig. 10-2F). Be careful that the distances between hole centers are exactly the same or the trellis will not submit to expanding and contracting or complete folding. Cut the ends to 45 degrees, which will come level when the meshes are square, but the slight unevenness will be attractive if the meshes are pushed to a diamond shape.

4. The joints are made with nails driven through and clenched. Drill all the hole positions slightly undersize. Then you can drive all, or most, of the nails and they will be gripped by the fibers while you turn the trellis over and clench them. Choose nails that will project about 1/4 inch.

5. At each nail position, support the driven nail on an iron block and curve the end over a spike (Fig. 10-2G) in a direction diagonal to the grain. Turning along the grain might split the wood. Remove the spike and bury the point in the wood (Fig. 10-2H). There is no need to knock the whole nail thickness into the wood.

6. Try moving the section of trellis from the mesh square shape to fully folded, with the intermediate diamond shape, to settle on which suits the situation. The supports can be arranged accordingly.

7. The trellis panel could be nailed or even tied in position, but it is best to fit it with brass screws in drilled holes. This way, even after long exposure, it can be taken down without damage.

Fig. 10-1. An expanding trellis attached to a wall provides a base for climbing plants.

TRELLIS SUPPORTS

If the trelliswork just described is to support climbing plants efficiently, it has to be supported so that the plants and their tendrils can work their way up without interference. They should be able to go all round and through, that means mounting the trellis away from a solid backing such as a house wall. Holding out about 2 inches should be enough. For the best appearance, any supports should be kept in from the edges (possibly at the first crossings of the laths).

The simplest supports on a surface are strips arranged horizontally (Fig. 10-3A), but the climbing plants will be coming on the trellis square to them and will not cross these obstructions unaided. Vertical pieces are better (Fig. 10-3B), but you will need more of them if the trellis is wide. Having the strips located behind trellis crossings makes them less obvious, but once foliage has started spreading they will be hidden in any case.

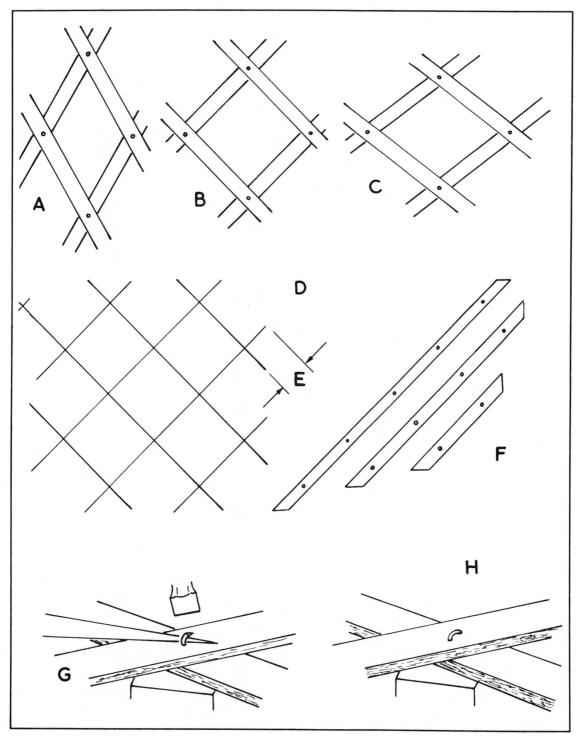

Fig. 10-2. Although a trellis can have different shapes (A-C), plan it square (D-F). Clench nail the crossings (G, H).

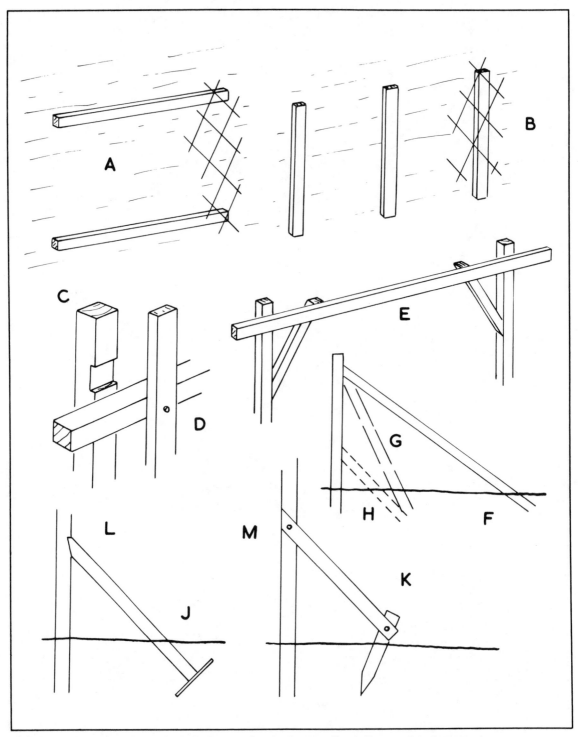

Fig. 10-3. Trellis supports can be attached to a wall or be free standing, with posts into the ground.

For free-standing trellis supports should go into the ground and have horizontal rails attached. Get adequate penetration in the soil for stability and treat the wood with preservative before driving. As posts are unlikely to go in the same amount, start with them over long and leave making any joints until after driving. Although shallow notches might be cut (Fig. 10-3C), it should be sufficient to nail the parts together. If you want to avoid horizontal rails obstructing climbers, there could be light vertical pieces between them and the rails (Fig. 10-3D). In a typical assembly with trellis up to 72 inches square, the posts could be up to 3 inches square, the rails 2 inches square, and the upright strips 1 inch by 2 inch section.

In some assemblies, it will be advisable to brace the supports to keep them square. Diagonal braces that match the angles of the trellis will do the job and be inconspicuous (Fig. 10-3E). They can be cut and nailed in after the other parts have been erected.Unless the structure is very shaky, one at each end should be sufficient.

If the ground is sandy or soft and the posts are not given much support by it, holes could be dug and the posts set in concrete. If there is a risk of wind moving the trellis, diagonal struts can be added. The greatest rigidity comes from having them large and at 45 degrees or even a flatter angle (Fig. 10-3F), but that means they could extend so far as to be a nuisance. A more upright angle will still give enough support (Fig. 10-3G), but in many cases struts at a reasonable angle lower down will stiffen enough and be out of the way (Fig. 10-3H).

For a strut to be most effective, it needs something to thrust against (Fig. 10-3J). That could be a piece of board or sheet metal, but you have to dig a hole and bury it. Another way to get a similar effect is to drive in a stake and notch or bolt to it (Fig. 10-3K). At the post, the strut can be notched in (Fig. 10-3L) or bolted through (Fig. 10-3M). It is unwise to depend only on nails or screws into the side of the post.

Struts are best able to take a load in compression. Arrange them so wind pressure is toward them. If there is a possibility of strong winds in both directions, there will have to be struts both ways.

If the trellis is to be arranged at an angle, possibly with two panels meeting at a corner, there is mutual support in the arrangement and the posts are unlikely to need struts to resist wind pressure.

LARGE ARBOR

An arbor is a support for vines, climbing trees, or anything more substantial than a simple creeper or climbing flowering plant. It is usually intended to be a permanent feature because what climbs it is expected to grow there for many years. How it is arranged depends on the situation. It could be attached to a house or form an extension of a shed or other existing feature. It is not roofed and it is not intended in itself to form a shelter, but in many cases the foliage growing over it becomes almost a complete cover. An arbor often provides shelter from the sun so it might contain seats that are separate or built in to the structure of the arbor.

One attractive form of arbor has four or more legs, and it supports a framework that the vine will grow over. The space below could be a path, possibly leading to a gate, or it could be a summer shelter. Some vines that grow over supports can become quite large and heavy. Wisteria and other climbers will develop strong trunks and spread their branches in all directions. Therefore the basic support has to be quite strong. This means that whatever you erect should be capable of standing there for many years with only the minimum of attention. A major repair after a few years would probably be impossible to make without damaging the vine that is being supported.

This design is the basic form of a large arbor that should be able to support any large climber (Fig. 10-4). Sizes will have to be arranged to suit the situation, but the parts should all be kept to large sections so that there will be little fear of breakages or sagging after long use. You could use softwood in stock sections, but a durable hardwood, if available, would be a better choice. The uprights are shown as square-sectioned wood, but they could be round poles with the bark removed. Treat poles in the same way with similar joints at the top.

Fig. 10-4. A large arbor needs substantial framing to support heavy growth over a long period.

1. Prepare the posts by allowing for at least 18 inches in the ground. In some soil, it will be possible to drive the posts in directly or into prepared holes. If soft soil will later let the posts sink deeper under load or there is a risk of them moving, it would be better to dig larger holes and set the posts in concrete (Fig. 10-5A). Treat the wood with preservative and slope the top of the concrete away from the wood so that rainwater will be drained away from the post.

2. Lay out the post positions while checking that they are parallel and square. Although you will have decided on a size, precision is not important, providing the posts will make a satisfactory pattern. Because of this, it is unwise to make the upper parts until the posts are located. Then you can allow for variations. Make the posts overlong at first because the ground might not be level and they might not enter the same amount. Check that the posts are plumb and put temporary stays between them for mutual support while the other parts are fitted.

3. Get the tops of the posts level. Use a temporary board across, with a level on it, using the lowest post as a guide for marking and cutting the others.

4. Mark down 6 inches for the notches (Fig. 10-5B). Use the board and level across where you have marked the notches before cutting them. It is these notches that settle the levels of the upper parts and it is less important if the tops of the posts are not level.

5. Cut the notches and bevel the tops of the posts to shed water (Fig. 10-5C).

6. Make the two stringers (Fig. 10-5D). With most assemblies, they can overhang the posts by up to 24 inches. In the example, it is assumed that a length of 12 feet will do. If the cross members are spaced at 18 inch centers, the end ones can

then be 9 inches from the ends of the stringers (Fig. 10-5E).

7. There is no need for deeply cut joints between the stringers and the cross members, but shallow notches in the stringers serve to locate the other pieces and ensure accurate assembly. With-out the notches the parts tend to slide during nailing. Put the two stringers together and mark the notches across them . A depth of 1 inch should be enough (Fig. 10-5F). Bevel the undersides of the stringers at the ends (Fig. 10-5G), but a small amount left square is stronger than cutting to a

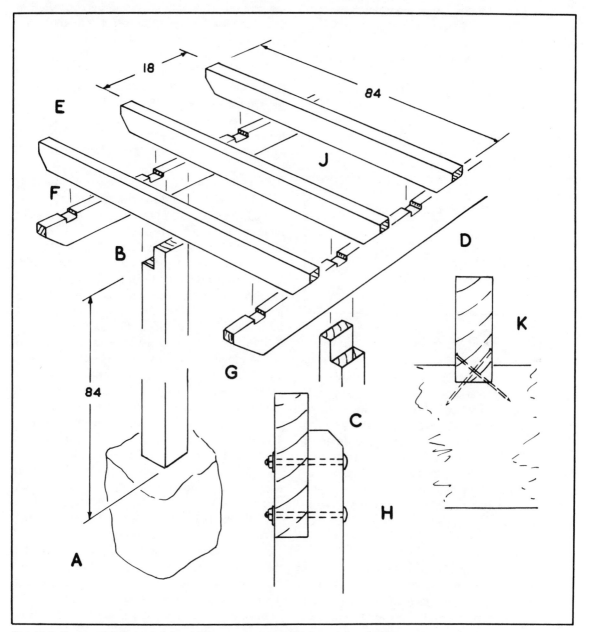

Fig. 10-5. Posts can be concreted and the upper parts notched as well as nailed.

177

sharp angle.

8. Mount the stringers on the posts, using two bolts at each place (Fig. 10-5H). Saturate the meeting surfaces with preservative before assembly. It is where water accumulates in joints that rot may start.

9. Make all the cross members to match each other and bevel their ends to match the ends of the stringers (Fig. 10-5J).

10. Join the parts with nails driven diagonally both ways (Fig. 10-5K).

11. Treat all the wood with preservative or thoroughly paint it, but leave the assembly long enough for the finish to become absolutely dry before allowing growing plants to come into contact with it.

Materials List for Large Arbor

4 posts	108	× 4 × 4
or	108	× 5 or 6 round
2 stringers	144	× 8 × 2
8 cross members	84	× 6 × 2

ROSE ARBOR

An arbor might be needed with a vista one way only and it might not have to support heavy vines or similar things that develop large trunks and branches. Such an arbor would suit climbing roses or similar climbing plants that need many years to develop. It is convenient to locate such an arbor at the boundary of a lawn or flower garden and provide it with a seat so that it is possible to sit in the shade and enjoy the views. The arbor shown in Fig. 10-6 is intended to be about 6 feet in each direction and be strong enough to take most kinds of climbing plants (except the heavier vines and trees).

Most of the top cantilevers forward, but its weight is balanced by the extensions at the back, tied to the uprights with diagonal braces. Besides ensuring the top keeps its shape, this allows the roses or other climbers to spread behind as well as in front and make an attractive canopy.

1. The posts are shown as 2 inch by 4 inch pieces, but they could be more substantial. They are shown sunk into the ground 18 inches (Fig. 10-7A), but how they are supported depends on the ground. They might have to be concreted as described for the previous project. It might be advisable to make a concrete platform to include the posts and extend along in front of the seat.

2. Make the cross members (Fig. 10-7B and C) the same and with 1/2-inch notches to locate the lengthwise pieces (Fig. 10-7D).

3. At the top of each post, attach a packing the same thickness as the brace (Fig. 10-7E). Drill through these and the cross members for 1/2-inch bolts.

4. Drill near the ends of the cross members for 1/2-inch bolts into the braces (Fig. 10-7F).

5. Temporarily bolt a post to its cross member and make a brace from the end hole to about 20 inches above ground level (Fig. 10-7G). Check the top in relation to the post and arrange it so the front comes higher than square to the post by about 3 inches. This will make the assembly look square. If you square it exactly, an optical illusion will make it appear to sag.

6. Bolt the end assemblies together and mount the posts in the ground. Check that the posts are plumb and use a lengthwise board with a level on it to check that the parts are correct lengthwise. Put a temporary piece between the two ends.

7. Prepare the lengthwise purlins (Fig. 10-7H). They are shown 2 inches by 2 inches, but they could be deeper if that seems desirable.

8. Fit the purlins in place. The cross members and purlins look best if they are beveled under their ends.

9. Put the seat back across behind the posts (Fig. 10-7J).

10. Arrange seat supports nailed or bolted to the posts (Fig. 10-7K) and legs into the ground and bolted to the supports (Fig. 10-7L). The seat (Fig. 10-7M) may be one wide board or several pieces with gaps between and cleats across underneath.

Fig. 10-6. A rose arbor has been arranged on two posts and a seat is provided.

11. Finish the wood with preservative or paint.

Materials List for Rose Arbor	
2 posts	90 × 4 × 2
2 cross members	72 × 4 × 2
2 braces	54 × 2 × 1
2 packings	4 × 4 × 1
6 purlins	72 × 2 × 2
1 seat back	60 × 6 × 1
2 seat supports	20 × 2 × 2
2 legs	24 × 2 × 2

CENTER POLES ARBOR

For some climbing plants and trees, it is best to arrange central uprights for the plant stems to climb. That way there will be support at the top for spreading branches. This is particularly suitable where the branches and foliage are expected to spread and hang in abundance. There could just be a pair of uprights, but the arrangement is also suitable for a long display—such as might be arranged to follow the edge of a path—that is not necessarily straight (Fig. 10-8).

The suggested project is comparatively light. If supports are arranged at not much more than 5-foot intervals, with a climber planted near the base of each upright, the arrangement should provide adequate support. If fairly heavy growth is expected or spacing is to be greater, sections should be increased. It would be possible to use round poles instead of the prepared wood by using methods of assembly described in Chapter 11. Sizes can be arranged to suit circumstances, but a height 7 feet above ground puts the main supports above head level, and a spread of 4 feet would be satisfactory. The uprights need not be central if a greater extension at one side would be more suitable.

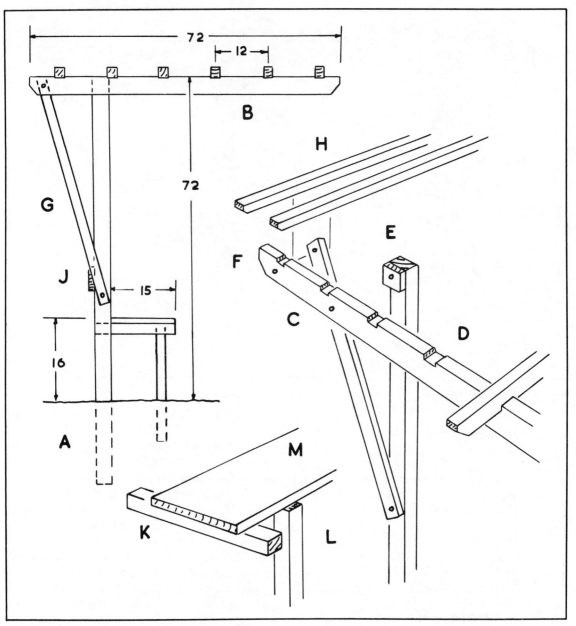

Fig. 10-7. Parts of the rose arbor are notched and the top is braced with diagonals at the back.

1. The wood need not be planed. Prepare the parts for all the supporting assemblies at the same time so that they are all the same. The crossbars (Fig. 10-9A) and the uprights (Fig. 10-9B) are the key pieces. Allow for the uprights entering the ground sufficiently (probably 18 inches). If

necessary, dig a hole for bedding the foot of the post in concrete.

2. Drill for 1/2-inch bolts a few inches from the ends of the crossbars (Fig. 10-9C) and mark where the uprights will connect.

3. Make joint covers (Fig. 10-9D) to nail or

screw both sides.

4. Assemble these parts by checking squareness between the top and upright.

5. Arrange two diagonal struts (Fig. 10-9E). They will provide most support if at angles slightly more upright than 45 degrees. If that angle makes a hazard for the head of anyone walking nearby, they could be brought to a flatter angle.

6. Bolt on the struts. Preferably, you should use large washers under the nuts and bolt heads to spread the pressure. It is advisable to put plenty of preservative in these and other joints before tightening in order to resist the onset of rot.

7. This arbor is shown without locating notches for the lengthwise parts, but shallow notches could be cut, if you prefer, in the same way as previous projects allow for joints in long

assemblies (see step 9).

8. Arrange the lengthwise parts at spacings to suit the expected growth, but having the outside pieces level with the ends of the crossbar and the others spaced at about 12 inch centers should suit most needs. At the ends, let the strips overhang their supports by about 12 inches (Fig. 10-9F).

9. In a series of supports, lengthwise pieces should preferably overlap three supports. Further pieces need not have fitted joints to the others, but it should be satisfactory to put them alongside (with an overlap nailed through). In a long assembly, that would mean pieces coming alternately inside and outside their partners. If a winding path has to be followed, lengthwise pieces can cross the supports on the skew.

10. Treat the wood with preservative or paint.

Fig. 10-8. An arbor for heavy climbers can be supported on central posts.

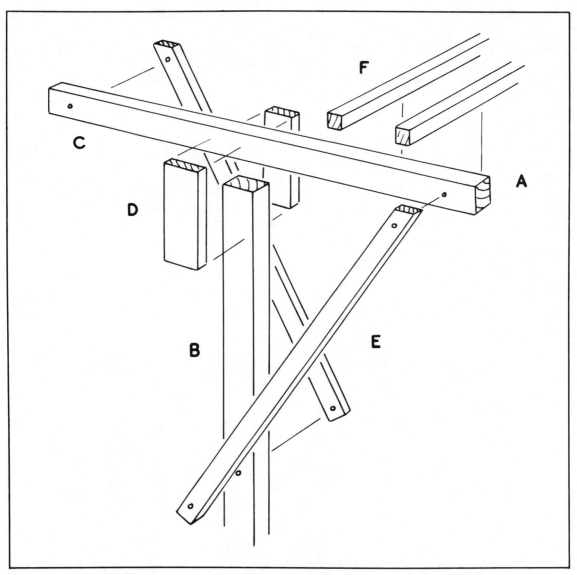

Fig. 10-9. The arbor parts are arranged to overlap so that they can be bolted.

Materials List for Center Poles Arbor
Parts for one support:

1 upright	90	× 4 × 2
1 crossbar	48	× 4 × 2
2 joint covers	12	× 4 × 1
2 struts	48	× 2 × 1
Lengthwise pieces	2	× 2 as needed

SUPPORTED ARBOR

An arbor might come alongside a building or it could be an extension of an existing garage or shed. It might be arranged in line or at one side. The design would then be similar to a freestanding arbor, but with posts and other parts omitted where the existing structure can take the load. Bear in mind what might happen in a few years time when the climbing plants have developed to maturity.

Will their coverage be what you want? Will the foliage admit enough light where needed? Will falling leaves be a nuisance? Will the structure still look good when the leaves are off the trees?

Supports for climbing vines and trees can improve a patio or deck. If the arbor adjoins the house, you can get some support from the house side. The posts can be arranged alongside the patio or deck, preferably where there is adjoining soil in which the vines can grow. It is possible to grow things in tubs, but these obviously restrict roots and you cannot expect to grow long-lasting and large plants in that way. Tubs might suit your annual and biannual growths.

A house-side arbor over a deck or patio can be made in a similar way to the large arbor (Fig. 10-4 and 5), but there will have to be a few structural differences. As it is closer to the living area,

you might want to relieve its severity by decorating in some way. It is primarily a support, however, and most decoration will come from the foliage and flowers.

1. At the side of the house or other structure, it will be best to fit a rail the same depth as the cross members and notch them fully into it (Fig. 10-10A). This will have to take increasing weights as branches grow. Therefore, it must be securely fastened to the house side, but some of the load could be taken by two or more uprights to the ground or floor.

2. The outer ends of the cross members can be beveled below, but a molded cut is more decorative (Fig. 10-10B).

3. The stringers and posts can be the same as in the large arbor, but you will have to arrange post spacings to suit steps or other features already

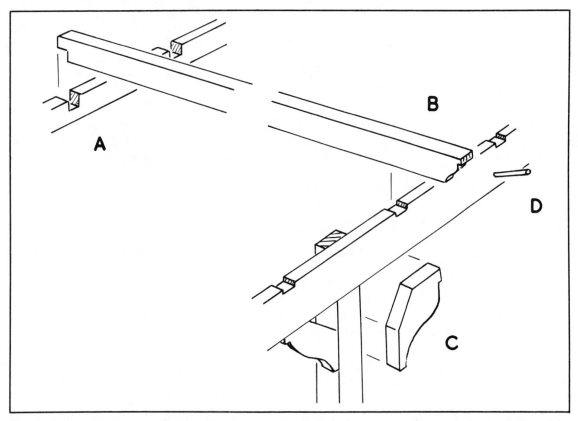

Fig. 10-10. If an arbor is to be built alongside a house or other wall, the inner part can be attached to a rail (A) and the outer part can be made more decorative.

there. The stringers can also be decorated in this way or their ends can be cut square, depending on the situation.

4. The decorative theme can be carried further by putting brackets between the stringers and posts, and you can have matching moldings (Fig. 10-10C). The brackets are not intended to provide strength; they can be nailed or screwed in position.

5. There could be a rail at a suitable height between the posts to enclose a deck. Hooks can be put under the stringers to take hanging plants or pots. Wood pegs or dowels (Fig. 10-10D) would serve the same purpose.

PERGOLA

Arbor, bower, and pergola are names for things that are so similar that it is difficult to separate them. For the purpose of this book, a pergola is an enclosed type of arbor. It has an open-topped support around which a vine or tree provides a covering, while the sides are open or may be enclosed with latticework. A pergola can be round, square, or many sided. There are structural problems in making a truly round pergola. A square pergola can be easier to build, but one with more than four sides has an attractive appearance and is not much more difficult to make.

Although the number of sides could be any total, there are advantages in choosing six sides. This makes a good-looking structure. In setting out six equal sides, you can use the fact that the radius of a circle can be stepped off six times around the circumference. In this assembly, all the cuts that are not square will be at 30 degrees or 60 degrees. The project has six posts equally spaced and a roof sloping at 30 degrees along the rafters to a central point (Fig. 10-11). The suggested size is 8 feet across the posts and most of the parts are 2-inch-by-4-inch section. This will be strong enough unless a much larger structure is planned. In that case wood sections should be increased.

The design shown in Fig. 10-12 has a full hexagonal base and is suitable for positioning where it can be viewed all round. It could make a centerpiece for a lawn or a focal point for paths. Of course, it is large enough for several chairs. If the pergola is to be at one side of a garden, it could be made as a half. The main frame then forms the back and the rest of one side of the design is made in exactly the same way as for the complete assembly.

1. The size of the pergola is decided by a main frame (Fig. 10-12A). This crosses the hexagon and is built of two posts with two rafters (all attached with halving joints). Set out the roof part and (a short distance down) the full-size posts on the floor. The slope of the rafters is not crucial, so long as both sides are the same. If you make the slope 30 degrees (Fig. 10-12B), that will simplify marking angles (if you are using a fence on a circular saw). Make sure the drawing has the two posts parallel.

2. Mark two rafters from the setting out (Fig. 10-12C). Cut the two posts to stand 7 feet above the ground and have enough at the bottom to go into the ground (Fig. 10-12D).

3. Mark and cut halving joints between the posts and the rafters (Fig. 10-13A). Cut another halving joint at the apex of the roof (Fig. 10-13B).

4. Assemble the frame. There could be waterproof glue in the joints, but use plenty of screws rather than nails. Put the parts together over the setting out and try the assembly both ways to check that it is symmetrical. Put a temporary piece across (Fig. 10-13C) to hold it in shape until it is brought together with the other parts.

5. The other four frames are like half of the frame just made, except for where they meet it at the apex. The posts and their joints to the rafters are the same. At the apex, cut back each rafter vertically (reduced by half the thickness of the main frame). Also cut there to 60 degrees (Fig. 10-13D) to make the two at each side into a pair (Fig. 10-13E).

6. The corners of the frames at the tops of the posts will fit the eaves pieces closely if they are beveled 60 degrees each side of the center (Fig. 10-13F). That could be cut after the posts are mounted in the ground, but it might be easier to do at this stage.

7. Set out the ground where the post holes have to come by using an improvised compass.

Fig. 10-11. This pergola has six posts and a top taken to a point.

Use any piece of wood and put a spike through a hole 48 inches from the end. Push the spike into the ground at what will be the center of the pergola and use a sharp piece of wood against the end to scratch a circle on the ground (Fig. 10-13G). Mark across the centerline in the direction you want the main frame to be, and then measure 48 inches from these points on the circumference to the posi-

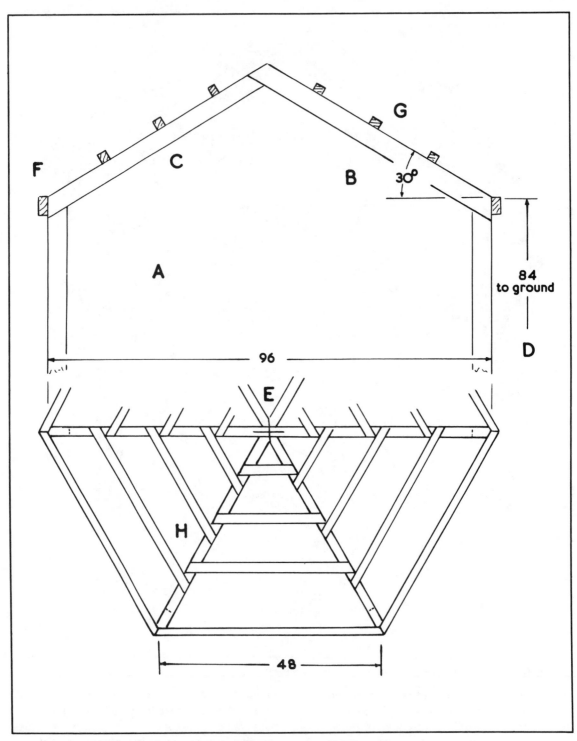

Fig. 10-12. The pergola is built with a central assembly and other parts brought up to it.

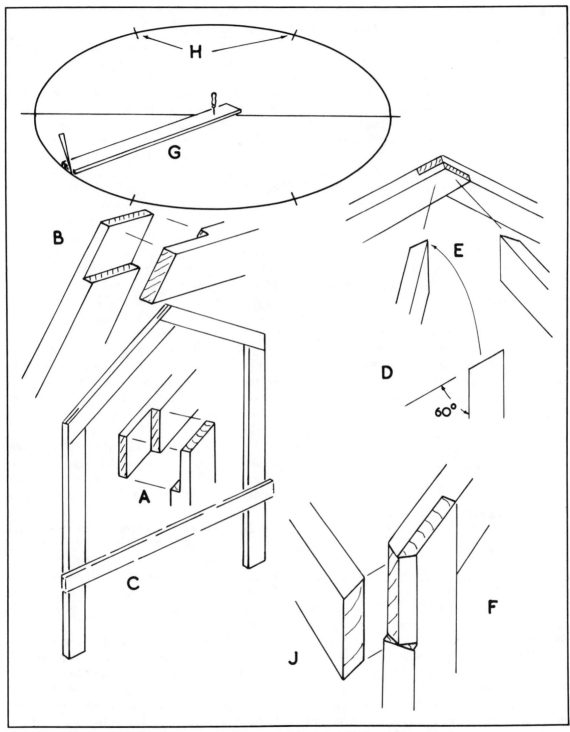

Fig. 10-13. Post positions are found with a circular layout. Joints are halved as well as nailed.

tions of the other posts on the circumference (Fig. 10-13H). Check that the distances between these positions is also 48 inches.

8. Erect the main frame. See that it is plumb in all directions and that a board temporarily clamped across the eaves corners is level.

9. Erect the other posts and bring the rafters to the center of the main frame and nail them there (Fig. 10-12E). Check distances apart around the eaves corners and adjust as necessary.

10. The eaves pieces (Fig. 10-12F), that go around and link the tops of the six posts, meet at the corners and will look best if cut to 60 degrees so they miter together (Fig. 10-13J). Nevertheless, they could be nailed satisfactorily even if their ends do not meet closely.

11. The number of purlins on each slope can be arranged to suit the type of climbing tree or vine, but a spacing of about 12 inches should be satisfactory (Fig. 10-12G). Put these strips first on three alternate sides of the roof, and then put the others on so they come against them (Fig. 10-12H).

12. The linked parts should provide mutual support and the pergola will be standing rigidly. Clean off any raggedness in the woodwork and finish it with preservative.

```
          Materials List for Pergola

     6 posts        102  × 4 × 2
     6 rafters       60  × 4 × 2
     6 eaves         52  × 4 × 2
     6 purlins       44  × 2 × 2
     6 purlins       30  × 2 × 2
     6 purlins       18  × 2 × 2
```

BEAN POLES

Beans, peas, and other vegetables that need something to climb on as they grow are often supported by a collection of sticks and poles that do not match. They are often tied together in such a way that the assembly is insecure and might collapse before the crop is ready for harvesting. If these are crops you grow every year, it is worthwhile making something that can do the job prop-erly and be suitable for taking down and storing out of the growing season.

How many supports and how high you take them depends on what you grow, but a height of 6 feet or 8 feet is probable. For rows of beans, you want poles 12 inches or more apart. The length of the row will tell you how many poles to make. A fault with many improvised assemblies is their tendency to sway. This assembly has diagonal braces to prevent this (Fig. 10-14). The poles are shown pushed into the ground, but they could be bolted to lengthwise pieces at ground level.

The wood chosen should be straight-grained and free from knots. Much spruce, fir, and pine can satisfy these requirements. The wood need only be 1 inch square. If you have to use wood that does not have such a straight grain, the section will have to be increased slightly to provide strength. Surfaces could be left as sawn—which is better than being planed—for the vines to grip.

1. Prepare all the uprights (Fig. 10-15A) with pointed ends, but do not go to fine points that would soon crumble or split. About 7 inches from the top drill for pivot bolts (3/16 inch stove bolts are suitable) and 2 inches below them, drill similar holes the other way for the horizontal bar (Fig. 10-15B).

2. Make the horizontal bar (Fig. 10-15C). For a long row you will have to use more than one bar and it will be convenient to change sides where they overlap. Drill for bolts at the spacing you want.

3. Assemble two sets of hinged uprights and erect them temporarily, using the horizontal bar as a guide to get them spaced correctly at top and bottom. From this assembly get the length of a diagonal (Fig. 20-15D). To allow for variations when you erect each year, drill a few extra bolt holes (Fig. 10-15E).

4. Grease the nuts and bolts when you erect the poles each year, to reduce rust and allow them to be released easily at the end of the season.

5. If you do not wish to push all the poles into the ground, there could be another horizontal bar near ground level each side (Fig. 10-15F), bolted in the same way as the top one. This might

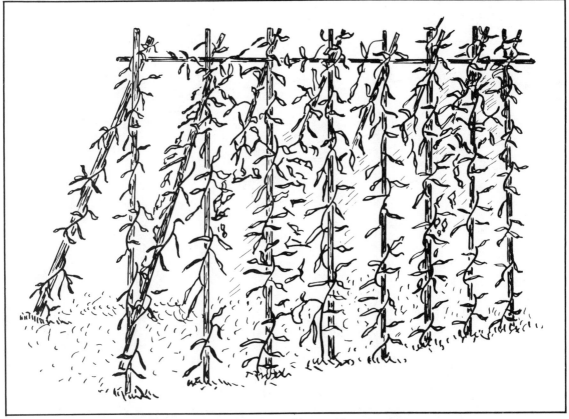

Fig. 10-14. These bean poles are designed to take apart and be used for several years.

be lashed down to stakes, or you can let the end poles continue with points into the ground (Fig. 10-15G). It would be unwise to expect end securing only to hold a long length, so there should be poles or stakes into the ground at least every 8 feet.

Materials List for Bean Poles

All parts 96 × 1 × 1
(quantity according to needs)

TOMATO POLES

Tomato and cucumber plants need something on which they can climb and spread. There could be poles with strings between, but it is better to have wooden horizontal pieces so that there is more for the vines and tendrils to grip. Construction could be with 1 inch square straight-grained strips, held together with bolts, as in the previous project. Alternatively, nails could be taken through and clenched so that the parts could pivot on each other for compactness in storage. Sizes depend on the plants you grow, but poles 60 inches or more should be satisfactory.

1. A single pole with crosspieces (Fig. 10-16A) will do if your crop is just confined to a corner of the plot. Make the pole with a point and holes for the bolts holding the crosspieces (Fig. 10-17A).

2. The crosspieces could all be the same length or you could taper them slightly (Fig. 10-17B). Drill centrally for bolts.

3. When assembled for use, it may be sufficient to rely on tightening the bolts to hold the crosspieces square. To be more certain they will

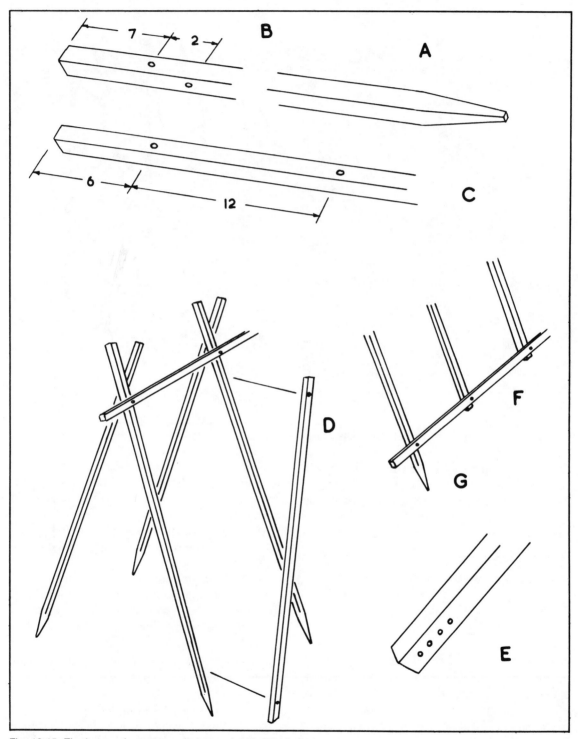

Fig. 10-15. The bean pole parts are square and drilled for bolts.

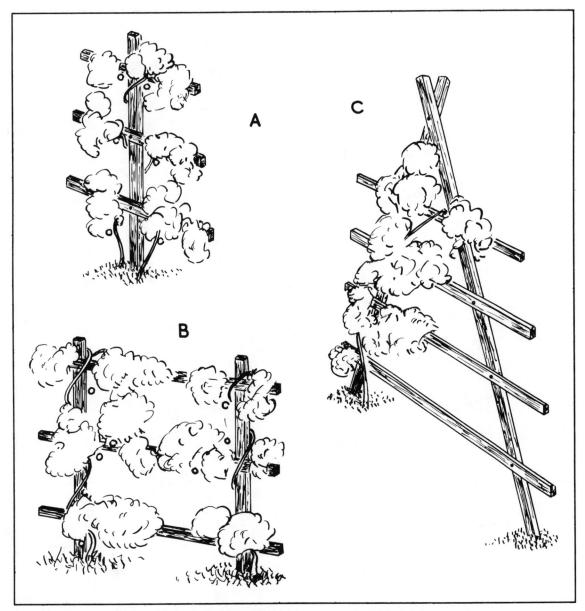

Fig. 10-16. Tomato and cucumber poles can be arranged on single or double uprights.

not move later, there could be shallow grooves in them (Fig. 10-17C). For storage, the bolts are slackened and the parts turned as far into line as they will go (Fig. 10-17D).

4. There could be two uprights with the strips across them (Fig. 10-16B). The assembly is similar to the single pole, but you can provide a

greater spread (Fig. 10-17E) and the pair of poles into the ground should be more rigid. The parts will fold for storage, but they will make for a rather long package.

5. An alternative to upright poles is to arrange them sloping (Fig. 10-16C). The arrangement could stand independently or you could slope a

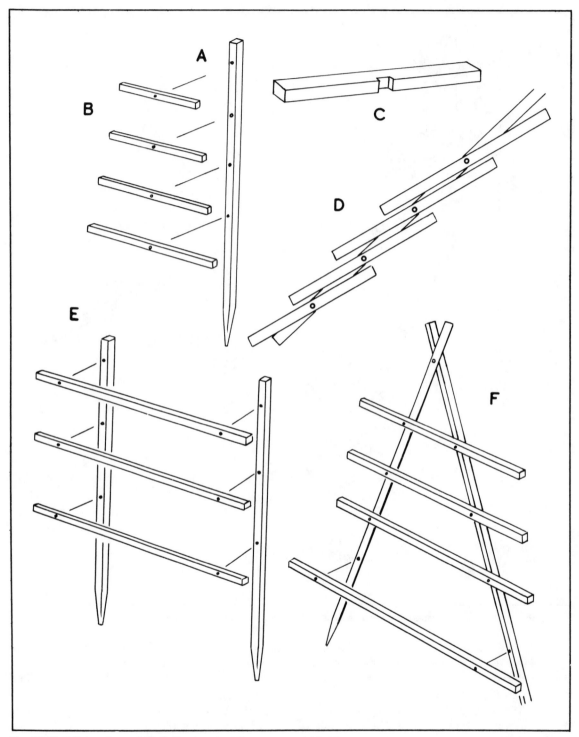

Fig. 10-17. If the parts are bolted, they can be taken apart or folded for storage.

pair towards each other. With the tops interlocked, there would be mutual support and a very rigid assembly.

6. Make a pair of poles with pivot bolts as for bean poles. Spread them to about 24 inches, and then mark where the crosspieces will come at even intervals (Fig. 20-17F). There should be no need to cut notches as the two bolts in each strip and the triangular shape of the assembly will provide rigidity.

7. If you do not want to fold the parts for storage they could be nailed. If you want to fold, you can take the bolts out of one pole so the crosspieces can swing almost in line on the other.

8. Any of the assemblies can be built up into groups so that the pattern has three, four, or more sides. The sides could be linked, and this would strengthen them as well as possibly allow for a greater spread for the crop. On the other hand, the inside will be sheltered and will not get as much sunlight. Fruit or vegetables there might not be as good as those on independently standing poles.

Materials List for Tomato Poles

All parts 1 × 1 (quantity according to needs)

WIRE SUPPORTS

Some climbing plants can be supported with cords or wires instead of strips of wood. They will climb hairy ropes or intertwine through wire netting. In some cases, such as grape vines, they will spread along wires in preference to anything thicker. The constructional problems are then in arranging supports for the wires or ropes.

1. For beans and other vegetables that climb, the ropes could go to a central bar on uprights (Fig. 10-18A). The posts could be 2-inch-square pieces, pointed at the bottom and drilled for a length of metal tube or rod (Fig. 10-19A), or wooden rods could drop into a slot at the top (Fig. 10-19B) and slip into loosely fitting mortises if they are also to come lower down (Fig. 10-19C). The lower bars might not be needed, but they allow shorter cords to be arranged intermediately.

2. How the cords are arranged at the bottom depends on your needs. They could be secured to notched stakes (Fig. 10-19D). A rod could be staked down at the ends (Fig. 10-19E) and the cords tied to it. Whatever method is used, you should make sure the cords cannot come away or slacken and damage plants climbing on them.

3. In some cases, it is better to spread the top supports by putting a crossbar on each post (Fig. 10-18B). That could be bolted on, and it could have a notch to keep it square (Fig. 10-19F). The crossbars can be drilled to take wires stretched between them (usually two, but there could be four). With the strain of the stretched wires, it is advisable to guy the ends down to stakes (Fig. 10-19G) or to very securely let the posts into the ground. This arrangement can be used at a lower position. Suppose the instructions on a packet of seeds says the supports should be 6 feet high. You could make this arrangement not more than 4 feet and the beans will climb first and go along the horizontal wires. This makes picking easier, and with the upright cords to the outer wires the insides get more sunlight and air.

4. Peas do not need high supports. Light trimmings of natural wood with many twigs and branches are ideal supports (if you have them). For another type of support, you can use wire mesh with large squares, such as turkey and pig wire, between posts (Fig. 10-18C). This is best erected before the peas are planted. The lower part of the wire mesh can have cut ends pushed into the ground or small stakes used there. The top need not be more than 36 inches above the ground, and it can be held level with a wire between the posts (Fig. 10-20A). An alternative is to use a piece of bamboo or a light lath that is pushed through the wire mesh and then nailed to the posts (Fig. 10-20B).

5. If you want to grow grape vines, they need a steady tight wire fence to train on (Fig. 10-18D). A shaky and loose arrangement would be unsatisfactory. The usual height above the ground is about 5 feet. The posts should be nearly 7 feet long to allow for sinking in the ground. The distance between the posts might be 8 feet (or not much

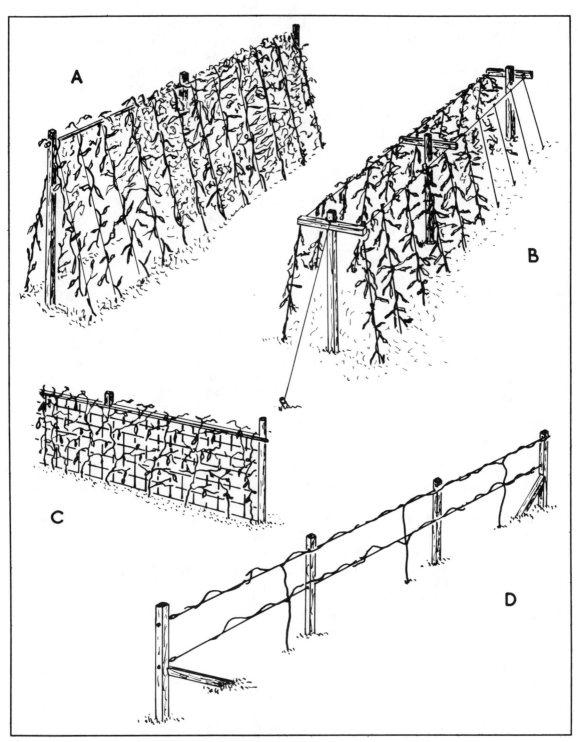

Fig. 10-18. Several crops will climb on wire. The wire can be supported in several different ways.

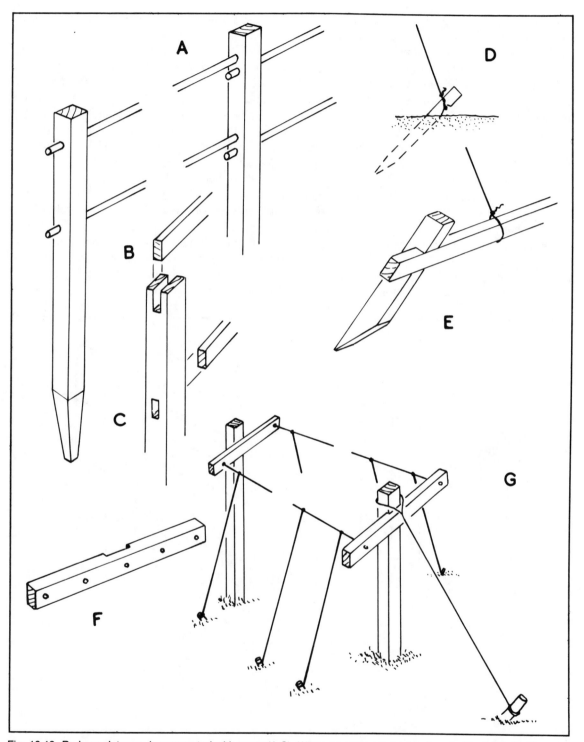

Fig. 10-19. Rods or slats can be supported with posts (A-C). Wires or cords can be tensioned with stakes (D-G).

more). Because the fence needs to stand for several years, use a durable wood for the posts. Put preservative on the posts and erect them truly in line and upright (Fig. 10-21A). Drill the posts for two horizontal wires. The wires go within a few inches of the tops and just above halfway between there and the ground (Fig. 10-21B).

6. The wire can be galvanized steel wire rope about 1/8 of an inch in diameter. The intermediate posts should be drilled to allow the wire to slide through easily. At the ends there have to be either 1/4-inch-diameter or 5/16-inch-diameter eyebolts. If you can get a type with a very long threaded portion or if you can cut the thread further yourself, the eyebolts might provide all you need to tension the wire rope (Fig. 10-21C). If not, you should include turnbuckles at one end of each wire (Fig. 10-21D) or at both ends if it is a very long assembly. Attach the wires to the eyebolts or turnbuckles with two wire rope clips (Fig. 10-21E).

7. It is unlikely that the end posts will be sufficiently rigid to withstand the pull of the tensioned wires. Therefore they must be stiffened. One way is to put a strut inside (Fig. 10-21F). Notch it to the post (Fig. 10-21G). At the bottom it must be prevented from being thrust deeper into the soil. One way is to dig down and put a board there (Fig. 10-21H).

8. If digging is impractical, you could drive in a stake and bolt the strut to it (Fig. 10-21J). Another method of support to resist the strain of the wires under tension is to arrange a stay at each end (Fig. 10-21K). If there is space, the longer this stay is the better because it gives a pull nearer horizontal. Ideally, it should come at an angle flatter than 45 degrees to the ground. Then the stake should

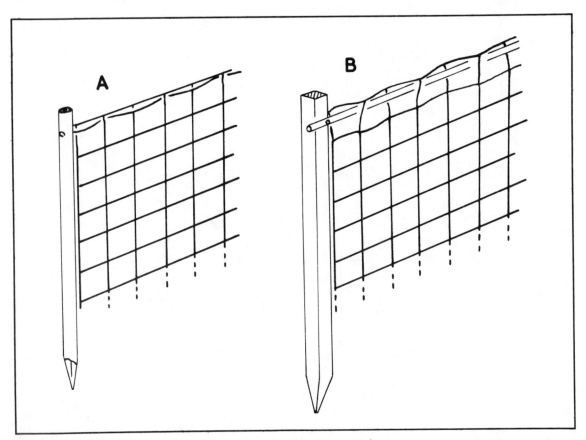

Fig. 10-20. Turkey wire mesh can be held between posts with wire or a rod.

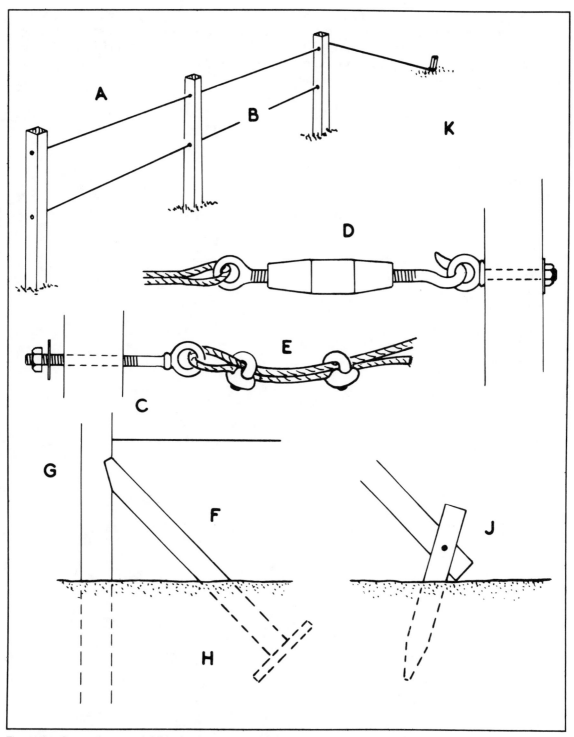

Fig. 10-21. Grape vines need tight wire that must be stretched between posts and held taut.

be driven only slightly more upright than square to the line of the wire stay. Loop the wire round a notch in the stake or use a ring bolt through it. At the top of the post, use a ring bolt and a turnbuckle in the same way as at the ends of the horizontal wires. Try to get the assembly tight so that the horizontal wires are reasonably rigid. There should still be some adjustment left on the ringbolt nuts or the turnbuckle to take up later if necessary.

Chapter 11

Rustic Construction

The use of natural poles and logs is particularly appropriate to the construction of things for use outdoors in the yard and garden. The wood in its more natural form will often look better in these surroundings than boards and posts that have been sawn square and possibly planed as well. Obviously, there are situations where the prepared wood is more appropriate, but if you have a supply of wood from felling or trimming you might consider using it for several projects outdoors. If the wood is unsuitable for sawing into boards, using it as it is gives it a new life.

Wood obtained by clearing land will be full of sap that will soon dry out. Such wood will shrink and might split. In particular, cracks are liable to pass through nail holes and weaken fastenings, even to the extent of joints collapsing. If you must use "green" wood, keep it for the cruder structures such as rough fencing. For better construction, the wood should be allowed to season in ventilated but dry space for some time (preferably a couple of years).

What you do about bark depends on the wood. With some woods, the bark is very firmly attached to the wood whether it is newly felled or has had time to season. In that case, the bark could be left on and you might find this improves appearances in a garden situation. If the bark is easy to peel with a hatchet or chisel, it should be removed before the wood is used. With many woods, the bark will peel unaided after the wood underneath has dried. If you use such wood with the bark on, next year you might find the structure you have built has become a patchwork of partly peeled wood that looks unattractive. In general, if bark will peel without too much effort, it is better to remove it before using the wood.

A drawknife is a good tool for removing bark (Fig. 11-1). It will also level inequalities and cut off the bases of shoots and small branches. A hatchet or stiff knife will also do the job. A broad chisel has possibilities. The traditional tool was a "spud" (a sort of long-handled, broad, blunt-edged chisel). Remove bark before seasoning.

A section of log more than a few inches thick will take a very long time to season if left as it is.

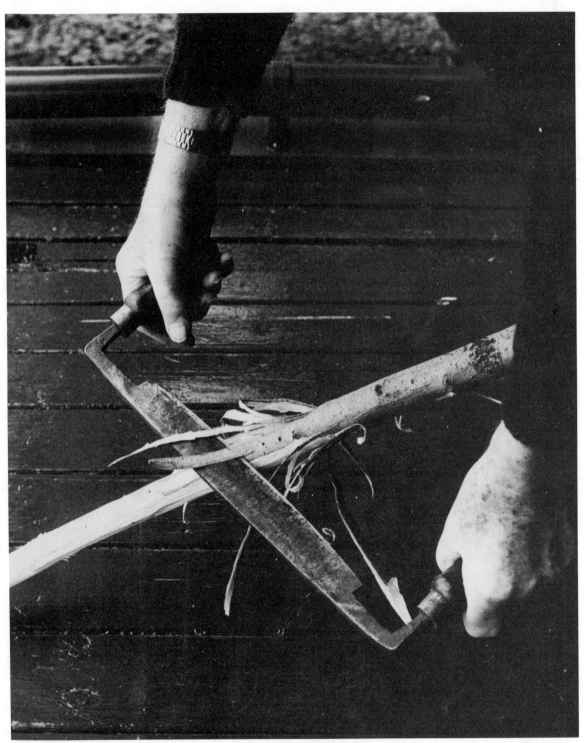

Fig. 11-1. A drawknife is a useful tool for stripping bark off natural poles.

It is better to plan what you will do with it, and then cut the wood to somewhere near size. You could saw it across to a little more than the final length. If something is to be made with half or less of the diameter, split the wood lengthwise. Seasoning times are related to thickness rather than length. The more you can reduce the cross-section the better. It is very probable that cracks will develop at the ends of pieces as they dry. If the wood is longer than necessary before seasoning, you can cut off any ends that split later.

If you have the skill, you might split a log centrally with one heavy blow with an ax. For most workers it is safer and more accurate to use

wedges. Ideally, the wedge should be steel. It is, however, possible to start a split with a hatchet, and then drive in a wooden wedge (Fig. 11-2A). As the split develops, another wedge can be driven into the side (Fig. 11-2B) to continue the split. Then the first wedge can be removed and entered again further along the split (Fig. 11-2C) and so on, in turn, if it is a long log.

The traditional tool for cleaving thinner wood is a froe (Fig. 11-2D). If a froe is unavailable, something like it can be improvised with a strip of flat stiff steel. In use, it is first driven into the end of the wood like a wedge. By rocking the handle (Fig. 11-2E), the split can be levered open and

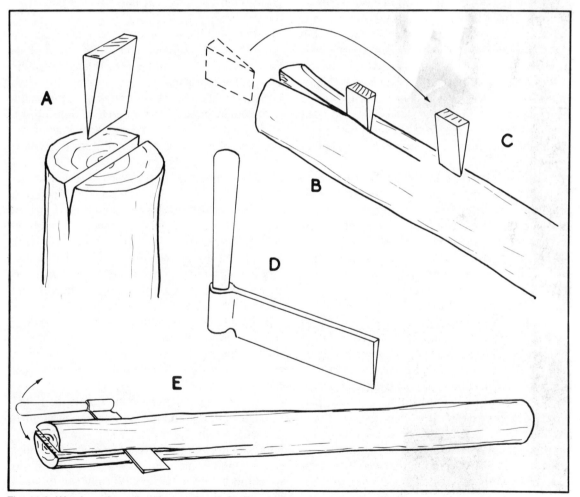

Fig. 11-2. Wood can be split with a wedge (A-C). The traditional tool is a froe (D, E).

extended along the wood. This is particularly successful with recently felled wood.

JOINTS

Much rustic construction is simple hammer and nail work that will suffice in many situations. In better assemblies, the nails can be supplemented with cut joints. These will not have the precision of many joints in sawn and planed wood, but they serve to increase strength where it is required. Unprotected steel nails will soon be attacked by moisture in the wood, as well and any in the atmosphere, so it is best to only use nails protected by galvanizing or other process.

There is a great temptation in rustic work to hammer in nails without preparation, but it is wise to assume that the wood you are using will shrink eventually. And that could mean splits at nail holes. To reduce this risk, drill clearance holes in the top pieces and, for all but the finer nails, pilot holes in the lower pieces. This is particularly important near ends. Clenching is often advisable if you can take a nail through and turn over its point while the head is supported with another hammer or an iron block.

Cleft wood can be joined with the flat faces together. So far as possible, in this and other nailed joints, drive two nails so they do not come in the same grain lines either way. This usually means arranging them diagonally across a joint (Fig. 11-3A). If the two parts are similar sections, the nails can be driven from opposite sides (Fig. 11-3B). If sections are different, it is stronger to nail through the thinner into the thicker.

Round poles can often be nailed directly to each other, but it is better to prepare flat meeting surfaces with either a hatchet or a saw and chisel (Fig. 11-3C). You could shave toward an end or chop out a hollow further along a pole. In any case, do not weaken the wood by cutting too deeply.

Two crossing poles can each be cut like a halving joint (Fig. 11-3D). In rustic construction it is unusual for poles to be crossed at the same level. Usually only a small amount is cut out of each piece. Saw across the rain at the limits of the cuts and chop out the waste with a chisel. Another way

of dealing with a crossing (which is appropriate when you are uncertain, until you assemble, where the crossing will come on one piece) is to leave a part round, but hollow the other to take it (Fig. 11-3E).

If pieces meet like a letter T, sometimes one can go over the other and be nailed. If they are to meet in the same plane, a simple nail through will not be very effective or strong. It is better to cut a notch for the end to go in (Fig. 11-3F). That would be even stronger if the end is shaved to make a parallel joint (Fig. 11-3G). Another joint that can be cut entirely with a saw has a V-shaped socket and an end to match it (Fig. 11-3H). Nails go through the long part into the end part in all these joints.

The V-cut is also suitable if the joint is diagonal (Fig. 11-3J). The squared end of the round piece then merely fits in, but the circumferences of the two pieces do not make a very close match. A better appearance is obtained by altering the shape of the notch and cutting the end to fit (Fig. 11-3K). These joints are often nailed into the end grain, but you get a better grip if the nail goes diagonally across the grain (Fig. 11-3L).

Another method of construction is very similar to doweling. The end of one piece is tapered to a smaller round and driven into a hole drilled in the other piece (Fig. 11-4). A drawknife or chisel will do the tapering. The hole can be made with a large bit in an electric drill, slightly more laboriously with a bit in a brace, or with an auger. In the simplest form of the joint, a hole is drilled about halfway through one piece, and then the tapered end becomes a drive fit in it (Fig. 11-5A). If the wood is dry, you can use a waterproof glue in the joint. Most glues are ineffective if the wood contains much sap. A nail could be driven across the joint.

A similar joint can have the hole drilled right through and the round end made long enough to pass through and project a little. Care is needed in tapering the end to leave a sufficient amount parallel, and in order to make a reasonably close fit within the hole. It might be sufficient to leave the joint as a drive fit or a nail can be driven across.

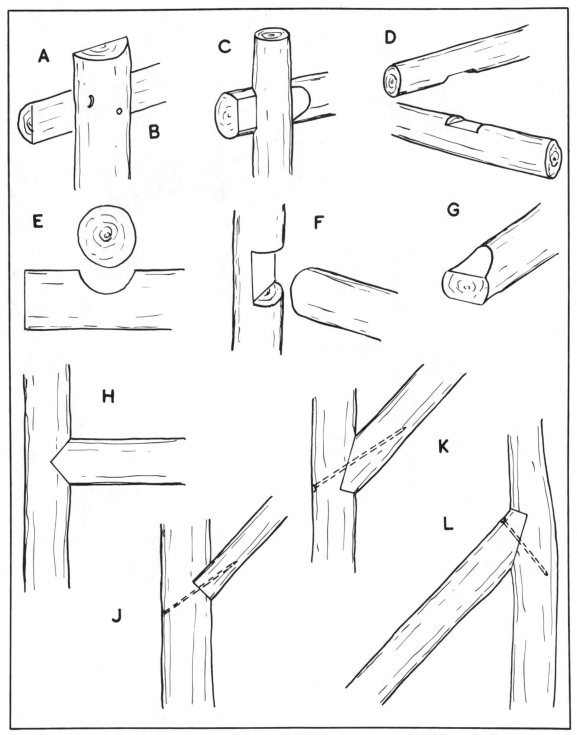

Fig. 11-3. Natural wood can be joined in several ways; usually it is a combination of notching and nailing.

Fig. 11-4. A tapered end into a hole makes a strong connection in rustic work.

A better way of securing is to put a saw cut in the end and drive in a wedge (Fig. 11-5B). This should be arranged across so that the spreading force is resisted by end grain in the holed piece. The other way could cause a split. It is advisable to make the wedge of hardwood even if the parts being joined are softwood. You can saw off the surplus end when the wedge is as tight as you can get it.

Even when it is not appropriate for the hole to go right through, it is possible to tighten an end by what is called *fox wedging* in the "blind" hole. This is sometimes done in cabinetwork. Drill the hole at least halfway through and make the end to fit it. Put a saw cut across the end and make a short hardwood wedge to fit it. It is common to give this a more obtuse angle than one for use outside. Put the wedge in the saw cut, arranged across the grain of the other piece (Fig. 11-5C), and then drive the parts together so the wedge pushing on the bottom of the hole spreads the end of the dowel (Fig. 11-5D).

There are not many uses for screws in rustic work, but you can use nuts and bolts (preferably galvanized). Screws do not hold very well in wood that is not fully seasoned, and neither do the square necks of coach bolts. It is better to use bolts with heads to take a wrench and put washers under them to spread the pressure. This is particularly important if it is wood with the bark still on. With a wrench on the bolt head and another on the nut, you can make a really tight joint.

DESIGN

Much rustic work is comparatively crude. That will not matter for many things and is acceptable, but it is important to design properly. It is possible to built what seems satisfactory at first and then find the assembly becomes shaky or goes out of shape. All of this can be avoided if you remember the value of the triangle. You cannot push a triangle out of shape. That is probably the most important design consideration when fashioning a structure from poles.

If you join three poles with one nail at each joint (Fig. 11-6A), it retains it shape. Do the same with four poles (Fig. 11-6B) and you can push it over (Fig. 11-6C). If you add a diagonal, that makes it into two triangles (Fig. 11-6D) and you cannot alter the shape. Every square does not have to be given a diagonal. Suppose you are making a tall, narrow frame for roses to climb (Fig. 11-6E). A diagonal in one panel will stiffen the whole thing (Fig. 11-6F).

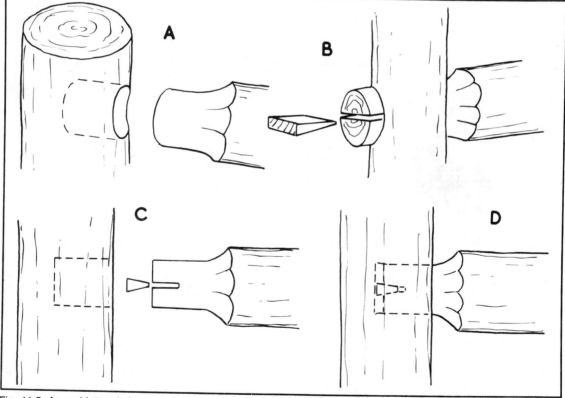

Fig. 11-5. An end into a hole can be strengthened by wedging.

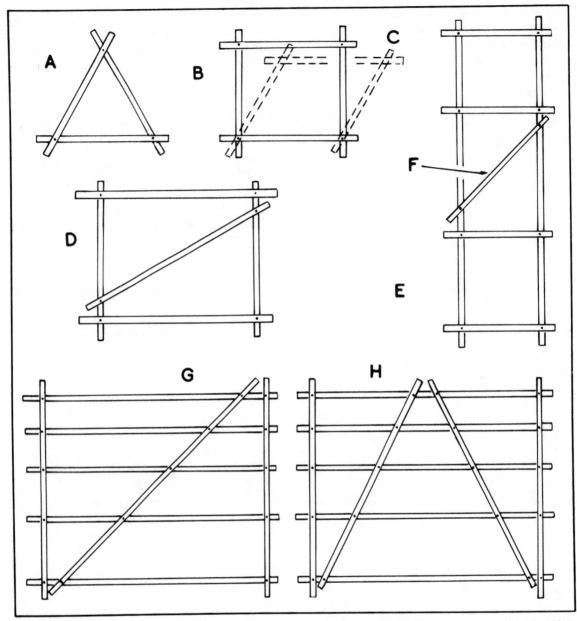

Fig. 11-6. A triangle (A) cannot be pushed out of shape like a four-sided figure (B, C). Diagonals are used to triangulate structures (D-H).

Suppose there are several horizontal poles on two uprights. Without diagonal bracing they could go out of shape. One diagonal across the lot provides triangulation (Fig. 11-6G) or a pair meeting at the center would serve the same purpose (Fig. 11-6H). Sometimes diagonals are taken both ways so that they cross. That will add a little more stiffness, but it is done mainly for the sake of appearance.

In some assemblies it is better to keep the

diagonals out of the way by making them struts at one or more corners of a four-sided assembly. This is almost as effective as full diagonals. Of course, driving uprights into the ground can provide all the stiffness in a frame that is otherwise four-sided without diagonals. Even then the stiffness might be imagined as coming from a diagonal from the point in the ground to the surface.

THREE-LEGGED STOOL

The idea of it being impossible to push a triangle out of shape can be taken a step further in noting that three legs will stand without wobbling on any surface. Our ancestors knew this and took care of unevenness in floors by making chairs, stools, and tables with three legs instead of the more obvious four. The milkmaid's stool for sitting anywhere in a cow shed is an obvious example, but three-legged seats can still have useful applications in a modern yard or garden. The average lawn might seem level until you find your usual seat will not stand without rocking. If you want to sit on an undeveloped surface, the usual folding chairs will not settle. Have a seat with three legs and it will be stable anywhere.

A version of the milking stool can have a round top (Fig. 11-7A) or you can use a split piece of log to make a rectangular seat (Fig. 11-7B). The round top could be a disc cut across a log, but some sections tend to dry out with radical cracks. Make sure your crosscut disc is dry and sound before using it. The alternative is to cut a disc with the grain across.

1. For the round stool, the disc can be about 12 inches diameter and 2 inches thick. To get the three legs equally spaced, draw a circle about 8 inches diameter—either on the disc or on paper—and step off the radius around it. The holes will come on alternate marks (Fig. 11-7C).

2. Prepare the pieces for the legs (perhaps 1 1/2 inches in diameter and 15 inches long). The holes and the tapered ends can then be about 1 inch in diameter.

3. The holes to be drilled at angles that will put the bottoms of the legs outside the rim of the top (Fig. 11-7D). This is advisable for stability.

4. If the holes can be made on a drill press, the wood can be packed up so the angles are drilled the same. If they are drilled freehand, a block of wood can be used as a guide to the angle (Fig. 11-7E).

5. Taper the legs to drive into the top, preferably to extend and be wedged, and then trim them level.

6. Invert the stool on a flat surface, measure equal heights for the legs (Fig. 11-7F), and cut them off. Remove raggedness and round the bottoms so there is no risk of a sharp stone breaking out the grain.

7. A stool with a split log top can be made in a very similar way. Arrange the leg holes so there is one central and two as widely spaced as the wood will allow (Fig. 11-7G).

8. Drill the holes at angles that will allow the legs to come outside the outline of the top (Fig. 11-7H).

9. Make and fit the legs in the same way as for the round stool. Level their bottoms after inverting and measuring, as before.

10. In both cases, level the tops by planing and sanding, but leave other parts as they are, to preserve the rustic effect.

FOUR-LEGGED BENCH SEAT

If a split log is to be used for a seat longer than needed for just one person, it is advisable to give it four legs. A long, three-legged seat could become unstable if the first person sits at the one-leg end. A bench seat suitable for two or three people, made from half a log possibly 12 inches in diameter, will be fairly heavy. Therefore, it is likely to be located in one position and rarely moved. The four legs can be bedded down level so the seat will not wobble. The legs could also be thicker than in the lighter seats described earlier. For a bench 6 feet long and about 12 inches wide, the legs should be about 3 inches thick (Fig. 11-8A).

1. The split log may need its top leveling if the split followed wavy grain. It need not be exactly half a log, if you want to make it lighter, providing there is sufficient width if the split is off-center. Of course, splitting one log gives you

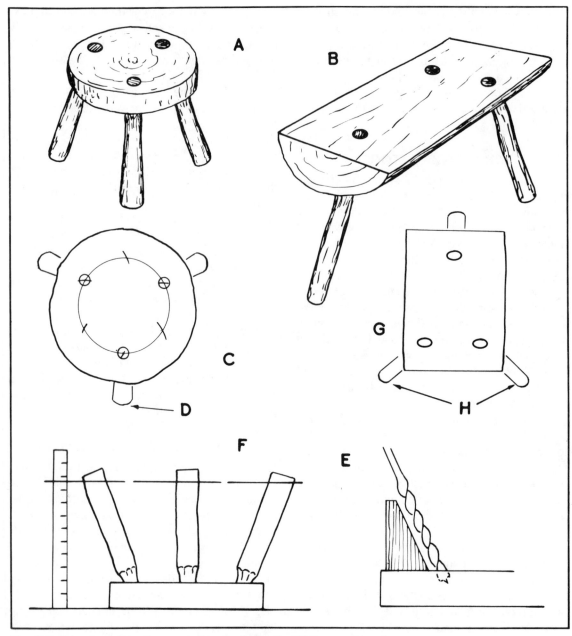

Fig. 11-7. Using three legs allows a stool to stand without wobbling on any surface.

pieces suitable for two bench seats, unless you have other uses for the second piece.

2. A long split log might leave edges that could be thin enough to be weak or sharp enough to be uncomfortable. This is particularly so if bran-

ches or other projections occur where the split comes. In that case, either remove just where these parts are (Fig. 11-8B) or make a straight cut along square to the top surface (Fig. 11-8C).

3. If the log section is fairly thick, there is no

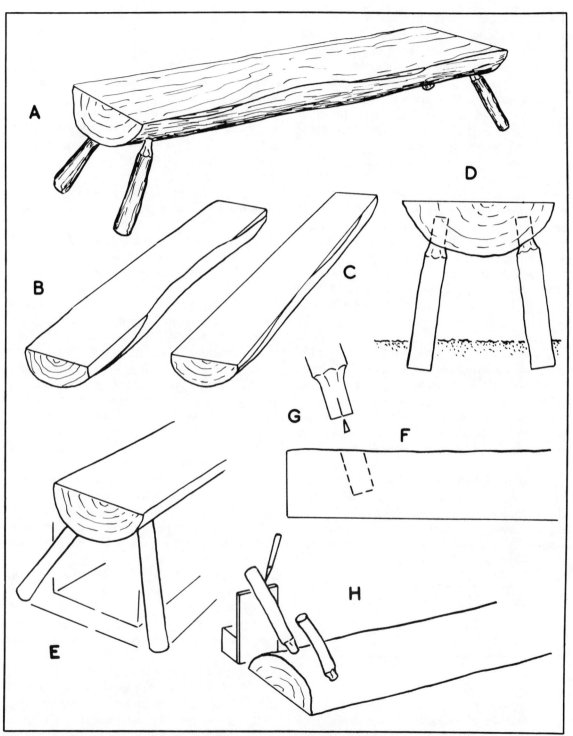

Fig. 11-8. A split log will make a bench top and splaying the legs gives stability.

need to take the legs right through. If the legs are 3 inches thick, the holes should not be less than 1 1/2 inches in diameter. If the bench is to be located in one position, it is advisable to let the legs into the ground. In that case, they could be almost upright (Fig. 11-8D). If they are actually vertical, you could not put a pair very far apart because there would not be sufficient thickness of log to drill nearer the edges.

4. If the legs are not to go into the ground, they should spread to come outside the width of the seat top and be near the end (Fig. 11-8E). Use an angled block of wood as a guide, but as you are drilling on the curved surface you will have to work mostly by eye. Slight variations between legs will not matter.

5. Take the holes in to a depth between 1 1/2 and 2 times their diameter (Fig. 11-8F). Anything less might become loose or let the legs wobble.

6. Prepare the legs to make a close fit. It might be sufficient to just drive them in, but fox wedging will strengthen the joints (Fig. 11-8G).

7. If the legs are to be let into the ground, it would be unwise to point them because that might cause them to penetrate more than you want when the seat is in use. It is better to leave them cut square and sink them in sunk holes (rather than try to drive them in). In very soft soil, a flat piece of wood could be buried under each leg.

8. If the legs are to stand on the surface, turn the bench over and measure from its top to get all the legs the same length. This can be done by measuring or a temporary gauge could be used (Fig. 11-8H).

Materials List for Four-Legged Bench Seat	
1 half log	72 × 12
4 legs	18 × 3

LOG TROUGH

A hollowed log trough in which plants can be grown makes a simple variation on the bench seat. Similar legs can be fitted, but they need only be short if all you want to do is steady the log just above the ground (Fig. 11-9A). Size can be whatever you prefer but there must be enough wood to make a hollow 6 inches or more deep (unless all you want to grow are small surface flowers).

1. Construction details are the same as the bench seat. It is advisable to complete the fitting of legs before doing any hollowing because the legs will provide stability for the wood while you remove the waste.

2. Decide on the outline of the hollow on the surface. Do not go too close to the sides and keep further in from the ends. The cut short grain might eventually open in splits if you do not leave much solid wood there. You could use a long ellipse, but it will probably be best to keep parallel to the sides and round the ends (Fig. 11-9B).

3. Fortunately, you do not have to produce a smooth inside to the hollow as it will be hidden by soil, but you must aim to get a reasonable shape even if you do not achieve it exactly. Bear in mind the shape you want, but remember to allow for any variations on the outside of the log and do not take the wood too thin. Much depends on the wood. With softwoods you should leave more thickness than you would with hardwoods. Allow for the legs going into more solid wood past the beginning of the hollow at each end or only just where it starts.

4. At the center of the hollow, make a series of holes approximating to the cross section of the shape you want (Fig. 11-9C). These do two things: they give you a shape to work to, and they prevent splits developing as you chop out wood towards the center.

5. It will help to drill more holes. You can do this with an electric drill or you can use a plunge router (if the router will take a bit large enough to be worthwhile). The holes are to break up the waste wood that has to be removed—so you can chop to a hole and break out the chip—without having to cut a long way each time (Fig. 11-9D).

6. You can remove a lot of waste with a wide stiff chisel, used with its bevel downward (Fig. 11-9E). If you use it the other way it will try to go deeper, but with the bevel down you can alter the

angle of cut and follow the curved bottom. Do all chopping from the ends toward the center.

7. A better tool is a large, stiff gouge that is beveled on the outside. Toward completion this will make a better shape than a chisel (Fig. 11-9F).

8. If you have to complete with chisels, a narrow one will follow the wide one to make a reasonable finish. It is only the visible part around

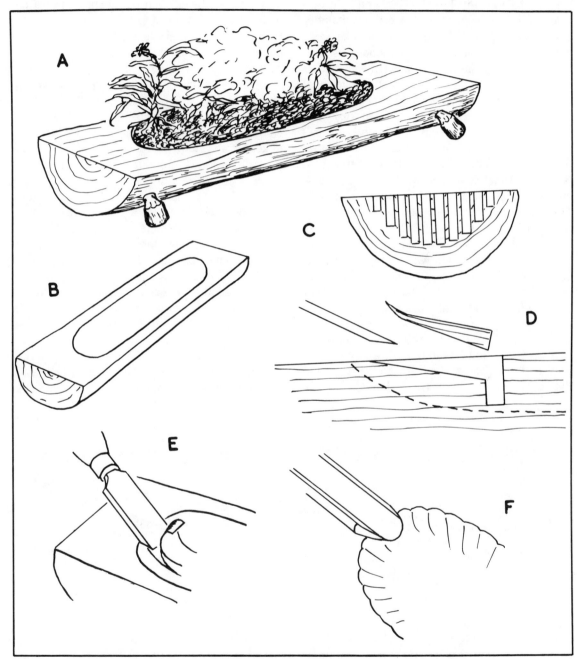

Fig. 11-9. A log can be hollowed by progressive drilling and chopping out with a gouge or chisel.

the edge of the hollow that matters in any case (providing you have scooped out enough for the soil).

SLAB-LEGGED BENCH SEAT

When a log is cut into boards at a sawmill, the outside has to be taken off to leave the remainder either with two parallel sides or with four flat sides making a rectangular section with rounded corners. If the log is irregular in length, the pieces cut off the sides might be thin in places and quite thick elsewhere. The slabs off the sides can be used for bench tops (although they are not half logs), and particularly if they came off logs of very large section and are plenty wide enough in themselves. If you use one of these slab offcuts, make sure there is at least 3 inches or 4 inches thickness to provide stiffness and adequate wood to take legs. There could be round legs, but in this case a pair of slab legs are suggested (Fig. 11-10).

1. These slabs will have finer edges than half logs and the edges might wander more than can be accepted. In that case you could make straight, parallel cuts square to the surface (Fig. 11-11A) in order to fully remove all waviness or to just take off the greater curves.

2. The legs are pieces with parallel thickness. In converting logs to boards, a sawmill will have to discard parts of boards cut after removing the rounded outer slabs. These slabs can be cut

for legs. If not, you must use boards 2 inches or more thick for legs under most tops (whether one-man seats or longer benches).

3. The legs can stand upright near the ends of the top or be splayed out slightly toward the ends. There is less need to get a wide splay as for individual round legs. Mark where the legs are to come and their thickness on the wood (Fig. 11-11B).

4. The slots for the legs can be cut with a chain saw. If you do not trust yourself to work accurately with a chain saw, use a handsaw, and then chop out the waste with chisel (Fig. 11-11C). Try to get the slots fairly deep. This depends on how thick the wood is, but a good depth is needed if the legs are to be a drive fit.

5. Have the grain upright in the legs. They could just have upright sides, but if there is enough width to cut they are better tapered (Fig. 11-11D). So that they are better able to stand on any surface without wobbling, cut away the bottoms with a V (Fig. 11-11E) or a curve (Fig. 11-11F).

6. Ideally, the legs will make a drive fit and will need no other fastening. Use a piece of scrap wood to spread the load as you drive them in (Fig. 11-11G).

7. If a leg is too thick, it can be pared thinner carefully. If it is too thin, shavings or thin pieces of wood can be used beside it in its slot. With the

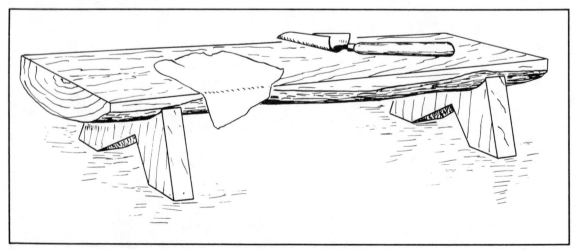

Fig. 11-10. A split log can be made into a bench with a pair of substantial slab legs.

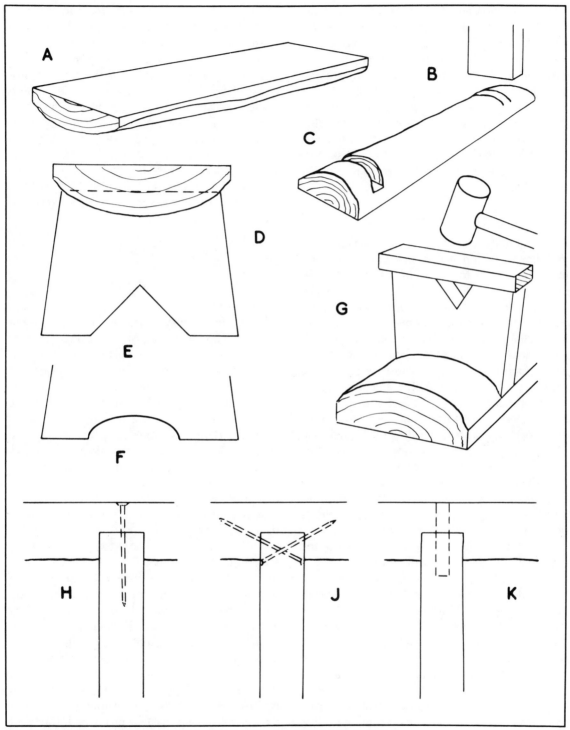

Fig. 11-11. Slots for the legs must match. They can be secured by nails or dowels.

risk of expansion and contraction in use, it is advisable to provide more fastening, even when the joints are tight at first assembly. Nails can be driven down through the top (Fig. 11-11H), but they would be more effective diagonal underneath (Fig. 11-11J).

8. If the wood is dry enough to take glue, you can glue the legs into their slots then drill down through the top for several dowels glued into each leg (Fig. 11-11K). There is no satisfactory way of wedging legs and screws would not be very successful.

LOG SEAT WITH BACK

Any stool or bench without a back can only provide limited comfort. If anyone wants to sit for long, they need a back to rest against. There are ways of fitting backs to log seats, but most of them involve prepared wood and are described later. It is possible to make a simple, one-man half-log seat into a chair with a back that still keeps the rustic appearance and will fit in with a wild garden background (Fig. 11-12). There may not be the comfort of a shaped or upholstered chair, but it is a step on from a simple flat seat.

1. Make a seat from half a log, with three legs, as already described. Allow for 12 inches to 15 inches at the two-leg end forward of where the back will come. The single leg hole must come far enough behind the back for the short grain not to be a source of weakness. That means a flat top 12 inches to 15 inches wide and probably 20 inches or more long. Round the front corners.

2. Prepare the seat parts, but do not fit the legs until after the back has been fitted.

3. The back is split from a log. It need not be as wide as the seat. Have it longer than needed until after making the joint.

4. Thin the bottom of the back to about 1 1/2 inches (Fig. 11-13A) and on that mark the width of the tenon (Fig. 11-13B). The sides should be parallel, but it does not matter if there is a slight taper in thickness.

5. Mark the mortise in the seat. The back should fit about 15 degrees to upright (Fig. 11-13C). Cut through the forward edge of the mortise to that angle, with enough waste to allow for working with the drill and chisel, but leave some waste wood at the rear edge of the mortise to trim later.

6. Cut the rear edge of the mortise progressively so you can try in the tenon. Get as close a fit as you can, but if it is not perfect the back will drive in and take care of slight inaccuracies. The tenon should go through and project slightly (Fig. 11-13D).

7. Round the top edge of the back to a curve you like the look of (Fig. 11-13E). The rounded back can be thinned toward the top if the full curve looks too bulky.

8. It should be sufficient to drive the back in. If it ever loosens, it can be driven further.

POLE CHAIR

If you have a supply of poles available, they could be made into a rustic chair. It will not have the comfort of one with upholstery or slung canvas or even a seat made from flat planed boards, but it is a piece of furniture that can be left outside and you can always put cushions in it for long use. The chair shown in Fig. 11-14 is intended to be made from poles all between 2 inches and 3 inches diameter. Their bark should have been peeled and they should be at least partially seasoned. Hardwood will be stronger and have a longer life, but a chair made from the more readily available fir and larch poles will have a reasonably long life. This is particularly true if it is soaked in preservative.

Sizes will have to be adjusted to suit available materials. Those shown (Fig. 11-15) will give a reasonably roomy chair. It helps if you can find a pair of curved poles to make the back legs. If you have to use straight ones, slope them back slightly and you can give the central support pieces a more comfortable angle by putting the crosspiece at the bottom in front of the legs and the top one at the back. If the legs have enough curve to provide a comfortable angle, both crosspieces are better at the back. The suggested construction uses bolts through for all parts that take much load. The fronts of the arms have dowel joints and the pieces mak-

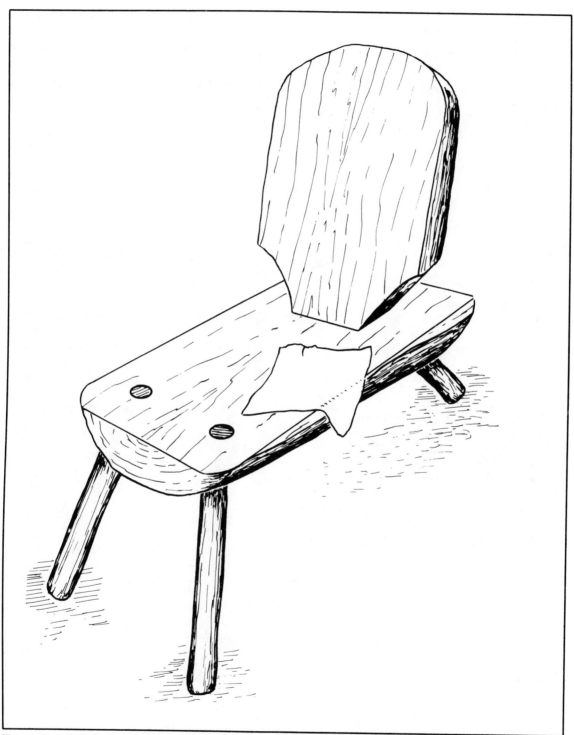

Fig. 11-12. A three-leg stool is made more comfortable by the addition of a back.

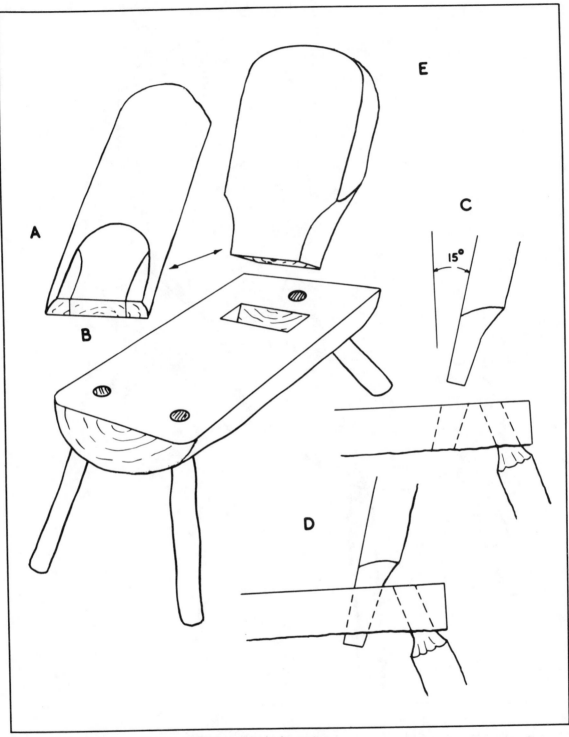

Fig. 11-13. The back is a split log cut to fit into a slot in the seat.

Fig. 11-14. This arm chair is made entirely from light poles.

ing the back and seat could be nailed. Bolts about 3/8 of an inch diameter should be satisfactory.

The sequence of construction has the two sides made first as a pair. Choose poles that will give a reasonable match. Otherwise you might finish with a chair that is not level or has a twist in it. The poles that are fitted closely to form the seat and back could be slightly thinner. If you are cutting long poles, the bottoms can be used for the structure and the tops kept for seat and back. It helps to sort your sections of poles before starting construction in order to make sure you are using the most appropriate pieces for particular parts and to check that you have enough. It would be possible to use flat boards for the seat and back.

1. Select the pieces for the rear uprights (Fig. 11-15A). See that they will make a pair and mark the positions of the bolts.

2. Make the front uprights (Fig. 11-15B). Mark bolt positions from those on the rear legs. The seat level could be up to 2 inches higher at the front. You could make it level, but it would be

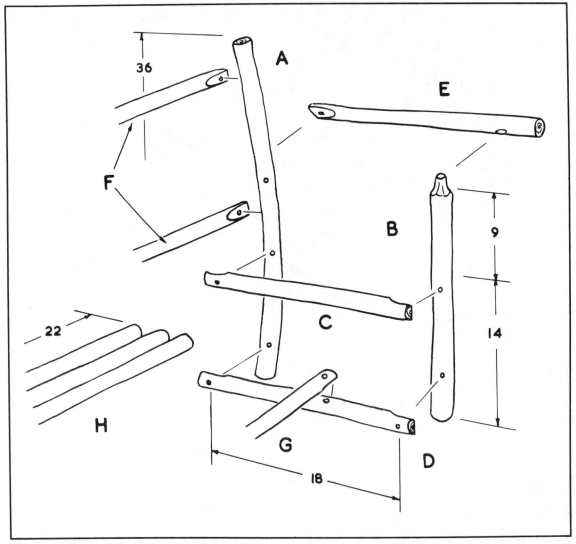

Fig. 11-15. Chair parts are drilled for bolts.

wrong to risk the chair finishing with the seat front lower than the back.

3. Prepare the tops of the front uprights to dowel into the arms. These are the only doweled joints shown, but you can use them for the lower rails if you prefer.

4. Make the seat rails (Fig. 11-15C) and the lower rails (Fig. 11-15D). All four should be the same (with flattened ends where they bolt against the uprights). Do not thin them too much. If a pole is 2 1/2 inches diameter, a flat about 1 1/2 inches wide would be enough.

5. Drill the bolt holes for the rails and assemble the pair of sides with the rails attached. Make the arms. Drill them for the front dowels, and then swing each arm to the rear upright so as to mark the part to be flattened and drilled (Fig. 11-15E). The dowels may finish as drive fits or be fox wedged. Round the forward ends of the arms.

6. Make the rails that go across the back (Fig. 11-15F) and the bottom rail (Fig. 11-15G). If you do not consider a single rail across the bottom will be stiff enough, there could be two. The poles forming the seat will supplement the strength of this.

7. Bolt on the back and bottom rails. Have the chair standing on a level surface and check that it stands upright when viewed from any direction. Tighten all bolts fully.

8. The seat poles are as many as are necessary to fill the space. If sizes vary, have the thicker at the front. If poles taper slightly, they can be put on in alternate directions. If the poles are reasonably parallel, they can be fitted as they are (Fig. 11-15H). If there are inequalities or lumps where twigs were attached, it may be better to get meeting surfaces reasonably matching by work with a chisel or plane.

9. Let the seat poles project through to come about level with the uprights. Nail them on. It would be wise to support under the seat rails while hammering to minimize shock and reduce the risk of splitting. In any case, drill clearance holes in the seat pieces and pilot holes, if thought necessary, in the rails.

10. The back is made up of vertical poles arranged similarly to those of the seat. They could be the thinnest pieces in your collection of poles. Tops could be cut straight across, but a curve improves appearance. In any case, take the poles high enough to provide back support. Remember, however, that this is not supposed to be a lounger with the back high enough to give head support.

11. The many parts tightly bolted and nailed provide mutual support. This should be adequate in a structure of this size, but if you find that your chair seems likely to develop loose joints in the back to front direction—possibly with users tilting back on to the two back legs—you could triangulate by putting diagonals between the legs and rails below the seat. Make the diagonals in a similar way to rails, and bolt them from near the lower rails on the rear upright to underneath the seat rails on the front uprights.

12. The wood could be left to weather to a natural greyish color, but it might be better to treat with a preservative. The posts could be given several coats of linseed oil that will finish most woods to a golden sheen. The oil takes a long time to fully dry so the treatment should be given a long time before the chair is used.

POLE BENCH

A longer seat could be made by extending the pole chair to make it wide enough to seat two or more, but it might need stiffening and bracing. The bench shown in Fig. 11-16 is similar in many ways, but it is braced and makes more use of dowel joints. The seat area is more substantial. Some of the parts shown with dowels could be bolted if you prefer. Sizes and layout will have to be adjusted to suit materials, but the measurements shown for the chair can be used as a guide to height and width (Fig. 11-15). The length will be about 48 inches to seat two persons.

Poles up to 3 inches in diameter are suitable. Preferably the poles should be hardwood and they should be stripped of bark. The uprights and main lengthwise parts should be from the thicker parts of the poles, but rails and diagonals could be thinner. The seat is made up of slab offcuts from a sawmill or from split logs, possibly 5 inch or 6 inch wide.

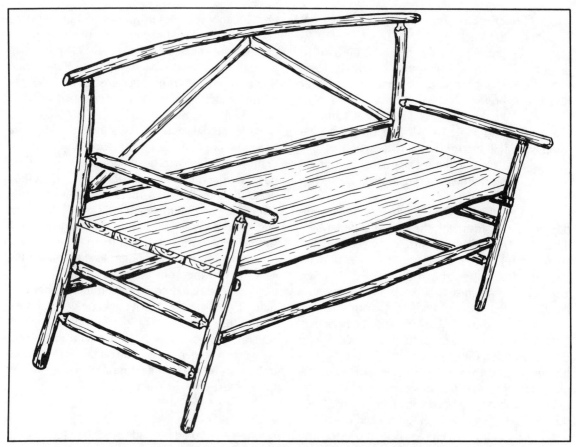

Fig. 11-16. The main parts of the bench are made from poles and the seat can be split logs.

Obtain sufficient wood, before you start making parts, so that you have enough and can match particular pieces to suit the construction. Do not use pieces with large knots, particularly for long parts, because these are weak spots.

1. Curved pieces that make a reasonable match are valuable for the rear uprights (Fig. 11-17A), but because they will be further apart slight differences in shape will not be as apparent as in the chair. If you have to use straight pieces, assemble the ends so they slope back slightly.

2. Choose straight pieces of similar thickness for the front uprights (Fig. 11-17B). Except for the seat bearers, which should be bolted, the parts between the end uprights are all doweled.

3. Mark where the holes for dowels are to come on all legs. Make the bottom rails (Fig.

11-17C), but do not drive in the dowel ends yet.

4. Make the seat bearers (Fig. 11-17D), but do not drill them until after the rails and uprights have been finally assembled. They can have their front ends slightly higher than the rear ends.

5. Make sure the tops of the rear uprights are at the same height, and then cut the dowel ends there (Fig. 11-17E). Do the same at the front.

6. Join the uprights with their rails. See that the ends match. Drill for and bolt on the seat bearers. If their top surfaces are not level, true them with a chisel or plane.

7. Make the arms to extend forward of the front uprights a short distance and round those projections (Fig. 11-17F). Fit their dowels into the rear uprights first, and then join the arms to the front uprights.

8. There are two lengthwise rails below seat level (Fig. 11-17G and H) and one forming the base of the back (Fig. 11-17J). These are all the same except for variations due to different wood sizes.

Make these long rails and drill the uprights for them.

9. Join the end assemblies with these lengthwise rails. As with all dowel joints, get them

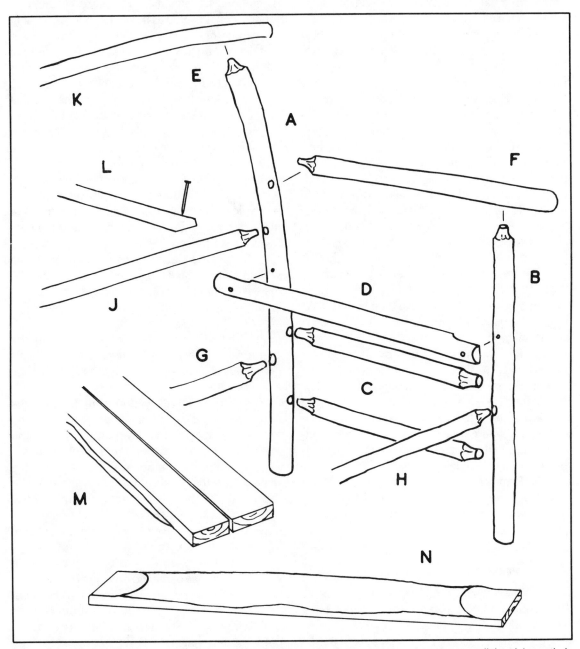

Fig. 11-17. Bench joints are made with tapered ends fitting into holes. The seat boards are cut parallel and have their rough surfaces downward.

as tight as possible with either good drive fits or fox wedging. For further security, nails can be driven across the joints.

10. Check that the assembly so far stands upright on a flat surface when it is viewed from any direction.

11. The top back rail (Fig. 11-17K) looks best if curved, but it could be straight. It might be thicker than the other poles. Drill it for the rear upright dowels and fit it in position.

12. The pair of diagonal struts are there to provide lengthwise stiffness as well as for the sake of appearance (Fig. 11-17L). For greatest stiffness they should be cut to fit closely into the corners at their outer ends and should butt tightly against each other at their centers. If they have to be forced in, that is an advantage. Secure them with nails.

13. The seat boards are made with the log section outline underneath. The tops can be left from cleaving or as sawn slabs from a log. Although they could be used with the thin edges together, it would be better to make them parallel, either completely (Fig. 11-17M) or partially, with just the greatest curves cut off. They can then be mounted almost touching, but with narrow gaps for rain to run through.

14. Prepare the undersides by paring down the ends (Fig. 11-17N) to rest on the seat bearers. Do not take the ends any thinner than essential or they will be weakened. If you have to reduce the width of a board to fit in, let the narrow one be at the back where it takes little load. If there are variations, put the thickest board at the front. Nail the seat boards to their bearers.

15. Remove any raggedness, but sanding would be inappropriate to a rustic piece of furniture. Leave the wood bare or finish it as described for the pole chair.

PERMANENT RUSTIC TABLE

Natural poles make very good supports for a table. They could be laid together as round rods for a rather crude table top, but it is probably better to use poles for supports only and have boards, plywood, or other smooth material for the top. The framework could be arranged to leave outdoors so that the top lifts off and is stored under cover when not required. This table (Fig. 11-18) has a permanent top made from cleft boards or sawn slabs. It is intended to remain in one place all the year round. It might serve as a bench while working in the garden or it could be used for picnics. Sizes will depend on available materials, but a width of 24 inches or 30 inches and a length of 48 inches might be considered. The usual height for use as a bench or for sitting at with normal chairs is about 30 inches from the ground to the working surface.

For a bench of this size, the legs and crossbars could be 3 inches or 4 inches diameter and the top could be made from split logs or slabs upwards of 6 inches wide. Construction is best done on site, with very little prefabrication, so the pieces should be too long at first to allow for cutting as they are fitted. Almost any woods can be used if they are treated with preservative.

1. Sort the pieces for the top. They settle the width you will make the table (Fig. 11-19A). Trim the edges straight and flatten the surfaces that will be on top. Leave the pieces overlength at this stage.

2. The supports should be about 9 inches in from what will be the ends of the table. Mark the positions on the ground. Check distances apart both ways and measure diagonals to see that the assembly is square.

3. Drive in posts (Fig. 11-19B). Measure the height you need (allowing for the crosspieces and top). Use a board with a level on it to check and mark the heights to cut off the tops of the posts.

4. Make the crosspieces (Fig. 11-19C) the same length the width of the top will be. Notch them and nail them over the tops of the posts.

5. Check the flatness and level of the tops. If necessary, plane off so there is a reasonable flat top to bear the top strips.

6. Start at one side and mark one top strip with the positions of the crosspieces. Then cut and chisel out the waste so that the strip will fit over the crosspiece (Fig. 11-19D). Adjust the grooves so the strips will rest in place without rocking. Do not fix at this stage.

7. Do the same with the next strip, but you

Fig. 11-18. The table has its legs into the ground and the top made with pieces of log with their rough surfaces downward.

will have to adjust the depth of the grooves to get the top surfaces matching.

8. Continue across with the other strips. Regulate the depths of the slots so you get a reasonably flat top. If too much is cut out, packing pieces can be put in. When you are satisfied with the level, nail on all the parts of the top.

9. Mark across the ends and saw them level. Remove sharpness all round. The table will probably be best left untreated.

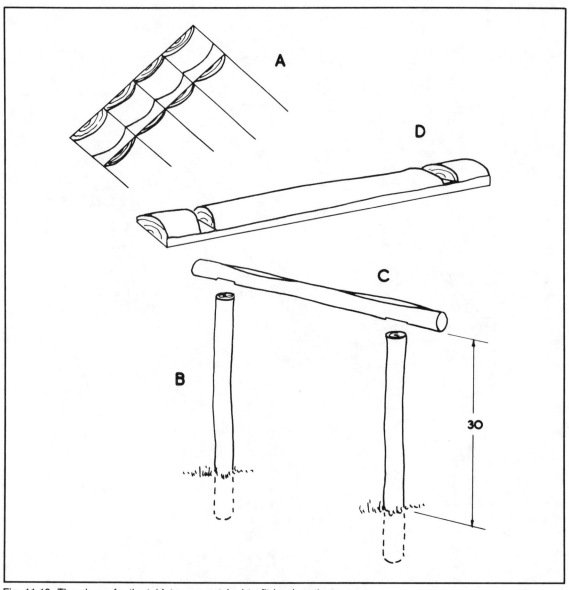

Fig. 11-19. The pieces for the tabletop are notched to fit level on the supports.

PORTABLE RUSTIC TABLE

A nonfolding portable table framework can be made from light natural poles. It could support a top made of plywood or boards held together with battens. Keep the top under cover when not in use.

Construction could be by overlapping parts, bolting them or just nailing them, but a neat construction is with doweled ends into holes in the legs. Because the legs should be thicker than the rails, the ends of the rails do not have to be reduced very much. The holes will not weaken the legs.

Choose straight poles for the top supports. The other parts do not have to be so straight and slight twists and bends will enhance the rustic appearance (Fig. 11-20). For a table about 40 inches by 20 inches and 28 inches high, the legs could be about 2 inches in diameter and the horizontal pieces not much more than 1 inch diameter after the bark has been stripped off.

1. Prepare the legs first (Fig. 11-21A) by marking the positions of the holes in all of them. Remember to pair the legs. Drill through at all positions (3/4 inch or 7/8 inch diameter may be suitable).

2. Make the straight pieces that will bear the top. Reducing the ends so they can go right through the holes and project slightly (Fig. 11-21B).

3. Use these as a guide to cutting the lower rails (Fig. 11-21C).

4. Assemble the opposite ends while checking them for squareness and that they match each other.

5. To hold the shapes, nail on diagonal struts (Fig. 11-21D). Flatten the ends slightly where they bear against the legs, but otherwise they need no special preparation. Nail through the dowels. They can be left projecting slightly as a design feature or you can cut them off level.

6. In the long direction, the parts are held with two rails each side (Fig. 11-21E). Make them all the same (with dowels long enough to go through and project slightly). Be careful to drill squarely so that the legs will stand upright in the finished assembly.

7. If the top is to be made of boards, they need not be thicker than 3/4 of an inch for the sizes suggested. Put together enough boards to make up the width, with battens underneath in positions to

Fig. 11-20. A light rustic table can be made with parts pegged and nailed together to support a flat board top.

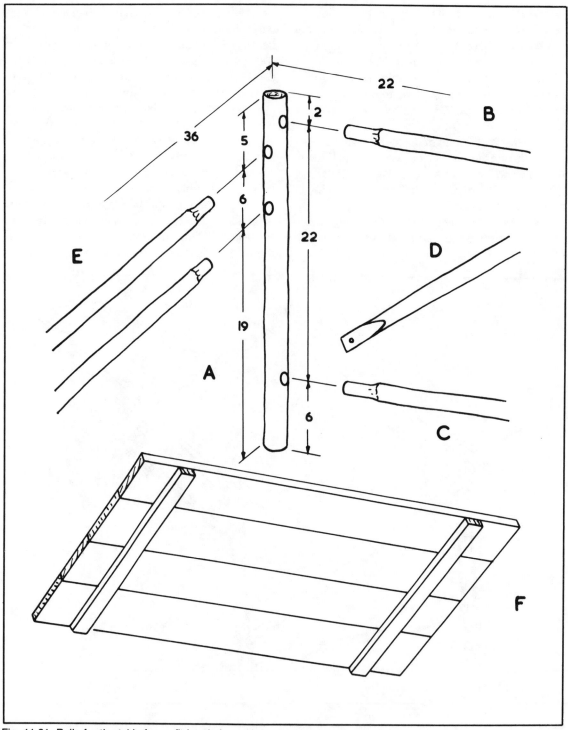

Fig. 11-21. Rails for the table frame fit into holes and the top rests on the crossbars.

come just inside the bearers, so they locate the top (Fig. 11-21F). If necessary, put another batten across at the center to prevent boards warping out of line. Tongued and grooved boards would make a firmer top than plain boards.

8. If the top is a piece of plywood, fit locating battens underneath in the same way.

Materials List for Portable Rustic Table	
4 legs	30 × 2 diameter
4 rails	24 × 1 1/4 diameter
4 rails	38 × 1 1/4 diameter
2 diagonals	30 × 1 1/4 diameter
4 tops	38 × 5 × 3/4
2 battens	22 × 2 × 1

GARDEN DIVIDER

An arrangement of natural poles to make an open fence between two parts of a garden will fit into most schemes better than anything more formal. The fence can then form a climbing frame for roses or other flowers or for vegetables.

Although the arrangement can be quite sim-

ple (Fig. 11-22), it will fail to please the eye if posts that should be vertical are not or rails that should be horizontal are not. If the divider comes on sloping ground, you will have to decide if the rails are to be parallel with the ground or are to be level. Posts should be upright in any case. A fence on uneven ground never looks right if it is allowed to tilt. If rails are to be horizontal, yet the ground is sloping, they will have to be arranged in step so that the rails at one level join a post nearer the ground than the next rows (Fig. 11-23A). The post lengths will have to be adjusted to suit uneven ground. Aim to get the rail spacing the same in each section. Remember, it is visual effect from a distance that matters.

1. For a divider with a gap for a path through is to be made, lay it out first with a stretched cord (Fig. 11-23B). Mark the position of each post with a peg.

2. Prepare the posts with pointed ends and keep them slightly too long so that the tops can be leveled after driving.

3. Erect the poles while checking that they are plumb. Sight along the row and this will help

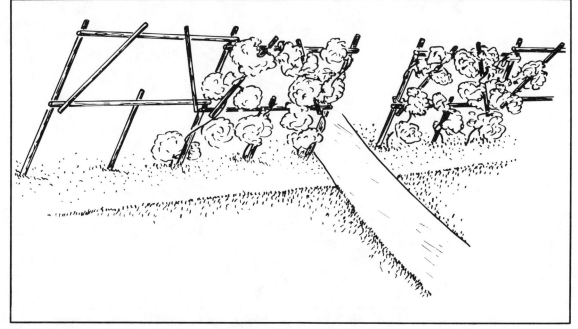

Fig. 11-22. A garden divider made from natural poles will support climbing plants to form a screen.

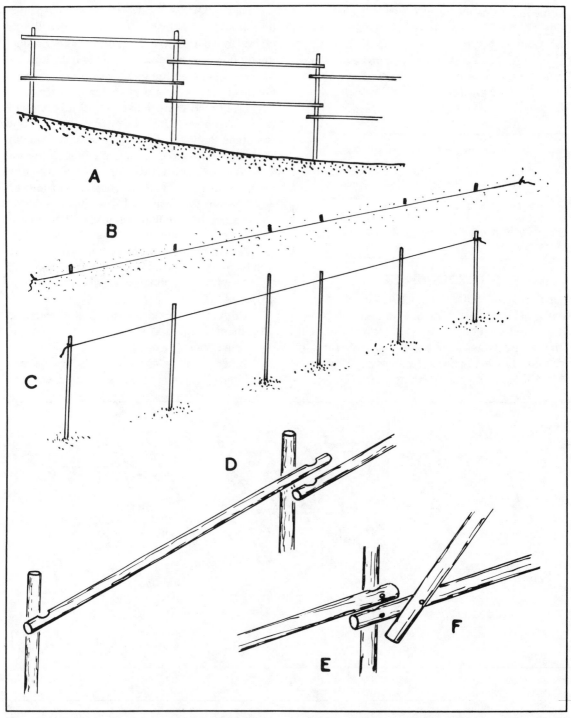

Fig. 11-23. On sloping ground, parts of a divider should be made level (A). Post positions should be kept straight (B, C). Parts can be notched and nailed or bolted together.

you check any that are out of true with others.

4. Use a cord tied to the end poles to check the levels of the tops (Fig. 11-23C), and then cut off the poles level. A sloping cut will shed water, but flat tops are common.

5. Mark the heights of rails on the posts. It is unlikely that the distances between the posts will all be the same. Work on pairs of rails in a section at one time.

6. Assuming the posts are reasonably straight, the distance between two at ground level should be the same at the top. Mark a rail at ground level and try it at the top position. If the distance there is very different, one or more posts might be out of plumb. Hollow the rail to fit around the posts (Fig. 11-23D) and nail it in position.

7. Mark the lower rail at its position, and then hollow and fit it. The rails could be cut off close to the posts, but they are shown overlapping slightly.

8. Do the same in the next section, but arrange the rails under the first ones (Fig. 11-23E). You can check proper positioning with a level. If you measure from the top of the posts, which were checked, the rails should come true. One nail through, or almost through, at each crossing should be adequate.

9. The diagonals can be lighter poles. Arrange them to overhang the rails and project upward to about the same level as the posts. One nail at each crossing should be enough (Fig. 11-23F). Their exact positioning is not important (providing you fit them in matching positions in each place).

10. A central post is recommended, and it should reach as high as the lower rail in each section. That can be driven after the other parts are erected. Much depends on what sort of climbing plants you have.

11. If you want a more closed lower section,

to obscure the view or to provide more for climbing plants to cling to, expanding trellis could be used (see Chapter 10).

RUSTIC PERGOLA

Natural poles make a good combination with climbing flowering plants such as roses. The round rods, whether left with bark on or peeled, often look better than sawn and planed wood in support arrangements. They can be used without the same precision. If there are irregularities or differences in spacings, it is not as important as with wood cut to regular sections. You can use up pieces of poles that do not always match, and it is possible to use hammer and nail joints with success. These advantages are apparent if you make a round climbing support.

Such a pergola could be any size from about 4 feet in diameter and upward. It should usually be high enough at the eaves to walk in, and the spacing of uprights will have to suit the roses or other plants; 18 inches is about right. The example shown in Fig. 11-24 is circular, about 6 feet across, and has a conical, open roof. Diagonal pieces brace the uprights and provide something for the climbers to cling to.

The uprights are straight poles with about a 3-inch maximum diameter. Similar poles can be used for the roof, but other parts can be pieces anywhere between a 1-inch and a 3-inch diameter. All of the construction is nailed. With the interconnected parts supporting each other, this is probably strong enough. If you prefer there could be some joints cut.

1. Mark out the circular base plan. You could use a strip of wood with a spike as center and a stick scratching against the end as it is pulled round. Alternatively, use a string that is tethered to a center spike and with another at the required radius scratching the circle (Fig. 11-25A).

2. On this circle, mark where the opening is to be. The gap can be 18 inches to 24 inches wide. Mark the positions of the other posts at about 18-inch intervals around the circle (Fig. 11-25B). Exactly even spacing is not important, but get the gaps about the same.

Materials List for Garden Divider

6 feet high and 8 feet between posts.
All stripped fir or other straight poles
Posts 3 inch to 4 inch diameter 96 inches long
Rails 2 inch to 3 inch diameter 108 inches long
Diagonals 2 inch diameter 60 inches long
Center posts 2 inch diameter 60 inches long

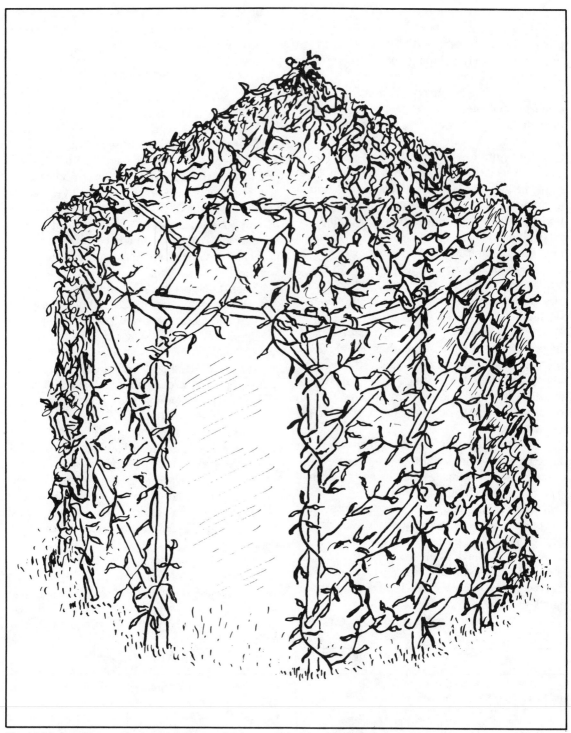

Fig. 11-24. A rustic pergola can become completely covered with a climbing plant.

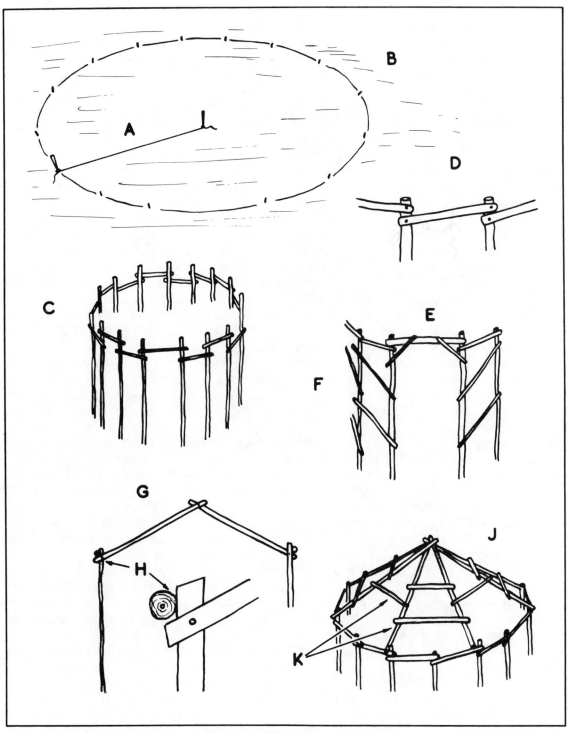

Fig. 11-25. The pergola is set out as a circle, and then it is built up around poles.

3. Drive the poles into the ground. There is no need to sink them to the depth they would have to be if they are to stand unaided, but get them upright and reasonably firm. Put temporary strips between them near the top (Fig. 11-25C) to hold the circle in shape.

4. Decide on the height you want the tops of the poles. Nail strips around at that level—with their ends overlapping (Fig. 11-25D)—and then cut off surplus wood above these joints. The assembly should now be rigid enough for the temporary strips to be removed.

5. Put light diagonal struts at the top of the opening (Fig. 11-25E) and go round adding diagonals to the sides (Fig. 11-25F). How many and how close depends on what you will be planting, but there should be no need to have strips closer than about 18 inches.

6. Choose two opposite uprights on which to mount a main truss. Pivot two poles together with a bolt and lift it into position so that it takes a pleasing angle (somewhere between 25 degrees and 45 degrees to horizontal), and then nail or bolt it to the posts. At the apex (Fig. 11-25G) and at the eaves (Fig. 11-25H), the ends can project slightly. Check that the assembly is put together with the rafters the same length.

7. Take other poles up to the apex. There is no need to do this from every upright, but if there are about six that should be ample. On a small-diameter pergola four may be enough. Attach to the upright poles in the same way as the main truss, but at the apex nail to the parts of the main truss (Fig. 11-25J) or carry one or two ends over them.

8. Unless the structure is very large, one or two strips between rafters should be enough for training flowers (Fig. 11-25K).

9. Remove raggedness at the ends. Cut off projections that might be knocked by a passing person. The wood could be treated with preservative, but it would be satisfactory if left in its natural state.

SIMPLE ARCH

An arch can stand anywhere on a path and provide a decorative feature with its climbing flowers or foliage. Its standard place, however, is at a divi-sion between parts of a garden. An arch can stand independently or it could be combined with a garden divider or fence. In that case, it can be simply made by carrying the divider end posts upward to support a shaped top, without doubling the posts or extending the thickness of the arch. If a broader arch is required, a suitable design is shown in the next project.

For a simple, single-pole-thickness arch, the uprights can be the end posts of the garden divider. If the arch is to stand unaided, you could have stout poles set into the ground (with struts if necessary). The project is a basic design (Fig. 11-26). All of the parts should be poles stripped of bark, and preferably at least partly seasoned so that they do not crack after being erected for a while.

1. Make the poles long enough to give clearance under the crossbar for anyone walking through even when there is trailing foliage. That means about 84 inches above the ground and probably 18 inches into the ground (Fig. 11-27A). Thickness should be about 3 inches or more.

2. Make the crossbar about the same diameter as the tops of the posts, or a little more, so as to cover the end grain and prevent rain from entering and causing rot. The bar can be notched to go over the flat post tops (Fig. 11-27B) or V notches can be used (Fig. 11-27C). In either case, drive nails downward into the posts.

3. If you want a ranch-style arch to serve as an entrance, with a hanging board carrying a name, a section cut diagonally across a log (Fig. 11-27D) would make a suitable name board. Hang it with chain or wire and make the assembly high enough for the board to clear heads.

4. For the more usual pointed arch, make two pieces that can be nailed or bolted to the posts and crossbar (Fig. 11-27E). This type of corner provides stiffness for the structure by triangulating. Make sure the nails or bolts are secure. At the top, the two pieces meet (Fig. 11-27F) with nails between them and a small brace across, or they can be notched into each other and allowed to extend slightly (Fig. 11-27G). There is no need to take the notches to half thickness; enough to flatten the meeting surfaces is all that is necessary.

Fig. 11-26. A simple arch can form a gap in a fence.

5. If you have doubts about the rigidity of poles into the ground with no other support, you can add diagonal struts. Much depends on the soil. Sinking the posts into concrete would be the most rigid structure. If the struts are to be fitted, it will probably be satisfactory to drive them in at about 45 degrees (Fig. 11-27H). Cut them too long and drive until they become secure, and then cut off

and bolt or nail to the posts (Fig. 11-27J). It should be sufficient to do this one way only, but they can be in both directions with the tops overlapping.

6. Many plants will climb almost anything, whether it is smooth or rough, but peeled poles can be fairly slippery. If your plants need help, there could be short pieces of wood nailed to the outsides of the posts to prevent turns of the plants

slipping down. Less obvious would be a few nails driven so that about 1/2 inch of the heads project.

DOUBLE ARCH

An arch based on four posts can be given thickness and the plants climbing over it will make a more impressive display than they could on a simple two-post arch. How thick you make it depends on needs and the situation, but an arch of normal size might be 18 inches thick. It would be less attrac-

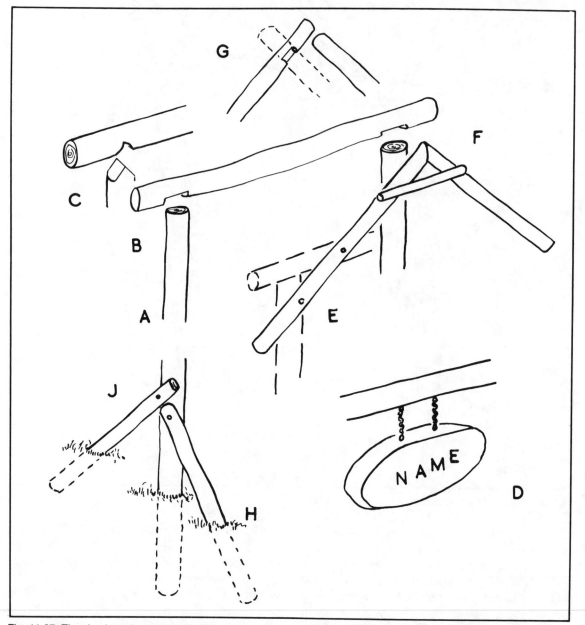

Fig. 11-27. The simple arch can have its parts notched together. Struts will be needed to the ground. A hanging name board might be appropriate.

Fig. 11-28. A double arch with its uprights in the ground is strong enough to stand unaided, and it forms a good base for climbers.

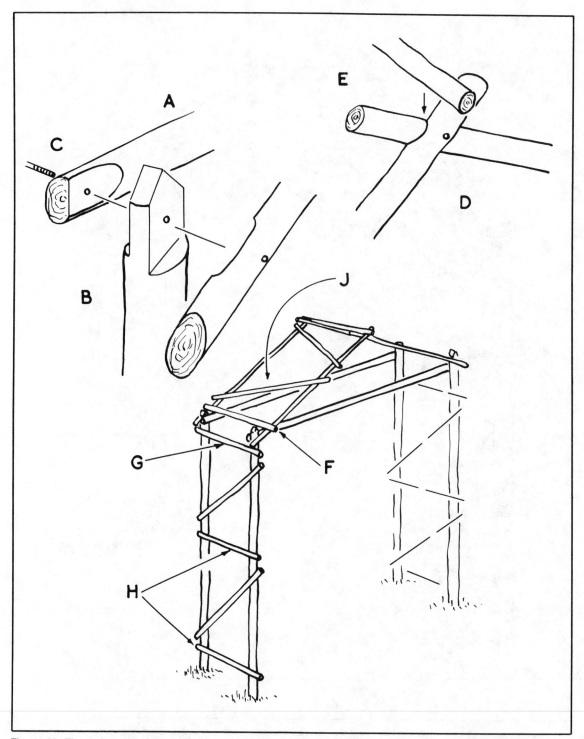

Fig. 11-29. The main parts of the arch should be bolted. Diagonal braces help to keep the assembly in shape.

tive if made rather thin; 12 inches ought to be regarded as the minimum for most double arches. In some situations, you might want to give more of a tunnel effect, and the arch could be 36 inches or more thick.

As shown in Fig. 11-28, the arch is assumed to be about 84 inches under the crossbar, about 48 inches wide, and 18 inches thick. For that size, the posts could be 2 inches or 3 inches thick and the other parts thinner. Much depends on the type of wood. The diagonals need not be much more than 1 inch thick (providing they are without flaws). All of the wood should be stripped of bark (unless the bark is very tight), and should at least be partially seasoned.

1. Select the wood for its locations. The main structures are made up of posts with the crossbars and rafters bolted through. Choose the best wood for these parts.

2. Lay a pair of posts flat on the ground with their tops square to each other and put a pair of rafters over them so as to mark the angle the posts tops are to be cut. The exact angles are not important, but rafters at 25 degrees to 35 degrees to horizontal will be about right. From this trial assembly, you can also mark the lengths of the rafters.

3. Cut the back of the top of each post with a notch to take the end of the crossbar, which will be flattened to fit (Fig. 11-29A). Cut a notch at the front. It will not matter if the cuts square across, but it will look better if it is about the angle of the rafter (Fig. 11-29B). Do not cut away the posts too much; there should be about half thickness left at the center. The tops of the posts can be pointed for appearance and to shed rain water.

4. Mark the positions of the posts on the ground. Besides being the correct distance apart, check that they are square by measuring diagonals.

Erect the posts while checking that tops are level.

5. Make the crossbars (with flats at the ends). Drill them and the posts for bolts (Fig. 11-29C). Put the bolts in with their ends extending outward.

6. Make the rafters. At the tops, notch each pair into each other (Fig. 11-29D) and bolt through. Check that the distance between bolt holes will be the same each side, and then drill and bolt to the posts.

7. The two assemblies have to be linked with short pieces. Put the first at the apex, resting in the V of the rafters (Fig. 11-29E), and nail it in place. This should steady the assembly.

8. Put more pieces on the rafters above the posts joints (Fig. 11-29F). Check that the assembly has not gone out of square by seeing that these pieces are the same length.

9. There could be two more pieces put across just below the crossbar joints (Fig. 11-29G).

10. What other pieces are put across depend on the pattern of climbing plants you hope to arrange. There could be another piece across level near the ground and one halfway, at each side, and then diagonals between them (Fig. 11-29H). Some of these could be merely nailed on without preparation, but the nailed joints are better if the ends of the pieces are flattened slightly where they contact the posts. Of course, the pieces brace the whole assembly, but only a few are needed for stiffening and the main concern is to provide places for climbers to grip.

11. Put a few more cross pieces on the rafters (Fig. 11-29J) and diagonals if you prefer. To get the plants to provide a good coverage at the top, closer supports are needed than on the vertical sides.

12. If the posts have a good grip in the ground, the whole arch should be very firm and rigid. If necessary, diagonal struts could be taken outward near the base.

Chapter 12

Seats

Seats of various sorts are the commonest outdoor furniture. Some seats are described in Chapter 11, but they are made from natural poles and logs. There is a place in a garden for more formal furniture that is made from wood sawn to thickness and usually to width as well. If it is planed, the furniture can be given a painted or varnished finish. Such furniture is durable and good looking in a planned garden with paths and lawns. Rustic seats and other furniture are more appropriate to natural surroundings.

Furniture of this sort is of a standard better than hammer-and-nail construction. Although the work might not be in the same class as cabinetry for indoor use, many of the same joints and techniques should be used. A few parts can be nailed, but where nails might be used in cruder construction it is more common to have screws. Mortise and tenon joints have more uses, but dowels can be substituted for many of them.

For this sort of furniture, the wood chosen should be of reasonable quality. It could be softwood. Many of the pines and firs that are resinous and with fairly straight grain are suitable. Hardwood should be more durable and some very long-lasting outdoor furniture is made of oak and teak. Most planed wood can be used in stock sizes. Allow for it being at least 1/8 of an inch less than the specified size (before planing).

There is not much use for plywood, but it can be built into table tops and other areas where a large, clean expanse is needed. It should be exterior or marine quality and preferably framed around the edges with glued strips that prevent moisture getting into the edges of the veneers.

If you will be cutting joints and using glue in them, the wood should be dry. If parts are only nailed or screwed, it is not so important that the wood is fully seasoned. Glue will not hold properly if there is excess moisture in the wood, and joints that are made tight at first might open as the wood dries out. If you obtain wood already cut and planed from a lumberyard, it should have been seasoned. It is advisable to get it ahead of your needs and keep it for at least a few weeks before working on it.

In general, it is better not to mix woods in construction, but you could make a framework of hardwood and fit slats for seat and back, for instance, made from softwood. Parts that are in contact with the ground are the first to develop rot. Oak and some other hardwoods have a better resistance to rot than softwoods. Keep in mind that wood can be treated with a preservative. If you are planning a painted finish, make sure the preservative is suitable for use below paint.

STOOL

There are many uses for a stool in your garden and yard. It is something steady to stand on to gain height, and it can be used for sitting by children. You will be glad to have a low seat as an alternative to bending or stooping when dealing with garden chores (Fig. 12-1). Two identical stools can be used

with a plank across for working or sitting.

The wood suggested is all the same section; for this stool it is 7 inches wide and 3/4 inch thick, before planing. The same method can be used for stools or benches of other sizes.

1. Make a drawing of one end to get the length and angle of the leg (Fig. 12-2A). For stability, the bottom of the leg should come below the end of the stool top.

2. Mark out and cut the two legs (Fig. 12-2B). The angles at the top, bottom, and notches should be the same angle as on the preliminary drawing. The V cutout is made toward a hole to reduce the risk of a split developing.

3. Cut a piece down the middle to make the two sides (Fig. 12-2C). Bevel the ends and mark where the legs will come. Drill for two screws at each position.

Fig. 12-1. A simple stool has many uses in a garden and yard.

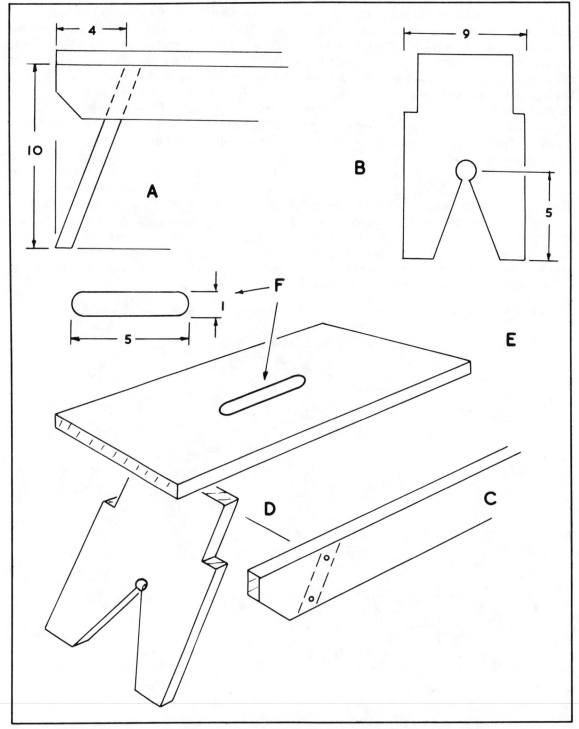

Fig. 12-2. The stool has feet angled to give stability. A slot in the top provides a hand grip for lifting.

4. Join the sides to the legs (Fig. 12-2D), preferably with waterproof glue as well as screws. Brass or galvanized steel screws should be used. An exception is if the stool will be kept under cover most of the time. In that case, plain steel screws might be good enough. Check squareness of the assembly when viewed from above, and that the legs will stand level on a flat surface. If there is a tendency to twist, leave the assembly for the glue to set with a weight on top.

5. Make a top to glue and screw on (Fig. 12-2E). The hand hole at the center is useful for picking up and carrying (Fig. 12-2F).

Materials List for Stool	
2 legs	12 × 7 × 3/4
2 sides	18 × 3 × 3/4
1 top	18 × 7 × 3/4

BENCH

A bench could be made like a large stool, but as you design higher and longer, for the sake of stability, it becomes advisable to provide a wider spread to the feet. That could be done by sloping the sides of the stool legs, but the bench shown in Fig. 12-3 has a different method of construction. Stiffness and strength are provided by a central piece of 2-inch-by-4-inch wood under the top (instead of the pair of pieces at the sides).

1. Set out the intended end view (Fig. 12-4A) in order to get the leg length and angle for cutting joints.

2. Make the two legs, but do not cut the top slots yet (Fig. 12-4B). They taper to the top, but the bottom is cut with a V into a hole. The top and bottom should be made to the angles found in the preliminary drawing.

3. Cut the center rib to length. Check that it has a flat top surface to fit against the bench top. Mark on it the angles the legs are to be and the depths of grooves that will leave about 1 inch solid wood at the center (Fig. 12-4C). The groove widths should be a close fit on the legs.

4. Mark the widths of the grooves in the tops of the legs and angle both the tops of the legs and

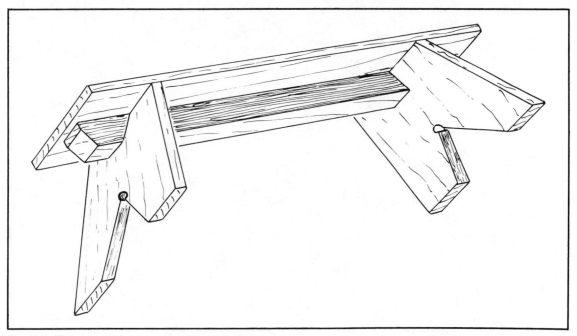

Fig. 12-3. This bench has a central stiffening member.

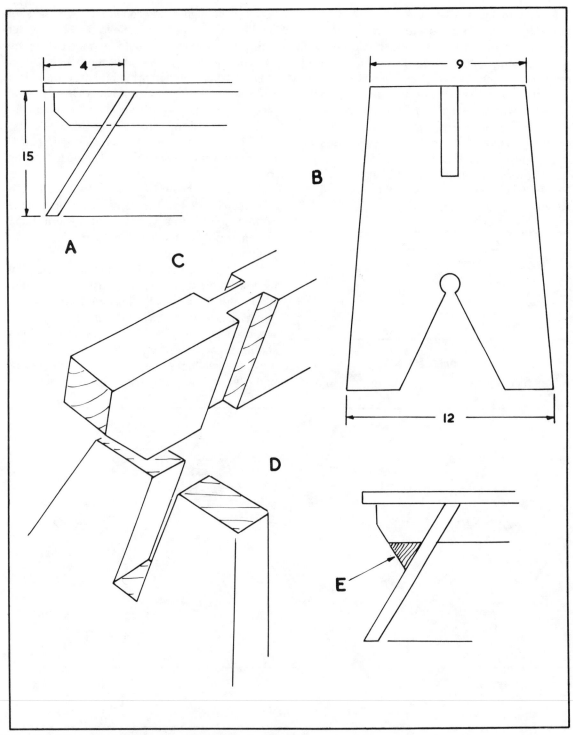

Fig. 12-4. The bench legs are notched into the central piece.

the bottoms of the grooves to suit (Fig. 12-4D). Leave a little extra length on the tops of the legs to plane level after assembly.

5. Drive in and glue the legs to the rib. With many woods and firm joints this should be all the construction necessary, but if the fit of the joints is not as good as you wish or you have doubts about the strength of the wood there could be stiffening blocks glued and screwed between the parts (Fig. 12-4E).

6. The top is a plain board and has rounded corners and edges. Use glue and screw it downward into the central rib and the tops of the legs. If you prefer not to have screw heads showing on top, they could be counterbored and have wood plugs glued over them. An alternative is to use dowels instead of screws. Screws or dowels located near the edges of the legs are important to make a close, firm joint.

Materials List for Bench

1	top	48 × 9 × 1 1/4
1	rib	48 × 4 × 2
2	legs	18 × 12 × 1 1/4

TENONED BENCH

If you have quite thick slabs of wood available, they can be made into a substantial bench (Fig. 12-5). It will be heavy but in a garden that can be an advantage. The bench is unlikely to tip over and others are less likely to move it from where you want it to stay. Thicker wood is less liable to be affected by exposure to all kinds of weather. There is more labor in working the thick wood, but the techniques are simple.

The wood suggested could be as converted in a sawmill with little further treatment before you start on it. It does not have to be planed. The sections to look for are about 12 inches wide and 2 inches thick. They could be greater, but very much thinner would not be strong enough without additional bracing. The wood may have waney edges, but they would have to be eased to allow for users sitting without sharp or rough edges

touching their legs. That could be done without destroying the character of the waney edging.

1. Prepare the top piece of wood. If it has a straight edge, you can mark out squarely from that. If there are waney edges on both sides, it would be better to draw a centerline and mark out the joints squarely from that.

2. Decide on the height and draw the angle of the leg at one end (Fig. 12-6A). Set an adjustable bevel to that and keep it at that setting for all marking of the joints (Fig. 12-6B).

3. Cut the wood for the legs, but leave the pieces slightly overlength at this stage.

4. The joints should be schemed so the tenons are about square in section and the gaps between are about the same. It is better to set the tenons in from the edge than to make open mortises there. Mark the chosen spacing across the top of one leg (Fig. 12-6C) and use that as a guide for marking other positions.

5. Mark out the mortises (Fig. 12-6D) in each position and the tenons on the tops of the legs (Fig. 12-6E). Use the adjustable bevel to transfer markings to the correct positions on opposite sides. Allow for the tenons being too long when you cut them so that they can be planed level after assembly.

6. Cut the joints. Much of the work on the tenons can be done with a saw, but the angled bottoms of the legs will have to be cut with a chisel. Some of the waste in the mortises can be drilled out, but because of the angles final shaping must be done with a chisel.

7. When you are satisfied with the joint cutting, mark the lengths of the legs, including the angles at the bottom. Check them against each other. The bottom of each could be a V cut, but it is shown scooped to a curve (Fig. 12-6F). The legs are shown parallel, but they could be broadened toward the bottom for increased stability.

8. It might be sufficient to drive in the tenons, with or without glue, but for long-term security it is advisable to use wedges. Make saw cuts in the ends of the tenons before assembly. These could be straight across (Fig. 12-6G), but

Fig. 12-5. A heavy bench is useful to work on as well as to sit on.

they will make an interesting pattern if driven diagonally (Fig. 12-6H). All the wedges at one end could be same way or you could alternate the angles or pair them if there is an even number of tenon ends to be dealt with. Before wedging, make sure all tenons are driven in as tightly as possible. Level the tops of the tenons and wedges to complete the bench.

Materials List for Tenoned Bench
Approximate sizes
1 top	60 × 12 × 2
2 legs	60 × 12 × 2

PLAIN BENCH WITH BACKREST

A seat without a backrest might be a welcome sight when you need a brief rest, but if you want to sit for long you need support for your back. There are various degrees of complication in seats with backrests, but the example shown in Fig. 12-7 is simple in appearance and construction. In addition, it can offer reasonable comfort to tired bodies.

Most of the construction is with screws, but the lengthwise stiffening rail has mortise and tenon

joints at the ends. The material is planed wood, which may be a softwood finished with paint, or a durable hardwood could be left untreated. Sizes can be varied, but a top 14 inches wide is suggested at a comfortable height for sitting. The rear support is at a height and angle that should suit most users. How long to make the bench will have to be decided in relation to the available space and what wood you have, but a length of 6 feet will suit three people or even four for a short time.

1. Sort the available wood and relate it to an end view, which will control most sizes (Fig. 12-8A). Make a full-size drawing. Have the seat at a comfortable height and locate the backrest in relation to it. A slope of about 10 degrees from vertical will give a suitable angle for comfort and for attaching to the ends without reducing the useful width of the seat (Fig. 12-8B). To allow for the need for resistance against tipping back, draw the feet further back than forward of the end (Fig. 12-8C).

2. The ends could be tenoned into the seat supports and the feet, but they are shown overlapped and glued and screwed. Make the pair of ends carefully squared and mark where the rail will come (Fig. 12-8D).

3. Make the rail and cut tenons at its ends.

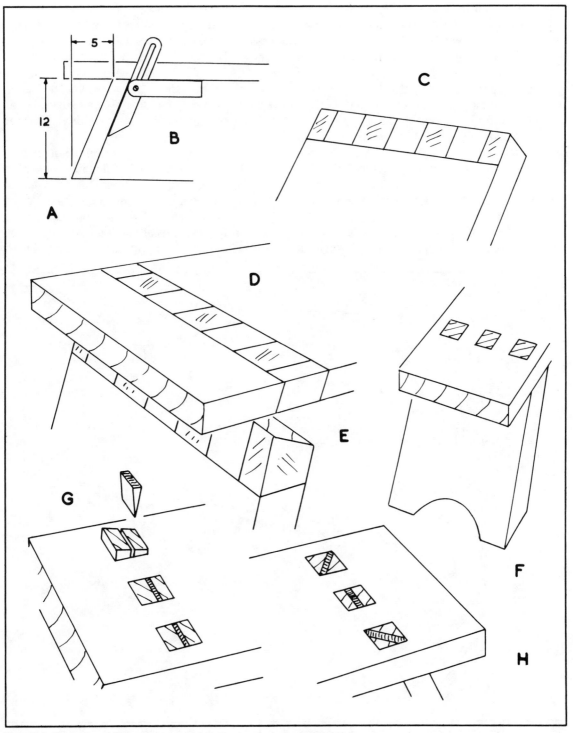

Fig. 12-6. The splayed legs are tenoned into the top and can be wedged.

They are the full thickness of the wood, but cut down to shoulders. If the tenons are a little more than half the total width of the rail, that will be right. Cut the mortises and tenons, but do not assemble these parts yet.

4. Glue and screw on crossbars on the upper surfaces at the tops of the legs (Fig. 12-8E), extending forward to support the seat.

5. Make the feet (Fig. 12-8F) and attach them to the outsides of the bottoms of the legs. Put pads under the feet (Fig. 12-8G). Make the pads wide enough to extend outward a little and come under the thickness of the legs. Check that the two legs match as a pair.

6. Make the backrest supports (Fig. 12-8H). Let the bottom of the support come close against its foot. At the top, cut away to let the backrest strip fit in. Round the top corners and take off the sharpness of all exposed parts. Glue and screw to the legs while checking that the two ends match.

7. Fit the rail to the legs. Put saw cuts across the ends of the tenons before assembly. Glue in the tenons and spread them with wedges. When the glue has set, level the tenon ends with the leg surfaces.

8. Make the seat (Fig. 12-8J). If you have to join boards to make up the width, they could have plain glued edges, be tongued and grooved, or there could be cleats across underneath. At the ends, allow the seat to project a short distance past the backrest supports around which they are notched (Fig. 12-8K). Round the extending corners

Fig. 12-7. A backrest increases the comfort of a bench.

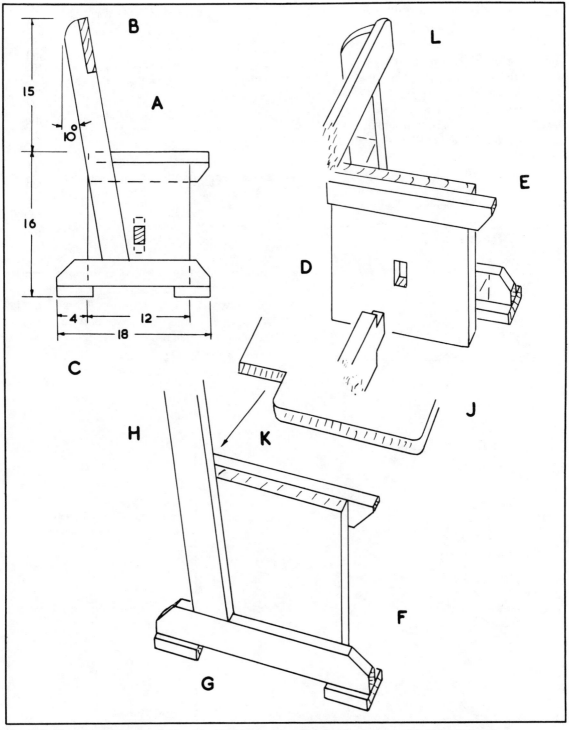

Fig. 12-8. The backrest is at a slight angle. Most joints are nailed, but the bottom rail is better tenoned.

and the front edge. Fit the seat by screwing into the supports and the tops of the legs. This will look best if the screws are counterbored and covered with wood plugs. Assemble on a flat surface and see that the seat will stand without wobbling.

9. Make the backrest (Fig. 12-8L). Let its ends extend the same amount as the seat. Round the corners and well round the front edges. Join to the supports with counterbored screws, in the same way as the seat.

10. There will probably be no need to sand the seat, but make sure there is no roughness left before painting or applying other finish.

Materials List for Plain Bench with Backrest	
2 legs	15 × 12 × 1 1/4
2 seat supports	14 × 2 × 1 1/4
2 feet	18 × 3 × 1 1/4
4 pads	4 × 4 × 1 1/4
2 backrest supports	30 × 3 × 1 1/4
1 seat	72 × 14 × 1 1/4
1 backrest	72 × 6 × 1 1/4
1 rail	70 × 5 × 1 1/4

BENCH WITH SHAPED SEAT

A flat seat becomes uncomfortable after a while. One with a hollow back-to-front seat is easier to sit on for a long period. A hollow can be arranged with a number of strips that run lengthwise instead of a single board. The lengthwise pieces can be of light section with frequent supports, or they can be stouter pieces that are strong enough in themselves. See Fig. 12-9. The method can be used for a bench of almost any length if supports are arranged not more than 60 inches apart. Here it is assumed that the bench is about 6 feet long and with two supports.

Although various sizes of wood can be used, it is suggested that all parts of this bench be made of 2-inch-by-4-inch standard sections. In some situations, the wood need not be planed. For good construction and a painted finish, it is better to have planed wood. It will not matter if there are a few small knots in the smaller support parts, but the lengthwise seat and back slats should be as clear of flaws as possible.

Fig. 12-9. A shaped seat is more comfortable than a flat one.

The support frames are made with halving joints. Other parts are held with screws and the back supports are bolted to the frames. The stout sections joined together will product considerable mutual support, but it is in the length that the benches often begin to become slack. This bench is braced with diagonal struts at the front.

1. Prepare the wood for the two frames. Check its width and use this information when making a full-size drawing of an end view (Fig. 12-10A). Start by drawing a line to represent the floor and another square to it for the bench front. Draw a line parallel to the floor 14 inches up and, on this line, measure 22 inches from the front to join at a slope to a point 24 inches from the front on the floor line. That gives your basic outline on which the other parts are drawn.

2. The pair of top pieces should be hollowed (Fig. 12-10B). Mark the width of the curve and its depth, and then spring a flexible piece of wood through the points so that you can pencil a curve.

3. So the bottom of each frame only stands at its ends, and is less liable to rock on uneven ground, mark similar curves in the bottom pieces (Fig. 12-10C).

4. From the full-size layout, mark and cut the parts of each frame (Fig. 12-10D). Cut back the top part at the front by the thickness of the front rail (Fig. 12-10E). Make a pair of frames with the joints glued and screwed.

5. Make the two backrest supports. They cross over the frame parts and will be bolted through (Fig. 12-10F). At the top, the backrest could be let in level, but it would be more comfortable if the notch is made so it comes at a slightly more upright angle (Fig. 12-10G).

6. Cut the bottoms of the backrest supports to match the bottom curve. Coat the meeting surfaces with preservative, if you are not gluing them, and bolt the supports to the outsides of the frames.

7. Have the four pieces ready for the seat. Drill them for counterbored screws into the frames (which will come about 9 inches in from the ends). Round all exposed edges and ends.

8. Make the front rail to fit into the notches in the frames (Fig. 12-10H). Screw it in place and

immediately screw on the seat pieces so that the assembly is held rigidly. Check squareness as you assemble and see that the frames will be upright. Work where you can stand back and view the bench from many directions.

9. Add the backrest (Fig. 12-10J). It should be the same length as the seat parts and it should be well rounded on the front edges and ends. Check that the backrest is level and the supports are upright when viewed from the front. Attach it with counterbored and plugged screws.

10. Make the diagonal struts at the front (Fig. 12-10K). They should be at about 45 degrees. Fit them behind the front rail (with bolts through). At their lower ends screw them into the frames.

11. Remove any roughness and finish the bench with paint or preservative.

Materials List for Bench with Shaped Seat

4 frame pieces	24 × 4 × 2
4 frame pieces	16 × 4 × 2
2 backrest supports	34 × 4 × 2
1 backrest	72 × 4 × 2
4 seat pieces	72 × 4 × 2
1 front rail	60 × 4 × 2
2 struts	24 × 4 × 2

CHAIRS

A chair could be made like a bench, but kept short enough to seat only one person. If all that is required is a stool, any of the bench designs could be made short and without a back. A short bench would make a satisfactory seat (with the same limitations of comfort as if made longer).

Individual garden seats are usually expected to be more comfortable and have wider seats for two or more people. They are generally too elaborate to be called benches. Arms are often included in these single or multiple seats. Besides their obvious additional comfort, they have a structural advantage. With the lengthening of the front legs and the arm framing, there is extra bracing involved that stiffens the chair. This provides better resistance to the sitter who tilts it back or sideways.

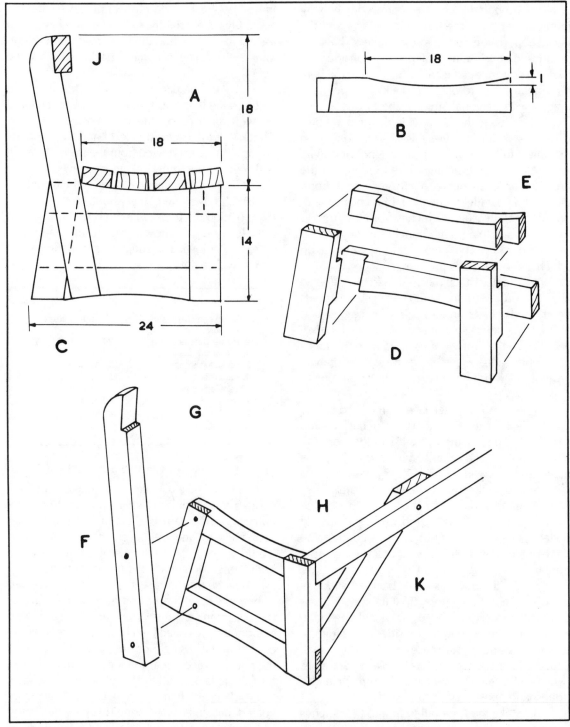

Fig. 12-10. The parts of the substantial assembly are mostly halved together and bolted.

FLAT STRIP ARMCHAIR

Although some of the better armchairs for use outdoors have joints very similar to indoor furniture, it is possible to make a satisfactory chair with flat strips and most joints screwed. They could be nailed, but it is better to use glue and screws to make a durable chair that will stand up to exposure.

All of the parts of this chair (Fig. 12-11) can be strips of the same section. However, there would be an advantage in making the four legs thicker. Although the parts of the chair are square with each other, the back support slopes and your posture when sitting should be comfortable (al-

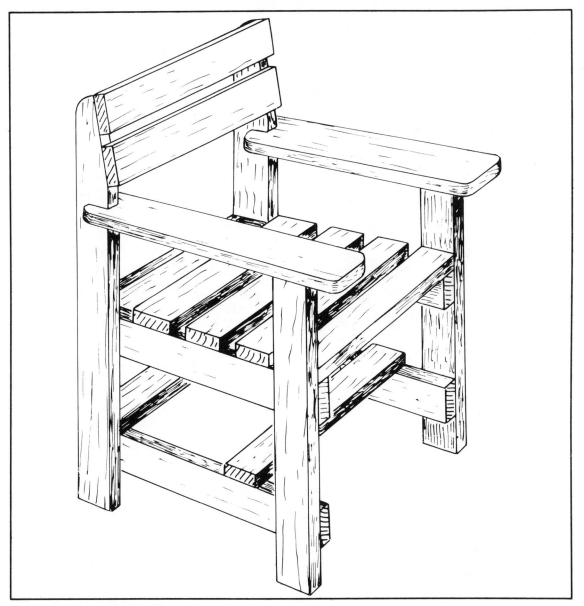

Fig. 12-11. A strong chair is suitable for leaving outside in all weather.

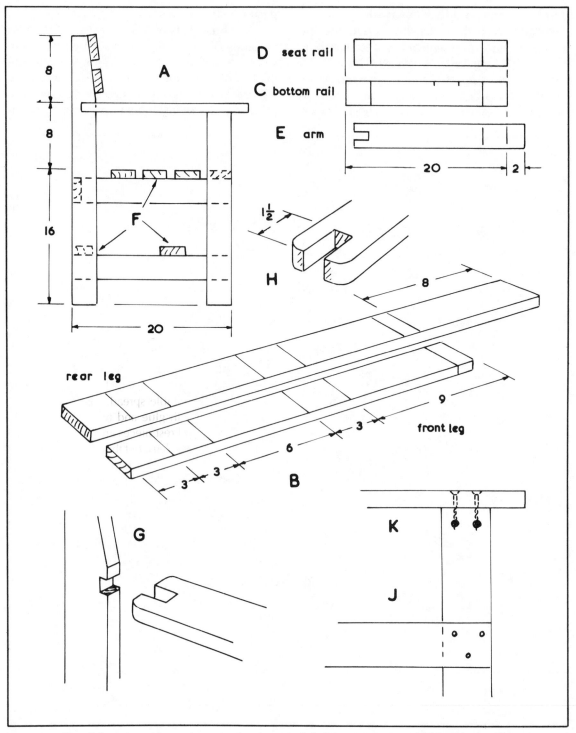

Fig. 12-12. The chair parts overlap and are glued and screwed, but the arms are notched into the back legs.

though it's obviously not a lounging chair).

This is a good project for a first attempt at chair-making. It is also a suitable project for a short run of quantity production either because you need several chairs or because you want to sell some. The parts are without angles to cut and fit. Therefore, a series of each part for many chairs can be prefabricated successfully. Even if you are only making one chair, prepare all parts that should match at the same time so that relevant measurements are the same. For instance, the front and back legs are different lengths, but many of the markings on them have to be the same distance from the bottom.

1. There is no need to make a full-size drawing because no bevels or shapings are involved, but study the side view (Fig. 12-12A) so that you understand the sizes and relationships of parts to each other.

2. Mark out the front and rear legs (Fig. 12-12B), showing the positions of the parts that will be attached to them. Allow a little extra at the top of the front legs at this stage. Mark a taper from just above where the arm will come on the rear leg. Taking it 1 inch back from the edge should be about right. If you leave fitting the backrest pieces until after the chair has been partly assembled, you can check the slope against your back and increase it if necessary before finishing the chair.

3. Prepare the pieces that go from back to front at each side. The bottom rail (Fig. 12-12C) is a plain piece of wood with the locations of the crosswise strips marked on it (Fig. 12-13A). The seat rail is similar, but it is cut back by the thickness of the rear crosswise strip (Figs. 12-12D and 12-13B). Cut the arms (Fig. 12-12E) to length, but leave further work on them until later.

4. The four seat pieces and the three crosswise strips (Fig. 12-12F) are all plain strips 20 inches long that fit on the seat rails (Fig. 12-13C) and the bottom rails (Fig. 12-13D).

5. Square off the tops of the front legs. Well round the edges and corners of the arms (Figs. 12-12E and 12-13E). Where the arm will connect to its rear leg, make a shallow notch (Fig. 12-12G) and cut the end of the arm to engage with it (Fig. 12-12H).

6. Start assembling the ends by joining the legs with the seat and lower rails. It is advisable to use waterproof glue in the joints. It should be sufficient to then use three screws in each crossing (Fig. 12-12J). Check squareness and make sure opposite ends make a pair.

7. Fit the arms. If the joints to the rear legs make a good fit, it should be sufficient to only glue them, but extra strength can come from a long screw driven across each joint. At the front legs the arms can be screwed down into the tops of the legs. Because this is end grain, it will help to drill across for dowels so part of the screw thread can go through them for a stronger grip (Fig. 12-12K). The screw heads should be counterbored and plugged for a better appearance.

8. Join the crosspieces to the bottom rail and to the rear ends of the seat rails. Check squareness with the chair standing on a level surface. Fit the four seat pieces to their rails (Fig. 12-13F) after rounding their top edges. Have one rail level with the front legs. Gaps about 1 inch between the strips should give a suitable spread. All of these joints can be made with glue and two long screws.

9. The backrest pieces are shown with their ends level with the legs, but they could be allowed to overlap with rounded corners. Round the exposed edges in any case and attach them to the legs (Fig. 12-13G). The tops of the rear legs can be left square or rounded to blend into the top backrest strips.

10. Remove any roughness and finish the wood with paint or preservative.

Materials List for Strip Armchair

2 rear legs	32 × 3 × 1
2 front legs	24 × 3 × 1
2 seat rails	20 × 3 × 1
2 bottom rails	20 × 3 × 1
2 arms	21 × 3 × 1
4 seat strips	20 × 3 × 1
3 crosswise strips	20 × 3 × 1
2 backrests	22 × 3 × 1

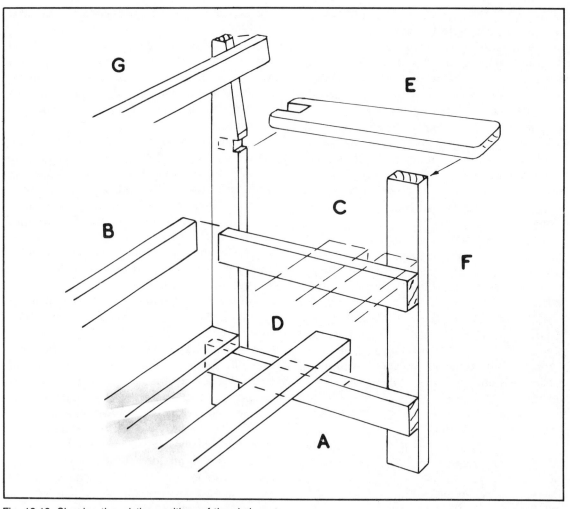

Fig. 12-13. Showing the relative positions of the chair parts.

FLAT STRIP BENCH

The flat strip armchair can be extended to make a seat for two or more. A few modifications are needed to give it the extra strength needed to allow for the greater weight and possible movements of the users. This has to be mainly stiffness rather than heaviness. A bench 48 inches long (Fig. 12-14) can be made stronger by using legs of greater section, notching parts together instead of relying only on surface joints, and providing some diagonal bracing under the seat. The drawings also allow for the seat sloping back slightly to give a little more comfort than a flat seat.

The parts could be all softwood and painted. Oak or other hardwood will be both more durable and perhaps better suited to a garden situation. In any case, the wood should be machined to size, planed all round, and reasonably free from knots or other flaws (particularly in the long parts). Joints should be made with waterproof glue and screws.

1. The side view of Fig. 12-15A gives the main dimensions. There is no need to draw all this full size, but you should draw the outlines of the legs up to the seat level and put the sloping lines across for the angled cuts that will have to be made for the seat rails (Fig. 12-15B). All other marking

out and cuts will be square, so you can measure them directly on the wood.

2. Mark out the rear legs (Fig. 12-16A). Get the widths of the slots by measuring the wood that has to fit them. It will probably be less than its nominal dimension and it helps to make all joints tight fits. Notches need not be more than 1/4 inch deep. Their purpose is to provide location and resistance to movement; screws provide strength. Cut the notches to make a pair of legs.

3. At the top of each leg, add the pieces that give slope to the backrest strips (Fig. 12-16B). They taper from 1 inch to almost a feather edge.

4. Mark out the front legs (Fig. 12-16C). Although the seat slopes the armrests are level. Leave some excess length for cutting the tenon flush with the top of its armrest after fitting. Cut the notches

in a similar way to those on the rear legs in order to make a pair of legs.

5. Prepare the bottom rails (Figs. 12-15C and 12-16D) that go straight across. Prepare the seat rails (Figs. 12-15D and 12-16E), which are similar, but allow for the slight slope and at the forward ends they have to be notched to take the lengthwise rail under the front seat slat (Figs. 12-15E and 12-16F).

6. The armrests extend forward of the front legs by 2 inches. At the rear legs, their inner surfaces come level with the insides of the rear legs, and then they go into the leg notches and extend outside the legs (Fig. 12-15F). At the front, they could be screwed downward in the same way as in the previous project. With the thicker legs, however, it is better to use mortise and tenon joints.

Fig. 12-14. A comfortable bench can be made from flat strips.

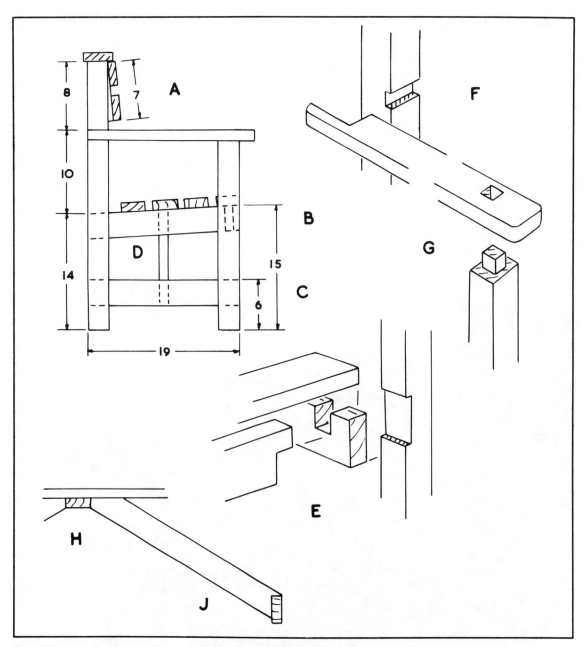

Fig. 12-15. Suitable sizes for the bench (A-D), leg and rail joints (E), arm joints (F, G) and bracing (H, J).

Mark the joints so the inner surface of an arm comes level with the leg. Cut the tenons back a little all round (Figs. 12-15G and 12-16G). Put saw cuts across the tenons so wedges can be used during assembly.

7. The two end frameworks can now be assembled. Three or four screws and glue in each joint should be adequate. Check that the legs are parallel and the bottom rails are square to them. Fit the rails first and then add the armrests. At the

rear legs, screws through the extending part will supplement glue in the slot. Well round the exposed edges and corners of the arms. At the front legs, glue the tenons tight and drive in wedges.

Leave the glue to set, and then level the tops of the tenons. See that the two frameworks match as a pair and are without twist.

8. Make the front rail so that it is notched

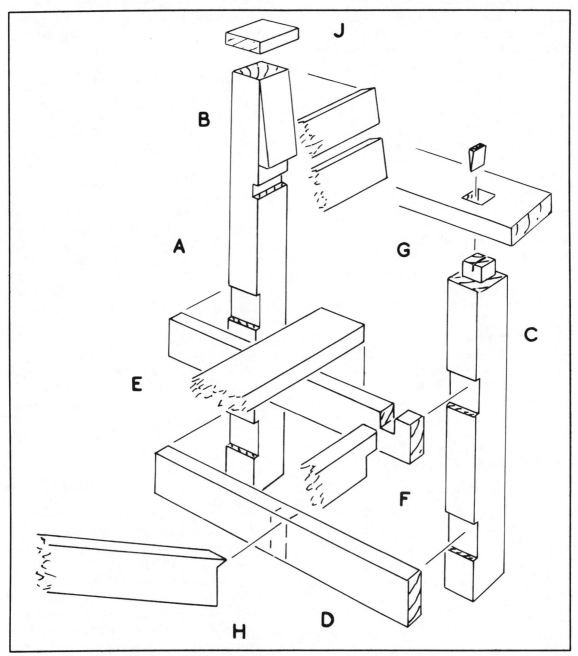

Fig. 12-16. The relative positions of the flat strip bench parts.

to fit into the seat rails (Figs. 12-15E and 12-16F). Check that it is straight. This is particularly important along its top surface where it has to bear under the front seat slat. Lack of straightness there would be very obvious in the finished bench.

9. Prepare the materials for the backrest and the seat slats. This should have rounded edges to the front and top. The seat slats should finish level with the outsides of their rails or they could extend a short distance and be rounded. The front slat has to be cut back to fit between the front legs. The backrest slats might also be cut level with the legs or extended and rounded. Drill all these parts for two screws at each crossing.

10. To get the bench assembled squarely, first fit the front rail, a seat slat near the back, and the top backrest slat. These three will hold the assembly while you check squareness by measuring diagonals. When you are satisfied with squareness, fit the other lengthwise parts. Screw the front slat to its rail.

11. Turn the bench over. At the center of the seat slats, put a cleat piece across underneath (Fig. 12-15H) to join the slats together and provide stiffness.

12. At the center of the third seat slat from the front, make diagonal struts to the bottom end rails (Fig. 12-15J). Cut the bottoms of the struts to fit over the rails (Fig. 12-16H). These struts are to provide resistance to lengthwise movement in the assembly and should be a close fit at each end (with screws to hold them in place).

13. The tops of the rear legs could be left square, beveled or rounded at the back, or square

caps can go over the tops (Fig. 12-16J). Make the squares to overlap about 1/2 inch all round and bevel the exposed edges.

14. Check that the bench stands firmly on a level surface and is upright. You might have to take a little off one or more legs. Remove any roughness and finish the wood with paint or preservative.

DOWELED CHAIR WITH LIFT-OFF SEAT

One problem with garden furniture that is left outside is the marking of the seat, by rain, falling leaves, or fouling by animals. If the seat can be taken off and stored under cover or even left outside with its surface downward, much of the trouble is avoided. This chair has a slatted seat that can be taken off (Fig. 12-17).

This is a simple chair without arms, of the type that might be used at a table for an open-air meal. The same ideas could be used for an armchair. The parts could be joined with mortise and tenon joints, but doweled construction is shown because many workers find it easier to make strong dowel joints with the aid of a jig than to cut mortises and tenons. The chair depends for its strength on all the joints being properly bonded with waterproof glue. The parts that have dowels in their ends are mostly 1 inch thick. If they are the full thickness, the dowels could be 1/2 inch in diameter. If the wood was finished 7/8 of an inch thick or less, they should be 3/8 inch in diameter.

The chair rear legs are cut from wood 3 inches thick, but that tapers to the floor and to the top to give a slope to the backrests. The seat has a slight slope for comfort, while still being suitable for sitting upright at a table.

1. The side view shown in Fig. 12-18A shows the slope of the seat and overall sizes. Draw the main lines up to the seat level to get the angle that the seat support parts make.

2. Mark out the rear legs (Fig. 12-18B). There is 6 inches left parallel at seat level, and then the front edges taper from there to leave both ends 2 inches square. Mark on the edge the position of the seat rail (Fig. 12-19A) and on the side the position of the rear rail. Cut the tapers.

Materials List for Flat Strip Bench	
2 rear legs	32 × 2 1/2 × 2 1/2
2 front legs	25 × 2 1/2 × 2 1/2
2 seat rails	20 × 3 × 1
2 bottom rails	19 × 3 × 1
2 arms	22 × 3 × 1
1 seat rail	48 × 3 × 1
4 seat slats	50 × 3 × 1
2 backrest slats	50 × 3 × 1
1 seat cleat	16 × 3 × 1
2 struts	30 × 3 × 1
2 rear leg caps	4 1/2 × 4 1/2 × 1

Fig. 12-17. For a chair that is to be left outside, it is convenient to be able to remove the seat for storage or cleaning.

3. Mark and make the pair of front legs (Fig. 12-18C).

4. Make the two bottom rails 2 inches deep and the seat rails 3 inches deep (Fig. 12-19B). The angles of the ends can be found from the full-size drawing.

5. Mark out the ends of the rails and the legs they connect for dowels. It should be possible to arrange three on the 3-inch depth (Fig. 12-18D) and two on the 2-inch depth (Fig. 12-18E).

6. Mark and make the rails that go across the chair back and front (Fig. 12-19C). Both have square ends and two dowels. A suitable width for the chair over the legs is 16 inches.

7. With all of these parts prepared partial assembly can commence. Prepare a supply of dowels. Assemble the two ends first, and then join them with the other rails. Use clamps where possible. It is advisable to assemble the two ends and let their glued joints set before fitting the pieces the other way. Squareness of the ends can be checked by seeing that the angle between the bottom rail and the front leg is 90 degrees on each assembly. See that the ends are without twist and that they match as a pair. When adding the rails the other way, have the chair on a flat surface and see that it stands level and upright.

8. Make the two backrest pieces (Fig. 12-19D). They can have their ends level with the legs or be allowed to overhang a short distance

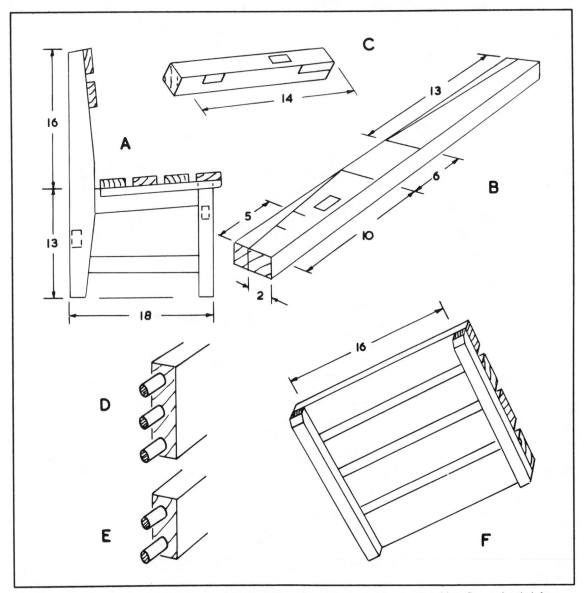

Fig. 12-18. Many parts of the chair are glued and doweled. The strips on the seat make an assembly to fit over the chair frame.

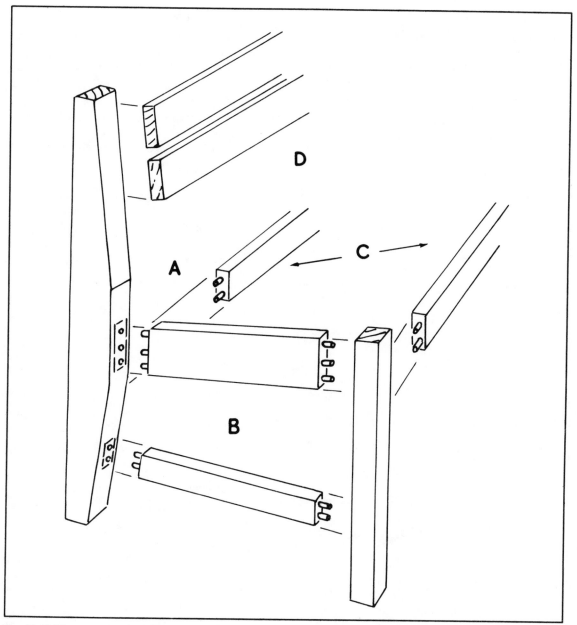

Fig. 12-19. The parts of the chair are assembled.

with rounded ends. Glue and screw the pieces to the legs.

9. The seat consists of four crosswise slats joined to pieces at the ends (Fig. 12-18F). This assembly drops over the chair frame. Get the seat sizes from the frame and make it so the end pieces press reasonably tightly over the parts that support it. The seat is unlikely to move out of place in use. There should not be any need for a fastener to keep it there. Have the tops of the seat slats well rounded and round the corners of the assembly. If everything is made exactly square and to size, the seat

should fit either way. Because this is unlikely, mark on the underside of the seat which edge is to come to the front.

10. Remove any surplus glue that has squeezed out of joints and finish the chair with paint or preservative.

Materials List for Doweled Chair with Lift-Off Seat	
2 rear legs	30 × 3 × 2
2 front legs	14 × 2 × 2
2 seat rails	14 × 3 × 1
2 bottom rails	14 × 2 × 1
2 crosswise rails	14 × 2 × 1
2 backrests	18 × 3 × 1
4 seat slats	20 × 3 × 1
2 seat ends	15 × 1 × 1

SAWBUCK CHAIR

A chair with legs arranged like a sawbuck or sawing trestle is novel and quite practical. The arrangement can give stability with lightness. This chair shown in Fig. 12-20 has the legs arranged asymetrically. There is an extension to the rear that prevents the chair from tipping backward and provides attachments for the backrest supports. The sizes given will make a chair of moderate size, but the same method could be used for a larger chair or extended in length to make a two-seat bench.

All of the wood suggested is 3-inch-by-1-inch section and this could be hard or softwood. If the chair is expected to be pulled about on a stone or concrete surface, a hardwood will be better able to resist the grain of the feet being torn and

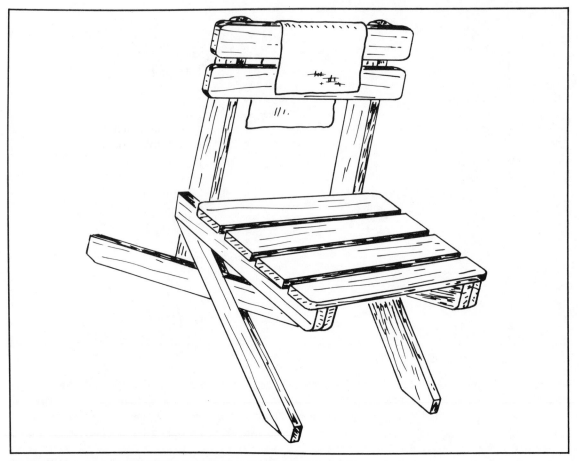

Fig. 12-20. A sawbuck chair gets its stability from the spread of the feet.

splintered. This would also be stronger at the halving joint in the legs. If softwood is used or you have doubts about the strength of the joint you cut, there can be a cover piece screwed on inside the crossing where it will not show. The parts should be glued, but the main parts are bolted and the others screwed.

1. Setting out the shape is not as complicated as it might first appear. The general shape is shown in Fig. 12-21A, but the first step is to set out using centerlines (Fig. 12-21B). Draw a floor line, and another representing the centerline of the seat support parallel to it (Fig. 12-21C), with a square line at what will be the front of the chair. Go 24 inches along the floor line from this and join that point to the top of the square line (Fig. 12-21D). Draw the other diagonal from 17 inches along the top line (Fig. 12-21E). Go 9 inches up the rear leg line and draw the backrest support through it (Fig. 12-21F). If you measure 1 1/2 inches each side of these centerlines, you will get the wood widths and you can finish off the drawing as in Fig. 12-21A. This completed drawing is necessary to get the shapes to cut most of the parts.

2. Make the two sets of legs from this drawing and cut halving joints between them (Fig. 12-22A).

3. Note how the parts will be put together on the front view (Fig. 12-21G). The seat supports are outside, the crossed legs come next, and the backrest supports are inside.

4. Make the seat supports (Figs. 12-21H and 12-22B). Leave some excess length at the rear for trimming off after the other parts are joined to it.

5. Make the two backrest supports (Figs. 12-21J and 12-22C). They will bolt at the marked positions to the legs and seat supports. Drill the holes and make a trial assembly. At the front of the seat, its support is screwed to the legs. If the trial is satisfactory, glue the joints and secure them permanently.

6. Make a bottom rail to screw to the backrest supports inside the legs (Fig. 12-21K). Prepare the backrest pieces (Fig. 12-22D). They overlap the supports and should have rounded corners as well as rounded front edges. Glue and

screw on these strips and the bottom rail. Check that the assembly stands upright.

7. Make the seat slats. Round their top edges and round the corners of the outside ones. Glue and screw them on, with the front one level at the front of the supports and the others evenly spaced.

8. This completes assembly and the chair can be finished with paint, varnish, or preservative.

Materials List for Sawbuck Chair

2 legs	24 × 3 × 1
2 legs	28 × 3 × 1
2 backrest supports	30 × 3 × 1
2 backrests	18 × 3 × 1
2 seat supports	20 × 3 × 1
4 seat slats	18 × 3 × 1
1 bottom rail	14 × 3 × 1

TUSK TENON SEAT

Construction where parts have tenons extending through to be held by wedges is particularly appropriate for garden furniture. That type of joint is suited to the fairly heavy boards of much exterior construction. There are at least two structural advantages. If wood shrinks, you can pull joints tight by hammering the wedges further in, and if the article is completely assembled with tusk tenon joints it can be disassembled if you want to pack it away for the winter. The method is not very suitable for light assemblies, but if you are using fairly thick wood it is a good structural technique and furniture made that way will give a novel appearance to the amenities of your garden or yard.

Use hardwood at least 1 1/2 inches thick; it need not be planed. Slabs cut across a log are particularly appropriate. Some parts have to be wide and you will need to find pieces of sufficient width. Boards can be joined, and some methods of making up width for exterior parts are described in Chapter 2.

The wood could be used with waney edges to give an interesting effect (Fig. 12-23) or the boards could be finished with parallel edges for a more formal design. Construction is the same, in any case, except that with waney edges on both

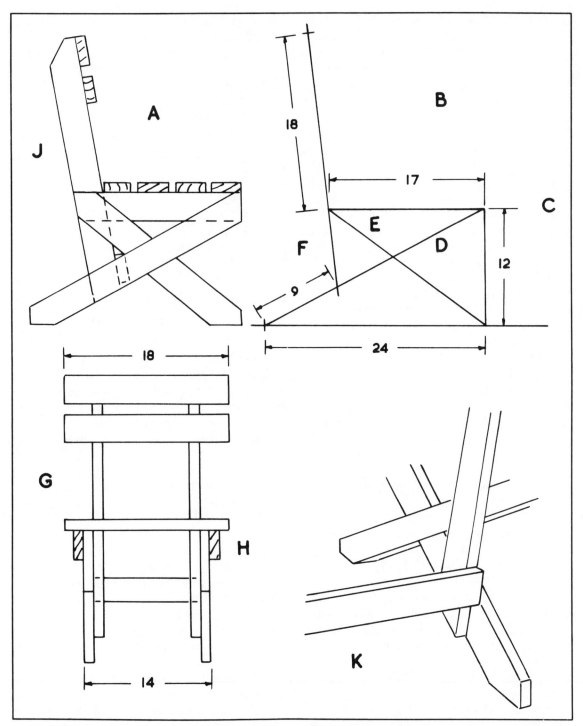

Fig. 12-21. The end of the sawbuck chair must be set out to get the legs in the correct position, with the back supports overlapping the legs.

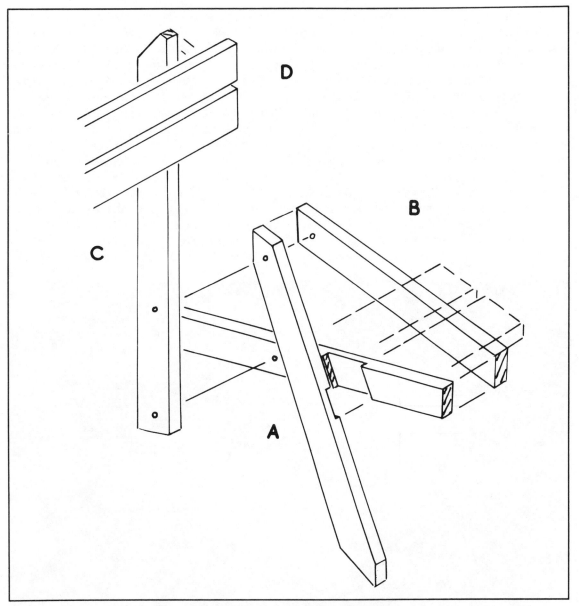

Fig. 12-22. The legs are halved, but other parts overlap and are screwed or bolted.

sides you should work from a centerline when squaring and marking joints. You cannot work from an edge; that is possible only if one or more sides are straight.

This design could be made as a single seat or extended to make a bench. A single seat might be about 24 inches wide. That would be rigid enough without a bottom rail, but if it is lengthened to 48 inches or more the extra stiffness of a rail would be advisable. As shown the tusks and wedges are plain. If the seat is to be given a formal finish for use on a patio or elsewhere near the house and a less rural appearance is preferred, they could be decorated with shaped ends.

1. The key shapes are the two ends (Fig. 12-24A). Set out the shape to suit the wood available, including end views of the lengthwise parts. Allow for mortises slightly more than half the width of the boards. If a seat board is 9 inches wide, a mortise 5 inches wide will be about right. Exact size is not crucial. Include the bottom rail position if it is a bench you are making, but omit it for a chair. The seat is given a slight hallow; a drop of 1 inch in a total width of 18 inches is suggested.

2. Prepare the wood for the lengthwise parts. The important measurements are the distances between shoulders each side of the tenons. The back, seat, and rail should be marked out together (Fig. 12-24B) with at least 6 inches of extra wood for the tenons extending at the ends.

3. Mark the tenon widths and the matching widths of the mortises. Cut the sides of the tenons, but do not trim them to length. Most of the waste in the mortises can be removed by drilling, but they should be trimmed to shape with a chisel. Each tenon should slide easily through its mortise. Excessive play can be avoided, but that would be better than fitting the parts for a drive fit.

4. It is advisable to adopt a standard size of wedge (Fig. 12-24C). Then it will not matter where you use them if you have to re-assemble. The slot in each tenon must allow the wedge to slot in easily, but its inner edge must come within the mortised part (Fig. 12-24D). When you drive the wedge in, it forces the tenon outward by its bear-

Fig. 12-23. Tusk tenons form a good way to join lengthwise parts to the end of a bench.

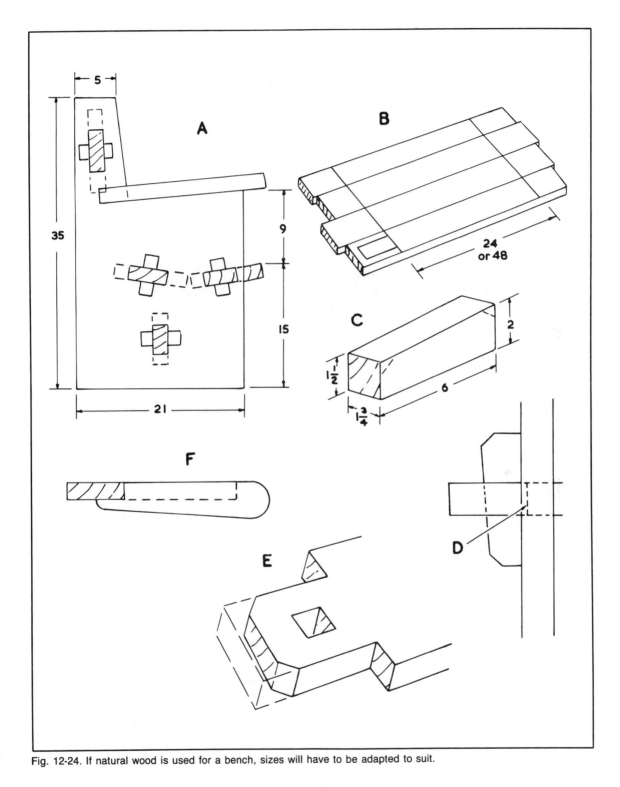

Fig. 12-24. If natural wood is used for a bench, sizes will have to be adapted to suit.

ing against the surface of the mortised piece and there is no risk of it touching the bottom of the slot (which would prevent further tightening).

5. Make a trial assembly. If that is satisfactory, trim and bevel the ends of the tenons (Figs. 12-24E and 12-25A). Do not cut them back too far because the wedges will tighten against end grain, and that could break out if the end is too narrow.

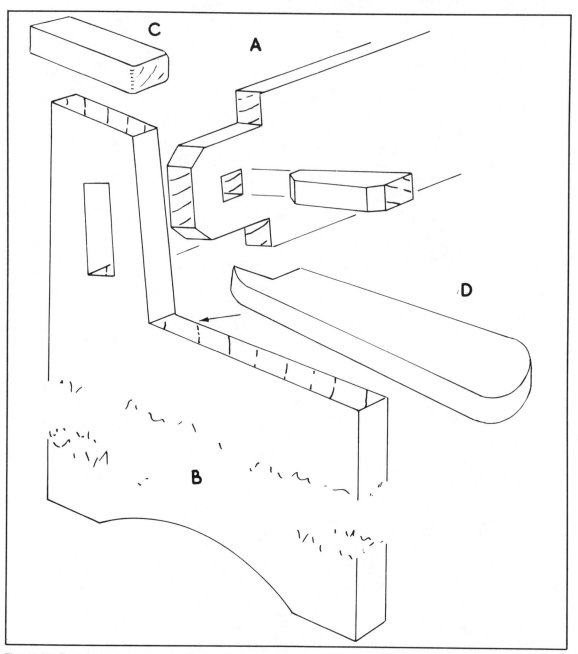

Fig. 12-25. Each end has mortises for the lengthwise parts. Tenons are large and pulled tight with wedges.

6. Complete the shaping of the ends. Hollow the bottoms (Fig. 12-25B) so that bearing only at the sides will reduce the risk of rocking on uneven ground. The top above the seat back can be rounded, but a capping nailed or screwed on (Fig. 12-25C) would match the arms and prevent rainwater from entering the grain.

7. The arms (Figs. 12-24F and 12-25D) could be parallel pieces, but they are shown with some shaping. Have straight inner edges over the seat end and a curved front end, with the outside shaped back to overlap with a notch. Screw down into the seat end, preferably with counterbored and plugged holes, or you could glue in dowels instead of screwing.

8. Assemble all parts and drive the wedges fairly tight. Usually, after exposure for a few weeks, you will be able to tighten them further. If the wood has a sawn finish and it is not a hardwood with its own resistance to exposure, treat it with preservative. If you have used planed boards, they could have a painted finish.

Materials List for Tusk Tenon Seat	
2 ends	35 × 21 × 1 3/4
2 arms	22 × 4 × 1 3/4
2 caps	7 × 4 × 1 3/4
wedges from	50 × 2 × 1 3/4
For chair:	
1 back	36 × 10 × 1 3/4
2 seats	36 × 9 × 1 3/4
For bench:	
1 back	60 × 10 × 1 3/4
2 seats	60 × 9 × 1 3/4
1 rail	60 × 5 × 1 3/4

PARK BENCH

Although much garden seating is crude and simple compared with chairs used indoors, there is a place for better made furniture. In a formal garden or on a well-equipped deck or patio, something that is not of a very high standard of construction will be rather obvious and not suited to its surroundings. Sometimes a seat is made to commemorate some event. It could be a special anniversary, a particular happening, or even the moving to a new address. Somewhere on the seat would be carved, painted, or a plaque added giving details. In that case the seat should be worthy of its importance.

A seat for an important situation should be made of good wood, with cut joints rather than screws or nails, and the total effect should be pleasing and functional. Seats of this type are often seen in public parks and gardens. There is a similarity about their designs due to comfort and appearance requirements having to be met. The seat shown in Fig. 12-26 is a basic form and possible variations are described. The material should be seasoned hardwood planed all round and free from large knots, particularly in the lengthwise parts. An overall length of 60 inches will accommodate three sitters, but other lengths are possible—down to a single seat. Two single seats might commemorate a wedding anniversary or other double occasion, but there is more wood and work than required for making a two-person bench. On the other hand, independent chairs allow you to locate them throughout the yard or garden.

The bench has a hollowed seat and a tilted back that is decorated with vertical slats. Except for the bend in the rear legs, shaping of the arms and possible shaping of the top back rail, nearly all the parts are straight. The wood may be machine-planed, but on the visible surfaces the plane marks should be removed by sanding or hand planing if the bench is to be given a clear or untreated finish.

1. A full-size layout of the end view will be useful, but it is not essential because most information is shown on the drawing. The back legs and seat supports can be laid out on the wood (Fig. 12-27A). Notice the positions of rails and other lengthwise parts in relation to the ends (Fig. 12-27B).

2. Mark out the rear legs (Fig. 12-28A). The bend comes above the seat level. Do not make this a sharp angle; curve between the straight sections, particularly toward the rear. Mark on the positions of all joints so that this leg layout can be used as a guide when marking other parts. Cut the legs to shape, but leave some excess length, at both ends, to be trimmed off after joints have been cut.

Fig. 12-26. A formal bench with parts made from planed wood can make a comfortable resting place in a garden.

3. Mark out the front legs (Fig. 12-28B) with joint positions matching those on the rear legs. The front seat rail will have its upper edge level with the tops of the seat pieces (Figs. 12-27C and 12-28C). Measure the actual wood being used for the seat to get the height of the top of the rail. At the tops of the legs, mark where the underside of the arm will come and leave more than enough above that for marking and cutting the tenons later.

4. The bottom end rail (Fig. 12-28D) is a simple piece with tenons at its ends and a mortise position slightly forward of halfway for a lengthwise rail (Fig. 12-29A).

5. Make the seat rails the same length between shoulders as the bottom rails. The amount

of hallow in the top is not crucial, but a drop of 3/4 of an inch at the center will be satisfactory (Figs. 12-28E and 12-29B). This can be drawn by penciling around a sprung lath (Fig. 12-28F). A rear rail (Fig. 12-29C) goes under the back seat piece and will have two seat supports (Fig. 12-29D) evenly spaced and attached to it and the front seat rail. Mark the curves on these now, so all parts have matching shapes, but do not cut them to length yet.

6. Make the pair of arms. They could be simple, mainly parallel, pieces (Fig. 12-28G) or have shaped outlines (Fig. 12-28H). In any case, well round the top and front edges. Leave more than enough for cutting the tenons at the back and mark

270

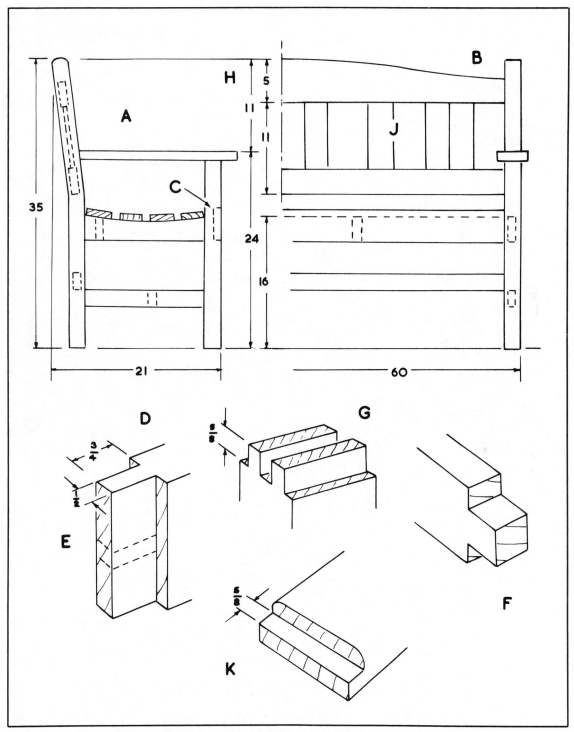

Fig. 12-27. These sizes make a good-looking bench. Structural parts should be tenoned.

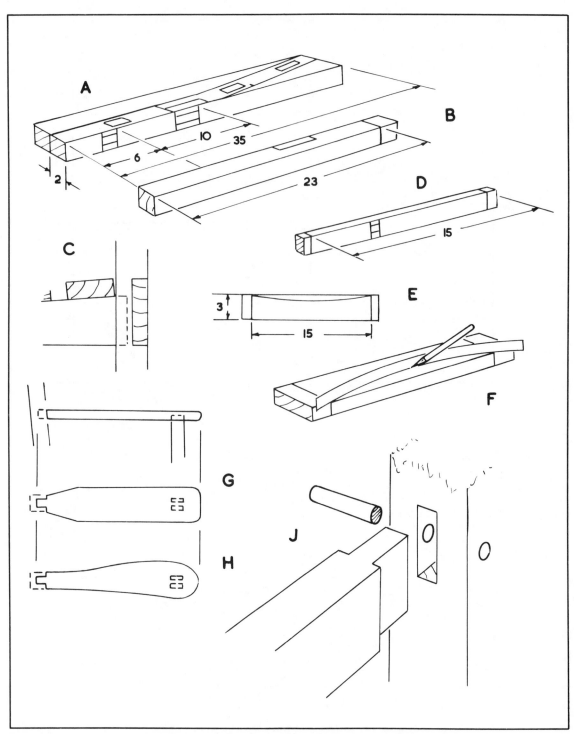

Fig. 12-28. Make the individual parts first. Mark and cut tenoned joints so they can be pegged.

where the front legs will join.

7. All of the end parts can be joined with stub tenons. It should be sufficient for them to enter mortises about 3/4 of an inch, with a tenon thickness of 1/2 of an inch on wood of the sizes specified in Fig. 12-27D. The parts of 2 inch or less depth can have the tenons as cut, but for 3-inch pieces the tenons could be divided (Fig. 12-27E) if you prefer. Where the rear seat and bottom rails join, allow for narrower tenons going right through (Fig. 12-27F).

8. At the arms, the tenon into the rear legs will be the same as elsewhere, except the shoulders should slope to match the leg angle. At the front legs, the tenons cannot penetrate very far into the arms and it is better to make them double (Fig. 12-27G) to give a greater glue area.

9. You could assemble the ends now and cut mortises for the lengthwise parts later, but it is easier to cut joints in separate pieces of wood. Determine the sizes of lengthwise parts and cut mortises in the legs and end rails now even if you do not make the matching tenons yet.

10. Assemble the pair of ends. Use clamps to draw the joints tight. Check squareness and that the opposite ends match and are without twist. Extra security of joints can be given by drilling for dowels across them; one 1/4-inch dowel in each joint should be sufficient (Fig. 12-28J).

11. Mark out the front seat rail (Fig. 12-29E) and use it as a guide to lengths between shoulders when making other lengthwise parts. Mark on it the positions of seat supports and round its top edges. On a 60-inch length, two evenly spaced supports will be enough. Allow for the supports having narrow tenons right through or stub tenons if you do not want end grain to show at the front.

12. Make the rear seat rail (Fig. 12-29F). This will be slightly longer than the front seat rail as it goes between end rails and not legs. Mark the bottom rail (Fig. 12-29G); it will be the same length. Both have narrow tenons at the ends.

13. Mark the positions of the seat supports on the two long rails. Cut these to fit and glue the joints. Check squareness as the accuracy of this assembly affects squareness of the complete bench.

14. The bottom rail between the rear legs is a simple piece (Fig. 12-29H) that is the same length between shoulders as the front seat rail.

15. The two back rails should also be this length. Figure 12-26 shows two parallel pieces, but if you want to carve, paint, or attach a plaque to the bench the center of the top rail is the place for this commemoration. The top rail is drawn with a curved top to provide this space (Fig. 12-27H). The ends are the same depth as straight rails would be. Therefore, the joints to the rear legs are the same. Make the two back rails to the shape you want. Ends are tenoned to suit the mortises in the legs.

16. The back could have a pattern of similar parallel upright slats (as shown in Fig. 12-26). If the top rail is curved up at the center, this could be complemented by having a wide center slat, and then reducing the widths of others toward the ends (Fig. 12-27J). This would provide enough space on the center one for an inscription in place of, or in addition to, any on the top rail.

17. As the slats are not very thick, they can have barefaced tenons on their ends (Fig. 12-27K). The front edges can be rounded. Make the slats and cut the joints. Assemble the slats to the rails while again checking squareness that will affect the finished bench.

18. All the lengthwise parts can now be joined to the ends. The seat and back assemblies should pull the bench square. Have it standing on a flat surface so that there is no risk of twist. Draw the joints tight and put dowels across most of them.

19. The seat pieces (Fig. 12-29J) should have their upper edges rounded and their ends extending a short distance over the end rails (where they can also be rounded). Mark where the crossings come and drill for two screws in each piece at each place. Brass screws could finish on the surface or you can counterbore and plug them.

20. The bench could be finished by painting, but if a good hardwood has been used it would look better if the grain is visible. If it is a durable wood that will withstand exposure unprotected, it could be left to weather to a natural shade. Otherwise, a clear varnish could be used. This does not

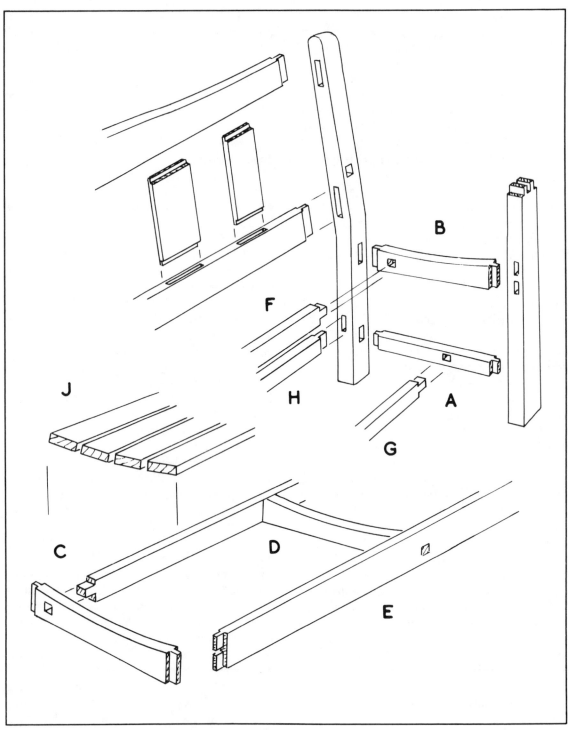

Fig. 12-29. All parts except the seat slats are tenoned.

have to be a high gloss, but several coats of semiglossy varnish can be more effective. Marine varnish will have the longest life.

Materials List for Park Bench	
2 rear legs	36 × 4 × 2
2 front legs	25 × 2 × 2
2 seat rails	19 × 3 × 1
2 bottom rails	19 × 2 × 1
2 arms	22 × 4 × 1
4 seat pieces	60 × 3 × 1
1 front seat rail	60 × 4 × 1
1 rear seat rail	60 × 3 × 1
2 seat supports	19 × 3 × 1
1 back top rail	60 × 5 × 1
or	60 × 3 × 1
1 back bottom rail	60 × 3 × 1
11 back slats	14 × 2 × 5/8
or	
1 back slat	14 × 6 × 5/8
2 back slats	14 × 5 × 5/8
2 back slats	14 × 4 × 5/8
2 back slats	14 × 3 × 5/8

SWINGING SEAT

A swinging seat or glider for two people makes a pleasant place to relax. It can be hung from a porch or it could have its own supports for use anywhere in the garden or yard. There are several ways of making such a seat and many sizes are possible. The seat shown in Fig. 12-30 is shaped to provide comfort as it is, but it could be improved with cushions. The size is intended to suit two persons with plenty of space. A bigger seat could be made in the same way, but if it is made much longer the sections of the lengthwise wood should be increased.

The ropes or chains attach to a strip that goes the length of the back and to reinforced front uprights. Details of a support follow. That needs to be fairly high to give a more comfortable swinging action than could be possible with short ropes.

All the parts can be made of softwood, but a durable hardwood, such as oak, would be better suited to exposure. If the suggested canopy is made, it will protect the wood from severe weather as well as shield the users from sunlight and showers.

1. The key assembly that settles the sizes of many other parts is the end (Fig. 12-31A). Draw this full size. How much slope to give the uprights is not crucial, but about 10 degrees is suitable. The curve of the seat can be drawn freehand. Let it dip about 1 inch from the top of the wood and curve down to vertical at the front (Fig. 12-31B). Allow for the 2-inch seat slats being spaced about 1 1/2 inches apart. Use a similar spacing at the back; it can be taken to a different height if you prefer. Curve the tops of the uprights (Fig. 12-31C).

2. Make the end parts and check that the opposite assemblies will be a matching pair. Although it would be possible to merely lap the parts and glue and screw them, notches help in locating the joints and preventing later movement. Keep the notches in the uprights quite shallow (Fig. 12-31D); 1/4 inch will be enough. Where the back hanging strip fits, the shallow notch will be in that and enough must be cut from the rear upright for the rear faces to come level (Fig. 12-31E).

3. Make the arms to fit into the uprights and come level at the outside (Fig. 12-31F). Round the front corners of the arms and round all edges that will be exposed. Take the sharpness off the tops of the uprights.

4. Assemble the pair of ends. The arms can be glued and screwed. The seat rails are better held with bolts through. Two 1/2-inch-diameter bolts at each crossing should be sufficient.

5. The front ropes attach to an eyebolt, in each end, where the front upright is strengthened with a block outside (Fig. 12-31G) below arm level (Fig. 12-31H). Its exposed edges can be rounded. The eyebolt should go through with large washers at each side of the wood to spread the pressure.

6. Although the seat and back slats provide considerable stiffness lengthwise, strength in that direction is mainly provided by the back hanging strip and another underneath between the seat rails (Fig. 12-31J). The one underneath should be tenoned into the seat rails (Fig. 12-31K). Make this before the other lengthwise parts and use it to hold the ends while getting their lengths.

7. Let the back hanging rail extend up to 6 inches beyond the seat ends. Drill the extensions

Fig. 12-30. A swinging seat can hang in a porch or be supported by a frame.

for the hanging ropes or shackles for chains. Round the ends. Assemble these two lengthwise pieces to the ends. Check that they fit squarely and the ends will be upright.

8. Make the seat slats to fit on the seat rails, either level with them or extending a short distance (Fig. 12-31L). Make the back slats in a similar way (Fig. 12-31M). Round all the slats' outer edges before screwing them into place. It is helpful to use a piece of scrap wood of the correct width to keep regular spacings. Uneven spacing can appear very obvious when the seat is unoccupied. An extended seat might require an intermediate support for the seat slats, but providing they are strong enough slight springiness is an advantage.

9. Modern synthetic rope is very strong and

most of it will stand up to exposure without suffering. Therefore the seat could be hung with rope about 1/2 inch diameter (knotted or spliced at the ends). Alternatively, there could be chains that would require shackles to the eyebolts and either

Materials List for Swinging Seat	
2 seat rails	30 × 6 × 1 1/2
2 uprights	27 × 4 × 1 1/2
2 uprights	23 × 4 × 1 1/2
2 support blocks	4 × 4 × 1 1/2
2 arms	33 × 4 × 1 1/2
1 hanging strip	72 × 4 × 1 1/2
1 bottom strip	60 × 4 × 2
7 seat slats	64 × 2 × 1 1/2
4 back slats	64 × 2 × 1 1/2

large shackles or eyebolts through the rear hanging strip for smaller shackles.

10. Finish the wood with paint or preservative.

SWINGING SEAT SUPPORT

If the swinging seat is to be located in the garden or yard, either in a permanent position or as a freestanding structure, there has to be a support that is high enough to allow a gentle swinging action, wide enough for the seat to move without touching the supports, and with a sufficient base to keep the assembly free from tipping. If the support is to be moveable, the base should be wide enough back to front to resist tipping with the most energetic swinging. That means feet should be about as long as the support is high. If the base is to be bolted or staked down, it need not project much more than the spread of the legs.

The support is for a seat, as just described, and is basically as shown in Fig.12-30. The height suits the seat, and its length should be sufficient to have the legs about 24 inches further apart than the overall length of the seat. As with the seat, the support could be made of softwood protected with preservative, but it would be better made of a durable hardwood. Details that follow are for a support without a canopy. If a canopy is to be fitted now or later, there are some slight modifications that should be allowed for during construction. See the following project.

1. Set out the main lines of an end view (Fig. 12-32A) to get the lengths of the legs and the angles to cut the parts. A half view at one side of the centerline will tell you all you need.

2. The wood for the beam and the legs should be chosen for straightness of grain and the absence of flaws. The beam (Fig. 12-32B) is a plain piece, extending far enough to cover the brackets.

3. At the tops, cut the legs to fit around the beam and against each other (Fig. 12-32C). Mark where the rail and foot come on each piece, but the bottom need not be cut until the foot is attached (Fig. 12-32D).

4. Prepare the feet (Fig. 12-32E) and mark where the legs come. Bevel the ends.

5. Bring the top of each pair of legs together and join them with gussets, cut with their grain running across (Fig. 12-32F). Arrange the width of the slot so that it will be a tight fit on the beam. Glue and screw the gussets (although there could also be bolts through) clear of where the brackets will come.

6. Bolt the legs to the feet and the rails to the legs. Cut off any surplus wood and take off any sharp edges or corners.

7. Add the beam and the bottom stiffener with the legs on edge. Screw and bolt the beam between the tops of the legs and use steel brackets underneath to provide stiffness (Fig. 12-32G). When you fit the stiffener to the feet, compare distances at tops and bottoms of the legs and check squareness by measuring diagonals. A bolt through each foot will be better than screws.

8. Bring the assembly upright and check stability and squareness.

9. The seat ropes could be taken around the beam, possibly located with small blocks of wood to act as cleats (Fig. 12-32H) to prevent the turns sliding along. If chain is used, there should be eyebolts through the beam (Fig. 12-32J) to take shackles. Locate them to suit the width of the seat. If they are wider apart, they will help to restrict lengthwise movement of the seat.

10. Finish the wood with paint or preservative.

Materials List for Swinging Seat Support

2 legs	102 × 4 × 2
2 feet	96 × 4 × 2
2 rails	48 × 4 × 2
1 beam	108 × 6 × 2
4 gussets	12 × 6 × 1
1 stiffener	100 × 4 × 2

4 steel brackets with 6 inch legs

CANOPY FOR SWINGING SEAT

A roof over the swinging seat and its support (Figs. 12-31 and 12-32) will make an attractive unit that

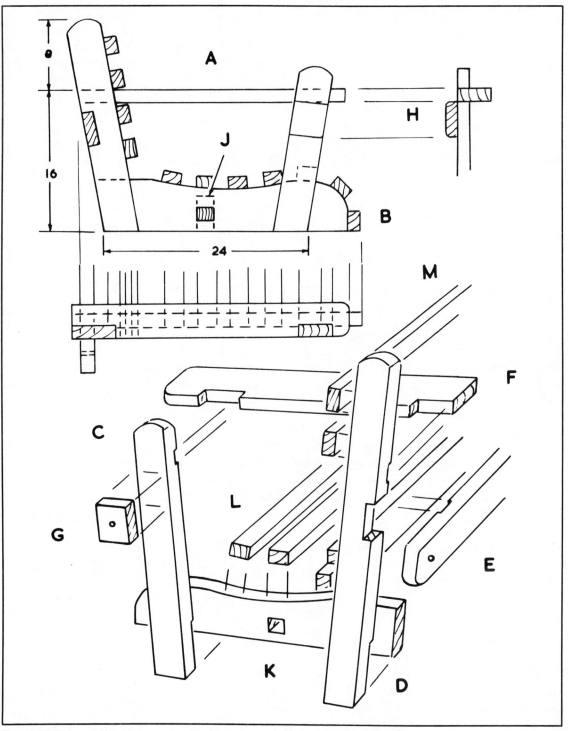

Fig. 12-31. The seat is built as a unit, with strong parts where the hanging chains come.

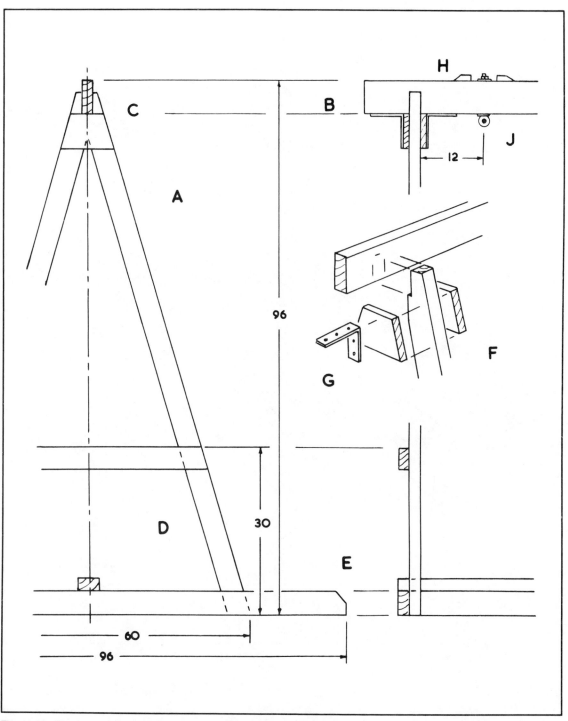

Fig. 12-32. The frame for a swinging seat should be reasonably high and with a broad base for stability and a satisfactory action.

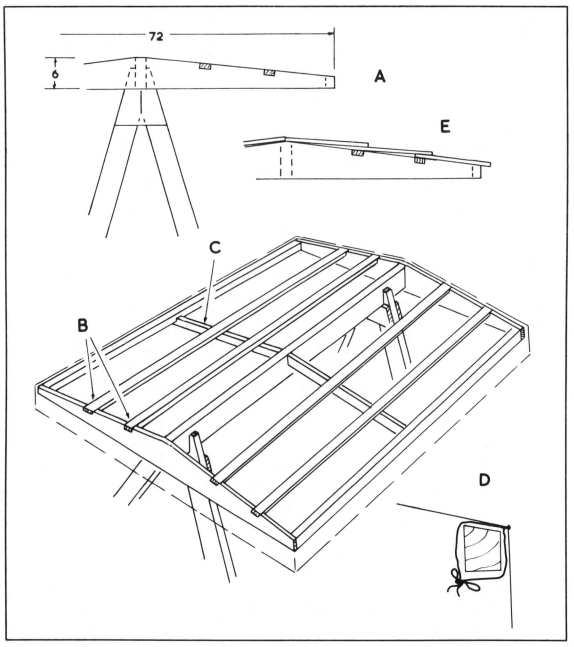

Fig. 12-33. The support for a canopy can be mounted on the top of the frame supporting a swinging seat.

should look good in any garden or yard situation. The roof can take the form of a canopy large enough to shield from overhead sunlight, as well as protect both the users and the woodwork from rain. Size can be adjusted to suit your needs. If the canopy is to be made longer, the beam length should be increased when making the support. As shown in Fig. 12-33, the canopy size suits the support as suggested in the previous project.

The basic framework can be covered in several ways. It can have a canvas top that is tied on and can be removed and stored under cover when not required. There could be plywood sheets permanently attached. An attractive finish could be achieved by using shingles. If they are to be used, their sizes will have to be checked and the lengthwise strips spaced to suit.

The framework should be kept light. As it is to be covered, softwood should be sufficiently durable. The suggested size has the ends the same depth as the beam, but if you make it much wider the ends should be deepened to give sufficient slope to the top.

1. Mark out and cut the two ends (Fig. 12-33A). At the eaves, the 2-inch-square strip goes between the ends and will be screwed there. At the other strips, cut notches for them to let in (Fig. 12-33B). Space the strips evenly for canvas or plywood covering, but arrange more, if required, to suit shingles.

2. Make the eaves strips the same length as the beam. Screw the ends to the beam and to the strips. Check that the pieces are horizontal in all directions. Stand back and see that the assembly looks right in relation to the beam and other parts. Check squareness as from above.

3. Put the two intermediate support pieces in (Fig. 12-33C) and add the lengthwise strips to complete the assembly.

4. If the top is to be covered with plywood, that should be exterior grade. Along the ridge put a cover strip to reduce the risk of water entering the edges of the veneers. Cover any joints with similar strips.

5. A canvas cover could be made with proofed canvas or with plastic-coated fabric, arranged with a hanging border that goes below the wood and is held on with tapes or cords around the eaves and other parts (Fig. 12-33D). If you prefer, this could be finished with a fringe. An overall green color would be appropriate if you do not want to attract attention to the seat. You could give it a bright effect with red and white stripes or other vivid colors.

6. With shingles, start at the eaves and nail (Fig. 12-33E). Support underneath with another hammer or an iron block as you progress along the strips. Along the ridge, use a cover strip or two shingles cut at angles and cemented.

7. Finish the wood appropriately to match other parts.

Materials List for Canopy for Swinging Seat.	
2 ends	72 × 6 × 1
2 eaves	108 × 2 × 2
4 strips	112 × 2 × 1

Chapter 13

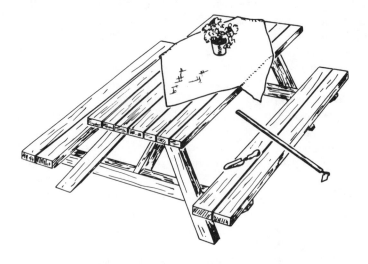

Tables

A fter chairs, tables are most in demand for outdoor use. There are many manufactured tables, some of which can be folded, and everyone is familiar with the picnic table with benches attached. There are several other tables that can be made for permanent outdoor use or to carry in and out as required. Many tables have similar construction to chairs so that they make matching sets. Some rustic tables are described in Chapter 11, but in a more formal garden—where chairs of the type described in Chapter 12 are used—the tables should mostly be of similar type with jointed construction and a good finish.

The notes at the beginning of Chapter 12 concerning materials and techniques are also applicable to the making of tables.

The main requirement of a table, whatever its design or construction, is a top that is level and held rigidly in place for normal use. The structure underneath is there to achieve this end and it fails in its purpose if the top slopes, is uneven, or is liable to fall over. This requirement should be borne in mind when planning and making a table.

If a table is to remain outside in all weather, the top will usually have to be made of solid boards. Even the best marine or exterior grades of plywood are liable to suffer if left exposed for long periods, but plywood will make effective tops for tables that are stored under cover. Most other manufactured boards suffer from the same problems as plywood when exposed to prolonged sunlight, rain, or frost conditions. The availability of suitable materials for the top could be the governing factor in deciding on the table you will make.

Table sizes should be related to seats. With chair seats about 15 inches from the ground, the tabletop should be 27 inches to 30 inches high. For most people, slightly less is better rather than slightly higher. If the table is only to be for drinks and magazines near a lounging chair, it can be lower—possibly down to 24 inches. If you make it much lower, someone will mistake it for a seat (so make it strong enough to sit on). Any table intended to be used for meals should have its top 12 inches to 15 inches above the chair or bench seat level. Anyone standing can use a table 30 inches high. If the table you make is not intended for anyone in a normal chair, it could be 3 inches or so higher.

A table needs a fairly broad base to stand steadily. In general, avoid making a table that is higher than its width and length. You might have to reduce one way in some cases. That means a tabletop should be at least 27 inches one or both ways. You can increase stability by letting the bottoms of the legs project outside the outline of the top, but extensions of more than an inch or so will be a nuisance.

Tabletops should be stiff enough to avoid warping, but that does not mean they should be thick if there is adequate framing. They need not be solid. Gaps between boards allow rain to run through. Light slats can be arranged with spaces to make a light top for a portable table. Obviously gaps should not be very wide. Even with a cloth over, anything wider than about 1/2 inch could cause some items to tip or small ones to fall through.

STRIP TABLE

Figure 13-1 shows a light rigid table that is easy for two persons to carry about. If made of suitable wood, it could be left outside, but it is the type of table that could also have uses in a greenhouse, playroom, or other indoor situation when it is not needed outside. The size suggested makes the table suitable for outdoor meals with many of the chairs described in Chapter 12.

The design is based on strips of wood all the same section. In the example, the wood is 3 inches wide and 1 inch thick, but the sizes could be adapted to suit wood of other sizes. For this method of construction, it is important that the top has an odd number of strips in it so that there is a central one over the lengthwise rail. The overall width suggested suits seven 3-inch pieces with narrow gaps between. If you are using other width strips, experiment with them to arrive at a suitable width top before planning the other sizes.

All of the parts are glued and screwed. There is insufficient thickness for screws to be counterbored, so use brass or other damp-resisting screws

and choose lengths that will go almost through the second piece.

1. Make the two end trestles (Fig. 13-2A and B), using glue and four screws at each crossing. Check squareness and that opposite ends match.

2. Notch the top bars of the trestles to take the rail (Fig. 13-2C).

3. Make the rail 6 inches less than the top is to be to allow overhang at the ends. Notch the ends to fit the trestle (Fig. 13-2D) and cut a notch at the center for a cleat that will go across under the top (Fig. 13-2E). Make that cleat to a length that will come to the outside edges of the top (or almost so). Bevel the undersides of its ends.

4. Prepare the top strips. Lightly round the top edges and round the ends, which will overhang the trestles by about 3 inches. Drill for two screws in each piece into the tops of the trestles. Use the rail as a guide to lengthwise spacing. Also drill the central strip for screws at about 9-inch intervals into the rail. Allow for the outside strips overhanging the trestle tops by 1 inch.

5. Glue and screw the central rail into the notches in the trestles. Put the cleat across in its notch and screw it there. Over this glue and screw the central top strip. Add the outer strips while checking that the assembly is square as you do this.

6. Position the other top strips evenly between those already attached.

7. Invert the table and drive screws upward through the cleat into each top strip.

8. Although the two diagonal struts come near the center of the table, their ends can be marked by having the table on its side. This way strips can be put across the edge and the contact places can be outlined. Allow for the bottom notch overlapping the depth of the trestle rail by about 2 inches. The overhang at the top bears on its edge and the surplus is cut off (Fig. 13-2F). At the top of a strut, allow it to go about 5 inches past the center of the table, and then cut its edge parallel with the top (Fig. 13-2G).

9. The struts are positioned on opposite sides of the central rail. Screw them first to the trestle rails. You can then move their tops a little along the central rail until, before screwing to it, you have

Fig. 13-1. A light table can be made from strips of all the same section.

checked that the legs are square to the top.

10. That completes construction and the table can be left untreated if it is a weather-resisting hardwood. If it is softwood it should be painted. Hardwood can be painted or varnished. In either case, the wood could be treated with preservative. If the table is to be used for eating from, it should be left some time before placing food on it.

Materials List for Strip Table

4 legs	27 × 3 × 1
4 rails	24 × 3 × 1
1 cleat	26 × 3 × 1
1 rail	42 × 3 × 1
2 struts	36 × 3 × 1
7 top strips	48 × 3 × 1

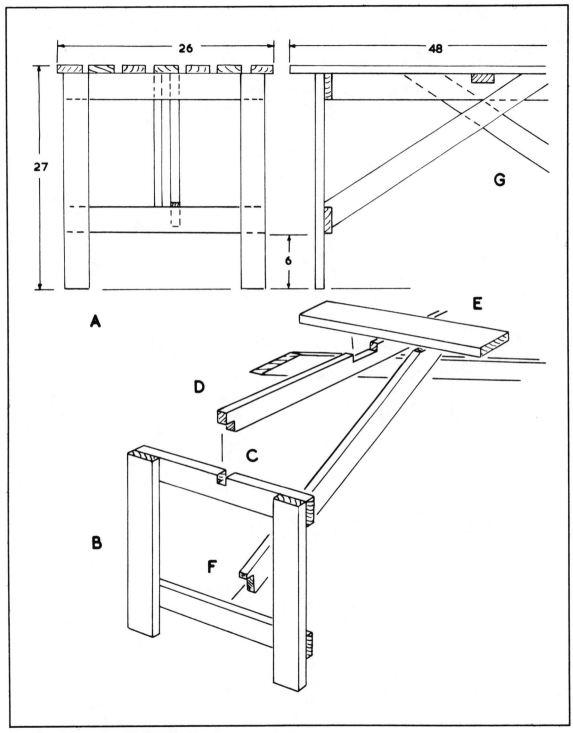

Fig. 13-2. The suggested table sizes allow the parts to overlap.

SPLAYED-LEGS TABLE

If table legs slope outward both ways, the appearance is improved and there is an advantage in stability. The outline covered by the feet can be at or outside the lines of the top. With vertical legs, this could only be arranged by having the legs joining the top at its corners (which is ugly and inconvenient).

Anyone interested in geometry will know that there is a problem if the legs splay much. The actual section of the legs will no longer be square, but will take on a diamond shape. This complicates the preparation of wood and the cutting of joints. If the splay is kept slight, however, any errors are also slight and can be taken care of in the practicalities of construction. Shapes and fits of parts

Fig. 13-3. A table with legs splayed both ways is very stable.

should be close enough not to be noticed.

The table shown in Fig. 13-3 has its legs sloping out to cover the same area on the ground as the top; it should stand firmly. It is shown as a small general-purpose size, but the techniques could be used to make a table of any other size. The top is drawn as made up of four 7-inch-wide boards. It could be framed plywood or particleboard if the table is to be kept under cover when out of use. Decide on the size of the top before making other parts.

Almost any wood could be used. A heavy hardwood might be most suitable if the table is to be rarely moved. Softwood would make it light for portability, but a softwood top on a hardwood frame would be strong and of moderate weight.

1. Although in precision construction the leg lengths would have to be developed geometrically, differences here are so slight that you can make the end frames as if there was no compound slope. Set out the end (Fig. 13-4A) with its main lines symmetrical about a centerline (Fig. 13-4B). This can be used as a guide to the slopes of joints the other way.

2. Mark the legs, using an adjustable bevel instead of a square, but do not cut off the ends yet. Mark the top rails (Fig. 13-4C); allow about 3/4 of an inch at each end for tenons. Mark the bottom rails in a similar way (Fig. 13-4D). Although there are slopes on the wider faces, lines in the other direction can be square across.

3. Make the mortise and tenon joints (Fig. 13-4E and F). Alternatively, cut the wood at the shoulders and use dowels (Fig. 13-5A and B).

4. In the other direction, mark and cut similar joints for the lengthwise top rails (Fig. 13-4G). With tenons, you can drill across and put dowels through for added strength, or you can use nails or screws from inside (Fig. 13-5C).

5. The bottom central rail (Fig. 13-4H) has tenons through the bottom and rails. Tenons here are preferable to dowels because they will have a better resistance to pulling apart under load.

6. The top can be screwed from above. If you want to attach the top without screw heads or plugs showing on top, there are two possible

ways of screwing from below. If you are to use either of them it is easier to prepare the rails before assembly than to do it after assembling the framework. Individual screws can be driven as "pocket" screws in hollows gouged out (Fig. 13-5D) or made by drilling (Fig. 13-5E). Another way uses "buttons." They screw to the top, but engage with plowed grooves inside the rails (Fig. 13-5F). Buttons allow for the top expanding and contracting without the risk of splits developing.

7. Prepare the rails for either method, if you wish, and then start assembly. Make up the end frames first. Measure diagonals to check symmetry. Join the frames with the lengthwise rails and check squareness of the parts by measuring diagonals while the legs are on a level surface.

8. The boards for the top can be put on without joining their edges, but it would be better to make them up into a solid piece. That can be done by simple gluing, using dowels, or by secret slot screwing (see Chapter 2). Prepare the top as a unit, with rounded edges and corners, and then fit it to the framework by screwing downward or by one of the methods of attaching from below.

9. Finish the woodwork with paint, varnish, or preservative.

Materials List for Splayed-Legs Table	
4 legs	27 × 2 × 2
2 top rails	30 × 4 × 1
2 top rails	21 × 4 × 1
2 bottom rails	25 × 2 × 1
1 bottom rail	28 × 2 × 1
4 tops	36 × 7 × 1

OVAL-TOP TABLE

Curves soften appearance as well as remove sharp corners that might be dangerous or inconvenient. Any curve can be used and parts of circles are common, but ovals are considered more aesthetically pleasing. If you are making a tabletop that measures the same both ways, you can use a circle. If it is longer one way, the circle is stretched to an oval. This is more correctly called an ellipse

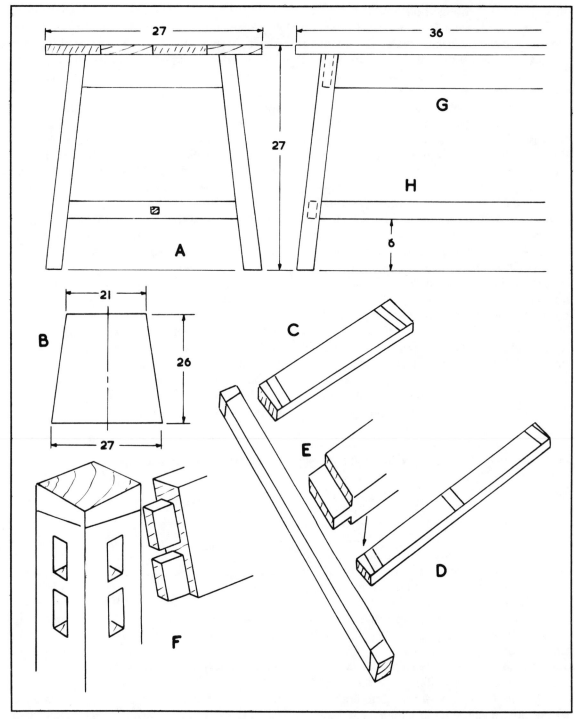

Fig. 13-4. The corners of the legs cover the same area as the top. End assemblies are tenoned first, and then the lengthwise rails added.

because oval means egg-shaped (wider at one end). A table with an oval top (Fig. 13-6) could be made any size and with various leg arrangements. Figure 13-6 shows splayed slab legs. A bottom rail is arranged flat so that it can be used as a shelf. The drawings show a similar table, but with the lower rail on edge. Using tusk tenons for that rail allows the assembly to be pulled tight even after

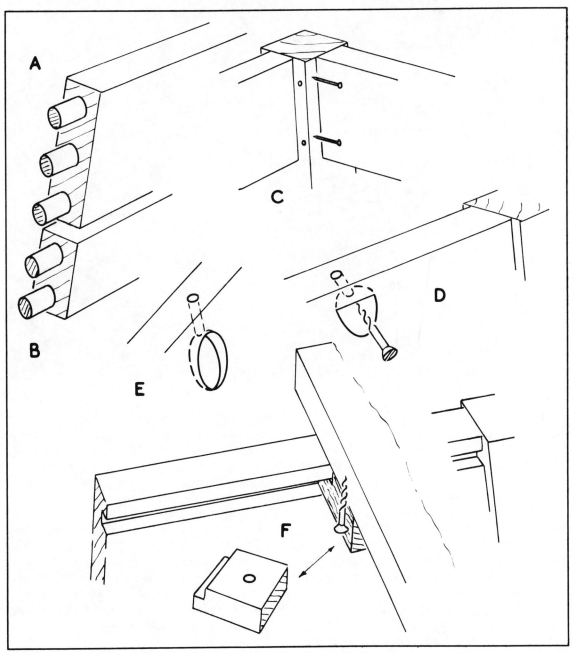

Fig. 13-5. Dowels could be used instead of tenons. The top can be held with slot screws or buttons.

Fig. 13-6. An oval top gives an attractive shape to a table.

swelling or shrinkage due to changes in the weather. The table is not meant to be dismantled.

The best wood is fairly thick hardwood and 1 1/4 inch or 1 1/2 inch is suggested. Softwood could be used, but it would not have as long a life. The table shown in Fig. 13-6 has a top made up of three boards with battens across and gaps between. It would be better to join the board edges so that the top can be treated as a single piece when marking out the shape. With separate boards, expansion and contraction will show an unevenness in the outline at the joints.

The legs will also have to be made up of several boards joined together. Avoid having a joint line through the mortise and top notch. Whether the wood is planed or not depends on

the situation. For a more rural part of the yard or garden, a sawn finish is appropriate. On a patio or deck, a smooth planed finish would be better. If the table is to make a set with tusk-tenoned chairs or benches, finish it in the same way.

1. Draw the main lines of the side view (Fig. 13-7A) to get the length and angles of the legs. The sizes given allow a slope of 15 degrees and bring the bottoms of the legs not quite to the length of the top, but wide enough for stability.

2. Mark out the legs (Figs. 13-7B and 8A). Get the actual length from your full-size drawing. Bevel the tops and bottoms and cut the curves, but leave cutting the joints until the other parts are ready.

3. Make the top rail (Figs. 13-7C and 8B). It

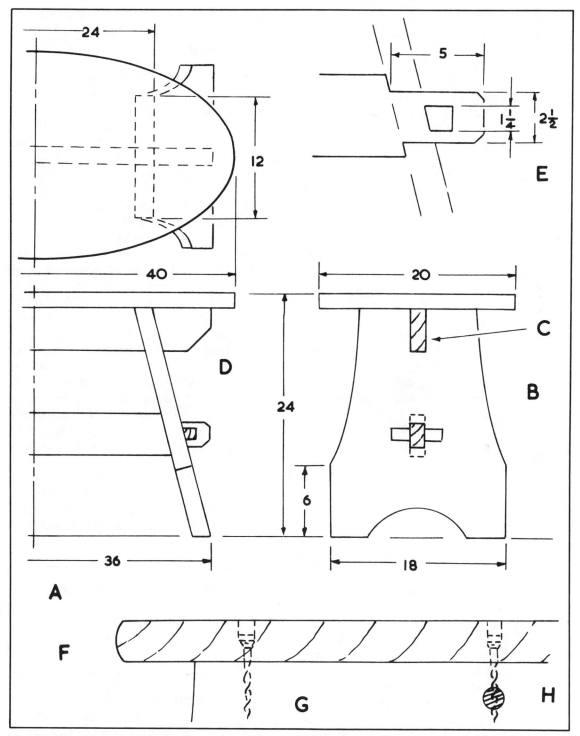

Fig. 13-7. The framework of the oval table uses tusk tenons in the rails (A-E). The top can be screwed to the legs (F-H).

has to be cut with halving joints into the legs (Fig. 13-8C). It is cut back shorter than the top will be and is beveled (Fig. 13-7D).

4. Get the length between shoulders of the bottom rail from your drawing. Allow some excess length on the tenons until after cutting the wedge slots. The shoulders of the tenons must match the slopes of the legs. Cut the tenons to width (Fig. 13-7E). Make mortises to match in the legs.

5. Mark out the wedge slots. The inner end of the slot should be at the same angle as the leg, but cut at least 1/8 of an inch inside its surface so that the wedge can pull in tight without binding on it. The outer end of the slot can be square. Make the wedges (Fig. 13-8D) too long at first and bevel their inner surfaces to match the leg. Cut through the outside of the slot to the same slope as the wedges.

6. Try each tenon in its leg. Trim the wedges so that they project about the same amount each side of their tenon, but it is wise to assume that they will drive further during later adjustments. Trim the ends of the tenons.

7. Assemble the parts. Because of the slope of the halving joints, you will have to progressively enter the tenons and the halving joints. Do not try to fix one rail before the other. Glue the top rail in, but allow for the wedges alone tightening and holding the bottom rail.

8. Join boards for the top, with battens below, that will have to be notched or glued into the top rail, preferably with dowels or secret-slot screwing (see Chapter 2).

9. The top can be made as a full oval or an ellipse. That takes away quite a lot of wood at the corners when compared with a plain rectangular top. That might not matter, but if you want to have a rather bigger top area, while still retaining curves, you could mark parts of circles across the ends (Fig. 13-8E). A full semicircle on the ends would leave short lengths straight at each side, but avoid sharp corners (Fig. 13-8F). For a larger area, just the corners of a rectangle might be rounded (Fig. 13-8G).

10. An ellipse of this size can be marked with pencil and string. Draw centerlines both ways on the top (Fig. 13-8H). Take half the length of the

long centerline up to the top of the short line and measure this amount to a point on the long line (Fig. 13-8J). Measure the same the other way. Put nails or spikes at these points.

11. Make a loop by knotting a piece of nonstretch string, around the nails, long enough to reach the top mark on the short centerline. Put a pencil in the loop and take it round (Fig. 13-8K). Keep a tension on the string all the way and you will get a true ellipse. If you want to make the ellipse wider, bring the nails a little closer together. To make it longer move them further apart.

12. Cut the top to shape. It could be left with square edges, particularly if the surfaces are left sawn, but for a better finish it could have the edges semicircular. A flatter curve looks better (Fig. 13-7F). This could be done with a suitable router cutter or by careful planing and sanding.

13. It would be possible to attach the top with secret-slot screwing, as in the last project, but in the end grain of the legs this will not hold very well. It would probably be better to use secret-slot screwing along both sides of the top rail and counterbored and plugged screws into the legs (Fig. 13-7G), and with dowels across (Fig. 13-7H) if it is a type of wood that does not allow much grip for screws in end grain. Because the top and the legs both have grain the same way, any expansion and contraction should match and be no problem.

14. Finish the table in a way to suit its situation. After it has been exposed to the weather for a few weeks, check the tightness of the wedges. Later checks will only be needed after prolonged changes in the weather.

Materials List for Oval-Top Table	
2 legs	25 × 18 × 1 1/2
2 rails	40 × 4 × 1 1/2
1 top	40 × 20 × 1 1/2
2 wedges	8 × 1 1/2 × 1 1/4

SAWBUCK TABLE

A table with crossed legs would match the sawbuck chair described in the last chapter, but

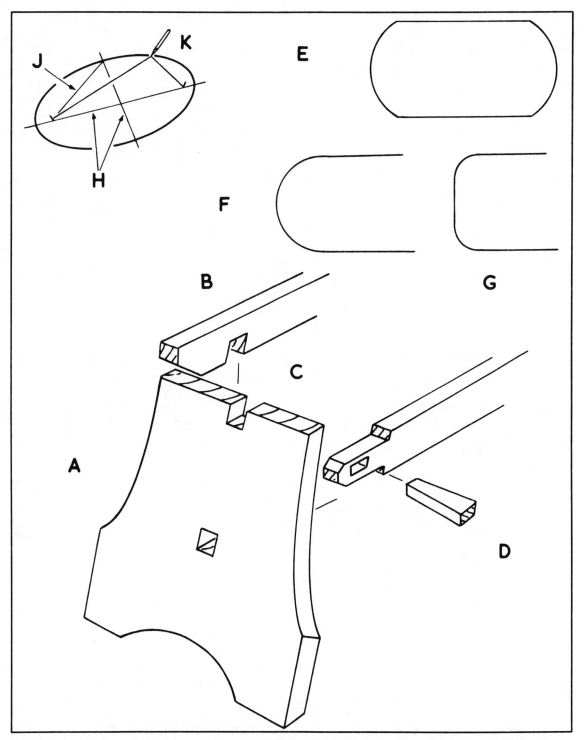

Fig. 13-8. Instead of an ellipse, there could be a parallel-sided top. Rails are notched and tenoned to the legs.

in itself it makes an attractive and interesting project (Fig. 13-9). The method of construction gives satisfactory bracing and a rigid table that might be considered more interesting visually than one with upright legs. There is slightly more wood in the legs, making the table heavier, but that could be an advantage where it is liable to be knocked and does not have to be moved often.

The wood used could be standard sections of softwood; hardwoods are also suitable. Whether the wood is left sawn or is planed depends on the situation. Sawn wood could have the main parts joined with bolts and screws used for joining the top and lengthwise rails. For a better table made of planed wood, the parts can be glued. They could also be screwed or bolted, but for an all-glued construction there might be dowels in nearly all joints. They could be taken right through the leg-framing joints and would make an assembly of adequate strength for use on a patio or even indoors. The table would also have uses in a large greenhouse. The broad slatted top would make a good work-

Fig. 13-9. A table with crossed sawbuck legs looks attractive in a yard.

ing bench or a stand for potted plants.

The sizes given are for a fairly large table of suitable size for meals. Use chairs of ordinary height. The same method of construction could be used for many other table sizes. This includes tiny tables for drinks and magazines alongside a chair. A small version would also be strong enough to use as a stool.

1. A full-size drawing of the main lines of an end is needed to obtain the sizes and shapes of the legs (Fig. 13-10A). They fit in a 27 inch square. At the ground the top edge meets the corner. At the other end it is 3 inches in from the corner. Draw the legs both ways and use this drawing to set them out and cut them.

2. It is inadvisable to make full-depth halving joints where the legs cross because that would weaken them too much. Nevertheless, some notching is advisable to keep them in correct relation under load. Mark where the legs cross and cut notches 1/4 inch deep (Fig. 13-10B). During assembly, one 1/2-inch bolt through the center of the joint will pull the legs tight together and the notching will prevent movement.

3. The end rail, which goes across under the top (Fig. 13-10C and D), has to be brought square to the line of the table with a packing (which will be about 1 1/2 inch thick). Check what is needed by measuring the overlap on the actual legs. Mark a halving joint at the center of the rail for the lengthwise top rail (Fig. 13-10E). A 1/2-inch bolt through each lap will join the legs to the end rail. Assemble these parts. If glued and doweled construction is being used, apply glue and clamp the joints while drilling for dowels. Four 1/2-inch dowels glued at each crossing should be sufficient.

4. Make the lengthwise top rail (Fig. 13-10F and G). Notch it to fit the end rails. If thick wood is used for the top, that will be stiff enough to hold its shape without further stiffening. Thinner boards should have bracing with cleats across underneath (Fig. 13-10H). Two evenly spaced cleats are suggested, but one at the center may be enough with some boards. Notch the top rail for the cleats.

5. The two stretchers are plain pieces screwed to the legs (Fig. 13-10J). Prepare them, and then complete assembly of the framework by fitting in the top rail and these stretchers while the legs are standing on a level surface and while you can see that the assembly is upright.

6. Any widths of boards can be used for the top, but there should be an odd number so that one covers the top rail. The suggested boards are a nominal 6 inches, which will probably be 5 7/8 inches actual size (leaving gaps about 1/4 inch wide). Take sharpness off the edges. Put the cleats in position. Screw the outside boards to the top end rails, and then space the others evenly between them and screw them in place. Either screw downward into the cleats or turn the table over and screw upward from the cleats into the boards. It will probably be sufficient to have the screw heads level on the top, but they can be counterbored and plugged for a better finish.

7. If the table is to stand on soft ground or you want to spread the load to reduce damage to a lawn surface, feet can be added. These could be offcuts from the stretchers screwed under the legs (Fig. 13-10K).

8. Round the corners and edges of the top, remove any roughness elsewhere and finish the wood to suit the situation for which it is to be used.

Materials List for Sawbuck Table	
4 legs	40 × 4 × 2
2 end rails	28 × 4 × 2
1 top rail	57 × 4 × 2
2 stretchers	53 × 4 × 2
2 top cleats	30 × 4 × 1
5 tops	60 × 5 7/8 × 1

HEXAGONAL TABLE

Tables do not have to be rectangular. There is an attraction about sitting around a symmetrical table. If you want to use an umbrella shade on a central support, it is logical to shape the table around that central rod or tube. The table shown in Fig. 13-11 has a hexagonal top and three splayed legs, with a shelf underneath, so the top and the shelf provide bracing for the umbrella pole. With the three

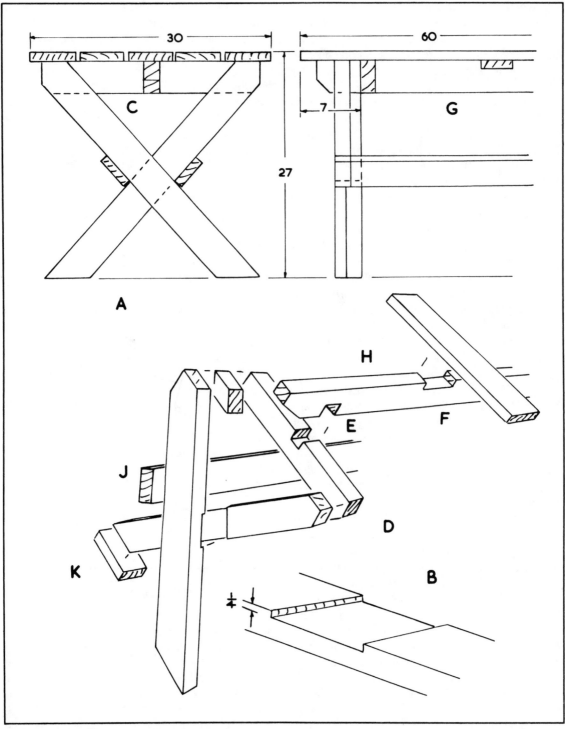

Fig. 13-10. The table framework is notched together.

Fig. 13-11. A hexagonal table can have three legs and a shelf below.

legs, there is the property of steadiness on an uneven surface. This will be an advantage if the umbrella is caught in a wind. Although the top is shown hexagonal, it could be made round with very little modification. The size and height should suit a meal or refreshments table with up to six people using chairs of normal height.

The top and shelf are made of exterior-grade or marine-grade, 1/2-inch plywood. The other parts are all 1 inch thick. Construction should be easy with hand tools if power tools are unavailable. With a regular hexagonal shape, all the angles that have to be cut for the top framing are 60 degrees. Leg joint angles will be found on the drawing.

1. It will help in getting the sizes of many parts to have the top piece of plywood set out so that the underframing can be marked out on its underside. Its outline is obtained by drawing a circle, stepping off the radius around the circumference, and then joining these points. The plywood is bordered with wood 1 inch thick (Fig. 13-13A). A suitable circumference for the circle is about 38 inches.

2. On the underside of the top, mark another hexagon on a 12-inch circle (Fig. 13-12A). From this draw the outlines of the top rails to the centers of three sides (Fig. 13-12B).

3. Make a center block to this hexagonal shape. It is 1 inch thick, but you can use pieces to make up its size if you do not have a single piece of wood large enough. It will be glued and screwed to the top so that will reinforce any joints needed to make up width.

4. Fit the block to the top plywood and drill through for the umbrella pole. Make it an easy fit; 1 1/2 inch will probably suit most poles (Fig. 13-13B).

5. Frame around the plywood top with strips underneath (Fig. 13-13C). Miter their corners. If you do not get a perfect fit, it does not matter. Aim to get the outer corners tight.

6. Cut the top rails (Fig. 13-13D) to fit in place, but do not fix them yet.

7. To obtain the shape and slope of the legs, set one out (Fig. 13-12C). From this cut the wood for the legs. Allow a little extra at the top for tenons.

Taper the legs from just below the tenon shoulders to 3 inches wide at the bottom. Mark the mortise positions at what will be 6 inches in from the outside of the top (Fig. 13-13E). Mark and cut the mortise and tenon joints. A pair of tenons is advised (Fig. 13-13F). Do not assemble these parts yet.

8. At the shelf level, mark out in a very similar way to the top. Make the shelf (Fig. 13-12D). It can be left unframed unless you want to add a lip to prevent things from falling off.

9. On the underside of the shelf, fit a center block the same as that under the top, and drill through with the same size hole.

10. From the leg setting out get the length of the bottom rails. Each bottom rail has to fit against the center block and be tenoned to the leg in a similar way to the top joints (Fig. 13-13G).

11. Frame around the outside of the top with mitered strips (Fig. 13-13H). Attach them with glue and screws. Make sure the edges of the plywood are thoroughly glued so water is unlikely to enter the end grain of the veneers. Round the outer edges of the top when the glue has set.

12. With all the joints prepared, assemble the legs and rails. It is advisable to first join the legs to the top rails. Wedge the tenons from above and plane level before fitting the rails to the top. The bottom rail tenons can also be wedged, but you can do that during assembly.

13. Check that all legs splay the same amount by comparing the angles they make with the top or shelf. Before the glue has set, view the table from above to see that all legs project the same amount. Stand back and look at the table from several directions to check its symmetrical appearance.

14. A painted finish is most appropriate.

Materials List for Hexagonal Table	
3 legs	29 × 4 × 1
3 top rails	12 × 4 × 1
3 bottom rails	15 × 4 × 1
2 center blocks	12 × 10 × 1
6 top frames	22 × 2 × 1
6 top borders	23 × 2 × 1
1 top	40 × 35 × 1/2 plywood
1 shelf	24 × 21 × 1/2 plywood

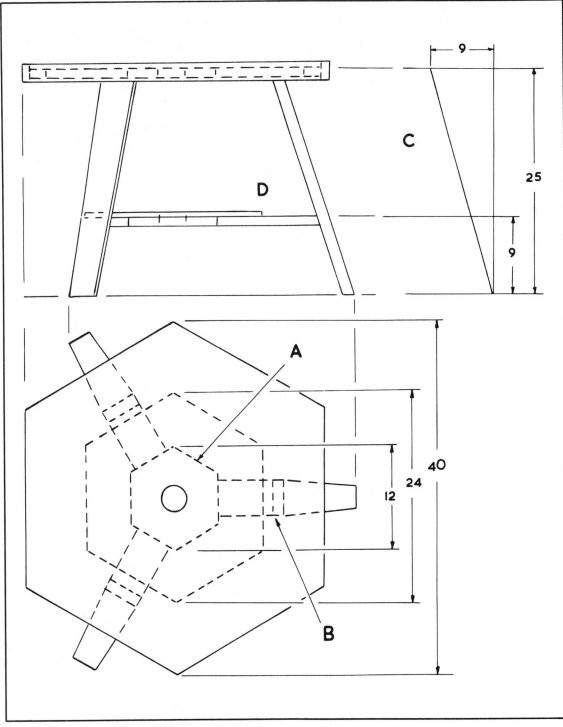

Fig. 13-12. The table shape is set from a pattern of regular hexagons.

PICNIC TABLE

Picnic tables are found everywhere from wayside rest areas to campgrounds, parks, and anywhere that people want to eat outdoors—including yards and gardens. The ubiquitous picnic table tends to follow a standard pattern. If you look at the details of the better ones, construction is basically the same. Sizes differ, but the way they are made does

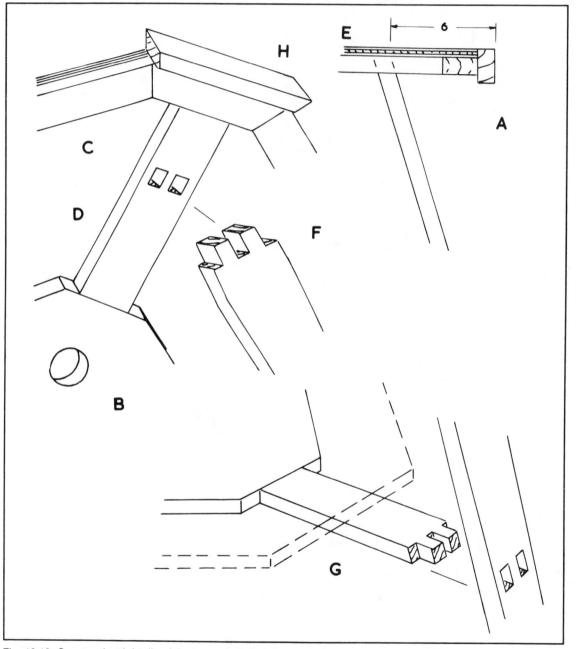

Fig. 13-13. Constructional details of the top and shelf of the hexagonal table.

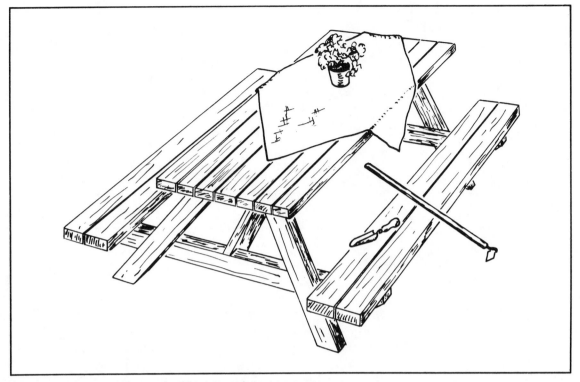

Fig. 13-14. A picnic table with built-in benches fits into any yard.

not vary much. The usual picnic table with built-in side benches has splayed legs at the ends, crosspieces to support the bench tops, and there should be some lengthwise bracing.

This picnic table is of moderate size, intended to be fairly heavy (and therefore stable), and it follows the common pattern (Fig. 13-14). Its sizes could be varied. As shown it gives roomy seating for at least six adults at a comfortable height. The end view (Fig. 13-15A) would be the same for any length, unless the wood sizes are altered considerably. If the table is made much longer, there should be one or more cleats across under the top boards and possibly under the seats. If longer seats become too flexible, they will need similar diagonal bracing to the tabletop.

All of the parts in this project are 2-inch-by-4-inch section. They might be left as sawn, but will be better planed when the sections will be about 1/8 inch undersize. The seven pieces making up the tabletop should have narrow gaps be-

tween them for drainage. Try the wood you have for total width and vary the size a little if necessary.

The main parts could be bolted together. One 5/8-inch bolt through the center of each joint should be enough. Alternatively, use two thinner ones, such as 3/8 inch, arranged diagonally across a joint so that the holes do not come in the same grain lines and possibly cause splits. The top and seat boards can be nailed on or screwed. If nailed, the heads should be punched below the surface and covered with stopping. Screws are best counterbored and plugged.

1. The only setting out needed is to obtain and measure the splay of the legs. The exact slopes are not crucial, but obviously they should be the same both ways. The measurements on the end view (Fig. 13-15A) will allow you to set out the main lines of the legs. At their tops they are 2 inches apart (Fig. 13-15B) and at the bottom they spread to 48 inches (Fig. 13-15C). Although shown taken to a fine edge at the bottom, the outer cor-

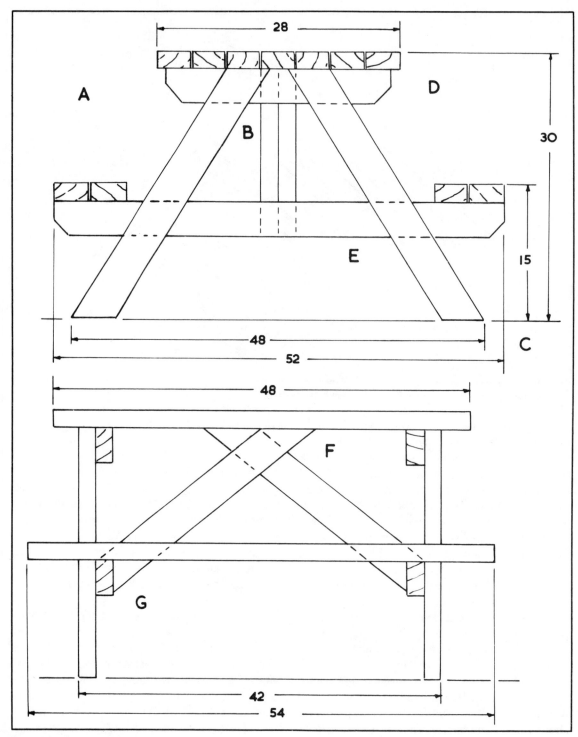

Fig. 13-15. Suitable sizes for a picnic table.

ner should be cut and rounded to minimize the risk of the wood splintering. Make the legs (Fig. 13-16A) from your drawing. Mark on them where the seat rail will cross.

2. Make the top rails (Figs. 13-15D and 13-16B) a little shorter than the overall width of the top will be and bevel the undersides of their ends.

3. Make the seat rails (Figs. 13-15E and 13-16C). If there are any variations in quality, choose your straightest wood for these parts.

4. With your full-size setting out as a guide, put the parts of an end together and drill through for bolts. There could be waterproof glue in each joint, but the bolts alone should be secure enough. Without glue, it is advisable with most woods to coat the meeting surfaces with preservative. Use the first assembled end as a guide when assembling the other end as a pair to it.

5. Prepare the boards for the top and seats. Take sharpness off the edges and round the ends (either now or after assembly). Outer corners of the seats and top should be well rounded.

6. Mark on the undersides of these boards where the end frames will come and drill for screws or nails.

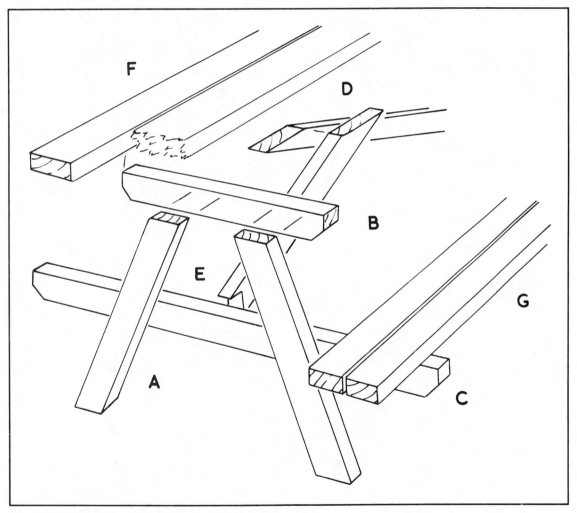

Fig. 13-16. The relative positions of parts in a picnic table.

7. Make a first assembly with the ends standing on a level surface for getting the shapes of the diagonal struts. Fit the center top board and one seat board at each side. Check that the ends are standing upright and squarely in relation to the boards you have fitted.

8. The two struts have their top edges meeting at the center of the top board. They overlap and will be bolted through (Figs. 13-15F and 13-16D). At their lower ends, the top surfaces should extend to the outsides of the seat rails, and then have notches to fit over (Figs. 13-15G and 13-16E).

9. Make the two struts. It is possible to make small adjustments by sliding the overlapping tops over each other until they fit closely at both ends while the framework is standing true. When you are satisfied, bolt the struts to each other and screw down into their tops through the top board. At their bottoms screw or nail in place.

10. Fit the other top and seat boards (Fig. 13-16F and G). A short piece of thin wood is a good guide to make gaps all the same width. Make sure all screws and bolts are as tight as possible. Washers under the bolt heads and nuts will prevent them from pulling in.

11. The finished picnic table could be painted, but for leaving outside indefinitely it is best treated with preservative—which is renewed occasionally.

Materials List for Picnic Table	
4 legs	38 × 4 × 2
2 seat rails	52 × 4 × 2
2 top rails	27 × 4 × 2
4 seats	54 × 4 × 2
7 tops	48 × 4 × 2
2 struts	33 × 4 × 2

Chapter 14

Fences and Gates

A wide-open vista at the limit of your property can be attractive, both for you looking out and for possible admirers looking in, but in many cases it is necessary to mark the limit of your land and to keep out trespassers and animals. In particular, straying animals, whether domestic or wild, can wreck your carefully nurtured flower beds or kill off your growing vegetables. This means that for at least part of your garden you need fences. If you have a fence, you must have some means of getting through or over it that is equally animal-proof. Usually there is a door or gate, but perhaps a stile will be appropriate in some situations.

Medieval owners of stately homes used one alternative to a fence and that was a ditch. They could sit and look over their garden into the farmland beyond, but cattle from the farm could not cross the ditch into the garden. Obviously this ditch, which was picturesquely called a *ha-ha*, had to be fairly wide and deep if the cows were to be discouraged. You might not have the space or energy to make such a ditch, but a smaller ditch might be worth considering to impede smaller

animals. If you need to drain water away, the ditch could serve that purpose as well.

Fences can be made in many ways and to different sizes. A few strands of wire stretched between posts would keep out larger animals and show people where the boundary is without having much effect on the view. A solid fence would also protect against animals and would be a windbreak. If you want privacy as well, the solid fence should be at least 6 feet high. If you want to keep geese or smaller animals from a vegetable garden, you need a fairly close mesh wire netting if you are not to build a solid fence.

The fences most of us build will be wood because we have the facilities for working it and are familiar with the techniques. For many purposes a wood fence is perfectly satisfactory. The vulnerable part is where wood posts go into the ground. There they can become loose and will be subject to rot. A better arrangement uses concrete posts for the full height or far enough above the ground for the wood posts to be bolted to them.

Some fences are wholly or partially made of

metal. Corrugated metal sheeting can be mounted on wood or metal framing. Corrugated or flat plastic sheeting could be used. Some of it will let sunlight through while providing a wind screen and some privacy.

The most solid fence is a wall built of stone. If stone is plentiful it makes a very attractive fence that usually fits in better with its surroundings than any of the other types. If sufficient stone has to be brought from a distance, cost would probably rule it out. Brick can be used in a very similar way, but it has a regular pattern of courses that will suit some situations, but tend to be rather too prominent in others. Concrete can be used alone or with prepared blocks. Finishing it with a stonelike surface disguises its often stark appearance.

Another type of fence is a grown hedge. It takes time to grow, but it can be decorative as a natural-looking boundary marker. The best type of plants or shrubs for the soil and locality will have to be chosen. It is possible to grow a high windbreak, a low arrangement of widely spaced plants or trees, or an almost impenetrable mass of intertwined branches and twigs. You will probably have to start with an arrangement of stakes, possibly with a few horizontal rails or wires, to serve as a foundation for the hedge as it grows. That arrangement will disappear inside the mass of foliage as it develops.

A stile can be made with any type of fence by providing steps on each side with built-up wood, projecting stones, or cast concrete. Gates are mostly wood. Metal gates are possible if you have facilities for welding, but a gate can put a considerable load on its hinges and there is an advantage in the comparative lightness of wood. Wood will also usually look better and can provide a decorative feature in an otherwise rather plain fence. An exception is a wrought-iron gate with its many curls and scrolls, but not many of us are smiths capable of making one of these.

For the entrance to your property, it is possible to fashion very elaborate gates. A pair of attractive gates will make a good impression on visitors as they turn into your drive (even if the gates are open most of the time).

POST TOOLS

If you want to build a fence with stone or brick, you have to dig a trench for foundations. This is straightforward hard work with pick and spade or, more likely today, a quick job with a hired excavator.

There are just a few wood fence methods that do not involve posts entering the ground some way, but for most fences you have to erect posts. So that they will stay upright indefinitely and not succumb to wind or other pressure on the fence, they should go into the soil quite deeply. How deep depends on the soil, but you should regard 18 inches as the minimum for a fence standing waist high, and go deeper for a high fence or softer soil.

It is very unlikely that a pointed post could be driven in by hand methods without a hole being made first. There are post drivers mounted on tractors for farm work that will push a post into the most stubborn ground. If you can get the use of one of these and the tractor will not damage your garden, it could be the answer to your post-driving problem.

A hole can be dug with an ordinary spade. The hole would be much bigger than the post. The post is then placed in position and the soil is put back and tamped down tightly around it. There are narrow, long-bladed spades made for this purpose so that you do not have to cut away quite such a large area. There could be a combination of digging and driving, with the spade used to make a hole and loosen the soil left in, and then the post driven and tamped firmly. If you only have a few posts to erect and no special tools, this is a satisfactory method.

There are post-hole borers of several types that are intended to remove soil from a hole not much further across than the size of the post. They can be successful if you have only soil to remove. If there are stones where the post is to come, you will still have to dig to remove them.

One type of borer is like a large auger. Blades cut their way into the soil and lift it (Fig. 14-1A). As the tool is withdrawn, it lifts the loose soil from the hole. A hand auger will have a cross handle to give plenty of leverage. A similar cutter can be

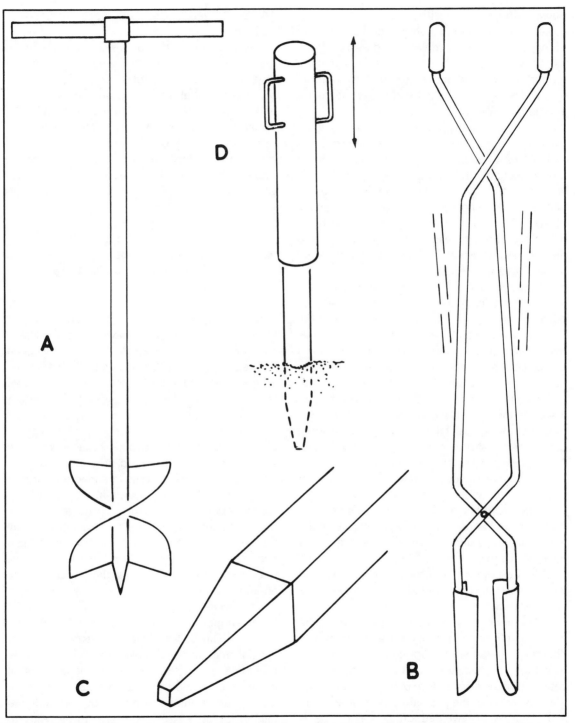

Fig. 14-1. Post hole borers (A, B) make holes with less disturbance than digging with a spade. A point makes driving easier (C). A tube for pounding is better than a hammer (D).

power driven, and either self-contained or mounted on a tractor. Another type has a pair of scooped blades operated with handles something like scissors (Fig. 14-1B). The tool is thrust into the ground. Handles are moved to pinch the soil between the blades so it can be lifted out, ready for another thrust to deepen the hole.

Ideally both tools should make a hole slightly smaller than the post—which is usually square—so it forces its way in and becomes tight without further attention. If the hole is larger, as it often is, you have to do some further tamping or you can pack around the post with strips of wood to make up size. If you do that, the packing should be as durable as the post, treated with preservative, and not just oddments you pick up. The wood could rot and give you trouble later on.

Fence posts should normally be pointed, but if you are digging a hole as deep as the pole is to go, a full size square end has the advantage of being less likely to sink deeper after the fence has been assembled. Sinkage of a post in soft ground could spoil the appearance of the finished fence. In most ground a point is an advantage. Do not cut to a fine point; it could crumble. An end about 3/4 of an inch across would be better. The angle of the end is not crucial and a length of 6 inches on a 4-inch post is reasonable for most soils (Fig. 14-1C). Usually the taper is square whether the post is round or square. It could be sawn or chopped with an ax.

A post could be driven with the heaviest hammer you can handle. An outsize mallet, called a maul (made by putting a piece of tree trunk on a handle), is also effective and less likely to split the post. In any case, the post should be too long and a piece of scrap wood is held over its end to take hammer blows.

Hammering involves someone holding the post. Apart from any risk of damage to them, it is difficult to keep the post upright. A one- or two-man tool, less hazardous and easier to keep on course, is made from a piece of heavy steel tubing that will slip over the post and an end welded in. Two handles are welded on and the tube is pounded up and down by a pair of workers (Fig.

14-1D). Its weight and fit are more effective than hammering.

A large pointed round steel rod, about 36 inches long and 1 inch in diameter, is useful for starting holes, levering out stones, and penetrating the ground. A flat steel rod about the same length and maybe 2-inch-by-1/2-inch section, with its end thinned, can be used like a chisel to square holes or use as a lever. For tamping down soil around a post, a tool consisting of a block of iron on the end of a handle could be used. A piece of fence post with its end cut square across is almost as good.

WIRE TOOLS

If a fence is made in any of the ways that use wood rails and other wood parts, the tools needed are only those used for other types of carpentry. Many fences are made with wires between posts supporting netting or other meshes to stop animals or birds. The horizontal wires have to be pulled fairly tight, and various tools and techniques have been devised for this purpose. It is unlikely that barbed wire will be used unless your garden adjoins farm land. The tools and techniques devised by farmers for dealing with barbed wire, as well as those used by telegraph workers for attaching wires to posts, can be of use in the more modest attaching of plain wire to posts around a yard or garden.

There are several tools intended for tensioning wire that can be found from secondhand sources, but it is possible to manage with improvised equipment. There are several tightening devices that depend on a screw action and remain with the fence. There is a limit to the amount of slack they can take up—and they might not be enough for a long farm fence—but for many garden fences they are adequate. Examples are shown in the supports for climbing vines (Fig. 10-21).

Wire can be attached to posts with staples. Special manufactured tensioning devices mostly provide a lever action for the second end post. If the wire is brought through a hole, it could be given a turn around a strip of wood and pulled to tighten it (Fig. 14-2A). You have to be ready to secure the wire with staples, but a small vise can

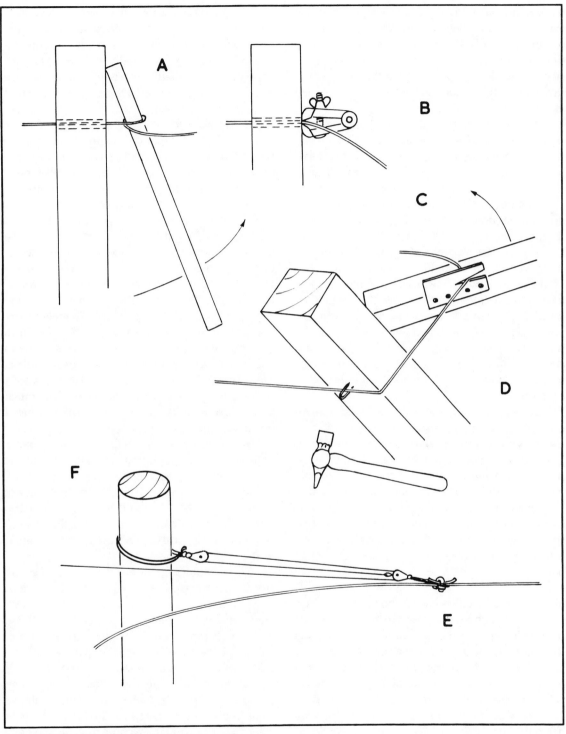

Fig. 14-2. Fence wires can be strained in several ways.

be put on the wire to prevent it pulling back through the hole (Fig. 14-2B) while you do this. Putting a turn of stiff wire round the lever can be difficult. An alternative is an acutely notched steel plate on the lever (Fig. 14-2C). If the wire is held down in the notch, the steel will grip the wire well enough while levering.

If the wire comes on the face of the end post, it can be strained over the edge and staples can be driven there before releasing the lever to allow more staples to be driven further round (Fig. 14-2D).

Another way of tensioning uses a grip on the wire further from the post. Manufactured devices for this purpose use one of many types of grip, including a vise action. Any small hand or metalworking vise could be used. A wire grip could be used, possibly with a short length of spare wire included to make up the thickness (Fig. 14-2E), and then a tackle made up of two blocks and strong rope is attached and used to pull the wire toward the post (Fig. 14-2F). With the tension on, you can deal with stapling with more space to move around the post than with the other methods.

Stapling can be done with your normal hammer, pliers and a screwdriver, to lever out staples that go wrong. If you have much fence wire to fit, you should consider special fencing pliers (Fig. 14-3) that serve as hammer, cutter, staple extractor, and tensioner. The amount of tensioning that can be given is limited, but the wire is gripped and the tool is rolled on the curved arm (which is also the staple extractor). You will probably find jobs for this tool other than fencing, as well.

PRIMITIVE FENCES

Where the early settlers had an abundance of wood left from clearing land, they devised fences that used poles laid in a zigzag form, without any posts or stakes into the ground in the simplest versions. Where the felled logs were too thick to use as they were, they were split into two or four. The method certainly uses a considerable amount of wood. One early authority said that a fence of this type 10 rails high, using poles about 11 feet long,

needed 8000 rails to the mile. Even for the more modest confines of a home garden, there would have to be a great many poles. If you want to provide a fence that reflects traditional form and have enough poles available, this is an interesting project even if you only build a token fence for a short distance (Fig. 14-4A).

If you want to mark the limits of your property or a particular part of it, without the need to restrict animals, this type of fence could be made only three or four poles high and the poles need not be as long as they would be for farm fencing. The result would be visually attractive.

To lay out such a fence, get together a stock of poles, either fully round, from about 3 inch diameter upward, or large ones split to about that size. The fence looks best if all poles are about the same size, but you can graduate sizes from the bottom upward. Decide on the length of poles and cut them all to size. You can vary panels to suit poles, but if the fence is to extend very far it will look best with panels of even size. You have to allow for overlaps. Suppose your poles are 10 feet long. They will overlap about 18 inches; the actual length covered by each panel is about 7 feet. If you have definite space to fill, work out panel lengths to suit.

You can lay out the fence with the bottom poles overlapped until you are satisfied with the experiment. For farm fences, the width of the zigzag arrangement was about half the length of a panel (Fig. 14-4B). If the fence is to be straight, it is a help to put down a central string (Fig. 14-4C) and arrange the crossings fairly regularly each side of it.

You can build up a little at a time all the way along, but if there is much length it is less laborious to work progressively from one end (Fig. 14-4D). Traditionally, the poles were just laid there. If you want to be more certain of the poles staying in place, you can drive a long nail down through the crossings as they are made (Fig. 14-4E).

If your fence is only the 12 inches or so high of a four-rail assembly, that will probably be all you want to do. The next step used by the settlers to make the fence stronger, without nails, was to drive in stakes where the poles cross. Stakes should be taller than the fence is to go, and they are driven in after two or three poles crossing have shown their positions. When the fence has reached the height you want, the poles are pulled together with wire below the top pair (Fig. 14-4F). The stakes could come in either of the opposite angles (Fig. 14-4G and H). The best way to get the grip tight is to pull the tops of the poles together with a clamp or a Spanish windlass, made by putting a loop of rope around the poles and twisting with a stick (Fig. 14-4J). While the pressure is on, tie the wire tightly and inconspicuously in the gap below. Remove the Spanish windlass. Nail in the two top poles, if you prefer, and cut off the tops of the stakes level.

Several other methods of strengthening farm fences of this type were used, but they involved supports set sawbuck fashion so they project each side. This could be an obstruction and nuisance in a garden.

RAIL AND POST FENCE

Rails nailed to posts have developed from the widely spaced rails of a farm fence (Fig. 14-5A) to the neater and more closely spaced fence of planed boards used around home property (Fig. 14-5B). For a board or rail fence, posts should not be more than 8 feet apart and could be down to no more than 5 feet. A closer arrangement of posts makes for stability and rigidity of the boards. This might warp and spoil appearance if used over a longer span.

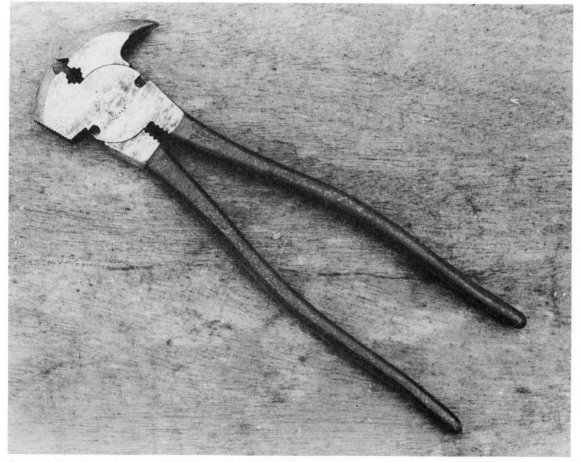

Fig. 14-3. Fencing pliers are multipurpose tools for dealing with wire.

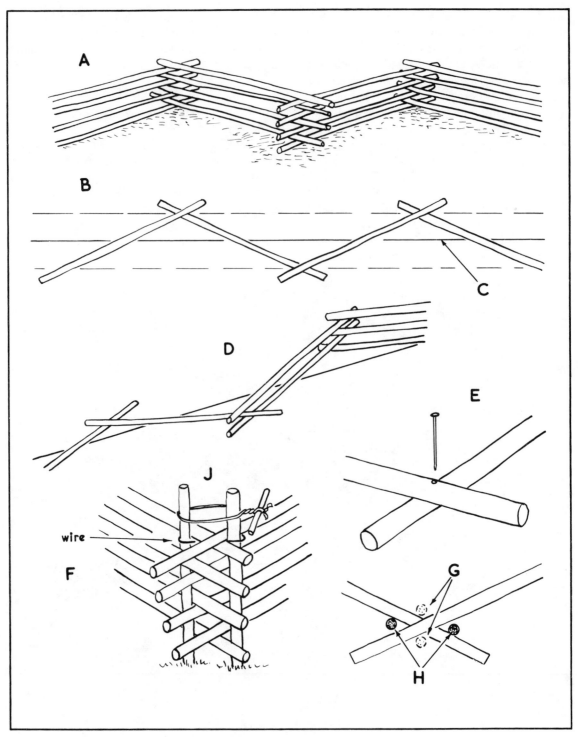

A

B

C

D

E

J

wire

F

G

H

Fig. 14-4. Primitive fences are made with poles supported on each other.

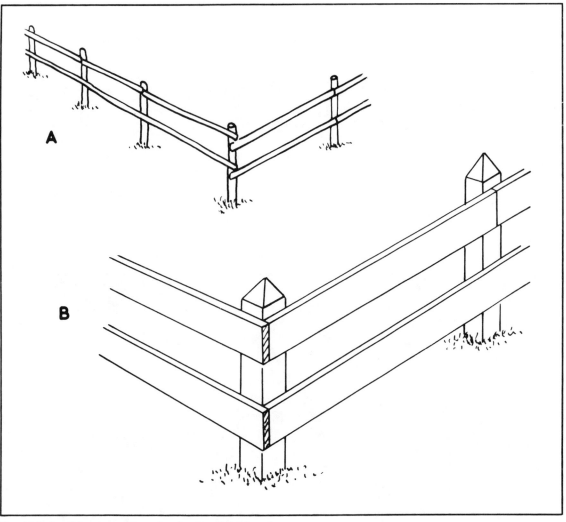

Fig. 14-5. A rail fence can use natural poles of flat boards.

If the fence is to be straight, set out the positions of post holes with a cord line (Fig. 14-6A) and use the line frequently as you progress to erecting the posts. It helps to sight along as well. If you look along a row of posts from one end, you can easily see any post that is out of line or not plumb. The further you can stand back to sight, the easier it is to see errors.

Make the post holes by any method described earlier. If the posts are to go directly into the soil, very thoroughly soak their lower ends in preservative. Creosote is often used, but there are many suitable prepared preservatives. Tamp the soil tightly around each post. Stones rammed in will help tighten the post.

If the post is to be set in concrete, treat its bottom with preservative as if for driving into soil. Have the hole reasonably parallel and about three times the size of the post (Fig. 14-6B). Set the post on stones for drainage and pour and ram concrete tightly into place. Trowel the top so any water is shed away from the wood (Fig. 14-6C). Check for plumb as you work. Correcting after the concrete has set is almost impossible.

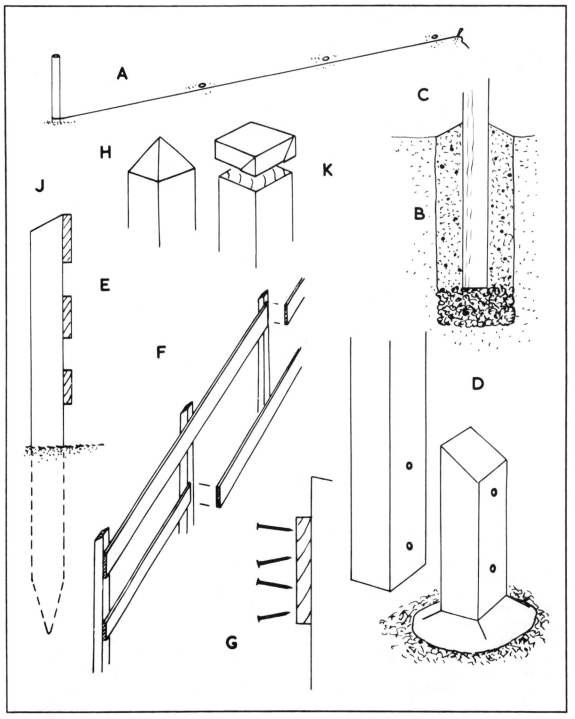

Fig. 14-6. Fence holes should be marked straight (A) and posts can be set in or attached to concrete (B-D). Nail boards to posts (E-G). Shape or cover post tops (H-K).

If the wood post is to be attached to a concrete post set in the ground, you may cast your own post or suitable ones can be bought. Although the concrete post could go directly into soil, it is better to set it into concrete. Then the wood post is bolted on with its foot above ground level (Fig. 14-6D).

For a yard fence, the posts could be 3 inches or more square with planed surfaces if the wood is to be painted. For a farm fence or more primitive fence. The wood need not be planed and it could be round or square. If a fence is liable to get thrusts square to it (from cattle or even a car backing into it), the posts could be thicker. You could have a 3-inch face against the boards and 6 inches or more the other way.

The boards could be any convenient width, but narrow widths will be too flexible for strength between supports. They need not all be the same width. For a three-rail fence, you could have 6 inches at the top and the others 5 inches and 4 inches (Fig. 14-6E). Thickenss should usually be at least 1 inch. Obviously, you must avoid boards with large knots that would weaken them. If possible, have the boards long enough to continue to a second post. Joints can be staggered (Fig. 14-6F). Let board ends meet closely and use sufficient nails; four in a 6 inch width should be satisfactory (Fig. 14-6G).

To get the boards level, use a stretched string. Preferably, it should be from one extreme of the fence to the other. If it is very long, you might have to level in stages. Check the top board level first. Waviness in the top edge of a fence becomes very obvious to a viewer. From the string, mark on each post where the board should come. Even then it is advisable to first fit each board with one nail only at each crossing, then stand back and see that the top edge makes a continuous level line.

With the top boards level, the others can be measured down from them. The post tops can be cut level with the boards or they can be allowed to project. Unless they are to be covered in some way, they should slope so water drains off instead of soaking into grain. Projecting posts can be taken to a point (Fig. 14-6H). They could be cut to a single slope whether they finish level with the boards or project (Fig. 14-6J). To completely prevent water from entering the end grain, thin sheet metal can be folded over and tacked on (Fig. 14-6K).

A board attached flat above the top vertical board can also cover the tops of the posts, making an attractive capping that gives a more solid appearance to the fence (Fig. 14-7A). Just a square over a post would have similar effect (Fig. 14-7D). If you do not want such a wide top, there could be a narrower shaped piece (Fig. 14-7B), taken partly over each post top, which is sloped outside it. Water has a tendency to run back underneath an overhang. It will not matter on a fence, but it can be prevented by plowing a groove a short distance from the edge (Fig. 14-7C).

Boards in this type of fence do not have to be left plain. They could be cut with curved outlines (Fig. 14-7E). They could be drilled or pierced (Fig. 14-7F). Painting rails in different colors can be distinctive.

If the fence is to have a painted finish, any wood that is not inherently durable should be treated with a preservative that can be covered with paint.

MORTISED FENCE

Instead of nailing rails to the surface of posts, they can be let into mortises. It is not easy cutting mortises in posts that have been erected. The method is better suited to positions where the posts can be prepared in advance and erected to the correct height in holes that allow them to be adjusted with packing stones or other means before tamping tight. The method can be used with natural wood or sawn boards. Cleft poles make good rails for this type of fence (Fig. 14-8).

Round rails, probably no more than 3 inches in diameter, could be used with posts 5 inches in diameter or square. Poles could be cleft along their centers and the fence built with all the flat surfaces to one side. If the fence is to withstand cows or horses pushing against it, the cleft poles could be up to 6 inches in diameter (particularly for the top rails). If you want a natural, rural look to the garden fence, you can use rather lighter posts and rails to get the same effect. The poles do not have to be straight and a fence of this sort with rails giving a slightly uneven appearance will look right if it separates the cultivated garden from a background of trees and bushes that have been left to nature.

If flat boards are used, they can be planed and painted in the same way as a nailed fence or they can be left as sawn and treated with preservative for a more natural appearance. Strength in the joints comes from having the posts fairly thick in relation to the rails. This is particularly important if you are using flat boards. This is less important, although still valuable, with round or cleft rails in a fence where the haphazard appearance of ex-

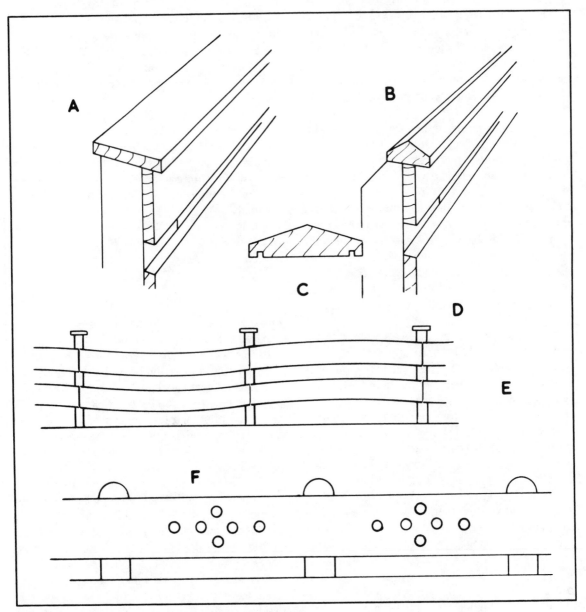

Fig. 14-7. Capping and decoration are possible on rail fences.

Fig. 14-8. With a mortised fence, the rails can fit against each other.

tending rail ends does not matter and may even be considered a feature.

1. For a fence with round or split rails, assemble the materials for the rails. These will determine the spacing of posts. Allow for overlaps at the joints. Short rails and more frequent posts will have the best resistance to sideways pressures. If it is only a garden fence where the loads will not be much, you can have the poles any reasonable length. Depending on the type of wood, bark can

be removed or left on; it will not affect construction.

2. The posts are best left longer than you need them eventually, and with sufficient length to go into the ground. Point them if they are to be driven or leave them square if they will be set in dug holes. If the ground where the fence will be is uneven and you want the rails to be horizontal, work to the highest level and make the posts longer for the lower parts.

3. The ends of split rails have to be reduced to a rectangular section (Fig. 14-9A). What this size will be depends on the wood, but you have to compromise between width and depth. A thickness about 1 1/2 inches and depth of 2 1/2 inches might be possible and is the proportion at which to aim. Do not reduce the ends too much, but the reduced size should extend for about the thickness of a post. Experiment with your poles or with offcuts to get a size that will suit your stock of rails. Precision is not important, but try to keep close to the size on which you settle. Reduce round rails from both sides (Fig. 14-9B). Tapering can be done with a saw, ax, or drawknife.

4. In the posts, the mortises should suit the thickness you are making the rails and be rather deeper than them. If the rails are 2 1/2 inches deep, the mortises could be 3 1/2 inches (Fig. 14-9C). They need not be chopped square and are best made by drilling several holes and removing the waste (Fig. 14-9D) with a chisel. Roughness and unevenness inside a mortise will not matter. Prepare posts in groups so mortise spacings match (Fig. 14-9E).

5. When you erect the fence, work along it by positioning posts loosely in their holes so you can move them a little. Add rails from one end and tighten the posts in the ground after their rails are fixed. At each post, the rails should be tapered to fit each other (Fig. 14-9F) so when they are forced tight they press against the top and bottom of the mortise. It is advisable to make the edge tapers as you go so that each one can allow for slight variations of the previous one and you may have to make some length adjustments. The ends that extend through could be left (Fig. 14-9G) or cut off at the post (Fig. 14-9H). If the ends are to be left, try to avoid tapering to a feather edge. It is better to leave 1/2 inch or so.

6. In a natural fence, there should be no need to do any more, but if joints shrink and loosen you can nail through the mortise.

7. If flat boards are to be used for rails, the method of assembly is very similar. Their thickness will settle the width of the mortises. If the depth of a rail is no more than the thickness of the post,

there is no need to reduce it (Fig. 14-10A). If it is deeper, there will have to be a shoulder at one or both edges (Fig. 14-10B).

8. The mortises can still be made by drilling (and left with rounded ends and the rails eased a little with a chisel), or you can chop the ends square (Fig. 14-10C).

9. The rails can have their ends cut to go through in a very similar way to the natural poles (Fig. 14-10D) or they can be angled to fit each other within the thickness (Fig. 14-10E). The second method is neater, but the joints will have to be secured with dowels (Fig. 14-10F).

10. It is unlikely that posts will be erected with the precision of spacing that you would expect in cabinetry. Differences of an inch or so do not matter, but this means that rails should be cut after the posts are loosely positioned, particularly if you will be making shoulders on them. Measure the distances between posts at ground level and use this as the distance between them where the rails will be.

11. In both methods of construction, get the fence erected with all posts still too long. When you are satisfied that it is as you want it, cut the tops off the posts—either at an angle or to a point.

PICKET FENCE

Probably the most common traditional garden fence has posts and rails, but between the posts are upright pieces attached to the rails. The whole fence can be quite low, it is commonly about waist-high, or it could be high enough to provide some privacy or act as a windbreak.

The variations are almost limitless. The upright pickets can be narrow or wide, they can almost touch or be wide apart, they could be on two, three or more rails. Instead of flat pieces, they could be round or square, the tops could be cut square or decorated, or they may be sloping instead of upright. In building a picket fence, there is scope for you to express your individuality. The instructions here are for straightforward picket fences of conventional design (Fig. 14-11) that can be adapted to suit your needs and ideas.

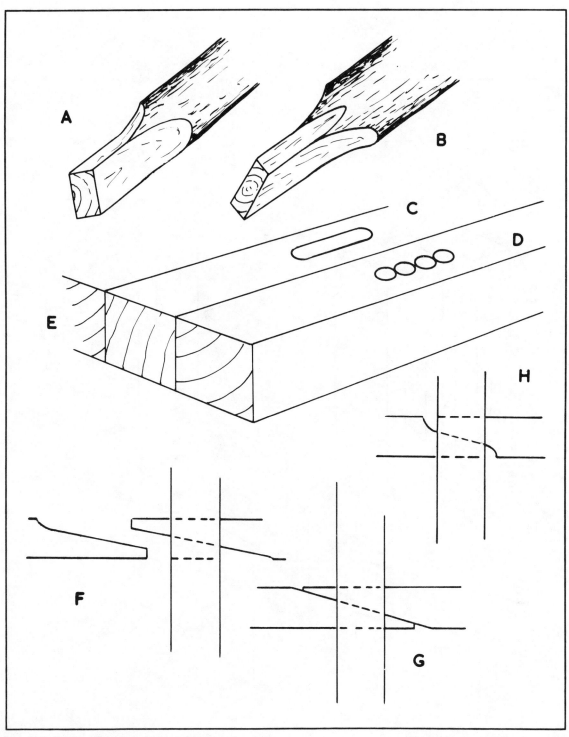

Fig. 14-9. Shape rail ends to fit the mortises in the posts.

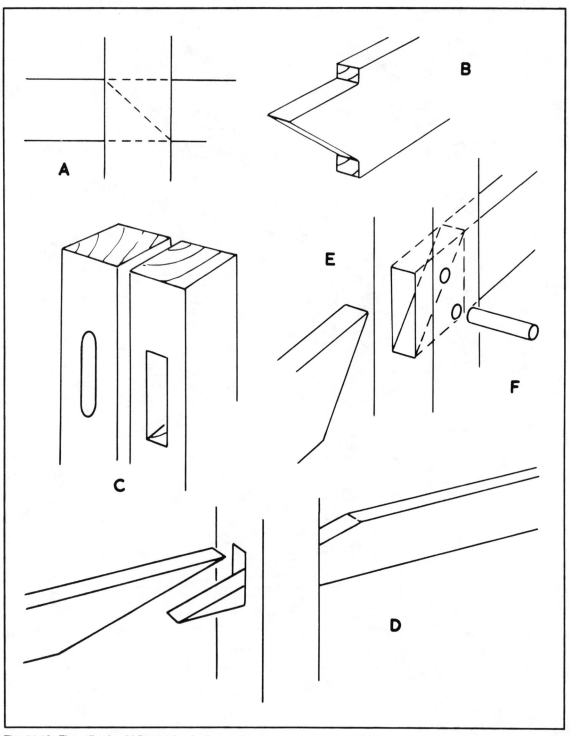

Fig. 14-10. Flat rails should fit together in the mortises.

1. Measure the place the fence is to be and decide on a suitable post spacing. If the fence is not expected to have to withstand much load, the posts can be wider apart than if you expect there to be occasional bumps. If the fence is to be at the boundary of your property and a public path or road, it is advisable to assume there could be unexpected occasional heavy loads.

2. If the fence is to keep in children, do not have spaces greater than 3 inches wide. This will also do for the majority of animals.

3. The number of rails depends on the height of the fence. Two rails should suit pickets standing 36 inches high or anything below that. If you are using light rods or other special pieces for pickets, there will have to be a third rail—even at this height.

4. The simplest way to make the fence is to nail the rails to the posts and the pickets to the rails, but this brings the pickets forward (Fig. 14-12A). To keep the appearance even along the fence, you must keep the posts inconspicuous and continue pickets over them (Fig. 14-12B).

5. Another way is to mortise the rails into the posts so the outside surfaces of the pickets will be level with the surfaces of the posts (Fig. 14-12C). The posts then form part of a line with the pickets and their tops can be decorated, in the same way, whether they stand up or are level with them (Fig. 14-12D).

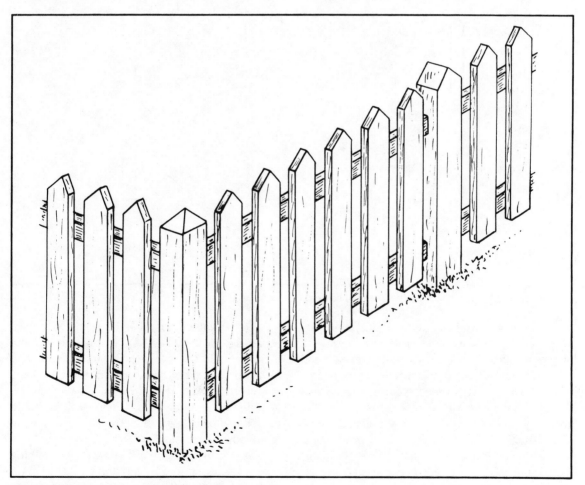

Fig. 14-11. A picket fence suits most gardens.

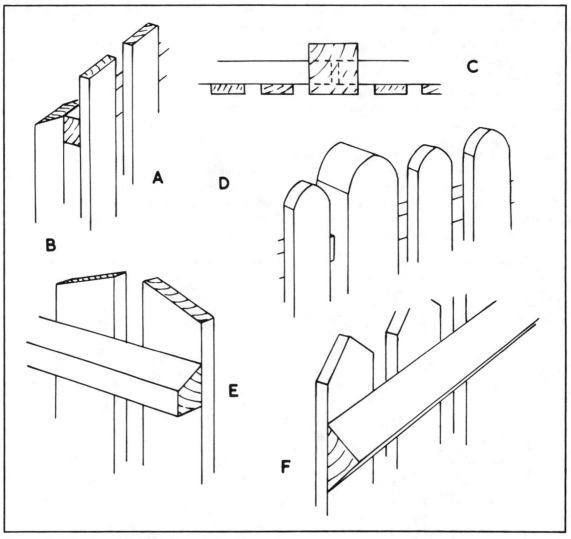

Fig. 14-12. Picket fence details can be varied to suit requirements.

6. For a waist-high garden fence, the posts might be about 4 inches square and the rails 2 inches square. It helps to slope the top of each rail (Fig. 14-12E) so that rainwater runs off instead of becoming trapped between the rail and the pickets (where rot could start). Even better is to use rails made by cutting diagonally across a square piece (Fig. 14-12F). To be as strong as 2 inches square, the wood cut should be 3 inches or more square. Rain is unlikely to be trapped behind such an *arris rail*.

7. Arrange the rail heights to suit your proposed design (Fig. 14-13A). The bottoms of the pickets should be clear of the ground. If you need to retain soil, a horizontal board could be used below the pickets (Fig. 14-13B). That might be regarded as expendable because it will probably rot. It could be nailed to the posts so that it is easily removed and replaced.

8. The widths of pickets can be anything from 2 inches up to 6 inches and will depend on what is available. Widths can vary. One wide

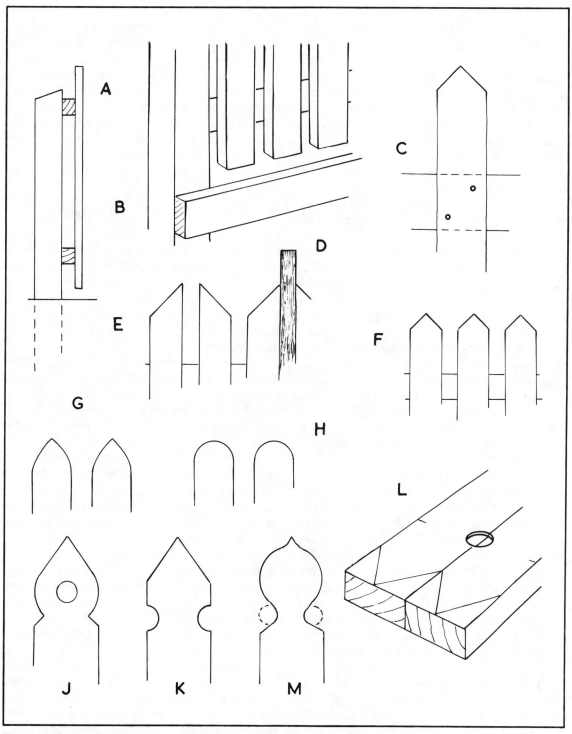

Fig. 14-13. Pickets should be evenly spaced and can have decorated tops.

picket between a regular series of narrower ones will be distinctive. You have to scheme out the spacing along the rails. Distances between posts should be kept the same or you will get different spacings. This will show when the fence is viewed from a distance. If there have to be different post spacings, work them out so that they are proportional and pickets will still have the same gaps. Pickets can be from 1/2 inch thick upward, but 3/4 inch to 1 inch is usual.

9. Use two nails at each crossing and arrange them diagonally in different grain lines (Fig. 14-13C). Have someone holding an iron block or heavy hammer behind the rail as you nail into it in order to take the rebound and get tighter nails.

10. Make sure one picket piece is upright (a post can be your guide). Use a strip of wood as a gauge to keep spacing even (Fig. 14-13D) while working from this first picket. Check squareness and spacing occasionally in case any error is developing.

11. The simplest pickets have square tops. Next simplest is a slope cut one way. Pickets can be nailed on alternate ways (Fig. 14-13E), or a series arranged one way, and then a similar number the other way. More common are simple points (Fig. 14-13F). Any slope is worth having because it sheds rainwater instead of letting it settle and soak into end grain.

12. Picket tops could go to rounded points or be fully semicircular (Fig. 14-13G and H). If the posts are in line with the pickets, they ought to have matching shapes. That will limit your choice of top design. Another consideration is the number of pickets. A complicated design might appeal to you and be interesting to cut on one picket, but will you feel the same if there are 50 to cut?. Use a template to mark tops so they are the same. If you have a bandsaw, the ends are easily shaped. Most will have to be cut individually. Cutting two or three in a pile will probably result in noticeable variations.

13. Drilling can be used. There can be a hole through inside a curved outline (Fig. 14-13J). Holes can also be used for edge decoration (Fig. 14-13K). A Forstner bit will make a half hole, but you can use a drill press to go through pickets held together (Fig. 14-13L). A development of this is a gingerbread pattern, with a pair of holes drilled and the bandsaw used to cut into them (Fig. 14-13M).

14. Avoid very sharp upward edges to prevent catching in clothing or scratching skin. If the design includes a point, round it with a file or abrasive. Although sawn shapes are satisfactory, remove raggedness and take off sharpness with a plane or abrasive. It helps to lightly plane off the sharpness of the straight edges of pickets before fixing them.

PRIVACY AND SHELTER FENCES

If you want to hide the view from outside, the fence has to be high and fairly solid. There are some plants that need shelter from the wind and some prefer shade to sunlight. Others flourish so prolifically that they would spread through any open fence. In these situations you need a closed fence, but not necessarily as high as when privacy is the main concern.

Open fences of most types are attractive to look at. A closed fence looks rather plain. You can break up its outline with higher posts or shaped tops, but its barrenness is best broken up by the plants growing in front of it or maybe climbing on it.

A simple solid fence can be made with exterior-grade plywood. This needs rails on posts. If the posts are at 8-foot centers, you can use standard sheets. A height of 4 feet might be all you need for a windbreak, but if you want to go up to 6 feet for privacy there will have to be a joint on a rail. A suitable arrangement would be posts 4 inches or more square, with rails 2 inches square nailed on to support the edges and center of each sheet (Fig. 14-14A). Where sheets join to make up the height, you will be able to nail to a 2 inch rail, but it will be better to have a wider joint rail. With the stiffness of 1/2-inch plywood helping the rails, supports only at the ends of each panel should be enough. If the result seems to be too flexible, there could be light uprights midway between the posts. Put a capping on the top edge to improve appearance and to prevent water entering the end

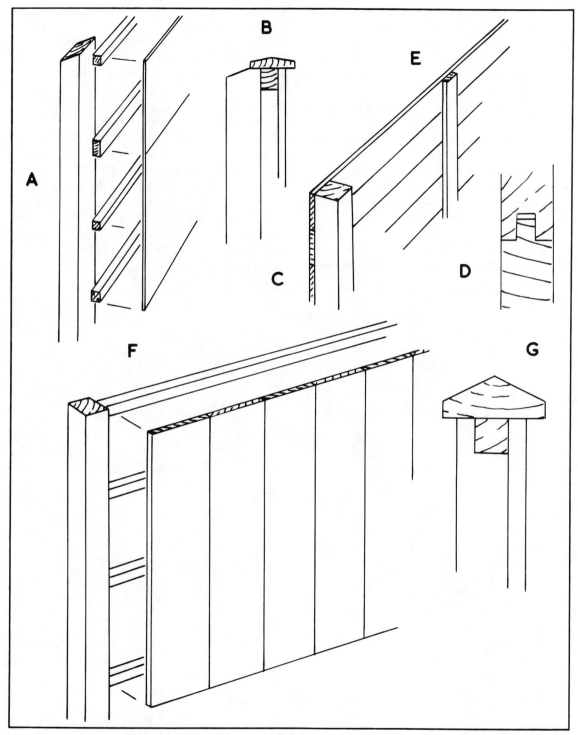

Fig. 14-14. A fence without gaps provides privacy and shelter.

grain of the plywood. This could be a flat piece, but a shaped strip looks better (Fig. 14-14B).

A closed fence could be made with boards nailed close together (Fig. 14-14C), but plain boards tend to warp. Tongues and grooves at the edges would prevent this (Fig. 14-14D), or you could put battens across at intervals between posts (Fig. 14-14E).

A closed fence could be made by arranging the boards vertically instead of plywood on rails (Fig. 14-14F). Boards nailed over rails at 24-inch intervals will be less likely to warp than those laid horizontally. Use a capping to keep water out of the end grain (Fig. 14-14G).

OPEN BOARDED FENCES

One problem with an expanse of high solid fence is windage. A high wind can put a considerable strain on such a fence, and this will find the weakest spots and cause breakages. There are ways of making fences that provide privacy and reduction of wind on delicate plants, but when some air is allowed through the loads on the fence are reduced.

Boards can be arranged on opposite sides of a fence, either horizontally or vertically, to make it difficult for anyone to see through. This also provides good circulation of air (Fig. 14-15).

A picket fence could be made in this way. An existing one might be modified with another row of pickets on the opposite sides of the rails over the gaps (Fig. 14-16A). This could be just to keep spreading plants within bounds or to act as a windbreak.

Fig. 14-15. A fence with boards on opposite sides lets air through, but provides privacy.

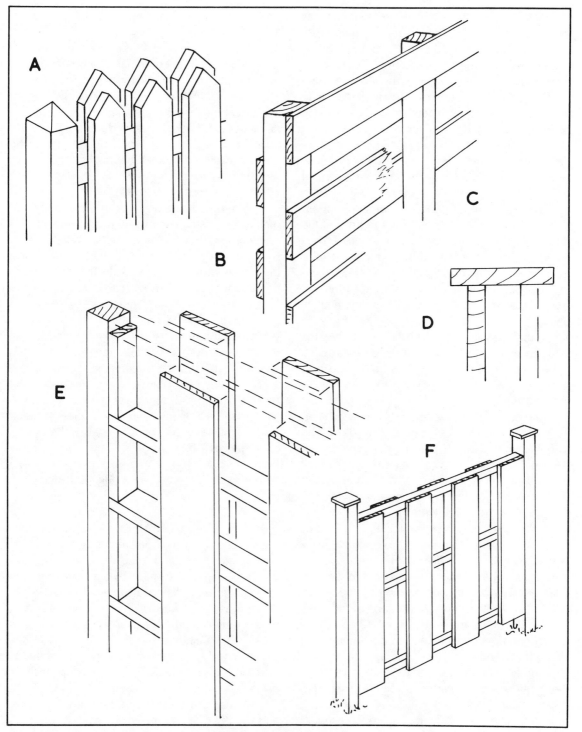

Fig. 14-16. Boards can be upright or horizontal in an open boarded fence.

With boards, the simplest arrangement has them horizontal and nailed alternately on opposite sides of the posts (Fig. 14-16B). That might be all that is needed. If the boards seem likely to flex in their length, one or more uprights—of the same thickness as the posts—can be included (Fig. 14-16C). They need not extend above or below the boards. A capping board is not essential, but it will improve appearance and could be just over the upper board or taken the full width (Fig. 14-16D).

There are several ways of supporting vertical boards on opposite sides of a fence so they alternate and obscure the view without stopping air. If the boards are to come outside the lines of the posts, the rails should be as thick as the posts. They might be tenoned into the posts, but it is easier to use spacers and nail to them (Fig. 14-16E). For a fence about 6 feet high, there should be rails at top and bottom of the boards and two intermediate ones.

In that type of fence, carry the boards over the posts so that you can space them along a fence with many posts without having to fit into post spacing. Arrange capping boards to overhang the tops a little.

Alternatively, arrange the boards between and level with the surfaces of the posts. That allows you to break up plainness by taking the posts higher (Fig. 14-16F). The rails could be fitted with tapered ends into mortises, as described for earlier fences, but it will be simpler to use the same method as the previous example—with the rails narrowed.

If the posts are 4 inches thick and the boards are 1 inch, that means rails 2 inches thick. They could be deeper for stiffness. If the posts are not too far apart, 2-inch-square rails should be adequate. Nail the rails to spacers, and then the boards will fit level with the posts. The tops of the posts could be cut level and a capping board continued over them, or you can take each post higher and shape its top or give it its own capping.

Another way to use vertical boards to let air through and provide partial privacy is to set them diagonal to make louvers (Fig. 14-17). You cannot provide intermediate stiffening. The boards should be selected for their straightness of grain. Warped

boards would spoil the appearance, if not the effect, of such a fence.

The angle used for the boards affects the degree of privacy. You could put 6-inch boards at 45 degrees with their edges opposite (Fig. 14-18A). This means that anyone looking through can get a fairly complete view at that angle as the gaps are fairly wide. If you want to reduce the view, the boards can be placed at a more acute angle to the line of the fence (Fig. 14-18B). The boards can also be arranged to overlap instead of having their edges opposite (Fig. 14-18C).

If the boards are arranged more acutely and their edges are to overlap, the spacers become narrower. They also need narrower rail surfaces (compare Fig. 14-18A and B). For these two examples, the rails could be 2 × 4s, with the 4-inch-width horizontal for a 45-degree angle or the 2-inch surface horizontal for a 30-degree angle. Leave small gaps at the posts or bring the boards close if you want to obstruct any view through there.

Make the spacers thick enough to take nails securely (1 1/2 inch deep should be enough). Draw a full-size section of fence, and from this get the sizes and shapes of the spacers (Fig. 14-18D) so you can make as many as you need before you start assembling the fence. There will have to be square-edged pieces against the posts. If you start assembly from one post, you can nail a board to a spacer before placing the next one (Fig. 14-18E).

GATES

A gate should close properly in its opening, swing far enough open, and keep its shape. In many gardens, the gateposts move, the gate distorts, and passage through a fence becomes a frustrating and disappointing performance. This indicates that more thought should be given to gate design and construction than is often considered. Most garden gates do not have to open more than is needed to push a barrow through. For the usual pedestrian passage, a width of 30 inches should do.

The pair of gateposts should be rigid, upright, and usually of a larger section than the ordinary fence posts. In particular, the one on the hinge side of the gate should be immovable. If possible, sight across the two posts to see that they are parallel in that direction. Of course, they should also be parallel in the direction the gate has to fit. You cannot make a good job of hanging a gate if there are faults in the gateposts.

A gate is supported by its hinges on one side and it has to be designed so it does not drop out of shape. If it is faced completely with plywood that will hold it in shape. If it is built up of pieces, they must be braced properly. If there is a piece put diagonally across an assembly of boards and

Fig. 14-17. Fence boards set at an angle will let air through and provide some privacy.

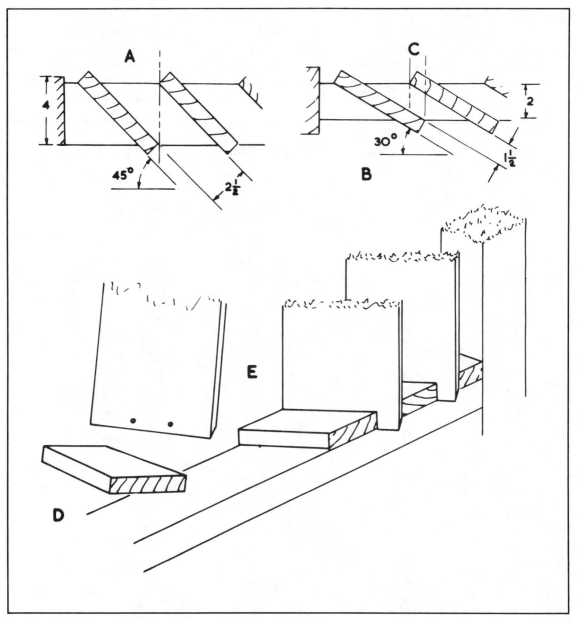

Fig. 14-18. Boards mounted at an angle are set between blocks.

it slopes down from the hinged side (Fig. 14-19A), it is in tension. If it slopes up, it is in compression (Fig. 14-19B). Because it is easier to make a small gate with a strut effective in compression, that is the usual way. Some large gates have diagonals in tension, but then loads have to be taken via bolts.

WICKET GATE

The most frequent need is for a gate in a fence at waist height. It might be a picket fence and the pattern of the fence could be carried on to the gate. Elsewhere there could be vertical boards that are perhaps wider than those to match pickets. In

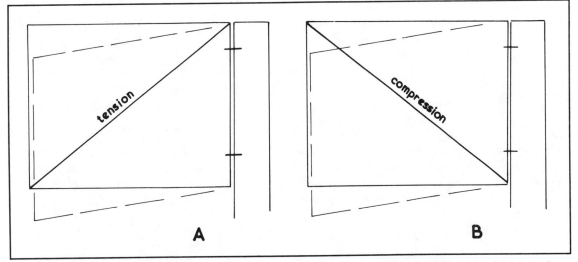

Fig. 14-19. When designing a framed gate, resistance to sagging can come from a diagonal in tension or one in compression.

general, the wider and fewer boards in a gate the less the risk of it falling out of shape. Figure 14-20 shows a satisfactory method of making a small gate that can be adapted to those of other sizes. It has a straight top, but boards can be shaped to match pickets.

The wood for a gate can be the same as for the fence. If you have used partially seasoned wood for the fence, it would be better to select fully seasoned wood for the gate in order to reduce the risk of warping, shrinking, and splitting. Gates are sometimes made of very light wood, but anything less than 3/4 inch thick is inadvisable. This gate should be all 1-inch (7/8-inch-planed) wood.

Unless there is a particular need for a closed-panel gate, it is advisable to make the gate with gaps between the boards. This allows for expansion and contraction with little effect on the overall width.

1. Prepare the boards for the upright parts. See that the edges are straight. Mark the lengths, but you can leave cutting the tops until after the crosspiece has been fitted.

2. Mark the positions of the two crosspieces (Fig. 14-21A). Make the crosspieces and mark on them the positions of the uprights (Fig. 14-21B), which will be evenly spaced. With these markings as a guide, drill the crosspieces for screws. Three

or four screws at each crossing are advisable (Fig. 14-21C). Although the gate might be nailed, screwed construction will be stronger.

3. Put the outside uprights and the crosspieces together face down on a flat surface. Check squareness and join them with one temporary screw at each crossing.

4. Lay the wood for the diagonal strut across and mark on it the line of the crosspieces. Mark on the crosspieces where it comes (Fig. 14-22A). The strut could be cut across on this line to fit close to the other parts, but the greatest resistance to gate distortion comes from notching it in. With the lines drawn as a guide, mark and cut the shaped ends (Fig. 14-21D).

5. Put the strut in place and from it mark on the crosspieces what has to be cut out (Fig. 14-22B). This should be a tight fit. Cut inside the lines after taking the assembly apart.

6. Re-assemble the four pieces and check that the shape is correct when the strut is in position. Fully screw these corner joints and put in the other uprights. Fit in the strut and screw it where it crosses the other parts. There could be glue in the notches if you prefer, but the gate should be satisfactory if assembled dry with screws only.

7. Trim the tops of the boards and add the capping (Fig. 14-21E). If the gate is to swing back

flat against a wall or fence, keep the inner edge level. Otherwise a small overlap can be allowed.

8. T-hinges are most appropriate, but other types could be used. Put the hinges on the crosspieces (Fig. 14-21F) and on to the gatepost (with a little clearance).

9. At the other side, put a stop strip on the post (Fig. 14-22C). This could get some rough treatment, and 1-inch-square hardwood is suitable even if the gate has been made of softwood.

10. There are several types of catches that can be used on a garden gate, but a strip of hardwood used as a turnbutton might be all that is needed (Fig. 14-22D). Put washers under the screw head and between the turnbutton and the post.

Materials List for Wicket Gate	
7 uprights	35 × 4 × 1
2 crosspieces	30 × 4 × 1
1 diagonal	36 × 4 × 1
1 cap	30 × 2 1/2 × 1

TALL GATE

If a fence is high and intended to provide privacy or act as a windbreak, any gate in it ought to also be high. This means having tall gateposts with a greater risk of the gate fitting badly later if they move only slightly. A move is more likely at the greater height unless the posts can be restrained.

Fig. 14-20. A wicket gate makes a pedestrian entrance through a fence.

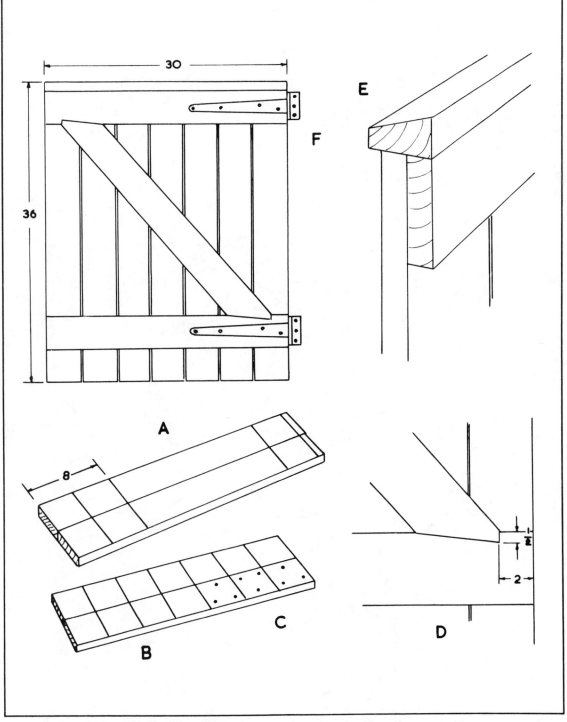

Fig. 14-21. Constructional details of the wicket gate.

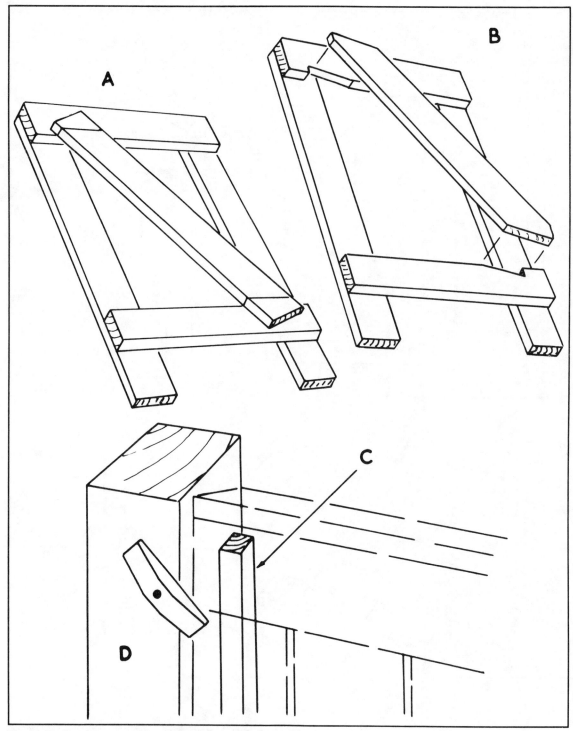

Fig. 14-22. Arrangements of the brace, stop, and catch.

Fortunately, it is possible to put a piece across above head height so that the posts are braced to each other and held parallel (Fig. 14-23). This depends on the fence height, but if you can take the posts to 6 feet 6 inches or more you can make a rigid gateway. The ranch-style piece across could have shallow notches to fit over the posts.

Something more than nails will be resisting movement.

The gate can be made in a similar way to the previous one, but there are a few points to note when working to a greater height. This gate is shown made of boards 6 inches wide and 1 inch thick (Fig. 14-24A). The top is shown cut to a curve,

Fig. 14-23. A tall gate in a high fence is best with a piece over the opening.

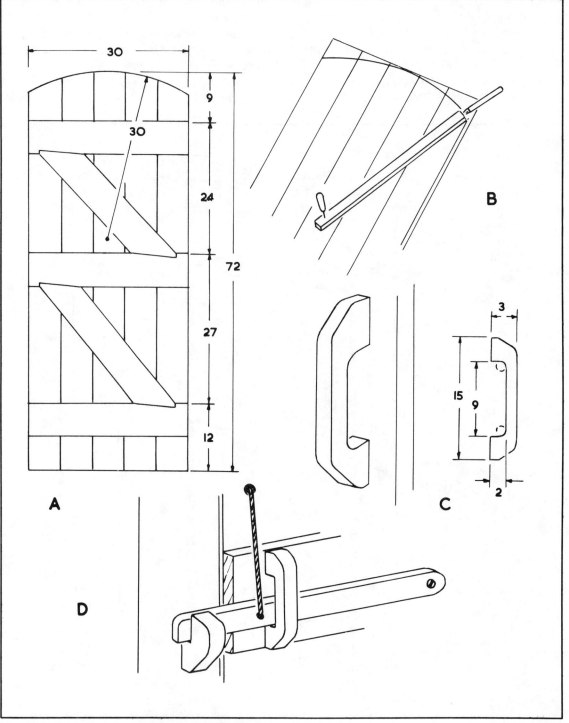

Fig. 14-24. Suggested sizes and details of a tall gate.

but it could be made straight across with a capping if you prefer. The three crosspieces (*ledgers*) are necessary, but the middle one is better not exactly midway between the other two. If it is central, an optical illusion makes it look lower. You might decide that does not matter. You cannot reach over to a fastener—as you can with the previous gate—so the latch or lock has to be workable from either side.

1. Set out the door and assemble the outside boards with the crosspieces each held with single screws. Have this square and position the diagonals so that you can mark their ends and the notches in the same way as described for the previous door. Because of the different spacings, the diagonals will be at different angles. If you want to keep the slopes the same, you can position one and arrange the other so it is at the same angle, letting its ends come as they will on the crosspieces.

2. The curve of the top is best left for marking and cutting until after the door is assembled,but you can make the ends approximately to shape. This is particularly appropriate if you want to use up short boards at the outsides.

3. Assemble the door with all the boards equally spaced. Planed wood will leave gaps up to 1/4 inch between edges.

4. Improvise a compass with a strip of wood, an awl, and a pencil (Fig. 14-24B). The curve drawn is 30 inch radius, but you can vary this if a flatter or greater curve would look better for your gate. Cut the top and take off any sharpness of the edges.

5. Fit a hinge central on each crosspiece. T-hinges 12 inches long would be a good choice. Hang the gate temporarily with one screw in each hinge and check its action. Position a stop to let the gate shut with the ledgers level with the post surface.

6. You could use purchased metal handles on each side of the gate and a latch of the type that allows opening from either side. If it is an outside fence, you might want to fit a lock or there could be bolts on the inside. Alternatively, you can make handles and latch.

7. Even if the gate is made of softwood, the handles and latches should be close-grained hardwood for strength and resistance to wear.

8. The handles are about 1 1/4 inch thick. Mark out (Fig. 14-24C), and drill the corners of the openings and cut the shape. Make sure the parts that come against the door are kept flat, but all the other edges and corners should be thoroughly rounded. Fit the handles at suitable heights by screwing through the door into them. Stagger them slightly so you can drive screws from both sides.

9. The latch is a strip of wood loosely pivoted on a screw, with washers under the head and between it and the door. Heavy hardwood about 1 1/2 inches wide, 3/4 inch thick, and 15 inches long would be about right. Within reason length is an advantage. This drops into a notched block on the post (Fig. 14-24D). The block is made like part of a handle. The bottom of the notch comes opposite the latch strip when it is level. Give its front a rounded slope so the strip will slide into it and drop in when the gate is shut.

On the door, there is a retaining piece over the latch strip. Get its size from the latch temporarily assembled. The bottom edge of the opening should come below the strip when it rests in the bottom of the block on the post. The top edge of the opening should allow the strip to lift clear of the notch. For raising the latch from the other side, use a cord through a hole in the strip and a loosely fitting hole in the door.

Counterbore the hole in the strip so the knot can pull in. Have a loop or large knot in the other end of the cord so it can be gripped and will not pull back through the hole in the door.

Materials List for Tall Gate	
5 uprights	72 × 6 × 1
2 crosspieces	30 × 6 × 1
2 diagonals	34 × 6 × 1
2 handles	15 × 3 × 1 1/4
1 latch	15 × 1 1/2 × 3/4
latches from	12 × 2 × 1 1/4

PLYWOOD GATE

Modern synthetic resin waterproof glues have such

a good resistance to moisture that it is possible to use plywood made with them and structures assembled with them outdoors with confidence. The only possible problem with plywood marked "exterior" or "marine" is that water might enter the edges of the veneers and cause them to swell or rot. Edges should be protected. If this is done, a gate can be faced with suitable plywood and used in a fence or elsewhere outdoors.

This project is a small gate (Fig. 14-25), but the same method could be used for a pair of gates or a larger one. The two faces are plywood. Framing inside strengthens it and provides solid places where attachments come. There is a lipping around top and sides where rainwater might otherwise enter. If the bottom is expected to get wet, that could be lipped as well.

The faces are exterior- or marine-grade plywood 1/2 inch or less thickness. The internal parts can be softwood. The lips can be hardwood or softwood and could be chosen to match the appearance of the plywood if there is to be a clear varnish finish.

1. Set out the size and shape of the door on

Fig. 14-25. A flush paneled gate can be covered with plywood.

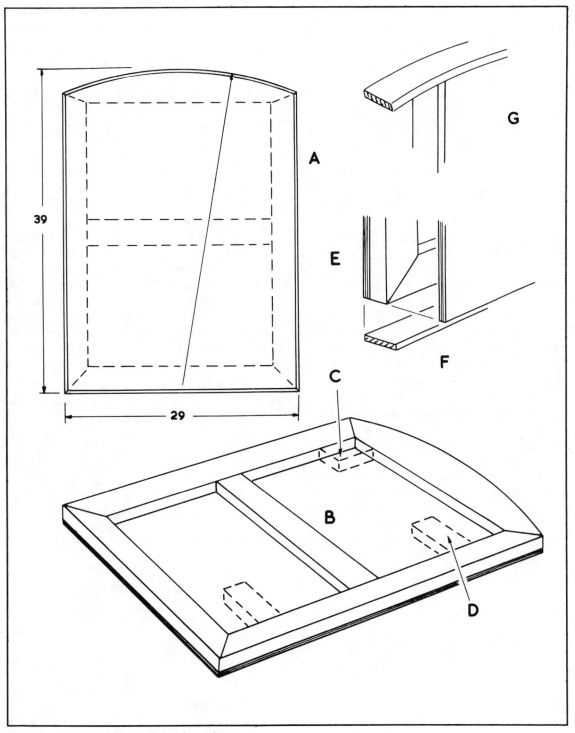

Fig. 14-26. Sizes and details of the plywood gate.

one piece of plywood (Fig. 14-26A). The top could be straight, but it is shown with a slight curve. Avoid much curve because there might be difficulty in making the lip conform and stay in place. Cut the plywood to size and check that it suits the gateway, if that has already been prepared.

2. Cut the pieces that will form the internal framing. They suit the outline, and one piece across the center should provide all the stiffness needed on a gate of this size (Fig. 14-26B). If you intend using a handle, lock, or catch that would be wider than the framing, have a block inside (Fig. 14-26C) to take any screws or holes. Ordinary hinges will probably come within the framing, but if you are using T-hinges place pieces to take their long arms (Fig. 14-26D).

3. Glue does not hold so well on end grain. Avoid it at the corners by mitering the frames (Fig. 14-26E). Expose side grain only to the lips.

4. Glue the framing to the plywood. Locate and secure it, while the glue sets, with nails through the plywood. There should be no need for screws providing the parts are kept in close contact. Clamps or weights can be used.

5. Level the framing surfaces if necessary. Cut the other plywood panel slightly oversize. Glue and nail it on, with clamps or weights, until the glue has set. Then trim the edges all round.

6. Prepare the material for the lips slightly too wide so that it can be planed level after attaching. It would be unwise to make it only just wide enough because planing the plywood surfaces should be avoided. That might be necessary if you found the lip edge slightly narrower than the plywood.

7. If there is to be a lip at the bottom, fix that first. Use plenty of glue so that the plywood is sealed. Use nails to hold the lip in place. Trim its ends to match the framing (Fig. 14-26F).

8. The lips at the sides and top are attached in the same way, but the top has to be pulled to the curve. It helps in doing that if the side lips are trimmed to the curve and the top piece is allowed to overhang a few inches at first (Fig. 14-26G). That allows you to put on pressure over the corners, where there is the greatest risk of the joint opening. Trim the ends after the glue has set. Many of these glues build up strength over several days, after they have apparently set, so delay trimming and planing edges of lips level for this period.

9. Completion of the gate involves the attachment of hinges and fastener, in a similar way to previous projects. Thorough painting is usually the best finish for this type of gate. The solid face of the gate is a good place for the name or number of your home. If that is painted on, there is no need for advance preparation. If you intend to screw on numbers or a nameplate, arrange a block inside to take the screws.

Materials List for Plywood Gate	
2 panels	39 × 29 × 1/2 plywood
2 sides	39 × 3 × 1
1 bottom	29 × 3 × 1
1 center rail	23 × 3 × 1
1 top	23 × 4 × 1
2 lips	38 × 2 1/4 × 3/8
2 lips	34 × 2 1/4 × 3/8

Chapter 15

Decks and Walkways

If you live in an area where the climate is suitable, one of the best ways of providing a suitable outside living area is to make a deck. A wood deck is attractive and less costly than providing a stone, concrete, or other hard surface deck or patio. If the ground is uneven or has a considerable slope, a wood deck on posts might be the only feasible way of making an outdoor extension to your home. It should be large enough for many chairs and tables, barbeque, and all the other things that make for comfortable outdoor living.

If part of your property is very uneven or "swampy," you might want to make a raised walkway for convenient access to another part of the garden. In general, the making of a walkway is similar to a deck. Posts and beams have to be provided in a similar way, and there will almost certainly have to be handrails. All are constructed in a way similar to parts of a deck. A shorter walkway would be better described as a bridge, possibly over a ditch. If it is on posts, rather than cantilevered out from the banks, it is made in a very similar way. You might want to make a walkway,

around your home, where the ground is uneven and a level path is required. That could be treated as a deck even though it may be narrower and simpler.

Obviously, you need to design and build to suit the situation. Broadly, they are divided into low-level and high-level decks. A low-level deck extends, usually from your house, over ground that might be slightly uneven. Perhaps at the edge it is no more than a step down to the surrounding ground. There is usually no need for protection around it.

A high-level deck might start high and continue over ground that is at a slope. It would have fairly high posts at its extremity. It could start at the ground and continue level although the ground below slopes away. In these cases, there has to be protection to prevent users from falling off and there will have to be stairs if you want an outside connection with the ground. In some places, a deck can be classed as low level for much of its area, and then it extends over sloping ground as a high-level deck to give you valuable outdoor living space where there was none before.

It is usual for the boards of a deck to have narrow gaps between. In most circumstances, this is a good arrangement as rainwater and dirt will fall through and the deck is easily kept clean. The deck might require a closed, solid surface as when it is over a working or living area that has to be protected. Then the boards can be laid close and caulked. The top edges must be prepared with bevels to take this.

Alternatively, plywood could be laid with joints close fitting and glued or caulked. Besides the plywood being exterior or marine grade, it is advisable to coat the surface with one of the mastic treatments that leaves a thick, hard-wearing waterproof skin. General construction for a close-fitting deck is the same as for the more usual open type.

The surface of a deck with narrow gaps can be formed with boards that are wider than they are deep (Fig. 15-1A) or by deeper boards standing on edge (Fig. 15-1B). The second type of deck is more costly because more wood is used, but less wood is needed for other parts in the supporting framing. The edgewise boards have greater stiffness and do not need as much stiffening below.

In the usual construction of a raised deck, the deck boards are supported on joists that are edgewise and close enough together to give rigidity

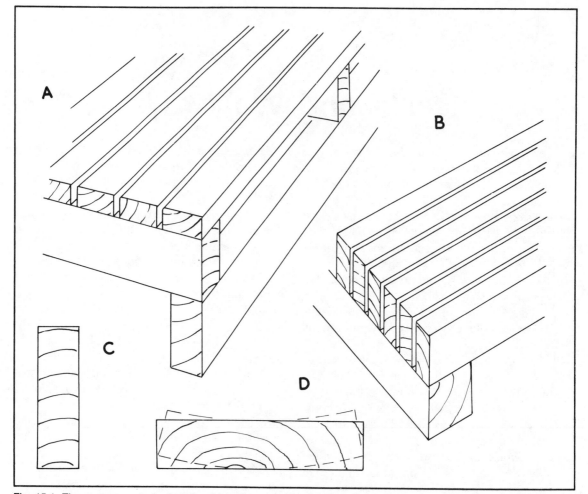

Fig. 15-1. The arrangement of parts of a deck. The probable direction of warping as seen from the grain lines.

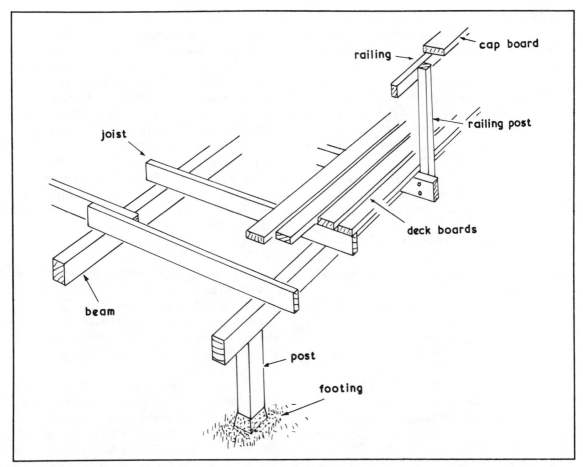

Fig. 15-2. The names of the main parts of a deck.

to the walking surface. These, in turn, are held up by beams that are larger in section and also edgewise. They are attached to the posts connected with the ground. If there is a railing around the deck, its supporting posts are bolted to the beams or joists (Fig. 15-2). When the deck boards are deeper than they are wide, the joists can be wider apart and there may be no need for beams in a low deck.

Although there are parts of a deck assembly where strips could be notched together or mortise and tenon joints used, it is more common to rely on nails, lag screws, and bolts. The parts merely overlap or rest on one another. Sections of wood are not then reduced so strength is maintained. If greater strength is required, joints can be reinforced

with metal angle brackets, and there are special metal straps and supports available to suit standard wood sections. Cutting away wood is then only done if necessary to bring surfaces level.

Lumber with a good resistance to exposure to all kinds of weather is needed. The ideal wood might not be available, but a deck should be expected to have a long life with little attention. Much depends on the wood from which it is made. You will have to depend on local availability. The wood should have a natural resistance to rot, but it can also be treated with preservative. It should have strength and stiffness, and its surface should wear well and have little tendency to splinter. Whatever the wood chosen, it is better if it is heartwood (cut from near the center of the tree). Sapwood (from nearer the bark) is inferior in all properties.

You will have to consider shrinking and warping. If a board is cut radially from the log, the grain lines are across and the effect of taking up or releasing moisture will be on the thickness and have negligible effect on the other direction (Fig. 15-1C). This means edgewise deck boards would not vary on the surface (whether wet or dry). If the wood is cut elsewhere from the log, the grain lines will show curves completely or partially toward one side (Fig. 15-1D). If the wood takes up moisture it will warp outward. Think of it as the grain lines trying to straighten. Deck boards are better laid with the outer bark side of the wood upward so that warping causes the edges to lift. This is less of a problem than having the center of the board try to lift. The edges can be leveled by planing or power sanding.

Some woods that have been found suitable for decks are Douglas fir, western larch, southern pine, redwood, cedar, cypress, and white oak. The man at the local lumberyard should be able to suggest which of his stock should suit your needs.

A simple inconspicuous deck might be your concern. If your plans are more ambitious, it will be wise to check that what you are doing conforms to building codes or planning ordinances before starting work.

The instructions that follow are for typical deck constructions. Every individual situation will have its own problems of design and techniques, but these examples will provide guidance and show possible ways of getting the results you want.

LOW LEVEL EDGE BOARD DECK

Figure 15-3 shows an example of a deck, not far above ground level, with the main area made with boards on edge. It is assumed that the deck will be about 7 feet from back to front and 10 feet wide. The ground does not have to be level, but variations should not be very great.

The suggested deck boards are 2 inches wide and 4 inches deep, with the supporting joists 4 inches square. Over most types of grade or soil, it should be sufficient to provide nine supporting

footings. If the rear of the deck is against a house, it might be possible to get support there without the need for footings.

1. Survey the area the deck will cover. Because the deck will be too close to the ground for maintenance after it is finished, clear away rubbish, remove large stones, and treat the area with weed killer. Excessive unevenness can be leveled.

2. Check levels. If the deck will be against a wall, you will know where you want its surface to be. Mark on the wall where the undersides of the joists will be to achieve this level or put a temporary board there (Fig. 15-4A). From this line, use a long, straight board and a spirit level to check where the heights will be at the limits of the deck (Fig. 15-4B). Drive temporary pegs to mark the heights at these points. Check in the other direction that the peg tops are level. This will show you if what you want to do is feasible on the land. If there are high spots where joists would have to go below ground level, you must remove soil because the wood must have at least a few inches clearance.

3. Leave the temporary pegs in place for future reference, but now—working square to the wall—mark where the lines of the joists will come and where three supports for each will be. At each of these points, there will have to be footings (Fig. 15-4C).

4. In the simplest construction, the supports can be short posts driven into the ground. With suitably treated wood of the right type, this will give a life of many years. Unlike a fence post that can be replaced or repaired fairly easily, a rotted support under a low deck is almost impossible to attend to without major work. It is better to use only concrete. If the ground falls away and you have to use a post anywhere, that should be arranged as described in the next project. If variations of height are not much, concrete supports can be made to the same height despite differences in grade level.

5. For concrete footings, dig holes to be filled with concrete. How big and how deep depends on the soil. Loose, sandy soil will need a greater spread than heavy clay. A typical hole

Fig. 15-3. Layout of a low level edge board deck.

will be about 12 inches in each direction.

6. Although the concrete in the ground will cover whatever area is necessary to provide support, the part that comes against the joist should be no wider than the joist (in this case 4 inches) and arranged to slope away (Fig. 15-4D). There should be a steel rod or bolt projecting to fit in a hole in the joist and locate it.

7. The support does not have to be made with the precision that would be needed when casting a concrete container or ornament that would be visible, but when you start concrete work have wood ready to make forms to give shape to these parts. The concrete in the holes can all be poured and well tamped down. Leave it until it begins to harden before adding the above-ground parts. There could be a few long nails or metal rods

pushed in where the supports will come to bond the two lots of concrete together.

8. At each line of supports, use a straight piece of wood on stakes driven into the ground to indicate the height and where one edge of the top has to be (Fig. 15-4E).

9. Make up simple forms for each place to the correct height and pour in concrete. Have an iron rod set in the top and projecting about 2 inches (Fig. 15-4F).

10. Leave all this for the concrete to harden enough for the forms to be removed. Leave a few more days for it to cure fully.

11. Make the joists. Drill overdepth for the pegs on the supports. Either cut the ends now or leave them until after the decking has been fitted. A slope back encourages water to run off and not

345

soak into the end grain (Fig. 15-5A). Treat the joists with preservative.

12. At each support, make a pad of roofing paper and waterproof mastic so the wood will bed down on that (Fig. 15-5B). If possible, fit all three joists during one working session. It is unlikely that you will achieve perfect level between them. Use your long straightedge and spirit level along the joists (across them and diagonally). You can get a good level by cutting away the wood where it rests on one support, but you are more likely to need to pack up to bring joists up to the highest point you discover. More roofing paper and mastic might be all that is needed. You might need wood packings, but make sure the whole support area is covered and everything you add is made waterproof with mastic. Press and hammer the joists tight. You do not want them settling further in use. Finally, if there is space, get back and sight across all joists to see that they are really level and paral-

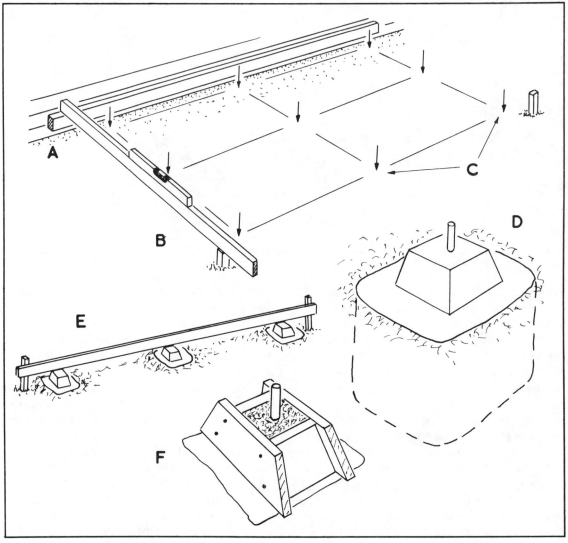

Fig. 15-4. Preparing the foundations of a low-level deck.

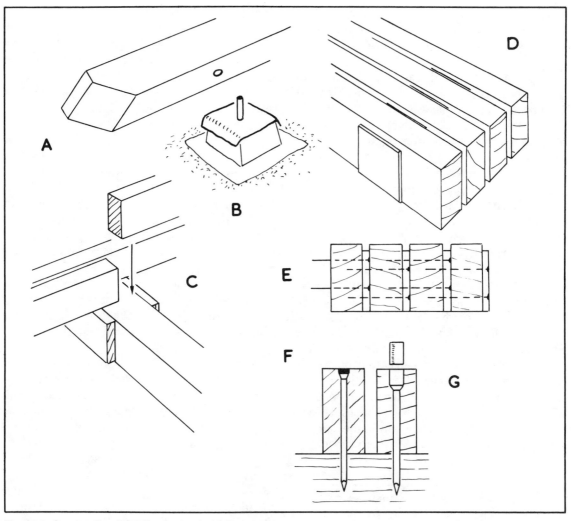

Fig. 15-5. Constructional details of a low-level deck.

lel. A twist in a deck is something to be avoided.

13. The foregoing instructions assume the deck is to be level. It could be given a slight slope so water drains away from the house and does not settle on the deck. That might seem a good idea, but you cannot provide much slope without it becoming noticeable, and only a slight slope is not very effective. If you want to provide a slope, use the leveling board with a packing under its end to arrive at the level at the outer edge. A drop of 2 inches in the 7 foot length is as much as might be provided without the angle becoming apparent.

14. In a deck of the size suggested, deck boards will almost certainly be full length. There can be an occasional joint on the middle joist if you want to use up short pieces. However, the joist should be thickened with cleats nailed on to provide support under the joint (Fig. 15-5C). Short boards should not come more often than every fifth piece laid.

15. The deck boards should have gaps between 1/8 inch and 1/4 inch. To maintain that, prepare spacers that can come over the joists. These could be pieces of shingle, tempered hard-

board, or strips cut specially. Have the grain the same way as the deck boards. Square pieces cut to come 1/2 inch below the top level will do (Fig. 15-5D).

16. The deck boards can be nailed through the spacers into each other in groups of a size you can handle; four at a time will probably be enough. Stagger the nails and leave the points projecting to go into a batch already mounted (Fig. 15-5E). The boards should have been treated with preservative, but as you assemble with the spacers also coat the joints with a waterproof mastic.

17. Predrill for nails into the joists to reduce the risk of splitting. Nails can be punched below the surface and covered with stopping (Fig. 15-5F), or they can be counterbored so they are deep enough for covering with a wood plug (Fig. 15-5G). As you fit each board or prepared batch, cover the joist with waterproof mastic or roofing paper or felt.

18. Nailing batches of boards together first will ensure that they finish upright, but where you fit single boards check that the ends are standing upright. Make sure the exposed ends of boards are level. Clean off any raggedness from sawing. If you make intermediate joints, the two pieces need not butt together tightly. The joists will not usually extend past the outside deck boards. If they are cut level and slope back, they should not suffer from water penetration.

Materials List for Low-Level Edge Board Deck	
3 joists	120 × 4 × 4
54 deck boards	84 × 4 × 2

HIGH DECK

If your home is on a hillside or you want to make a deck higher than ground level, it has to be supported on posts for at least part of the area. Much depends on the actual situation, but this deck is 20 feet long and extending 8 feet from the house wall. Its inner edge is supported on the house side a short distance above the ground, and the further edge is supported on posts arranged to suit variations in the sloping ground (Fig. 15-6). The surface

is made of 2-inch-by-4-inch boards laid flat on joists that are supported at their outer ends on a beam with posts. There is a railing all round. One possible stair arrangement is suggested in the next project.

In this arrangement, the beam is joined midway over a post and the gap between post centers is 60 inches. The joists on this are 24 inches apart, and they can span the distance to the house side without intermediate supports. If your arrangement involves spacing the posts more than 60 inches apart, the beam depth should be increased. The joist spans should not be increased very much unless they are deepened. It is assumed that the 4-inch-square posts will not have to be more than 60 inches high. A larger section should be used for higher posts.

Treat the wood in the way described in the previous project (with preservative and waterproof felt or paper in joints). If any metal is not rustproofed, use a rust-inhibiting fluid on steel and protect it with paint.

The actual fitting of deck boards is to joists and joists to beams. The adding of a railing is all straightforward, but there are some other details of construction that should be settled before starting work. In particular, you need to know how the deck will be attached to the house side.

1. With the deck boards laid parallel to the house side, the ends of the joists will come to the side and have to be supported there. The strength of the house structure must be checked. Usually there are strong members that will take lag screws or other fasteners through the siding or other covering. The locations of nails will give you a clue to positions. It may be possible to fix a ledger along the side and have the joist ends rest on it (Fig. 15-7A). If that is securely fastened it should take the weight. To prevent the joists from pulling away from the house, there could be a steel bracket at each joist or you could use a long piece of steel angle (Fig. 15-7B) with screws upward into the joists.

2. If it is inconvenient to use a ledger or you need to spread the fasteners, a board of a similar section to the joists can be attached to the house.

The joist ends are then held by metal joist hangers (Fig. 15-7C), with screws through both ways.

3. With the house connections decided, it will be a help to make a light assembly of scrap wood to the outline of the deck and with other pieces in the place of the posts to check on positions of footings and the general layout.

4. The footings can be dealt with in a similar way to those of the last project. The projecting bolt or spike goes into the end grain of the post, and a packing of roofing felt and mastic seals the wood.

5. Other ways of mounting the posts, to keep them clear of the ground and the risk of rot, involve steel anchor straps that might have to be made specially. One type uses steel (about 2-inch-by-3/8-inch section) forged to a loop that can be set in the concrete. Then the foot of the post is held by bolts between the two arms (Fig. 15-7D).

6. At the beam, the posts are best held with metal connectors. There could be angles with two lag screws each way (Fig. 15-7E). There could be steel strips each side bolted through or with lag screws (Fig. 15-7F). A further step would be to take a strip as a band over the beam (Fig. 15-7G).

7. For a joint over the center post, the two parts would not get much bearing on the post top.

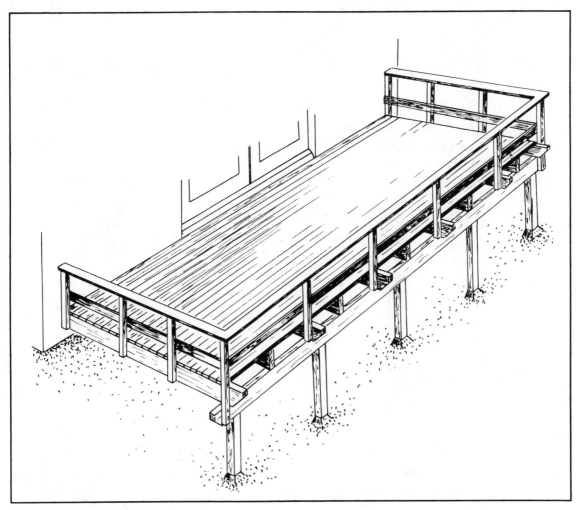

Fig. 15-6. A typical high-level deck.

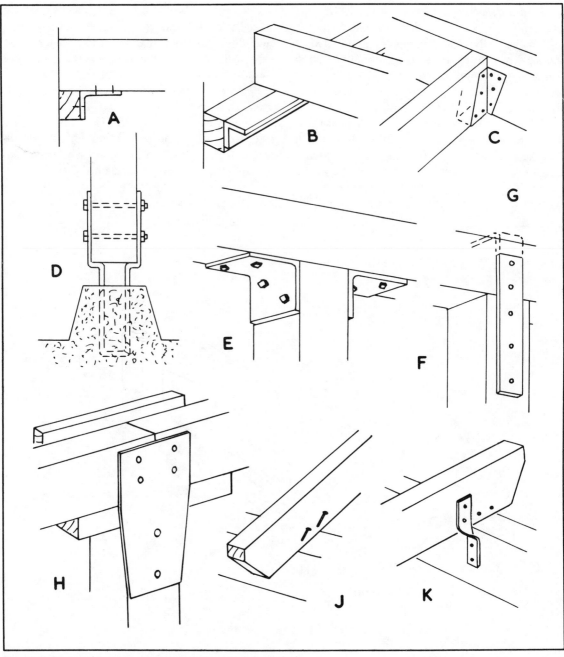

Fig. 15-7. Post and framing arrangements for a high-level deck.

The post could be widened with a strip across. A cover piece goes inside and there is a metal strap outside (Fig. 15-7H).

8. The joists on top of the beam can be held down in various ways, but toe nailing is simple (Fig. 15-7J). Drill for the nails to reduce risk of splitting. For additional strength, particularly where high winds might be expected to produce lifting

forces, there can be twisted strip-metal straps (Fig. 15-7K).

9. Plan the deck layout so that alternate joists extend over the beam about 12 inches to take the railing posts. For a stronger railing, allow for posts on every joist. At the ends, let the beam also extend far enough to take railing posts, and have the end joists level with the end of the deck boards so more railing posts can be mounted along them (Fig. 15-8A).

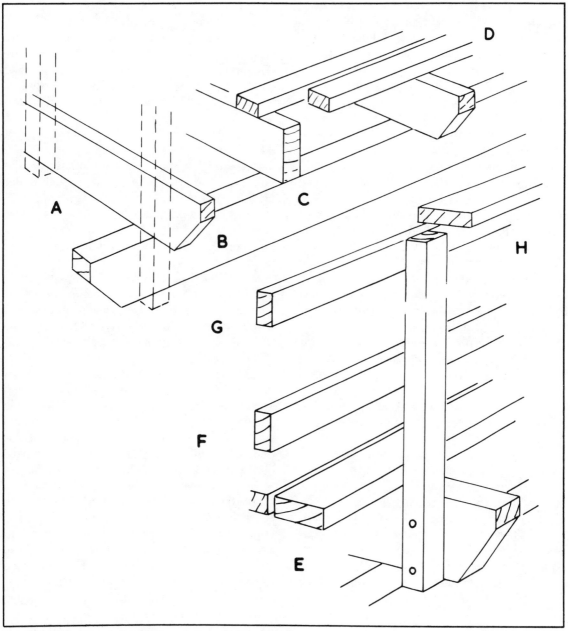

Fig. 15-8. Arrangements for railing posts on a high-level deck.

10. Prepare the posts. Level their tops with each other and check their level in relation to the attachments on the houseside. Mount the beam on the posts. Set them vertically before making the joints. Use temporary struts to the house side and others to the ground, if necessary. Fit the two end joists (Fig. 15-8B). Mark out for other joists at 24-inch intervals (Fig. 15-8C). Fit one near the center next to steady the assembly, and then add the other joists. Check diagonal measurements to see that the assembly is square.

11. Depending on the lengths available, there will have to be joints in the deck boards. Stagger the joints and thicken the joists where they come. You will be able to arrange some joints at the center, and probably have to divide the total length into about thirds.

12. Nail the deck boards with two nails at each crossing. Drill at the ends to reduce risk of splitting, and elsewhere if you wish to counterbore and cover the nail heads with plugs. Lay the outside boards directly over the beam (Fig. 15-8D). Space the others inward from this. with boards laid flat, there is no need to include spacers. Use a short length of 1/4-inch-thick wood as a gauge as you fit boards alongside those already laid.

13. With the deck boards fitted, the assembly should be rigid. Trim the board ends, if necessary, and remove raggedness from sawing. Check that all joints are tight. This is particularly important for lag screws and bolts.

14. The railing is intended to be 30 inches above the deck boards and have one intermediate rail. It could be arranged like a closed fence (as already described) or the height could be varied. Cut the posts from 3-inch-square wood that is long enough to overlap the joists at the ends and sides. The two longer posts go over the beams at the corners. Bolt the posts to the alternate joist ends (Fig. 15-8E). Check that they are vertical and sight along to see that they are in line. At the corners, put the posts on the outsides of the beams so that they will be inline with the other posts both ways. At the deck ends, bolt the posts to the joists at about 36 inch intervals.

15. In most situations, the lower rail can be inside the posts about 12 inches above the deck (Fig. 15-8F). It could be 2-inch-by-4-inch wood or rather thinner. Make joints on posts as needed. At the corners, one rail could go above the other. Long screws could be used or bolts could be taken through.

16. At the top, there is a similar rail level with the tops of the posts (Fig. 15-8G). A flat capping is put over it (preferably) wide enough to cover the posts and prevent water entering the end grain (Fig. 15-8H). If you cannot cover all of the post, taper the exposed part to encourage water to run off. Miter the capping corners.

17. Trim the ends of the joists and beams, but do not cut back close to the railing posts because that would leave short end grain in line with the bolts. The end grain might break through under pressure.

18. The edges of the capping and rails should be rounded, and any other parts that could come into contact with skin should have sharpness removed.

19. If the deck is firmly secured by attachment to the house and none of the posts are more than 5 feet high, there should be no fear of unsteadiness or movement due to activities on top or high winds blowing underneath. If stiffening is required due to tall posts, there will have to be some bracing.

20. The most effective bracing comes from diagonal struts from the base of one post to the top of another. They could come inside and outside and be bolted through so that they slope alternate ways (Fig. 15-9A). However, this makes access underneath difficult. If you want to use the space below, bracing can be with shorter struts arranged at the tops of the legs. Plywood gussets inside are simple (Fig. 15-9B). If they are outside as well, the edges should be protected with glue or wood strips to prevent entry of water. Better stiffening is with diagonal struts (Fig. 15-9C). The longer they are, the more effective they will be, but you will have to compromise if you need clearance for access. Even shorter struts can provide good stiffening due to their triangulating effect.

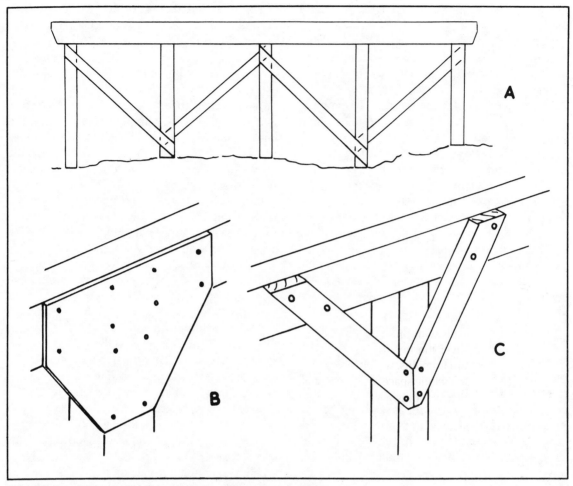

Fig. 15-9. Bracing is needed if the deck supporting posts are high.

Materials List for High Deck

(lengths to suit situation)

posts	4 × 4
beams	8 × 4
joists	8 × 2
deck boards	4 × 2
railing posts	3 × 3
rails	4 × 2
capping	6 × 2

DECK STAIRWAY

Stairs are often needed between a deck and the ground or with another level of deck or the house. They have to be planned so steps taken are the same all the way from ground level to the deck level. Having a higher or lower step at an end could cause the user to falter and have an accident. It is usual for the rise of stairs to be no more than 8 inches. If you measure the total height between surfaces, you can divide that into the nearest rise under 8 inches. The amount one step projects ahead of the one above is its *run* (Fig. 15-10A) and this is best if it is more than the *rise*. Shallower rises usually have wider runs. With a rise of 8 inches, the run might be 9 inches. If the rise is only 7 inches, the run would be better 10 inches or 11 inches.

Obviously you have to adapt to the available space. You cannot do anything about the total height, but you could make one more or less riser. Adjust the spread of the stair to fit within the available space. Most stairways are a compromise, but for ease of use aim at the suggested relation between rise and run. The angle of a stairway is flatter than 45 degrees to horizontal, and that must be allowed for (it extends more than it rises).

The two side supports are called *stringers* and they can support the treads in several ways. Because of the stringer angle in relation to the tread widths, they have to be fairly wide—usually 2 inches thick and 10 inches or 12 inches wide.

Treads are best as wide as the run, or a little more, but some stairways have the rear edge of each tread slightly forward of the nose of the one above. Stair widths are usually between 24 inches and 36 inches, and can have treads 2 inches thick.

1. It is possible to partially notch treads into stringers and support them with wood cleats securely bolted on (Fig. 15-10B). There could be steel angle instead of wood cleats (Fig. 15-10C). Notching treads into dadoes, as is often done on indoor stairways, is not recommended for exterior work. If the treads are to come wholly within the stringers, they are better on bolted cleats (Fig. 15-10D).

2. At the top, the stringers must be secured to the decking. If there are joists at convenient spacings, they can be bolted through (Fig. 15-10E). The stringers could be notched over ledgers and toe nailed (Fig. 15-10F), but there would be less obstruction to feet with cleats outside (Fig. 15-10G).

3. If the foot of the stairway is at ground level, it should be a concrete pad to avoid rot. The stringers could have cleats or steel angle outside, with anchor bolts set in the concrete (Fig. 15-10H). Another way to take any thrust uses stout strip iron bolted down and the wood stringers fit into the bends (Fig. 15-10J).

4. A stairway could go off the deck squarely at any point. Usually the deck boards are carried out on extended joists (Fig. 15-11A). If the boards are met end on, they should be cut back over a piece added inside and a cover strip fitted (Fig. 15-11B).

5. It might be more convenient to have the stairs alongside the deck. In that case, the joists have to be extended to take boards to form a landing (Fig. 15-11C). In most constructions, this can be allowed to cantilever from the deck—providing the extension is no more than 30 inches—but there will have to be another post at the corner.

6. Less commonly the stairway top can be set back into the deck. If the cutout is much, there are problems of support and railings will have to be arranged around the top for safety.

7. A stairway of just a few treads can be safe without a hand rail, but in most cases there have to be railings or bannisters. Construction can be the same as for the deck. This will give a uniform and attractive appearance.

8. Bolt the rail posts to the outsides of the stringers (Fig. 15-11D). Attach rails to them in the same way as around the deck (Fig. 15-11E). Maintain a similar height above the treads so that anyone using the stairway and the edge of the deck will not have to change the height of their grip.

9. How close you arrange the posts depends on your needs. Posts opposite every tread will give a balluster effect, but placing them at every second or third step—with a rail parallel with the stringer lower down—will provide ample protection.

At the top, link the rails with those of the deck. At the bottom, have a pair of posts near the end of the stringer. The greatest loads will have to be taken there so these posts could be stouter. They could be braced with struts outward (Fig. 15-12).

DECK SEATS

Seats of various sorts are the commonest furniture used on a deck. They could be loose chairs, benches, loungers, and other portable things, but permanent bench seats around the sides of the deck have at least two advantages. They are always there for use, without having to carry seating from

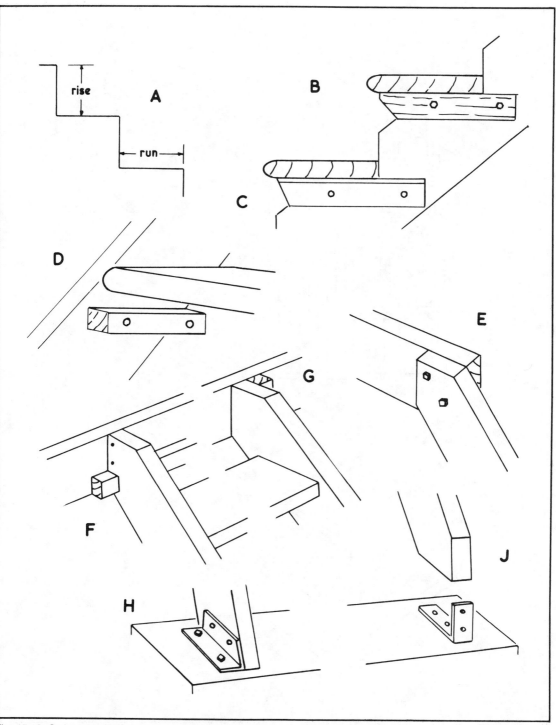

Fig. 15-10. Stairs to a deck must be planned so steps are the same throughout.

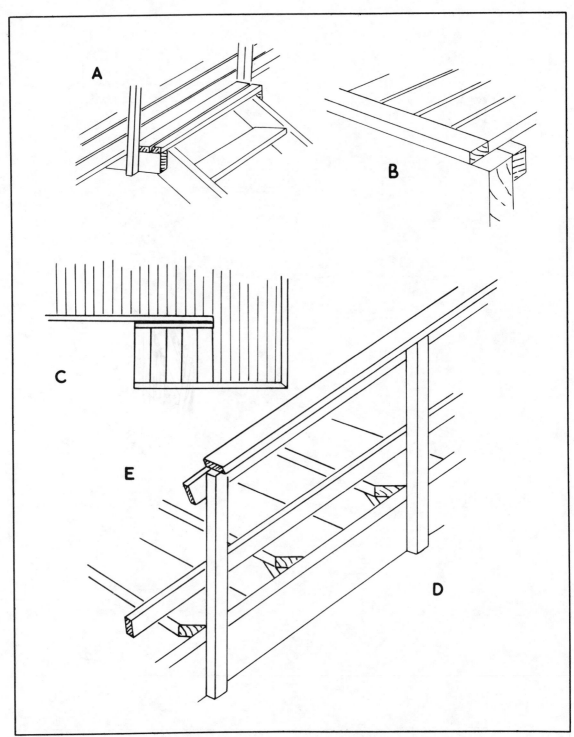

Fig. 15-11. A stairway can lead squarely or parallel to a deck. Rails should be provided.

Fig. 15-12. A stairway and its rails should be firmly bedded on a concrete base.

elsewhere, and they can strengthen the structure if built in when the deck is made. Of course, it is always possible to add benches inside railings on an existing deck, but when they are made at the same time as the deck it is possible to bond them to the structure so they become part of it. Bench seats inside the railings fit into the whole visual effect and are an added attraction (Fig. 15-13).

Seating is best planned and made after the joists have been fitted and before the deck boards and railing posts have been fitted. This allows the seat parts to become structural members instead of additions. If seats are to extend only partially along a side, you have to allow for the line of rail-

ings to match where they are open and where they form seat backs. In most situations, allow for the fronts of the seats to be about 15 inches above the finished deck. If the capping of the railing is between 30 inches and 36 inches above the deck, that will be satisfactory for both a barrier when standing and a seat back.

1. The railing posts will have to be upright to suit places where there are no seats, but a seat is more comfortable with a slight slope. Posts to joist ends can be attached at a slight angle (Fig. 15-14A); 10 degrees should be satisfactory. If the posts are to attach to the sides of joists or beams, they will have to be beveled. They can be reduced

at the top for neatness (Fig. 15-14B).

2. Where the seat will be square to the joists, front supports can be taken through and bolted to them (Fig. 15-14C). The same spacing as the railing posts should do, but 60 inches is about the maximum for a seat to be stiff between supports (depending on its material).

3. Where the seat will be in line with the joists, the front supports could be on top of the deck boards. For strength they are better taken through to pieces put between the joists (Fig. 15-14D).

4. The seat top could be level, but it is more comfortable if it slopes back a little. Making it square to posts sloping at 10 degrees should be about right (Fig. 15-14E). If you want to take the seat around a corner, the slope introduces complications and you might prefer to leave it parallel with the deck.

5. If there are no railings, you could settle for simple benches. In that case, double supports are needed (Fig. 15-14F). Otherwise construction can be the same as for seats against railings.

6. There is a choice of seat tops. You could join boards to make solid seats, you could use boards similar to those on the deck, or there could

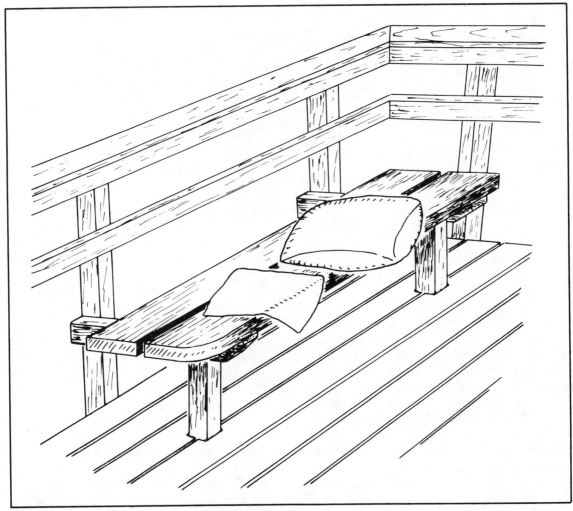

Fig. 15-13. Seats inside deck railings can contribute to strength.

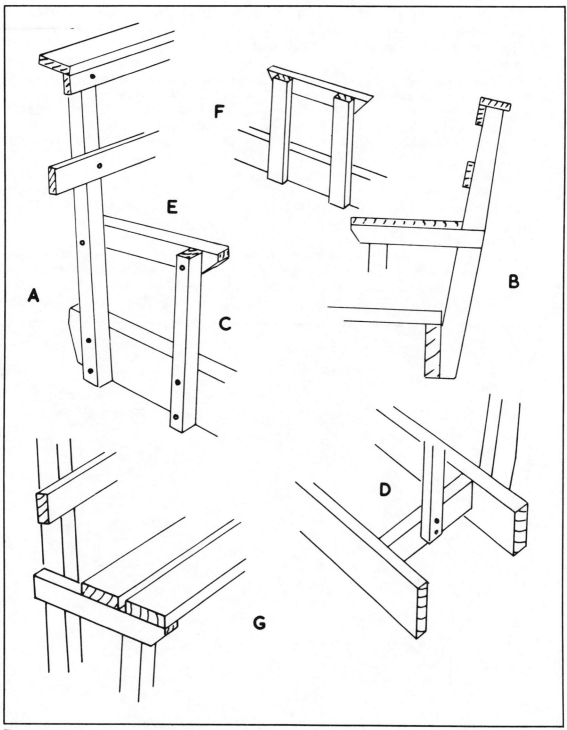

Fig. 15-14. Constructional details of deck seats.

be wider boards. Leave narrow gaps (Fig. 15-14G). The seat front should be about 15 inches forward of the strips that form the railings, but the boards need not go fully back.

7. At a corner with a horizontal top, you can take one seat top through and support the other over a cleat on it (Fig. 15-15A).

8. If the seats slope you cannot do this. Instead, it is better to miter the boards. Have supports as close as you can on each side, and then run the boards over. They need not make a close fit to each other (Fig. 15-15B).

9. If the deck is covered with boards standing on edge, matching seat tops can be made in a similar way (possibly with a 2-inch width and a depth fo 3 inches or 4 inches). Use spacers at intervals in the same way as suggested for the low deck. On the seat, the gaps could be wider than on the deck; up to 3/4 of an inch is reasonable (Fig.

15-15C). At a corner of a seat laid horizontally, you can get an interesting effect by overlapping alternate strips (Fig. 15-15D).

10. Consider how the decking will be laid. Where the seat supports are bolted to joists, it is convenient to arrange them symmetrically in a space (Fig. 15-15E). If much has to come out of a deck board, nail on a cleat below to support it. Where the supports are on pieces between joists, they can be adjusted in the preliminary layout so they come in gaps and little has to be cut away (Fig. 15-15F). If much has to be removed from a board, put a supporting cleat below.

WALKWAY

A boardwalk or raised walkway can be made like a deck, but usually it will be simpler. As it is narrower than a deck, there is no need for joists on beams in most cases. The posts that support the

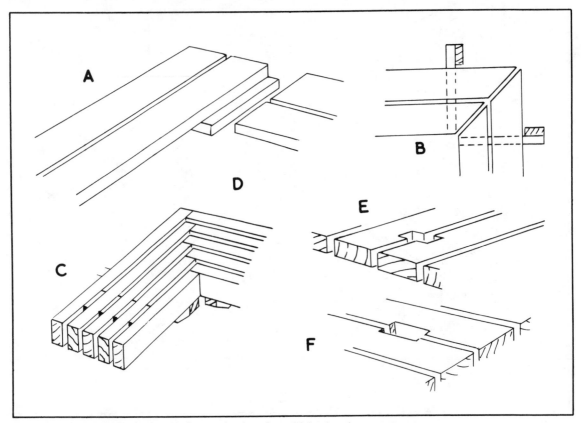

Fig. 15-15. Seats can be made with flat or edge boards and joined at the corners.

Fig. 15-16. A walkway can be made in the same way as a deck.

decking can continue up to form railing posts. Any length is possible, but in most gardens the assembly is more likely to be fairly short to cover a ditch, an uneven patch, or marshy ground. In many situations the walkway might even be regarded as a bridge. Figure 15-16 shows such a walkway, but the same methods could be used for much longer structures.

It is assumed that the walkway crosses a hollow and a pair of posts to the ground are used. They can be 3 inches square for most structures. If the span between them is not more than 7 feet, the joists could be 8 inches deep and 2 inches wide. You can have 2-inch-thick boards forming the decking if the joists are not more than 36 inches apart. Railings can be similar to those already suggested for decks, but the extended posts will provide support.

1. Use strings to lay out the two sides. Decide on the way you will treat the ends. If you want to take anything with wheels across, the approach should be level. The joists could fit into concrete blocks (Fig. 15-17A) that are arranged so the top of the concrete and the deck level will match the approach surface. If it is not important that the deck be level, you could rest the joists on flat concrete pads and make two shallow wide steps. The total height of 10 inches is too much for a single step, but you can cut the ends of the joists to take one wide tread midway between the surface level and the top of the deck boards (Fig. 15-17B).

2. The joists in position can be used to locate the posts. Check that they are level and parallel, and that there is no twist when you view from one side.

3. Make the posts long enough to extend about 36 inches above the deck level. The bottoms can be treated and driven into the ground, but they will be better set in concrete or on concrete pads

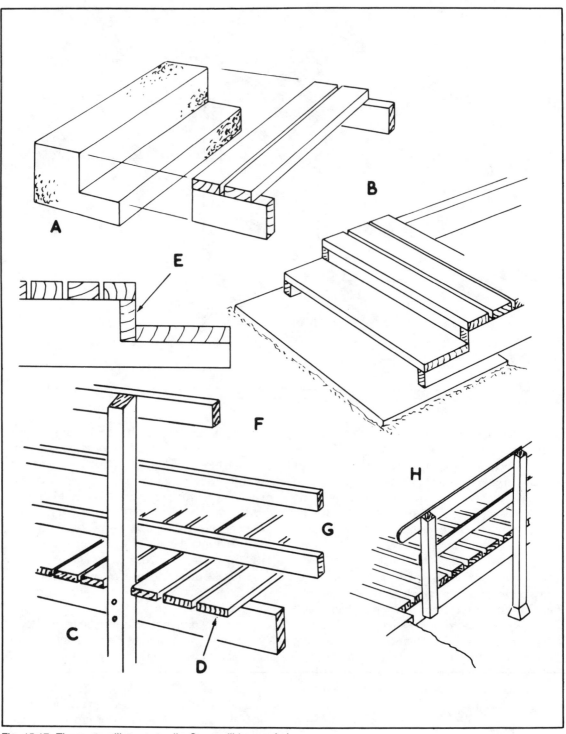

Fig. 15-17. The posts will support rails. Steps will be needed.

as described earlier in this chapter. Check that they are vertical and bolt them to the joists (Fig. 15-17C).

4. Lay the decking strips across the joists; use 1-inch gaps. The strips need not be cut level, but they should extend an inch or so each side (Fig. 15-17D).

5. At each end, if there is a step, put a piece across between the joists to support the deck strip. The strips will then receive most loads and wear (Fig. 15-17E). You will find this also advisable with a level approach.

6. Bolt or screw on top rails (Fig. 15-17F).

They can extend a little at each end. There could be a capping strip on the rails but if not slope the top of the posts to shed rainwater.

7. One lower rail might be enough, but it will probably be better to have two rails that are evenly spaced (Fig. 15-17G) or closer to the deck if you want to prevent wheels from running over the edge.

8. If the walkway has to be arranged so that the posts are some way from the end, have short railing posts near the ends that are bolted to the joists, but not projecting below them (Fig. 15-17H).

Chapter 16

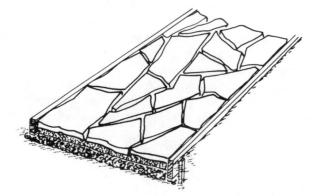

Concrete and Masonry

Stone blends with soil and vegetation in a garden to keep a natural appearance, and can be used to break up the mass of flowers and leaves with a solid, more somber contrast. Stones can also be used structurally for walls and other constructions. If a garden is to be broken into different levels, stone walls are often the most attractive way of retaining and supporting higher levels.

There are now many manufactured substitutes for natural stone. The regular shapes and sizes make assembly easier, but the effect will be a more formal appearance. Perhaps that is what you want. Precast concrete blocks with decorative surfaces or piercings can make a suitable surround for a patio or divisions in a garden, possibly between a formal layout and a more natural one.

Bricks are more traditional than precast blocks. Bricks with color and texture give a more earthy and natural look than those used in houses. Nevertheless, that type of brick would be appropriate if you are making a wall or other structure near the house.

Concrete can be regarded as stone that you

can shape and it will hold that form and be structurally strong. The finished thing will still be concrete and will never fool the viewer into believing it is stone, but concrete has many uses in a garden or yard.

MIXING CONCRETE

The active part of concrete is cement that is usually bought in bags. It must be kept dry until it is used. Sand should be free of soil and other impurities, and should also be dry. Because sand is usually stored outdoors and will have absorbed moisture from the air, you might have to use it while it is damp. Avoid sand that is saturated because it will not mix properly and the result will be weak concrete.

Aggregate is another name for gravel and stones. The stones can be anything from not much more than sand size up to an inch or so across. The aggregate should be clean and dry.

The proportions can be varied according to the intended use. For much garden concrete work, you can be wide of the theoretical ratios and still achieve satisfactory results. Aim to get them right. An easy to remember proportion is 1:2:3 (1 of cement, 2 of sand and 3 of aggregate). For foundations the amount of aggregate is increased. If it is mortar you are making, where there will not be aggregate; 1 of cement to 3 or 4 of sand will do. There are theoretical proportions of water to be added, but this is difficult to assess because the sand may already contain water. It is more usual to rely on the appearance of the mix.

If there is much concrete to be mixed, it will be advisable to hire a power-driven mixer. If the site is accessible to a truck, you might prefer to take a delivery of ready-mixed concrete. If you do that, get your quantity right as most suppliers will not want to take away unwanted mixture.

If all you want is a small amount, work on a clean surface. A piece of plywood is suitable. Put down the sand and aggregate and add the cement. Then very thoroughly mix dry with a spade. This is important. Spray on a little water and mix again. You could pour some water into a hollow at the center. Mix by turning over with the spade.

After working in that water, add more and mix again, usually by lifting the outside and turning into the center. For such purposes as post holes, aim to get the mixture wet right through, but barely pourable. When you work the spade up and down in it, the concrete mixture should be plastic and stay in the ridges you make. Wiping over with the flat of the spade should leave a smooth surface. Use the mixture within an hour or so (depending on the conditions). If the heat of the sun makes water evaporate rapidly, you will have to work quicker.

LAYING CONCRETE

If you are laying foundations or filling a post hole, there can be stones and gravel in the bottom, rammed down. Then the concrete can be poured and shoveled in. Tamp it with the spade or shovel edges and perhaps ram it with the end of a piece of post so that air is excluded.

You can build up the bulk in a foundation with larger stones, but make sure they are clean and wet them as you bury them in the concrete. If it is a post you are laying concrete around, support it and ram the concrete around it. Then use a flat trowel to smooth the surface to a slightly conical form at the top (Fig. 16-1A). A raised top can be shaped with a simple form made from boards (Fig. 15-4F). The boards can be pulled away after the concrete has set.

It is possible to make a slab away from where it will be used, but in most gardens it will be simpler and better to cast it in position. If the concrete is to be walked on, it should be about 2 inches or more thick over a firm foundation of stones and gravel. Dig out and make a frame of boards with straight tops held in place with pegs (Fig. 16-1B). Check that the tops are horizontal. If the slab is to be rectangular, check squareness by measuring diagonals. An inaccurate shape will be rather obvious. Ram stones and gravel into the bottom; leave enough depth above for the concrete. Lightly water the stones just before pouring the concrete. Otherwise too much moisture will be drawn out of the concrete too soon.

Use a straight board on edge to level the surface of the concrete (Fig. 16-1C). At first, this can be bounced up and down as it is moved along slowly. That leaves a generally level surface but with small ridges. Such a surface gives a good foot grip. If you want a smooth surface, go over with sweeps of a float made from a flat piece of wood and a handle (Fig. 16-1D).

A path can be made in the same way as a slab, but it is inadvisable to attempt a very long length in one operation. Prepare the form boards for the whole length and put in the stones for the base. Then divide the path into convenient lengths (about 6 feet). Put pieces across and lay alternate bays. When they have set, remove the dividing boards and lay concrete in the spaces between. A path can be flat, but there is an advantage in giving it a slight camber or crown so that water runs off to the sides. Plane a board to the curve you want and use that on the surface (Fig. 16-1E).

If you want to make concrete blocks or slabs of a size that can be handled, make simple forms with two angles (Fig. 16-1F). Use nails or screws

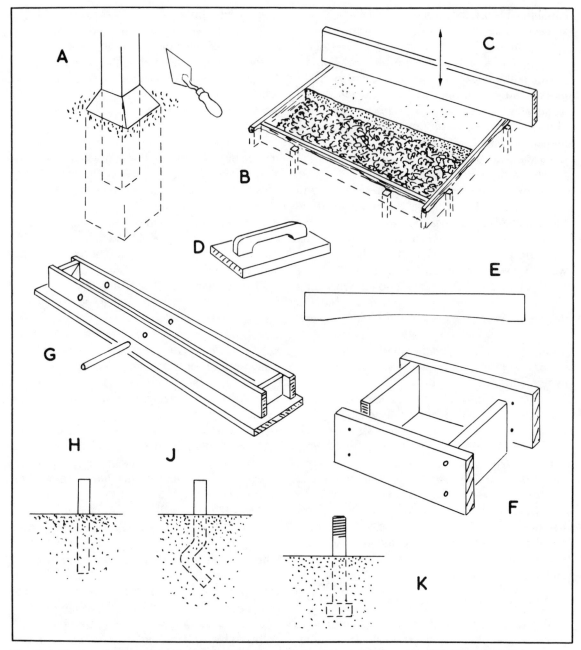

Fig. 16-1. Much concrete work involves wooden forms and tools. Pegs and bolts can be set into the concrete.

so they can be taken apart. There are nails with twin heads for this purpose.

With the form on a smooth surface, you can put in the concrete and level the top. After a few hours, the block will have set hard enough for the form to be opened carefully and removed, and ready for use again. Items of other shapes can be cast in this way. Much depends on your ingenuity in making forms. Remember that the form has to be tapered so it will pull away or it must be suitable for disassembly.

Concrete posts can be made in forms with dowels through to form bolt holes (Fig. 16-1G). Remove the dowels before the concrete has fully hardened.

For the attachment of wood, you will have to set in spikes or bolts. A plywood template duplicating the holes in the wood is useful as an indication of positions. A simple spike will give locations (Fig. 16-1H), but it could pull out. It is better with a few bends (Fig. 16-1J). A bolt head buried deep enough will provide its own security (Fig. 16-1K). When to put in the metal depends on the mix. If it is rather runny, let it begin to harden, and then put in the metal and trowel around it. If it is a thick, barely plastic mix, you can put the bolt or spike in as you level the top.

Concrete is strongest if it does not dry too

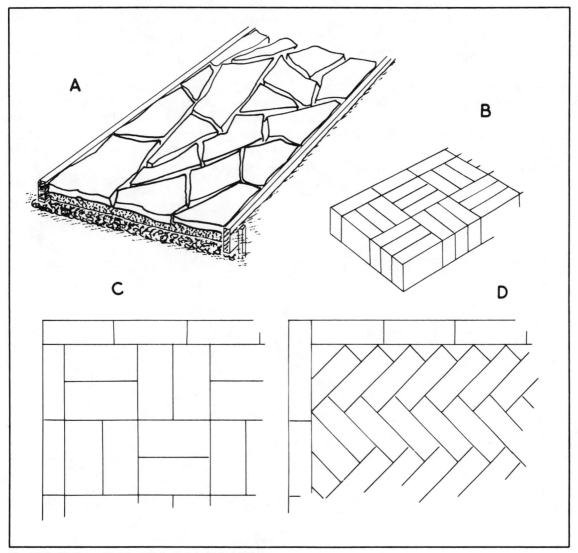

Fig. 16-2. Stone and brick paths can be set in patterns.

quickly. In moderate temperatures, it can just be left. Wet burlap laid over it will delay drying in hot or windy conditions. It must not be allowed to freeze before it has set; cover it when frost is expected.

STONE AND BRICK PATHS

A supply of flat stones or bricks can be used to make a path. Estimate your needs carefully because a surprising number are needed to go very far. Isolated stones of interesting shapes can be used like stepping stones in a lawn. Very little preparation is required.

Paths are often "crazy paved" with stones of irregular shapes. Unfortunately, you need many stones to fit into each other because gaps must not be very large. Such a path needs fairly straight edges. A temporary margin of board can be used to indicate width and height. Unless the soil is very firm, use a base of gravel. Over this can come sand only or a sand and cement mix that will grip the stones and discourage weeds growing between them (Fig. 16-2A). You could use this mortar between the stones as well, but open gaps, or those filled with soil, are usually preferred.

If you have to cut stones, the correct tool is a wide chisel sometimes called a *bolster*. You can use an engineer's cold chisel. To bed the stones down and level them, a heavy log bounced up and down is better than a hammer that might break the stones.

Bricks can be laid in a similar way to stones. There are many possibilities for various patterns (Fig. 16-2B, C and D). Mortar can be placed under the bricks and allowed to come almost to surface, which is usual, or allowed to come right to the surface to be troweled level.

Stone or brick paths do not have to be straight. There is an attraction about a slightly winding path or those that broaden in suitable places. It is not so easy to give a crown or camber to these paths, but a board with a suitable curve can be laid across as a guide as the parts are laid.

Chapter 17

Carts

Some means of transporting things is needed in almost every garden and yard. You could carry some items in a basket or box, but it is often better to have something on wheels. It need not be big or have a large capacity, but it gets tools and plants to where you want them and allows you to take away trash or produce. How it is made and its size and shape depends on your needs and the layout of the garden. If there are broad tracks or paths, the cart can be quite large. You could even have a trailer to go behind a mini-tractor. If the routes about the garden are narrow, you have to make something more compact.

The traditional garden-size transport has been a barrow with one wheel. The attraction is that it can go anywhere wide enough to walk. It lowers on to two legs and is then quite stable, but when you are using it, your arms take at least half the load. Some older barrows were made of such heavy wood that it took quite an effort to manage the barrow without anything loaded into it. There are much lighter versions, but stability depends on

your skill and not everyone is happy with a wheelbarrow.

There are two-wheel barrows and others that use a wide roller instead of the one wheel. Both are more stable, but you still have to take much of the weight on your arms. If the two wheels are brought back to come on each side of the load, the wheels take nearly all the weight and you need be concerned only with steadying and pushing or pulling.

The next step is to use four wheels to take all the weight and are steady, but one pair has to be steerable. With any cart having wheels at the side, you must have paths wide enough. You cannot take this sort of cart everywhere that a barrow would go. The ultimate in effortlessness is a trailer behind a tractor, but that needs even more space, and there may be places in the garden that you cannot reach.

You have to weigh up your needs and facilities against what you would like to have. The following projects are examples of the various types that can be built or adapted to your land.

GARDEN TROLLEY

A lightweight means of carrying tools, transporting plants, or gathering weeds is useful in a flower garden or a small vegetable plot where a larger barrow or cart would not be justified. The trolley shown in Fig. 17-1 has a pair of wheels and two handles. It has space for long and short tools, and there is a bin that could have a plastic bag fitted for trash, plants, or young trees would stand inside.

If necessary, the whole trolley can be tilted forward to release the contents, but it usually stands firm on the wheels and two legs.

The construction is almost entirely of 1/4-inch or 1/2-inch plywood on wood 2 inches wide and 1 inch thick. The sizes suggested in Fig. 17-2 are based on wheels about 8 inches diameter of the type that fit on a 3/8-inch or 1/2-inch rod axle and are retained by washers and cotter pins. The wheels and axle should be obtained first in case sizes have to be modified to suit. If glue is used

Fig. 17-1. A garden trolley will transport tools, plants, and other equipment.

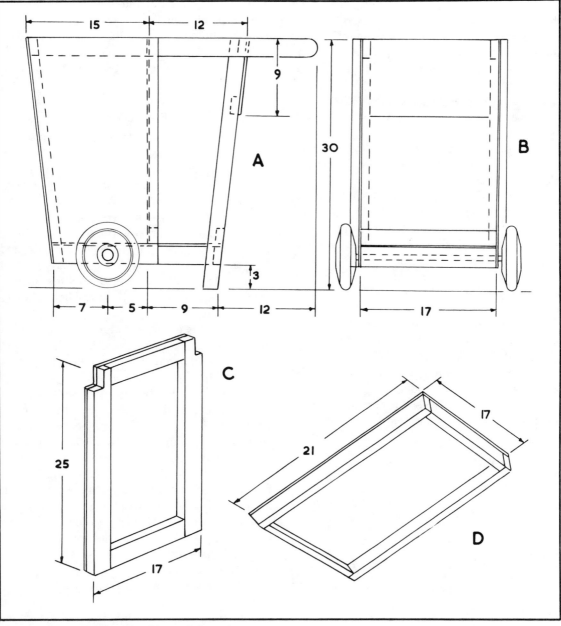

Fig. 17-2. The trolley is made of framed plywood.

between the plywood panels and the strips of wood, that will provide considerable strength and corners or other joints need only be nailed or screwed. Dowels or mortise and tenon joints could be used between some parts, but glue, nails, and

screws should be sufficient.

1. Set out the outline of the side view (Fig. 17-2A) to get the angles of the ends. The center panel is upright and the ends are sloping outward. In the other direction (Fig. 17-2B) the sides are par-

allel and the width may have to be modified to suit the axle, if a plain rod cannot be used.

2. The basic part, around which the others fit, is the center panel (Fig. 17-2C). Glue and nail the strips to it and cut out the corners for the handles to pass through.

3. Next comes the bottom (Fig. 17-2D). This is the same width as the center panel. The ends slope.

4. Attach the panel to the bottom, with the plywood forward (Fig. 17-3A). Screws as well as glue are advisable.

5. Make the handles (Fig. 17-3B) and use them parallel with the bottom to check the height of the front panel. Make and frame that panel (Fig. 17-3C). Glue and nail it to the bottom and glue and screw the handles to both panels.

6. Make the plywood sides (Fig. 17-3D) and glue and nail them to the other parts to complete the bin.

7. Drill through for the axle and temporarily put the wheels in position. This will allow you to make and fit the legs (Fig. 17-3E).

8. Put a strip across the bottom (Fig. 17-3F) to prevent tools from slipping off.

9. At the top between the handles and legs, stiffen a piece of plywood to fit inside the legs. After

painting the wood, put a strap in loops across this to hold small tools (Fig. 17-3G).

10. Thoroughly paint the wood. Fit the axle and wheels. Put large washers inside the wheels to prevent wear by rubbing on the plywood.

CYCLE WHEELS CART

Many wheels used on garden carts and similar load carriers have plain bearings and are stiff. Some of your energy is used in overcoming that resistance, but bicycle wheels have some of the easiest-running bearings available. Two bicycle wheels will support as big a load as you are likely to want to push. And make it easy to push. They can be back or front wheels, complete with their axles and nuts, from an old bicycle. The sizes suggested in this project suit 26-inch wheels, but the method of mounting allows other sizes to be fitted with little difficulty.

This cart is intended to be pushed or pulled with a pair of handles, but it can be adapted to suit towing behind a mini-tractor (see next project). It will stand level on its wheels and single leg, but its shape allows it to be tipped forward to empty a load of soil, sand, or stones. If you use wheels of another size, arrange them so the forward edge of the tread is at or forward of the bottom corner of the sloping front. The cart will then tip to bring the front almost flat on the ground (Fig. 17-4).

The main parts are made of plywood framed around with solid wood, but they could be made of solid boards assembled edge-to-edge. If all joints between plywood and solid strips are glued as well as nailed, there should be ample strength with corners glued and screwed.

1. The side view (Fig. 17-5A) is the key shape that governs certain other sizes. The back is upright and the front slopes forward at about 30 degrees. Mark out one side on a piece of plywood, but do not cut it to shape yet. You can use it as a working drawing when making other parts.

2. Make the wheel assemblies first (Fig. 17-6A). These are strip mild steel. If you have the means of bending it, sections about 2 inches wide and 1/4 inch thick are advisable. For easier work-

Materials List for Garden Trolley	
middle panel	
1 piece	25 × 17 × 1/4 or 1/2 plywood
2 pieces	25 × 2 × 1
2 pieces	14 × 2 × 1
bottom	
1 piece	21 × 17 × 1/4 or 1/2 plywood
2 pieces	21 × 2 × 1
2 pieces	16 × 2 × 1
front	
1 piece	28 × 17 × 1/4 or 1/2 plywood
2 pieces	26 × 2 × 1
1 piece	16 × 2 × 1
2 sides	27 × 17 × 1/4 or 1/2 plywood
2 handles	36 × 2 × 1
2 legs	31 × 2 × 1
1 back	17 × 9 × 1/4 or 1/2 plywood
3 backs	17 × 2 × 1
2 wheels 8 inch diameter with 25 inch axle	

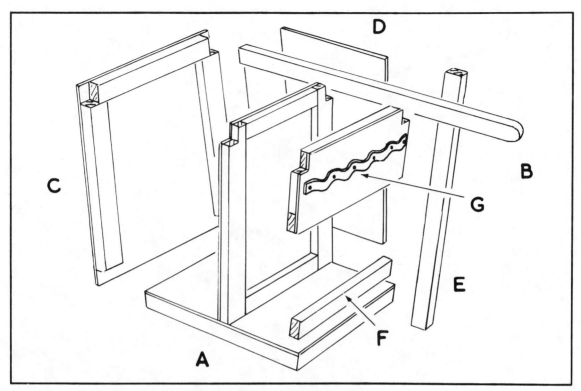

Fig. 17-3. The trolley parts assemble over the base. Loops will hold small tools.

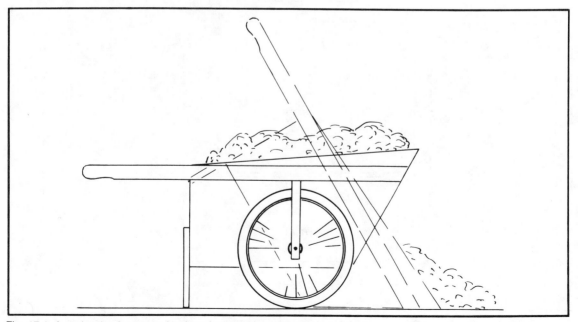

Fig. 17-4. A cycle wheel cart can be tipped to shed its load.

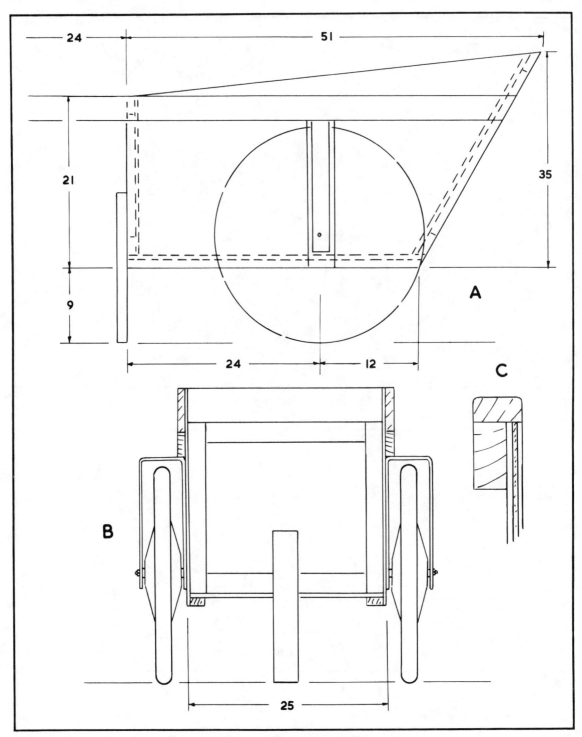

Fig. 17-5. The cart sizes will have to be adjusted to suit available wheels.

ing, you can come down to 3/16 of an inch or even less. Make the width to fit over the axles and the top high enough to clear the tires.

3. Drill the inner sides for bolts that will go through the cart sides (Fig. 17-6B). When the wheels are mounted, hollow the pads to clear the inner nuts (Fig. 17-6C).

4. Decide on the width you want the cart to be. It can be anything reasonable. Figure 17-5B shows a 25-inch width that is convenient for handling.

5. The assembly is based on framed ends over a bottom (Fig. 17-7). Make the upright end first (Fig. 17-7A), with strips glued and nailed to the outside.

6. Make the sloping end next, in the same way (Fig. 17-7B), using the layout on plywood as a guide to size and angles.

7. Cut the bottom piece of plywood and put stiffeners under its sides (Fig. 17-7C). Its ends will be stiffened by joining front and back.

8. Join the ends to the bottom and add the two sides (Fig. 17-7D).

9. Make the two handles (Fig. 17-7E). They will be parallel with the floor and other pieces are needed above them to strengthen the top plywood edge (Fig. 17-7F).

10. Unprotected plywood edges would soon suffer during rough use and it is advisable to put capping pieces on all round (Fig. 17-5C).

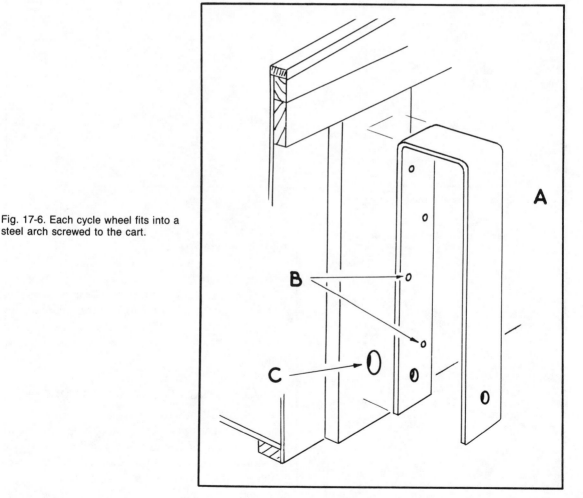

Fig. 17-6. Each cycle wheel fits into a steel arch screwed to the cart.

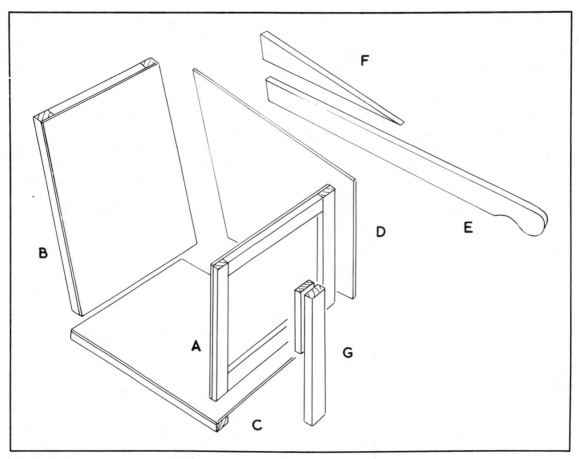

Fig. 17-7. The cart parts are framed plywood.

Materials List for Cycle Wheels Cart	
back	
1 piece	25 × 21 × 1/2 plywood
4 pieces	21 × 2 × 1
front	
1 piece	31 × 25 × 1/2 plywood
2 pieces	31 × 2 × 1
2 pieces	21 × 2 × 1
bottom	
1 piece	36 × 25 × 1/2 plywood
2 pieces	36 × 2 × 1
2 sides	51 × 36 × 1/2 plywood
2 cappings	54 × 2 × 3/4
2 cappings	26 × 1 1/2 × 3/4
2 handles	76 × 3 × 1 1/2
2 packings	51 × 5 × 1 1/2
1 leg	18 × 3 × 1 1/2
1 leg pad	9 × 3 × 1
2 wheel pads	18 × 4 × 1
2 pieces steel	48 × 2 × 1/4 or 3/16

11. Fit pads for the wheel assemblies and bolt them on temporarily.

12. Make a central leg and pad (Fig. 17-7G) for the back of the cart to support the bottom level.

13. If the cart performs satisfactorily at this stage, it is advisable to remove the wheel assemblies so the wood can be painted all over and the steel strip also can be painted all round.

TIPPING CYCLE WHEELS TRAILER

If you have a mini-tractor or a ride-on mower, it is convenient to be able to hook your cart on to it. The body of the cart just described could be mounted on a simple chassis for hooking to a tractor and it could be arranged to tip.

The body could have a box shape with its top sloping to a tapered end. Make it as described except there are no handles, pads for wheel assemblies or a leg.

The chassis will have to be made to suit the box. Sizes are suggested in Fig. 17-8. Use wood 4 inches wide and 2 inches deep. In relation to the box, the wheel positions are about the same as in the last project.

1. Make the box complete. With that as a guide, mark out the central piece of the chassis (Fig. 17-8A). The end crossbar comes with its center at the wheel position and the other one (Fig. 17-8B) supports the upright end of the box (with its edge level with it). Bolt these parts securely and squarely together, without projections on top.

2. Under the box goes a 4-inch-wide strip across to come level with the lengthwise strips and locate over the end chassis members.

3. Fit strong hinges to the chassis (Fig. 17-8C) and to the piece under the box.

4. The wheel assemblies are similar to those on the cart. An exception is that they have to be extended under the chassis crossbar (Fig. 17-8D) to which they are bolted. Keep the bend close to the end of the wood in order to gain stiffness from it. The steel used must be stiff enough because it does not gain strength from the box sides in this case.

5. The box will keep level, due to gravity, but to prevent inadvertent tipping use a hook and eye (Fig. 17-8E).

6. At the forward end, there must be an attachment to the tractor and this will have to be arranged to suit. A bar with a hole for a pin is shown in Fig. 17-8F. The bar will have to be cranked up

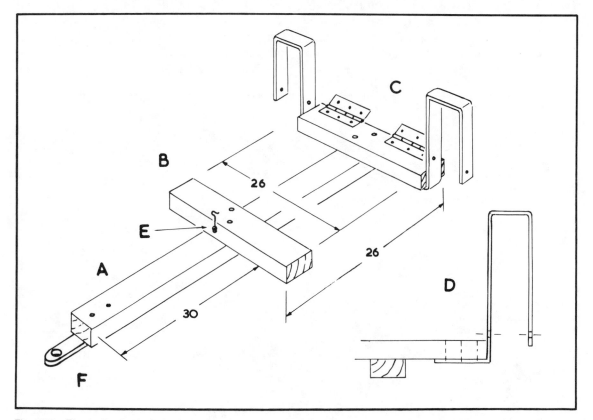

Fig. 17-8. The cycle wheel cart body can be adapted to mount on this chassis so that it can be towed by a mini-tractor and be arranged to tip.

or down to suit the level of the tractor attachment.

WHEELBARROW

A traditional wheelbarrow is the sort of equipment that is almost essential in a yard or garden—from the tiny backyard to property of several acres—even if you have other means of transporting things about. With its single wheel it will go almost anywhere.

The wheelbarrow of not so many years ago was a very heavy assembly of wood. There are light metal alternatives that can be bought, but they would be difficult to make with the usual home craftsman equipment. You can make a barrow with a framed plywood box on a light wood framework.

The important part is the wheel and its axle. It should be a free-running wheel with a 12-inch overall diameter. Many types are possible, and you might be able to buy or recycle something suitable. A breadth of tread of about 3 inches will prevent the wheel from sinking in the soil too much, and that size wheel will have a hub broad enough to withstand the rocking loads that are sometimes imposed. A wheel with a solid rubber tire is ideal. There could be an iron rim. You could make a solid wood wheel with several thicknesses laid across each other and glued and screwed together. However, get the wheel and an axle at least 10 inches long before planning the other parts.

The box should be flared in all directions. This is complicated by the tapered width of the bottom, to suit the supporting handles, while the rim should be rectangular or nearly so (Fig. 17-9). This results in outlines of box parts that are odd shapes and different angles. One way of getting over this problem is to make the bottom with parallel sides and have the box sides upright, but that removes some of the advantages of the traditional shape. It is not difficult to make a box with a flare all round (Fig. 17-10) if you work in steps. This shape allows the

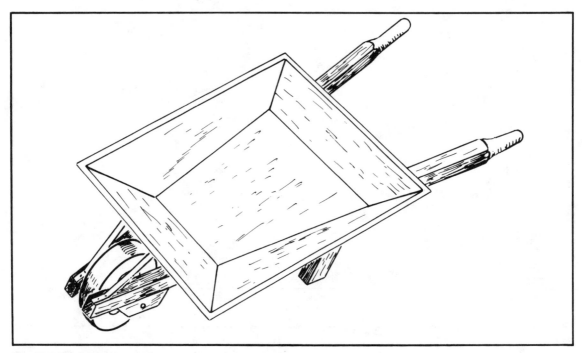

Fig. 17-9. A wheelbarrow is the most versatile cart in a garden.

contents to be tipped forward or sideways without difficulty.

Figure 17-10 shows sizes that will give a reasonable proportion for a light wheelbarrow that should suit the average home garden. The box could be deepened if most of your loads are bulky rather than heavy, and all sizes could be increased if you want to deal with really heavy loads. The drawing is based on a 12-inch wheel.

1. Start with the box; it is made of 1/2-inch plywood. Work from centerlines to get the bottom and ends symmetrical. Cut the bottom plywood to size (Fig. 17-11A). Frame it around with 1-inch-thick wood 2 inches wide against the plywood. Use nails and waterproof glue. At the ends, bevel at 60 degrees (Fig. 17-11B). Leave the sides square, but keep the nails far enough back from the edge to allow for some beveling there later.

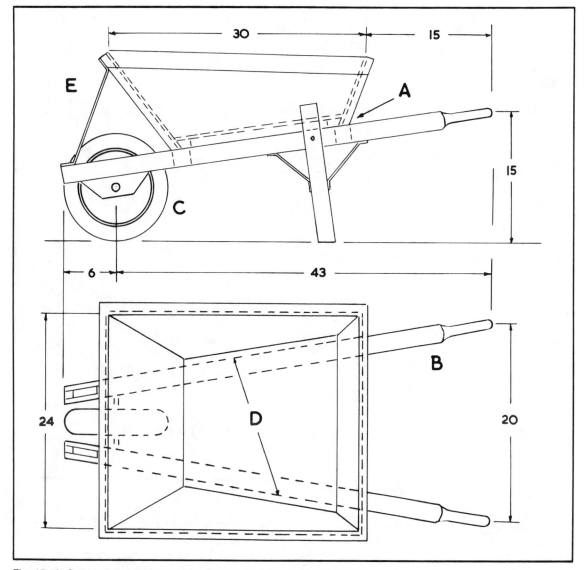

Fig. 17-10. Suggested sizes for a wheelbarrow with a framed plywood body.

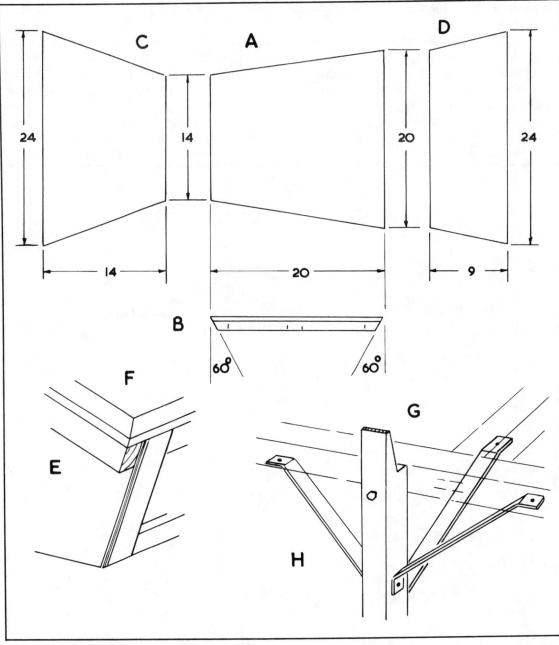

Fig. 17-11. Sizes of panels (A-D) and constructional details (E-H).

2. Cut the plywood front (Fig. 17-11C) and back (Fig. 17-11D). Frame them around in the same way. The top edges will finish square. The bottom edges should match the box bottom (Fig. 17-10A). Leave the sides square, but allow for them being beveled later.

3. Join the ends to the bottom temporarily with one screw near each corner. Hold a piece of

plywood for one side against this assembly and mark its outline. Check that the other side matches. Cut both pieces of plywood. If you hold a side against the other parts, you can see what bevels are needed on their edges. Plane the bevels. When you have a satisfactory fit, join all the box parts with glue and screws. Plain nails might not be strong enough, but annular ring nails could be used.

4. There is no need to frame outside the side panels because they are stiffened where they join the other parts. Put a strip along the top edge (Fig. 17-11E). There should be a capping all round to protect the plywood edges (Fig. 17-11F). The bottom plywood will be stiff enough as it is, but if you want to reinforce it there can be another strip across under its center.

5. Make the two handles (Figs. 17-10B and 12A). Reduce the ends to comfortable round grips; a 1 1/8-inch diameter is a suitable size. At the other end, thicken with blocks glued and screwed on to take the axle that will be about 1 inch below the handle strip (Fig. 17-12B).

6. For very light work, the handles should get enough steadiness from being attached to the box, but it is advisable to give them their own cross

bracing. These are 2-inch-square pieces between the handles and under the ends of the box. You can lay out their lengths and angles by using the box. Have the box inverted and put the handles in position on it. They should come not more than 1 inch in from the sides of the box bottom (Fig. 17-10D).

7. The pieces across could fit between the handle parts and be held with brackets (Fig. 17-12C), but this is a place where mortise and tenon joints are preferable (Fig. 17-12D). If you want to give a traditional appearance, let the tenons project so you can shape their ends.

8. If the axle is a rod through, you can assemble the under frame to the box now and leave it until later. If the axle is part of the hub assembly, drill to suit and fit the wheel now. Attach the box with screws down through the stiffening framing into the handles.

9. The legs are bolted to the handles and can be extended up the sides (Fig. 17-11G). Bolting alone will not resist the many loads liable to come on the legs. They should have struts along the handles and to the cross bracing (Fig. 17-11H). Strip steel about 1 inch wide and 3/16 of an inch thick is easily bent cold in a vise, and it should be

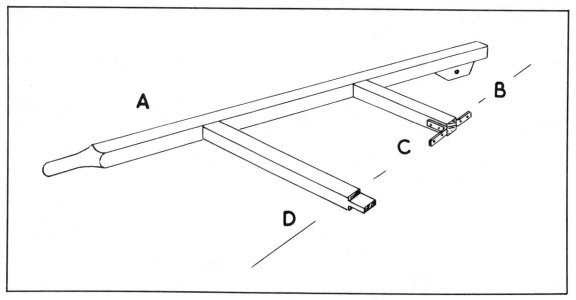

Fig. 17-12. Handle and support details.

strong enough.

10. Similar struts can be put between the ends of the wood on each side of the wheel and the top front framing (Fig. 17-10E), but that is not so important. Check the stiffness of the front wood assembly.

11. Trimming the bottoms of the legs to length can be left until everything has been assembled. Then you cut them to get the barrow to the angle you want and the handles to a comfortable height.

12. Finish the wheelbarrow with paint. If all the box joints have been made with waterproof glue, it should be capable of carrying water or any liquid mixtures.

Materials List for Wheelbarrow

1 bottom	20 × 20 × 1/2 plywood
1 front	20 × 14 × 1/2 plywood
1 back	24 × 9 × 1/2 plywood
2 sides	33 × 17 × 1/2 plywood
6 framing	25 × 2 × 1
6 framing	16 × 2 × 1
2 cappings	33 × 1 1/2 × 3/4
2 cappings	25 × 1 1/2 × 3/4
2 handles	56 × 2 × 2
1 bracing	20 × 2 × 2
1 bracing	14 × 2 × 2
2 axle blocks	9 × 2 × 2
2 legs	18 × 2 × 2
8 struts	14 × 1 × 3/16 steel

Chapter 18

Buildings

You can store tools and equipment in lockers or other small containers, but in many gardens there is a need for a small building for storage or for use as a greenhouse. It might be possible to build a shed on the side of a house or against a fence, but in many cases it will have to be a freestanding structure. Building such a shed or greenhouse need not be very complicated and you do not have all the restrictions that come with building a house. The structure can range from a simple shelter made from available material to a well-finished structure that looks like a smaller counterpart of your house.

Construction is usually of wood, but walls could be partially or completely made of bricks or precast blocks with wood above. It is not usually necessary to include insulation in walls or roof, and many sheds have nothing in the walls except the sheathing that is visible outside. Roofs can be treated in a similar way, but they can include two or more layers to ensure weatherproofing.

A fairly large building will have to be built in position, but for sheds of a size often needed in a garden prefabricated panels can be bolted together on the site. This means you can make the parts in your shop or elsewhere (perhaps when the weather is unsuitable for work outside). It also allows you to take a building apart and move it to another position with the minimum trouble.

There are several ways of covering shed walls. Simplest is to use sheets of exterior plywood or exterior-grade particleboard. This has a plain appearance (Fig. 18-1A), and contributes more strength to the structure than any type of boarding made up of strips.

Boards laid vertically with battens over the joints (Fig. 18-1B) are more appropriate to barns. Boards can be laid to overlap (Fig. 18-1C) and fit better if they taper in thickness. Shiplap boarding makes a tight attractive covering (Fig.18-1D). Tongued and grooved boards can be laid horizontally or vertically (Fig. 18-1E). Laying diagonally would give an interesting effect and help to brace the building. Metal siding can be used, but it is less common on garden buildings.

Exterior-grade plywood or particleboard can

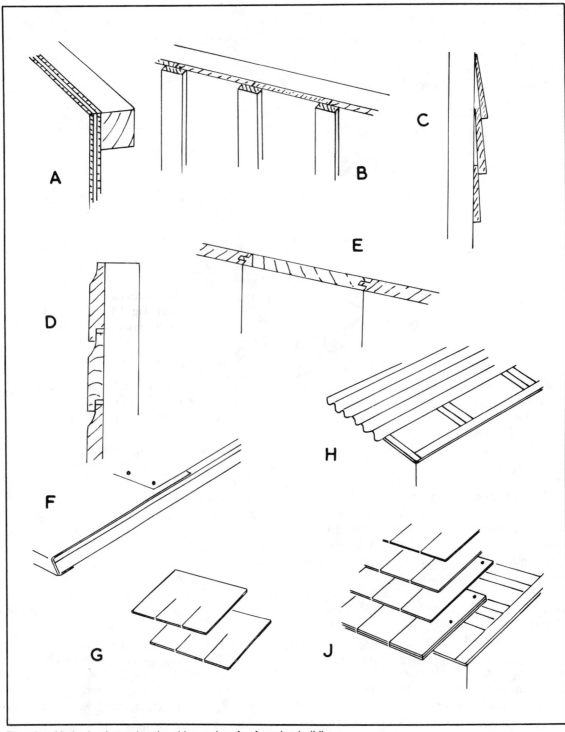

Fig. 18-1. Methods of covering the sides and roofs of garden buildings.

be used on the roof, but it then has to be covered. Asphalt roll roofing is suitable. Follow the maker's instructions and arrange overlaps in the direction of the slope (Fig. 18-1F). There are asphalt shingles (Fig. 18-1G) that have a similar effect with a shingle appearance. Use the special roof nails with large heads. Corrugated metal sheets can be laid over widely spaced purlins (Fig. 18-1H). Wood shingles are attractive. Arrange the lengthwise purlin spacings to suit the amount of shingle overlap (Fig. 18-1J).

A shed could stand directly on the ground, but that would obviously encourage rot. There could be a wood floor raised on concrete blocks or bricks. A concrete slab would make a foundation and a floor.

SIMPLE SHED

A storage shed with enough space inside for tools and a small bench on which to deal with seed trays and similar things need not be complicated. The shed shown in Fig. 18-2 is intended to be made in sections and bolted together. It is shown covered with plywood, but any of the other methods of sheathing could be used. There is a wood floor, but a concrete one would be just as suitable.

1. The sizes suggested in Fig. 18-3A allow the plywood covering to be made with the minimum of joints. The same method can be used for a shed of other sizes adapted to suit your available space. Although this is a free-standing shed, it could be made as a lean-to against an existing wall.

2. There are several ways of dealing with frame corners. Bridle, or open mortise and tenon, joints might appeal to a craftsman (Fig. 18-4A), but with plywood providing some strength simple nailing will do (Fig. 18-4B). For that or other covering, you could include a block to give extra nailing surface (Fig.18-4C). Another way of strengthening for any covering is to nail on triangles of galvanized sheet steel or aluminum (Fig. 18-4D). In general, let uprights overlap horizontal and sloping members.

3. The ends provide the key shapes. Make

the back first (Fig. 18-3B). The covering is trimmed level at the edges. If there is to be a wood floor, let the plywood project below enough to at least partially cover it. If you are using shiplap boards, allow for the bottom one going over the edge of the floor, but it need not be fitted yet.

4. Assemble the other end over the back so that it makes a pair (Fig. 18-3C). Include the framing for the door and check this opening for squareness as you join the strips.

5. Make the low side (Fig. 18-3D). With a plywood skin, there is probably no need for diagonal bracing. With other sheathing it is advisable, and this is especially important if the shed will be exposed to high winds.

6. At the corners, allow for the uprights bolting together and the side skin overlapping (Fig. 18-4E). Three or four coach bolts will be used at each corner. The skin edges can be covered with a batten after assembly (Fig. 18-4F). Allow for the sheathing going over the floor in the same way as at the ends. The top edge could be left square, but for the best construction it should be cut to the same angle as the ends (Fig. 18-4G).

7. Make the high side (Fig. 18-3E) with its length to match the low side and height to match the ends. Frame the opening for the window and cut the sheathing level with it. If there is a vertical joint in the plywood, cover it with a batten. Treat the edges of the assembly in the same way as the back.

8. The roof could be prefabricated. If you will be assembling the shed straight away, it would be advisable to wait until after the four walls are erected in case there are slight errors of size or squareness to be allowed for. There is need for little framing in a plywood roof of this size. Allow the plywood sufficient overlap and frame it all round (Fig. 18-4H). Two other strips across inside the walls should give sufficient stiffness (Fig. 18-4J).

9. If there is to be a wood floor, it could be plywood or particleboard on framing (Fig. 18-3F). Nailed construction is all that is needed, but it is important that the overall sizes match the sizes of the assembled walls. Attach the walls to the floor with coach screws or long nails and nail the

Fig. 18-2. A simple shed covered with plywood.

sheathing around the outside (Fig. 18-4K).

10. If the plywood roof is to be covered with asphalt roofing, screw it down to the wall framing first. Covering should be wrapped over the roof

edges, where appropriate.

11. The window can be a single piece of sheet glass or stiff plastic. It can be fitted with strips around the opening to project over the sheathing

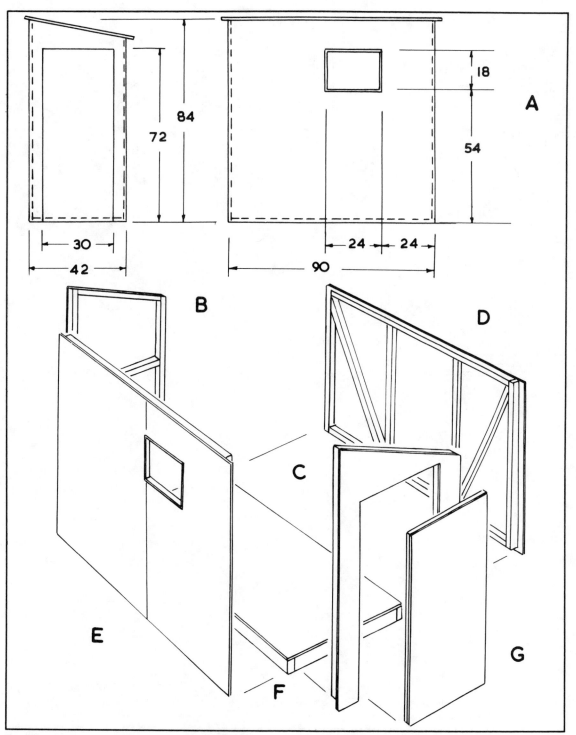

Fig. 18-3. Sizes and assembly of the simple shed.

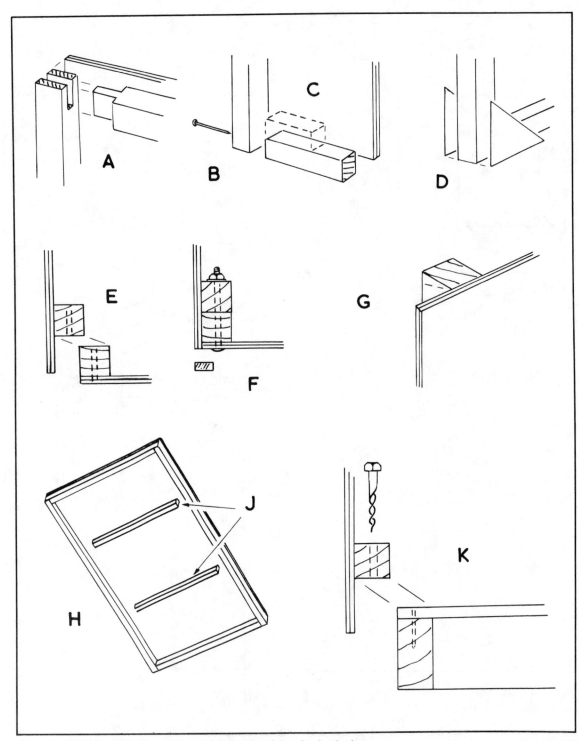

Fig. 18-4. Methods of framing and assembling parts of the simple shed.

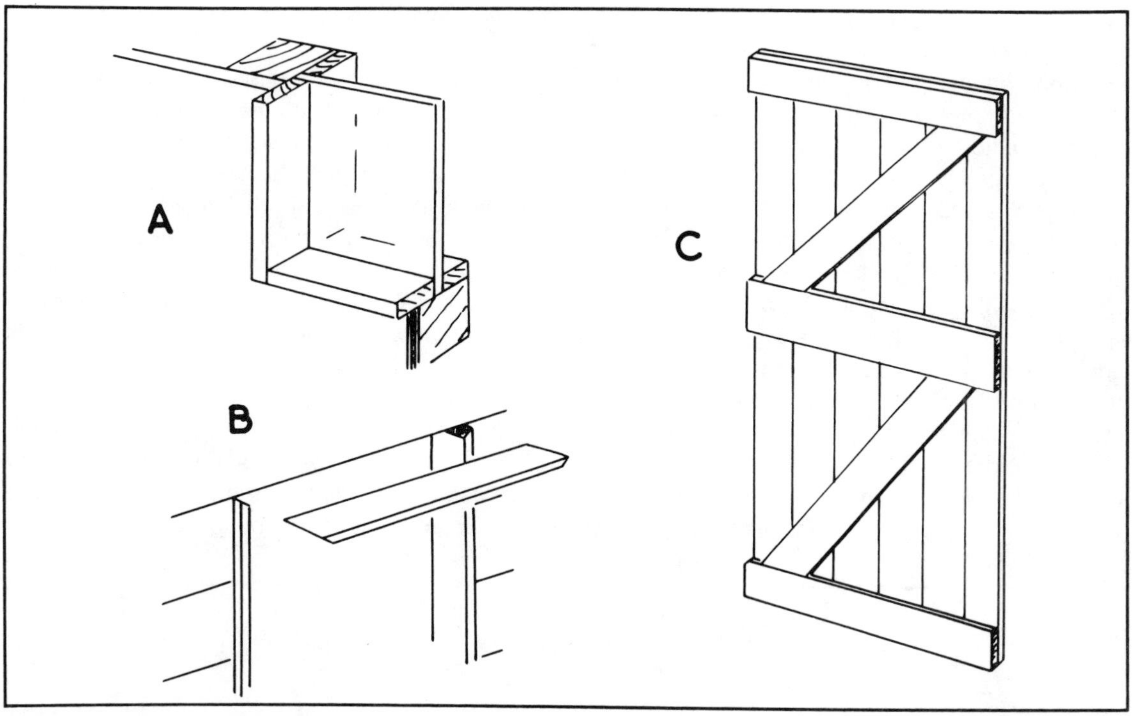

Fig. 18-5. Window and door details.

outside. Other strips hold the glass from inside (Fig. 18-5A). If the inside strips are lightly nailed, you can remove them easily if you have to replace glass.

12. Frame the doorway with strips that overlap the sheathing slightly (Fig. 18-5B).

13. The door (Fig. 18-3G) can be plywood or vertical boards with framing inside (Fig. 18-5C). Hinge it whichever side is convenient and fit a latch and lock.

14. For the most durable shed, the wood should be treated with preservative either before or during assembly so that parts that would be inaccessible later can be reached. This would also apply to painting. Meeting surfaces can be painted before they are brought together, and then the finished shed is finally painted all over.

15. Although a painted plywood roof might seem adequate, you will get a longer life out of using asphalt sheet materials over it. Arrange any overlaps in the direction the water will run. Use plenty of galvanized roofing nails.

Materials List for Simple Shed

2 roof frames	96 × 2 × 2
4 roof frames	48 × 2 × 2
6 end frames	44 × 2 × 2
2 end frames	84 × 2 × 2
2 end frames	78 × 2 × 2
4 side frames	90 × 2 × 2
4 low side frames	78 × 2 × 2
3 high side frames	84 × 2 × 2
3 window frames	28 × 2 × 2
4 window frames	28 × 2 × 5/8
4 window frames	28 × 1 × 5/8
2 door frames	72 × 3 1/2 × 5/8
1 door frame	31 × 3 1/2 × 5/8
2 door frames	90 × 4 × 2
4 floor frames	40 × 4 × 2
6 door boards	72 × 5 × 3/4
3 door ledgers	30 × 5 × 3/4
2 door braces	48 × 5 × 3/4
1/2 inch plywood:	
2 ends	84 × 42
3 low sides	78 × 30
1 high side	84 × 48
1 high side	84 × 42
1 floor	86 × 38
1 roof	96 × 48

PLAYHOUSE/SHED

If you have space to build a playhouse, your children will get a lot of satisfaction out of using it, but children grow up and you can reach a stage where a building that is just a playhouse has no further use. If it is a scaled-down size, there is not much you can do with it. If there is space, it is better to start with a building that can have other uses. That means it should be large enough for adult use. Children will quite happily play in it.

This building shown in Fig. 18-6 has an enclosed part large enough for most adults to stand in and a porch area large enough for them to sit in. The whole thing gives plenty of scope for several children to use. The back is a large lift-out door. Quite large garden equipment can be put inside for storage, and that end might be used for

access even when children are playing at the other end.

The suggested sizes (Fig. 18-7A) allow for cutting plywood sheets with the minimum waste, but covering could be with wood siding or any other means suggested at the beginning of the chapter. The enclosed area is about 7 feet by 8 feet, and this gets natural light through windows at one or both sides and in the front door. The porch extends 5 feet and can have fixed side benches or there is ample space for several chairs. A wood floor is shown, but the building could go on a concrete slab.

Modifications are easy at the planning stage. Check on available space and compare access and sitting arrangements to see that they are feasible if you intend very different sizes.

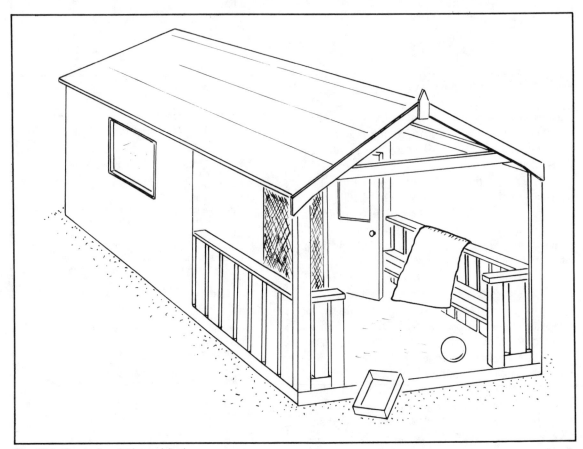

Fig. 18-6. Front of a playhouse/shed.

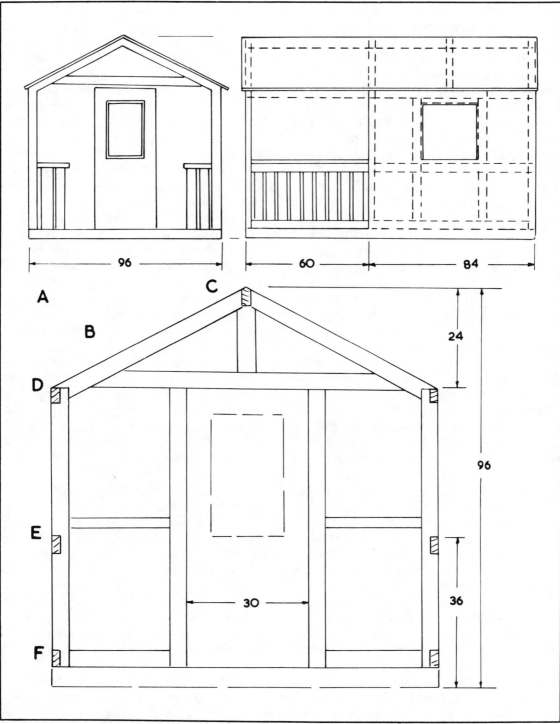

Fig. 18-7. Sizes of the playhouse/shed.

1. The key part is the central partition (Fig. 18-7B). Other parts have to be matched to it; make it first. Most of the wood is 2 inch by 4 inch. Check the actual dimensions; they could be undersize. There are five lengthwise pieces that should go right through from one end of the building to the other (without joins if possible). There is a ridge (Fig. 18-7C) and two eaves (Fig. 18-7D), with other pieces at the side (Fig. 18-7E) and foot (Fig. 18-7F). They could be notched fully into the uprights, but it is better to cut a small amount (5/8 inch is suitable) out of the long piece and more out of the upright (Fig. 18-8A). At the ridge, the rafters can be nailed against the lengthwise piece (Fig. 18-8B). Include a central upright piece over the door.

2. At the eaves, notch the lengthwise piece into the upright. Then arrange the rafter to fit over (Fig. 18-8C). The piece across above the door should have its underside level with the eaves (Fig. 18-8D). Nail it to the rafter.

3. With all the partition parts prepared, assemble them on two sheets of plywood that meet over the central upright. It is advisable to use plywood for this partition even if the outside is to be covered with shiplap or other boarding. Assemble with glue and nails. Be careful to keep the doorway sides parallel. If the plywood needs stiffening, put pieces across the side panels at half door height. Use this assembly as a pattern for making other parts.

4. For the back of the shed, make an assembly to the same overall sizes as the partition. Alter the door opening to almost full width (Fig. 18-9A). Unless you need absolutely the maximum door width to get your equipment in, it is advisable to have a little width left each side of the doorway for the sake of stiffness.

5. For the front of the porch, allow for strips forming the outline. You can arrange the horizontal piece higher than in the partition for more headroom (Fig. 18-9B) and it can overlap the inner surfaces of the rafters. Even if you will not be fitting side benches, it helps in stiffness and appearance if there is some framing each side.

6. There should be a truss midway along the enclosed part. That is like the top part of the partition framing, but the horizontal piece could be higher (Fig. 18-9C). It can overlap the rafters instead of meeting at the edges.

7. There will have to be some preparation of the rafters to suit the chosen roof covering. If you are using 1/2-inch, exterior-plywood or particleboard it might have sufficient stiffness, but it is advisable to use at least one lengthwise purlin midway between the ridge and eaves. That can be 2-inch-by-2-inch strip notched in (Fig. 18-18E). If you have to make up lengths, do that in a joint. If there are to be shingles or other covering, space purlins to suit. If you need a large number, they could go on the surfaces of the rafters, but you would have to cover their ends later.

8. If the floor is to be framed plywood or particleboard, make that next. If you build it in one piece, it will probably have to be assembled in position. It could be in sections, all full width, but one for the porch and two for the other part. A one-piece floor is easier to keep flat and in shape. There are several ways it can be framed.

For the stiffness of most covering you should not exceed framing 2 feet by 2 feet or the equivalent (if one way is longer, make it narrower the other way). The width could be divided into three, and then pieces fitted across at about 18 inch intervals. You can stagger meetings to make nailing easier (Fig. 18-8F). Make sure the overall width agrees with the partition and its matching parts, but slight errors in the length can still be allowed for.

9. Position the floor and mount the partition and back on it. Check squareness and temporarily nail these parts in position. Put the long side strips (Fig. 18-7D, E and F) in position. See that the main parts are upright. You will have to steady them with temporary diagonal struts. Add the other uprights to the sides of the closed part and frame around where the windows will come (Figs. 18-9D and 18-10A). Fit the plywood or other skin to the sides of the building. This will hold the main parts in shape.

10. Fit the truss to the closed part (Figs. 18-9C and 18-10B) and the porch at the front Figs. 18-9B and 18-10C). Put the ridge (Fig. 18-7C) in place.

11. At the sides of the porch, there can be

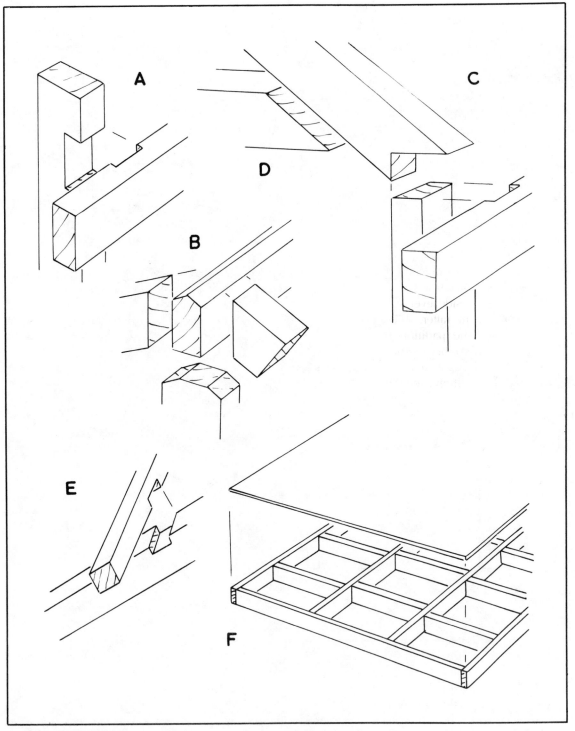

Fig. 18-8. Details of the framing and floor of the playhouse/shed.

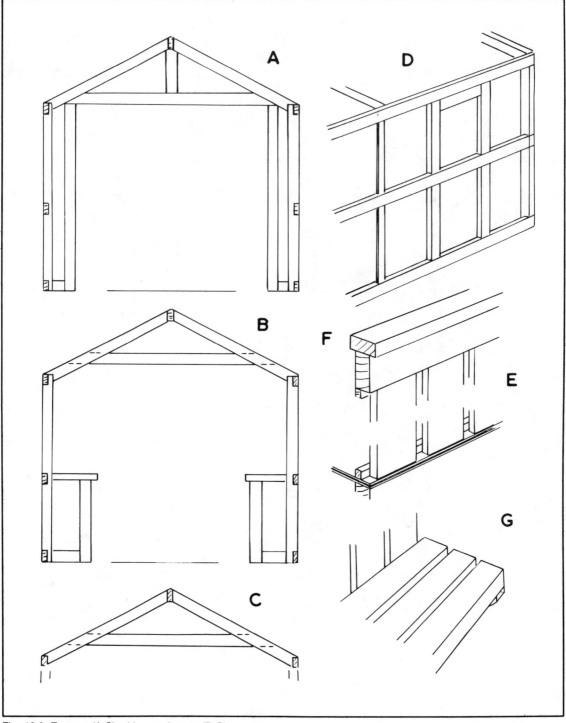

Fig. 18-9. Trusses (A-C), sides, and seats (D-G).

plywood closing the lower part or you can arrange palings between the long strips (Fig. 18-9E). Arrange the top piece (Fig. 18-9F) with rounded edges along the rail. This can be continued about 18 inches around the front (Fig. 18-7A) whether you want to fit bench seats at the side or not. Bench seats are simply made with strips on end supports (Fig. 18-9G).

12. Cover the roof with shingles. At the porch there could be a decorative barge board (Fig. 18-10D).

13. The window can be framed around and glazed in the same way as described for the previous project.

14. The front door could be ledged and braced as in the previous project, but another way to make it is to use two pieces of plywood—with framing between (Fig. 18-11A). Make sure there is solid wood where the hinges, lock, and window come. The plywood edges can be left exposed or covered with thin strips. Frame around for the window and hold the glass in with strips (Fig. 18-11B).

15. The back door could be a frame covered with plywood or shiplap boards and then hinged at one side, but it is rather wide and heavy for that support. It could be made as a pair of doors hinged at both sides and meeting at the middle. Another way is to make it like a single door (Fig. 18-11C), but arrange for it to lift out when you want to get large equipment in or out.

Projections on the bottom can fit into slots in the floor (Fig. 18-11D). Bolts and a stop inside the top will hold it up (Fig. 18-11E) and cannot be opened from outside.

GREENHOUSE

An enthusiastic gardener needs a greenhouse. It could be a small lean-to against a wall or a freestanding one of any size. The example shown in Fig.

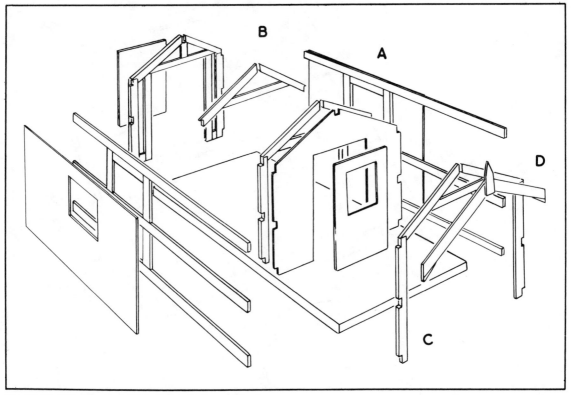

Fig. 18-10. The subassemblies of the playhouse/shed.

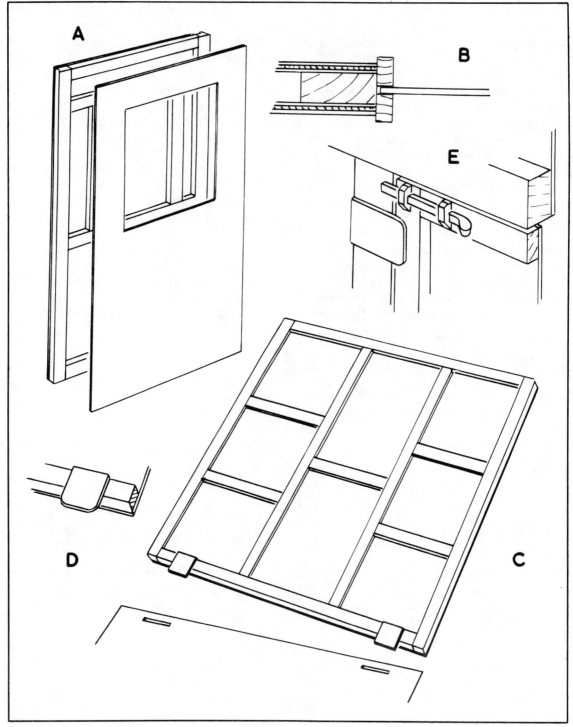

Fig. 18-11. Door details.

18-12 is a project about as small as could reasonably be used. The method of construction can be adapted for a freestanding greenhouse of almost any size. It could be glazed to the ground, but it is shown with shiplap boards to bench height. There is a door at one end, with a low ventilation flap, and another ventilator is high in the opposite end.

Much of the structure is made from 2-inch-square wood, and with 2-inch-by-4-inch wood where extra strength is needed. There is a sill all round above the lower boarding. The glass is intended to be puttied in. Some modern glazing compounds, however, are better than traditional putty. Glass can be cut to approximate squares and overlapped as it is set in putty. The wood could have rabbets cut in it for the glass, but it is simple to nail on strips of about 1-inch-by-3/4-inch section (Fig. 18-14A).

The main sizes (Fig. 18-13) allow a door with sufficient headroom and a roof sloping at about 30 degrees.

1. Using Fig. 18-13 as a guide, make the door end. The pieces each side of the door and

Fig. 18-12. A greenhouse with the lower part boarded.

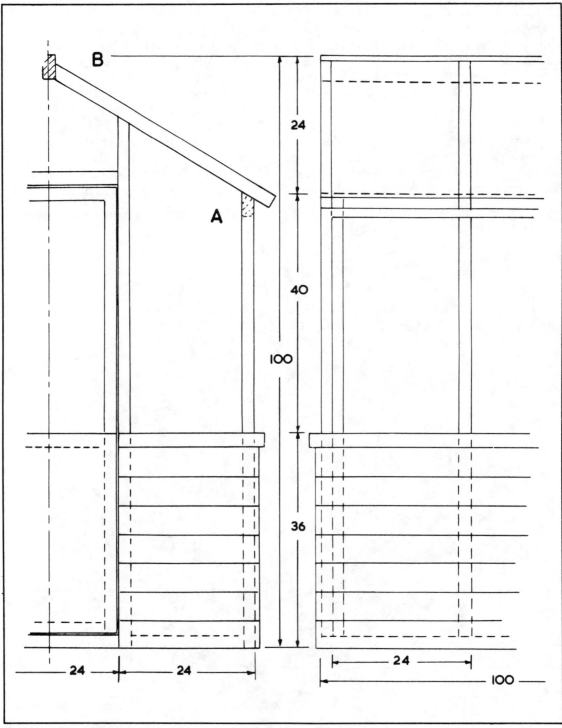

Fig. 18-13. Sizes of the greenhouse.

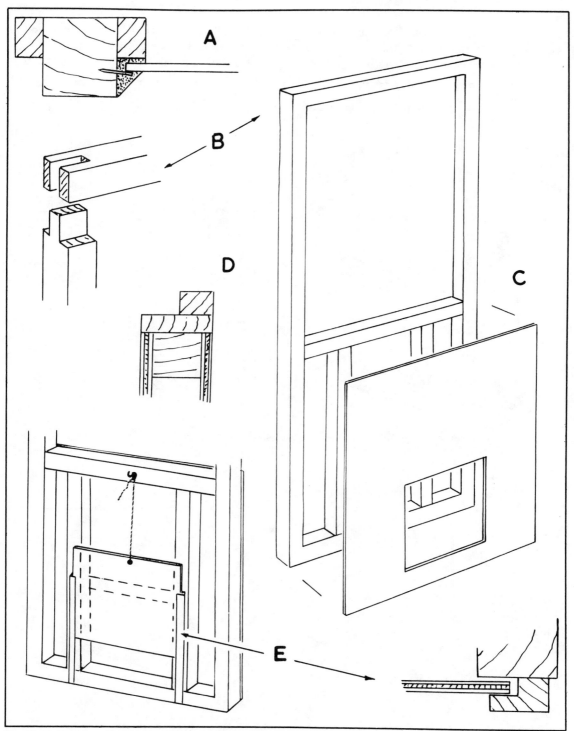

Fig. 18-14. Framing, door and ventilators of the greenhouse.

the strip above it should be 4 inches thick, but all other parts are 2 inches square. Corners and other joints can just be nailed, but notching in allows nailing both ways (Fig. 18-15A and B). Above the door, locate the strip with shallow grooves (Fig. 18-15C). At the sill level, notch the strip in to the door and corner posts (Fig. 18-15D). Leave at least 2 inches extra at the corner to be mitered or fitted

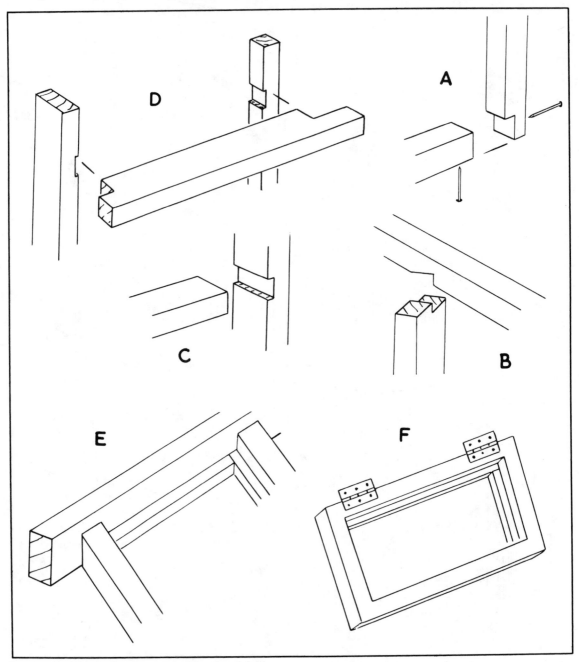

Fig. 18-15. Joints in the upper part of the greenhouse.

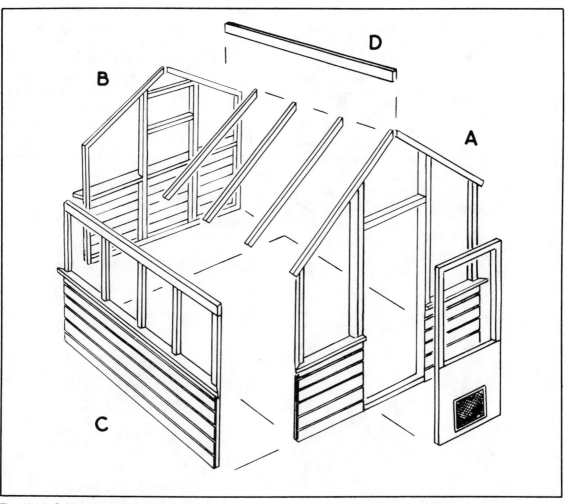

Fig. 18-16. Subassemblies of the greenhouse.

to the side sills during assembly.

2. Assemble the door end (Fig. 18-16A) with the shiplap boards cut level.

3. Use this as a guide when making the opposite end (Fig. 18-16B). That can all be made with 2-inch-square wood. Put an extra piece at the top between the uprights to support the ventilator. At sill level, take one piece right across and do the same with the shiplap boards.

4. The sides are identical. At the eaves, prepare 4-inch pieces at an angle to suit the roof (Fig. 18-13A). All other parts, except the sills, are 2 inch square. Make up the two sides (Fig 18-16C).

Use corner joints as suggested for the ends. Fit the sills level with the inside surfaces of the uprights and with a little extra at each end.

5. There could be a wood floor, as suggested for earlier projects, or the greenhouse could go on a concrete slab. In some situations it could stand on bricks or rammed gravel.

6. Assemble the sides and ends with bolts through the ends that overlap the side uprights. Miter the corners of the sills. Check squareness by measuring diagonals.

7. Fit a 4-inch-deep ridge (Figs. 18-13B and 16D) into the tops of the ends.

401

8. Make roof glazing bars that are nailed to the ridge (Fig. 18-15E) and overhang the eaves by about 4 inches.

9. For the high ventilator, make a frame with strips for the glass and hinges at the top (Fig. 18-15F). It can swing outward and be held by a stay.

10. The door is made of 2-inch-square strips, preferably with glued bridle joints at the corners (Fig. 18-14B), and covered with plywood to the sill level (Fig. 18-14C). There can be a sill to cover the plywood (Fig. 18-14D), but do not let it extend because that would interfere with the house sill and prevent the door swinging very far. When you mount the door, bevel the end of the sill beside it on the hinge side to allow more movement.

11. The ventilator in the door is an opening with wire mesh over it and a flap inside (Fig. 18-14E).

12. Nail on strips where the glazing is to come (Fig. 18-14A). This includes over the eaves and across the ridge. Except for the final coat, paint all of the woodwork before glazing. Nongloss paint in the rabbets will help the glazing compound to bond to the wood.

13. Glaze the sides and roof from the bottom up so that joints in the glass will have their overlaps downward. Locate the glass in the putty with fine pins or headless nails that will be puttied over. Let the eaves glass overhang to the ends of the wood bars.

Glossary

The making of outdoor tools and equipment forms only part of the crafts of woodworking and metalworking. The selection of words that follows are some that are particularly appropriate to the subjects of this book, and may be helpful to readers unfamiliar with the language of craftwork.

aggregate—Stone, gravel, or sand used with cement to make concrete.

alloy—A substance composed of one or more chemical elements, at least one of which is metal. Brass is an alloy of copper and zinc.

anchor bolt—Bolt set in concrete with its threaded end projecting.

annealing—Softening metal. To anneal steel it is heated to redness and cooled slowly.

apex—The top or peak of a roof.

backfill—Fill an excavation around a post or foundation.

barrel bolt—Sliding door fastener.

batten—Narrow strip of wood.

beam—A horizontal, load-bearing structural member.

blind—Not right through, such as a stopped hole.

brass—An alloy of copper and zinc.

brazing—Joining parts by flowing a thin layer of nonferrous filler metal in the space between them. This is ordinarily done at temperatures above 800 degrees F. At lower temperatures the process is called soldering.

bridging—Wood fitted between joists to spread load.

butt—End to end.

carriage bolt—Bolt with shallow round head and a square neck.

cast—Pour metal or concrete into a mold. Twisting of a surface that should be flat.

cement—Fine powder, which is the active ingredient of concrete when mixed with sand and stones with water.

check—Split in wood in direction of grain.

cleat—Strip of wood used as a support or a brace

across other wood.

clench (clinch)—Turning over the extending end of a nail.

concrete—Mixture of sand, cement, aggregate, and water.

conversion—The general term for cutting a log into boards and smaller pieces of wood for use.

counterbore—Let the head of a screw or bolt below surface.

countersink—Set the screw or bolt head level with the surface.

course—Row of stones, bricks, or shingles.

dado—Groove cut across the grain of a board.

dead pin—A wedge or dowel.

drift—Tapered punch used to drive through holes to bring them in line.

eaves—Overhang of roof over wall or an angle between them.

feather edge—Thinned edge of a piece of wood.

ferrule—Metal tube at end of handle to reduce risk of splitting when a tool tang is driven in.

float—Flat wood tool for smoothing surface of concrete.

footing—Masonry or concrete form to support wall.

foundation—Support in ground for a structure.

foxiness—Sign of the first onset of wood rot.

frost line—Depth frost is expected to penetrate into soil.

gable—Vertical end of a building with inverted V end of roof.

galvanized iron—Iron or mild steel coated with zinc as protection against rust.

girder—Wood or metal beam.

glazing—Glass pane. Fitting a glass pane.

glazing compound—Sealing and glass-setting compound as alternative to traditional putty.

grade—A slope (gradient).

grout—Thin mortar to pour into cracks.

gusset—Wood or metal joint cover.

haft—Long handle of hammer or similar tool.

handed—Made as a pair.

hardware cloth—Woven steel mesh.

jamb—Side or head lining of window or door.

joggle—Offset double bend in a strip of metal.

kerf—Slot made by a saw.

lag screw—Large wood screw with head for a wrench.

laying out—Setting out the details of design and construction.

ledger—Strip of wood fitted in position to support board ends.

level (spirit level)—Instrument to determine horizontal direction.

lintel—Support for a load over an opening.

mild steel—Iron with a small amount of carbon content.

mortar—Sand, cement, and water mixture used to bond bricks and stones.

particleboard—Board made by bonding wood chips with a synthetic resin.

pegging—Dowels or wood pegs through joints.

pier—Masonry column.

pilot hole—A small hole used as the guide for a drill point when making a larger hole.

pitch—Slope of roof. Distance between tops of a screw thread.

quartered (quartered sawn)—Board cut radially from a log.

rabbet (rebate)—Angular notch in the side of a piece of wood, as letting in glass.

rail—A horizontal framing member.

retaining wall—Supporting wall subject to lateral pressure.

riddle—Sand or soil sifter.

ridge—Top or apex of roof where sloping sides meet.

rive—To split wood.

roll roofing—Roof covering consisting of felt impregnated with asphalt.

run—Lumber quantity can be described as so many feet run.

sash—Frame containing a pane of glass.

screw—A screw for wood has a tapered thread, but a bolt with its thread almost to the head is also a screw.

seasoning—Drying out wood to an acceptable low level of sap.

shake—Natural crack in wood that develops in the tree.

shank—Neck or part of a tool between the handle and the blade.

sheathing—A covering such as plywood over a frame.

shiplap—Boards rabeted to fit into each other.

siding—Covering for outside of a framed structure.

sill—Lowest member of a frame construction or of an opening.

slat—Narrow thin wood.

span—Distance between supports.

splay—To spread.

spud—Chisel-like tool for removing bark.

square—Besides an equal-sided rectangle, this also means corners at 90 degrees.

steel—Iron alloyed with carbon. With the correct proportions it can be hardened and tempered.

stringer—Support for cross members, as at the sides of stairs.

stud—Vertical support in a wall.

tang—The tapered end of a tool, such as a file or chisel, to fit into a handle.

template (templet)—Pattern to be used to check or mark pieces to be cut or drilled.

tines—Prongs, as in a fork.

toe nailing—Nailing diagonally where the end of one piece of wood meets another.

tongue and groove—Board edges meeting with a projection on one fitting a groove in the other.

truss—Structural members joined to provide strength and shape, as in a roof truss.

vent—Arrangement in a wall or roof to allow air to flow through.

waney—Edge of board showing shape of outside of log.

warping—Going out of shape as wood dries.

winding—Board twisting in its length.

Index

Other Bestsellers From TAB

☐ **BUILDING OUTDOOR PLAYTHINGS FOR KIDS, with Project Plans—Barnes**

Imagine the delight of your youngsters—children or grandchildren—when you build them their own special backyard play area complete with swings, climbing bars, sandboxes, even an A-frame playhouse their own size or a treehouse where they can indulge in their own imaginary adventures. Best of all, discover how you can make exciting, custom-designed play equipment at a fraction of the cost of ordinary, ready-made swing sets or sandbox units! It's all here in this practical, step-by-step guide to planning and building safe, sturdy outdoor play equipment. 240 pp., 213 illus., 7″ × 10″.

Paper $12.95   **Hard $21.95**
Book No. 1971

☐ **PRACTICAL LANDSCAPING AND LAWN CARE—Webb**

Make your lawn the envy of the entire neighborhood . . . *without* spending a fortune or putting in never-ending hours of maintenance time! Here's absolutely everything you need to successfully plan, plant, and maintain lawn grasses and groundcovers, vines, and flowering ornamentals . . . annual, biennial, and perennial flowers . . . shade trees, lawn trees . . . even decorative (and delicious) fruits and berries. It doesn't matter whether your climate is cold and damp or hot and dry . . . whether your soil is sandy, rocky, or gummy clay . . . *everything* you need is here! 240 pp., 84 illus., 7″ × 10″.

Paper $13.95   **Hard $21.95**
Book No. 1818

☐ **HOW TO BE YOUR OWN ARCHITECT—2nd Edition—Goddard and Wolverton**

The completely revised version of a long-time bestseller gives you all the expert assistance needed to design your own dream house like a professional! You'll save the money that most custom-home builders put out in architects' fees—an estimated 12% to 15% of the total construction costs—to pay for more of those "extras" you'd like your new home to include! 288 pp., 369 illus. 7″ × 10″.

Paper $14.95   **Hard $22.95**
Book No. 1790

☐ **PRACTICAL HERB GARDENING . . . WITH RECIPES**

Imagine the satisfaction . . . and the savings . . . of being able to whiz by the high-priced herb section in the supermarket, secure in the knowledge that your garden is full of *fresh, organically grown herbs* that are costing you next to nothing! All the how-to information you'll need is included in this practical, down-to-earth guide . . . even a sampling of mouth-watering recipes! 216 pp., 25 illus.

Paper $11.50   **Book No. 1661**

☐ **58 HOME SHELVING AND STORAGE PROJECTS—Blandford**

From a two-shelf book rack or table-top organizer to a paneled chest, basic room divider, or hall locker . . . from shelves or a spoon rack to a period reproduction of a Shaker cabinet or a Welsh dresser, you'll be amazed at the variety of projects included. And, each one includes easy-to-follow, step-by-step directions, plenty of show-how drawings, and complete materials lists. 288 pp., 227 illus. 7″ × 10″.

Paper $14.95   **Book No. 1844**

☐ **TROUBLE-FREE SWIMMING POOLS**

Here is the ideal sourcebook for anyone thinking of installing a swimming pool—in ground or above ground from wading pool size to large indoor public pool. It shows how to plan, excavate, construct, and safely maintain all types and sizes of pools. You'll find out how to have your own pool for as little as $1,000 . . . or how to get more pool for the money no matter how much you're able to spend! 176 pp., 306 illus. 7″ × 10″.

Paper $11.95   **Hard $18.95**
Book No. 1808

☐ **ATTRACTING, FEEDING AND HOUSING WILD BIRDS . . . with Project Plans—Moorman**

Here is a thorough, up-to-date look at how you can provide a total environment that will attract the most birds—both common and rare varieties. It's also a rich source of project plans for practical and easy-to-construct bird feeders and birdhouses that can be expensively built from space age materials. Includes a year-round bird feeding schedule, recipes for custom seed mixtures, and detailed plans for birdhouses and bird feeders. Plus landscaping ideas for making your yard more attractive to birds! 154 pp., 33 illus.

Paper $8.95   **Hard $15.95**
Book No. 1755

☐ **BUILDING WITH SALVAGED LUMBER—Williams**

Build an $80,000 home for as little as $15,000 . . . have new paneling, decks, furniture, and more *for next to nothing!* This first-of-its-kind guide lets you in on a surprising, money-saving secret—how to find top-quality wood virtually FREE in old buildings, begin salvage operations, transport and store lumber, then use it on your own amazingly, inexpensive do-it-yourself building projects! Here are all the work-in-progress photos and step-by-step directions you need to turn painted lumber studded with rusty nails into beautiful, polished wood! 272 pp., 122 illus. 7″ × 10″.

Paper $10.25   **Book No. 1597**

*Prices subject to change without notice.

Look for these and other TAB BOOKS at your local bookstore.

TAB BOOKS Inc.
P.O. Box 40
Blue Ridge Summit, PA 17214

Send for FREE TAB Catalog describing over 900 current titles in print.

Popular Science Books offers a wood identification
kit that includes 30 samples of cabinet woods. For
details on ordering, please write: Popular Science
Books, P.O. Box 2033, Latham, N.Y. 12111.